SULTANIC SAVIORS AND
TOLERANT TURKS

Gentzler

INDIANA SERIES IN SEPHARDI AND MIZRAHI STUDIES

Harvey E. Goldberg and Matthias Lehmann, *editors*

SULTANIC SAVIORS AND TOLERANT TURKS

*Writing Ottoman Jewish History,
Denying the Armenian Genocide*

Marc David Baer

INDIANA UNIVERSITY PRESS

This book is a publication of

Indiana University Press
Office of Scholarly Publishing
Herman B Wells Library 350
1320 East 10th Street
Bloomington, Indiana 47405 USA

iupress.indiana.edu

Manufactured in the United States of America

Library of Congress Cataloging-in-Publication Data

Names: Baer, Marc David, [date]- author.
Title: Sultanic saviors and tolerant Turks : writing Ottoman Jewish
history, denying the Armenian genocide / Marc Baer.
Description: Bloomington, Indiana : Indiana University Press, 2020. |
Series: Indiana series in Sephardi and Mizrahi studies | Includes
bibliographical references and index.
Identifiers: LCCN 2019021136 (print) | LCCN 2019980961 (ebook) | ISBN
9780253045416 (paperback) | ISBN 9780253045447 (hardback) | ISBN
9780253045423 (ebook)
Subjects: LCSH: Jews—Turkey—History. | Antisemitism—Turkey. | Armenian
massacres, 1915-1923. | Holocaust, Jewish (1939-1945) | Turkey—Ethnic
relations.
Classification: LCC DS135.T8 B333 2020 (print) | LCC DS135.T8 (ebook) |
DDC 956/.004924—dc23
LC record available at https://lccn.loc.gov/2019021136
LC ebook record available at https://lccn.loc.gov/2019980961

1 2 3 4 5   25 24 23 22 21 20

CONTENTS

PREFACE

Decades ago, in graduate school, an Armenian friend once asked me, "Why is it that you Jews deny our genocide?" I remember answering meekly, "Not all of us do." In reflecting on my own emotional introduction to these issues, I realize that I have written this book as a more detailed answer to the question, a kind of exegesis on the feelings, convictions, and material circumstances that have compelled Jews in the Ottoman Empire, Turkey, and abroad to promote the tenacious image of sultanic saviors and tolerant Turks.

Here is the path I took. I am a Jewish American raised in the Reform tradition, which emphasizes social action and social justice. Compassion is a central focus of belief and practice. Growing up in Indianapolis in the mid-1970s and early 1980s, I was fully exposed to the Holocaust from a young age. I remember watching the *Holocaust* miniseries on television at the tender age of eight. Each year at religious school, I studied the Nazi annihilation of the Jews. A number of survivors with the telltale numbers tattooed on their left forearms inhabited my world. They included a best friend's father and an Auschwitz survivor, the stern referee at our Jewish Community Center soccer league. When we visited my mother's relatives in Chicago, I listened engrossed as elderly women with thick accents talked about Hitler's Germany, they sipping tea with lemon, I eating jelly fruit slices. In 1978, neo-Nazis even dared plan a march on Skokie, Illinois—a Chicago suburb where relatives lived—one of the highest-density areas for survivors in all the United States. Two years later we cheered when Jake Elwood declared "I hate Illinois Nazis" and drove them off a bridge in a scene in the *Blues Brothers* film.

My family moved to Kaiserslautern, West Germany, where our rabbi was a fiery US Air Force chaplain. Under his tutelage, I celebrated my bar mitzvah there in 1983, the first that town had witnessed in many years. A year later, I was astonished to learn that anyone who completed Kaiserslautern's hiking club trek was given a medallion featuring the city's magnificent gold-domed synagogue, destroyed during the November 9–10 pogrom of 1938, the Kristallnacht. I never visited a concentration or death camp, but I did not need to understand what the absence of Jews meant. The medallion said it all for me.

Grandpa Harvey, my father's father, a first-generation Russian Jewish American, refused to visit us in Germany. He had served in the US Air Corps, making bombing runs over southern Germany during World War II. When his plane was shot down over Nazi-occupied Slovakia, he used his Russian skills to link up with Soviet guerrillas fighting against the Nazis. He would never go back to Germany.

When I began to travel to Turkey during graduate school in the early 1990s, Grandpa Harvey told me bluntly he would not visit me there either, on account of what the Turks had done. What had the Turks done? I had not heard about the Armenian genocide until I was in my early twenties, when an elderly aunt told me about donating money for the "starving Armenians." I began to explore the topic on my own and learned about how the Jewish American ambassador to the Ottoman Empire, Henry Morgenthau, had stood up to the Ottoman architect of the genocide, Talat Pasha, as it was happening. I read a 1930s historical novel by German Jew Franz Werfel, *The Forty Days of Musa Dagh*, set in the Ottoman Empire of 1915, which uses Armenians as a stand-in for German Jews under Hitler. Jews read the novel in the besieged ghettos of Poland, identifying with the Armenians and their similar plight. I learned that it was the Polish Jew Raphael Lemkin, a man who had witnessed the trial of Talat Pasha's assassin in Berlin two decades earlier, who, reflecting on the common fate of the Armenians and Jews and watching it happening again, coined the term "genocide" during World War II. His own family was murdered in the Holocaust. I read Holocaust survivor Robert Melson's comparative history, *Revolution and Genocide: On the Origins of the Armenian Genocide and the Holocaust*. All these readings and experiences led me to believe that Ashkenazi Jews were constitutionally sympathetic to the Armenian plight, likening theirs with our own.

I was to be disabused of this notion in 1992, however, when I began to pursue a PhD in history at the University of Michigan. Advanced graduate students made it clear to me that not only did the most prominent Jewish historians of the Ottoman Empire lack sympathy for Armenian suffering, but, worse, they publicly denied that the Armenian people had been subjected to genocide. I could not comprehend why Ashkenazi Jewish historians, not subject to the same pressures as their Sephardic Jewish counterparts in Turkey, would deny the Armenian genocide. Why could they not empathize with Armenians? Where were the Morgenthaus, Werfels, Lem-kins, Melsons, and Grandpa Harveys among them? It brought to mind how I had felt when I first came face to face with a notorious Holocaust denier at my undergraduate college. I was in the microfilm room at Northwestern University Library when I caught a glimpse of him—sporting a Hitler-style haircut and mustache, no less—the electrical engineering professor who had written a book in the 1970s denying that Jews had been murdered in gas chambers at Auschwitz. Seeing him made me angry and hurt. In the face of overwhelming evidence—including the testimony of both perpetrators and survivors, testimony I had heard firsthand—what could motivate him to deny the murder of Jews? My outrage, the normal reaction to someone promulgating malicious lies that fly in the face of all evidence, could not have been sincerer.

In graduate school I quickly discovered that, whether through silence or open denial of the Armenian genocide, Turkish Jews and their historians proffered a utopian perspective on Turks as having been sent by God, time and again, to save His persecuted people from European barbarity. What were the origins of this claim, where was the evidence to support it, and why was it still being repeated? Such a view could not be reconciled with the nightmare that the Armenians experienced in 1915, a set of events that in the early 1990s only a handful of professional historians of the Ottoman Empire referred to as a genocide.

To learn more about the Armenian genocide, I took an undergraduate course in Armenian history at the University of Michigan taught by professor Ronald Grigor Suny. The other students, two dozen Armenian Americans, were hostile to him. They resisted his efforts to rid them of their notions of primordial national identities and to show them instead how identities are socially constructed. All hell broke loose in the classroom when Professor Suny dared to invite professor Fatma Müge Göçek, a sociologist at the University of Michigan, to discuss the fate of the Armenians in the late Ottoman Empire. The very idea of even a liberal Turk explaining the event to such an audience was viewed as an outrage. What could a descendant of the perpetrators possibly have to say to descendants of the victims, and why should anyone listen?

My fellow students were equally antagonistic to my presence in the classroom. They were full of rage and jealousy that my genocide was recognized and commemorated—given a capital letter and its own special word, *Holocaust*—while theirs was denied and dismissed. They were well aware that American, Israeli, and Turkish Jews frequently, publicly denied the Armenian genocide. At the annual Ann Arbor Armenian dance that year, held per usual in the old blue-domed Greek Orthodox church on Main Street, an argument between me and some of the more hotheaded among them nearly turned into a fistfight when they referred to me with a derogatory term for Jews.

I also socialized with Turks. At the Del Rio Bar, I downed pints of beer with well-dressed, well-coifed secular Turkish medical and engineering students and professionals who insisted all Armenians were liars, and that *their* ancestors were the true victims of genocide at the hands of Armenian terrorists. Was I unaware of the fact that dozens of Turkish ambassadors had been assassinated by Armenians over the past two decades? And I had thought that studying Ottoman history would be less contentious than the Israeli-Palestinian struggle, for which I had initially pursued graduate education.

Fortunately, a year after my arrival, a group of open and critical Armenian American, but especially Turkish graduate students in history, anthropology, and sociology began to gather around Professor Göçek. And elsewhere in Ann Arbor, other descendants of victims were encountering descendants of perpetrators. Around that time, I started dating fellow graduate student Esra Özyürek, who, hailing from a family of secular Turkish elites, had received the best education available in her country. Yet she had never been taught about the genocide. Her roommate was fellow graduate student Lucine Taminian. As soon as they met, Lucine made Esra a pot of tea in their kitchen and explained what had happened to her ancestors in the Ottoman Empire in 1915. I wondered how it felt for this descendant of survivors of genocide to face a descendant of the perpetrators who had not even heard of the tragedy. When Professor Suny invited us over for dinner, his wife, Armine, took Esra aside the moment we entered their house and asked her whether she had accepted the fact that the Armenian genocide had happened. As Jew and Turk, we faced the wrath and hurt of those who experience genocide twice over: the physical annihilation of their forbears, followed by the denial of their annihilation. Rather than promote the myth of Turkish-Jewish coexistence, as might be expected, we were compelled to reappraise the ethnonational myths we had both been reared on.

When deciding to pursue Ottoman history exclusively, I was recruited and received a generous fellowship offer from Princeton University but declined it. Admittedly, I had to choose between an ethical rock and a fairly hard place. One choice was to study at Princeton, whose Atatürk Chair in Turkish History had been endowed by the Turkish government. The chair was held by a professor who had worked hand in hand with the Turkish Ministry of Foreign Affairs as the coordinator of Armenian genocide denial in North America. My other choice was to study at the University of Chicago, whose Kanuni Suleyman Professorship of Ottoman and Modern Turkish Studies had also been endowed by a gift from the Turkish government, and whose holder would receive the Order of Merit of the Republic of Turkey, Turkey's highest honor given to foreigners. Along with most US-based professors of Ottoman history at the time, the professor in question had signed a notorious anti-Armenian genocide petition in the 1980s, part of Turkey's public campaign against genocide recognition. For reasons that should at this point be obvious, there were in the early 1990s very few historians of the Ottoman Empire who both conducted research in Turkey and recognized the Armenian genocide.

I first lived in Istanbul in the summer of 1994, continuing my study of Turkish at Boğaziçi University. Two sets of generally negative experiences from that summer left a lasting impression. My interactions with Turkish Jews were mixed. When I inquired at the offices of the Jewish weekly *Şalom* about Ladino lessons, I was asked what (Jewish) language my grandfather spoke. I responded, "Yiddish," as my grandparents originated in either Austria-Hungary, Poland, or Russia and are named Wolf, Braun, and Baer. "Then you can never learn Judeo-Spanish," I was told. "It is not on your tongue." I was also not allowed to conduct research at the library of the chief rabbinate. I did meet with the official historian of the community, Naim Güleryüz (b. 1933), in his book-lined office at his home in seaside Moda, but he only repeated the mantra that Jews and Turks had lived together in peace and brotherhood for five hundred years. He would not discuss the messianic movement of Sabbatai Zevi and his followers, about whom I planned to write a dissertation. In fact, I would find it easier to enter the secret community of the Dönme—the descendants of Sabbatai Zevi's followers who had abandoned Judaism for Islam in the seventeenth century—than the community of Turkish Jews. I also became good friends with Turkish Jewish researcher Rıfat Bali, who dared like no other to publicly criticize the myth that there was no anti-Semitism in Turkey. Only after several attempts was I allowed to pray at Sephardic synagogues in Ortaköy, Kuzguncuk, and Büyük Ada, but I found it difficult to follow the unfamiliar liturgy and melodies, prayer books sometimes written in the

Rashi script, and sermons delivered in Turkish and Ladino. I did appreciate the tables laden with cucumbers, feta cheese, spinach *börek*, tea, and *rakı*, and the warm welcome I received after the services, however. At one of these synagogues I met an Ashkenazi family whose narrative of a life of discrimination and violence in Turkey contradicted the story promoted by the chief rabbinate and its spokesmen. More off-putting were the many levels of security enveloping these houses of prayer forever flying the Turkish flag at their gates. Despite several attempts, I never was allowed in to Neve Şalom synagogue in Beyoğlu, showing my US passport and speaking Hebrew or English (rather than Turkish). In the middle of the street outside one of these synagogues, I was stopped and questioned by an Israeli security guard. If Turkish Jewry felt so safe, secure, and welcomed by brotherly love in Turkey, I thought, then why did they feel the need to hire Israelis to protect them? I realized that, despite their public face, perhaps this was a sign that these communities did not trust their own government and police to defend them.

Connected to this first set of experiences was a second: coming face to face with pervasive anti-Jewish sentiment expressed by young and old, secular and religious, right-wing and left-wing, Kurd and Turk. I did not grow up in a naïve Jewish bubble. I had had anti-Jewish epithets shouted at me by children my age, Grandpa Harvey received anti-Semitic tracts in his mailbox, I read ads placed by the Ku Klux Klan in the *Indianapolis Star*, and I witnessed a Klan gathering in southern Indiana. At Kaiserslautern American High School in Germany, my elder brother Steve was viciously and repeatedly targeted by an underground student group calling itself USA, which circulated its own samizdat gossip newspaper. Members of the appropriately named student group Kaiserslautern Kar Klub (KKK) tried to run him over in the school parking lot. Despite such experiences, I had never seen, heard, or read the likes of what I found in Istanbul, whether it was in conversation with academics, taxi drivers, or imams or encountered in the daily newspapers, on television, or in the bookstores of Taksim. Along with Turkish translations of anti-Semitic classics such as *Mein Kampf, The Protocols of the Elders of Zion*, and the *International Jew*, there were vicious Turkish-authored pieces. These included *Soykırım yalanı* (The Holocaust lie), which claims there were no gas chambers at Auschwitz and that six million Jews were not murdered in the Holocaust; *Yahudiler dünyayı nasıl istilâ ediyorlar?* (How do the Jews take over the world?), whose cover depicts a globe entrapped within a Star of David; and *Nasıl bir dünyada yaşıyoruz?*

(What kind of a world do we live in?), illustrated with a globe surrounded by a question mark made up of Stars of David. Worse was a Turkish translation of an Arabic work, *Yahudilerin kanlı böreği* (The Jews' bloody börek), whose cover depicts a Hasidic Jew cutting into a flaky pastry, which, rather than being filled with spinach and feta cheese like the böreks I had enjoyed at Turkish synagogues, was stuffed with bleeding children. It was an Islamification of the medieval Christian calumny of Jews as Christ-killers and child murderers. I was troubled by how, facing an onslaught of such anti-Jewish hate, Turkish Jews continued to present themselves as being grateful for Turkish tolerance. This jarred my Jewish American sensibilities. But it also made me wonder why this pervasive Turkish anti-Semitism and the Turkish Jewish response to it did not also bother other Jews raised in liberal societies, particularly those who become historians of the Ottoman Empire.

I have been studying, researching, and writing about Ottoman and Turkish history and the interactions of Jews and Muslims for nearly three decades. Having lived on and off in Istanbul since that first summer, I am perpetually impressed by the passionate feelings aroused when the topic turns toward Jews and Armenians, for good and ill. But it is only very recently that I have begun to openly confront the emotions and questions that marked my first two years of graduate study and those first summers spent in Istanbul all those years ago. What moral responsibility do the descendants of the victims of one genocide have to the descendants of the victims of another? What role have Jews played in genocide denial? What is the relationship between the utopian depiction of the experience of Jews in the Ottoman Empire and the Turkish Republic and efforts to counter recognition of the annihilation of the Armenians? Finally, what are the moral and ethical obligations of historians on these counts?

ACKNOWLEDGMENTS

ALTHOUGH I HAVE BEEN ENGAGED WITH THE TOPIC of this book for nearly three decades, the stimulation for writing came in the form of an invitation to give the 2014–2015 Poullada Lecture Series at Princeton University. I thank the Poullada family, whose generous contribution enabled this endowed lecture series, and my host, Cyrus Schayegh, who invited me. At Princeton, I presented versions of chapters 1 and 2 as "Ottomans and Jews in the Literary Imagination of the Other, from the Fifteenth through the Twentieth Century," receiving stimulating audience feedback, as well as insightful criticism and commentary during the final roundtable discussion from Mark R. Cohen and Molly Greene. I also presented a version of chapter 1 as the David Patterson Lecture at the Oxford Centre for Hebrew and Jewish Studies, University of Oxford (2015); at the international conference, "Visions, Vows, and Wonders: Religion and the Sea in the Eastern Mediterranean, 15th–19th Centuries," organized by Gelina Harlaftis and Nikolaos Chrissidis at the Forth Institute for Mediterranean Studies, Rethymnon, Crete (2018); and as part of the Middle East Lecture Series organized by Ebru Akçasu and Stefano Taglia at the Department of Middle Eastern Studies, Charles University, and Oriental Institute, Czech Academy of Sciences, Prague, Czech Republic (2018). Paul Bessemer and Shimon Morad assisted with Hebrew-language scholarship cited in chapter 1. Yorgos Dedes and Baki Tezcan helped with difficult Ottoman-language material. Chapters 1 and 2 also benefited from the insights of my undergraduate and graduate students in my courses at the London School of Economics and Political Science: "The Ottoman Empire and its Legacy" and "A History of Muslim-Jewish Relations" (2014–2018).

I presented the theoretical framework of the introduction at the London School of Economics Contemporary Turkish Studies Conference organized by Rebecca Bryant, "Interrogating the Post-Ottoman" (2016), and received valuable insights from fellow presenters, including Amy Mills, Christine Philiou, and Müge Göçek. I also presented the introduction, along with much of chapter 1, at Cornell University (2016). I thank Ziad Fahmy in the Department of Near Eastern Studies and Jonathan Boyarin of the Jewish Studies Program for having invited me, and for the stimulating discussions.

I presented material on the Turkish novels discussed in the book at several conferences: at the German Studies Association Annual Conference in Washington, DC, as part of the panel entitled "Berührungspunkte: Triangulating the Discourse on Jews, Turks, and 'Germanness'" organized by Leslie Morris with discussant Deniz Göktürk (2015); at the "Nationalism, Revolution & Genocide: A Conference Inspired by Professor Ronald Grigor Suny" organized by the University of Michigan (2016); and at the "Past in the Present: European Approaches to the Armenian Genocide" Workshop on Armenian and Turkish History in Potsdam, Germany (2017). I received valuable insight about the novels from Aslı Iğsız and Kader Konuk.

I also discussed ideas regarding the tangled relations of Armenians, Jews, and Turks presented in this book at the "Turkish-German Studies: Past, Present, and Future" seminar organized by Ela Gezen, David Gramling, and Berna Gueneli as part of the German Studies Association Annual Conference in Kansas City, MO (2014); at the "Jewish History/General History: Rethinking the Divide" roundtable organized by Lisa Leff with discussant Leora Auslander as part of the American Historical Association Annual Meeting in New York City (2015); at the "Coming to Terms with the Armenian Genocide: 100 Years On" international workshop organized by Kader Konuk at the Institute of Turkish Studies at the University of Duisburg-Essen and the Institute for Advanced Study in the Humanities (KWI), in Essen, Germany (2015); at the Conspiracy and Democracy Project, Centre for the Research in the Arts, Social Sciences and Humanities (CRASSH), Cambridge University (2015); "Genel'de Yahudi Çalışmaları" (Trends in Jewish Studies), Türkiye'de Yahudi Çalışmaları Çalıştayı (Workshop on Jewish Studies in Turkey), İstanbul Bilgi University, Yahudi Toplulukları Çalışma Birimi (YATOÇ) (2015); at the "Christians and Jews in Ottoman Society" international workshop organized by John-Paul Ghobrial at the Faculty of Oriental Studies, Oxford University (2017); at the "Jews in Muslim-Majority Countries: History and Prospects" international conference organized by Yasemin Shooman at the Jewish-Islamic Forum of the Academy of the Jewish Museum in Berlin (2017); at the Europäische Sommeruniversität für Jüdische Studien, "Krypto Jüdisches im Verborgenen," Hohenems, Austria (2017); at the "Jewish-Turkish Entanglements: Resilience, Migration and New Diasporas" international symposium organized by İpek Kocaömer Yosmaoğlu and Kerem Öktem at the University of Graz, Austria (2018); and at the workshop "Talat Pasha: Father of Modern Turkey, Architect of Genocide," organized by Rolf Hosfeld at the Lepsiushaus, Potsdam, Germany (2018).

Former Ann Arbor housemate Theresa Truax-Gischler did a marvelous job editing the complete manuscript. Lerna Ekmekçioğlu and Esra Özyürek read the entire manuscript and offered helpful criticisms.

I am fortunate that Esra is still with me all these years later, after I left Michigan to pursue a PhD at the University of Chicago. We have spent the past two decades mainly in Istanbul, Berlin, San Diego, and London, and some unique places in between, including Pittsburgh and New Orleans. Our daughters, Azize and Firuze, have arrived at an age where they are beginning to ask questions about evil men like Hitler who kill children. Literally stumbling over *Stolpersteinen* in Berlin, brass-plated cobblestones inscribed with the names and life dates of those murdered by the Third Reich, we began to teach them about the Holocaust and the Armenian genocide. As German-speaking Turkish Jewish Americans growing up in London, they will find their own myths against which to rebel, as have Esra and I.

SULTANIC SAVIORS AND
TOLERANT TURKS

INTRODUCTION:
FRIEND AND ENEMY

I N January 2014, high-level Turkish government officials
participated for the first time in the Turkish Jewish community's public
commemoration of the Holocaust—an annual event first authorized only a
few years earlier. Mevlüt Çavuşoğlu, the Turkish minister of foreign affairs,
gave a speech on that day filled with meaning for the Turkish Jewish community. He began by honoring "the memory of millions of Jews, Roma
people and other minorities who lost their lives in a systematic annihilation
by the Nazi regime. This crime against humanity is the common grief and
shame of humankind."[1] He then quickly pivoted to Turkey, which "not only
embraced Jews who were sent into exile from Spain in 1492 in the Ottoman
period, but also helped and protected its Jewish citizens and became a safe
haven for all Jews, especially scientists and academicians, during World
War II."[2] Based on these events, his conclusion was unambiguous: "There is
no trace of genocide in our history. Hostility towards the other has no room
in our civilization."[3]

In his statement, originally available in English on the Turkish Jewish community's official website, Çavuşoğlu contrasted European Christian persecution of Jews from the medieval era to the Holocaust, which he
termed "the shame of humankind," with five centuries of Turkish tolerance
of Jews.[4] Embedded in his short speech is the straightforward implication
that because Turks have always rescued Jews, they could not possibly have
committed crimes against humanity, certainly not the Armenian genocide,
perpetrated in the waning years of the Ottoman Empire by their ancestors.
Thus, in a spare five sentences at an event meant to commemorate the murder of European Jewry—itself remarkable, as Holocaust denial is rampant
in Turkey—the foreign minister of Turkey shifted the focus from the Holocaust to a performative conscience clearing of his own country.[5] To deny
the Armenian genocide, the foreign minister deployed a specific, dominant,
utopian narrative of Ottoman and Turkish Jewish history. That historical
narrative, how it came to be, and how it functions is the focus of this book.

Representatives of the Turkish Jewish community also deny the genocide by contrasting Turkish Muslim tolerance with Christian persecution
of Jews. In 1989, Turkey's chief rabbi, David Asseo, wrote in a letter sent to
all one hundred US senators that the resolution to recognize the Armenian
genocide then pending before the US Congress "is of great concern to our
community. . . . We cannot accept the label of 'genocide'; the groundless
accusation is as injurious to us as to our Turkish compatriots." Asseo went
further in his grateful praise of the Turks. "As Turkish Jews, we have received
for the last five hundred years the protection, the rights and the freedom
granted to all Turkish citizens, at times when the concepts of human rights,
liberty and tolerance were unknown in most Western countries."[6] Using
the same logic that the Turkish foreign minister would use a quarter of a
century later, the rabbi argued that the Armenian genocide never happened
because Turks have always tolerated Jews. What both Çavuşoğlu and Asseo
are asking us to accept is an if/then assumption about tolerance and genocide: if one buys the myth that Turks and Jews have lived in harmony as
friends for five hundred years, then one trusts that Turks could not possibly
have committed genocide against the Armenians.

In fact, Jews have been giving the Ottomans and Turks favorable press
for five centuries.[7] Here, I analyze the emotional frames of mind that have
driven them to do so, demonstrating how for the past century Jews have
been joined by Ottoman and Turkish Muslims in promoting a historical
narrative of sultanic saviors, tolerant Turks, grateful and loyal Jews, and
anti-Semitic Armenian and Greek traitors, a narrative that has simultaneously served to deny the very possibility of an Armenian genocide. Even
during the genocide, Talat Pasha asked Jewish American US ambassador
to the Ottoman Empire Henry Morgenthau why he bothered complaining
about persecution of the Armenians when the Ottomans had always treated
the Jews well. Such views have in fact been predominant in Jewish historiography until only recently.

As a historiographical analysis of the treatment of Muslim and Jewish relations in the Ottoman Empire and Turkey, this book examines early
modern and modern primary sources, history writing, and other forms of
literature. Its focus is on historical events, perceptions, and motivations,
and in particular how history is depicted by modern historians and what
kinds of emotional worlds propel them. The book is therefore also an
exploration of how entangled modern Jewish accounts of the Turks and
early modern Jewish accounts of the Ottomans are. Its primary focus is on

Jews: how Ottomans and Turks have treated them, how they wrote about that experience, and how their writing has changed over time.

Much scholarship has been devoted to understanding genocide denial, mainly focusing on the perpetrators and their descendants at the level of the state and public memory.[8] In the Turkish case, this has involved denying intentionality as well as rationalizing, relativizing, and trivializing the mass murder of Armenians carried out in the Ottoman Empire in 1915.[9] This book concerns another type of denial—that expressed by members of a group that was neither perpetrator nor victim of the genocide in question. How can we understand that group's identification and alliance with the perpetrators and their propagation of denial? What emotional world or affective disposition compels them to take this public stand?[10]

Where Ronald Suny and Müge Göçek have written of the "emotions and events" that are "utilized to mobilize Muslims in general and Turks in particular" to commit genocide against the Armenians and deny its occurrence afterward, I explore instead Jews' "public expression of affective states" toward Ottomans and Turks.[11] To do so, I tell a story that pivots on a key historical legitimating event that first gave rise to this emotional state: the welcome given Jews expelled from Iberia in 1492.[12] Memory of that event in turn was used to shape collective emotions during the four-hundredth-anniversary celebration of the arrival of the Sephardim in 1892; the five-hundredth-anniversary celebrations in 1992; and the invention of the claim in 1993 that Ottomans and Turks have continuously given Jews refuge from the Expulsion to the Holocaust. It was only at the turn of the new millennium that certain Turkish Jews ceased publicly ascribing to this affective disposition and instead began to criticize the mantra of "five hundred years of peace and brotherhood."

In the fifteenth and sixteenth centuries, Jews depicted the Ottoman sultan as their redeemer, as "God's rod" who had struck down their enemies the Byzantine emperors as part of a divine plan. Giving refuge to Jews expelled from Christian Spain in 1492, the sultan thus also opened the way to Jerusalem and the dawning of the messianic age. After Jews proclaimed Sabbatai Zevi the messiah in 1665, they ceased referring to the Ottoman ruler in messianic terms. But in the nineteenth century, Ottoman Jewish intellectuals recycled medieval and early modern tropes, thereby converting the sultan—and by extension all Turks—into tolerant hosts of their Jewish "guests." In 1892, during the four hundredth anniversary of the 1492 "welcome" given Iberian Jewry, Ottoman Jews promoted this new version of the Turk as humanitarian protector. Identifying with the Muslim, with whom there could be no conflict, Jews depicted themselves as loyal subjects. Armenians and Greeks, both Christian minorities within the empire, became eternal traitors and enemies, alleged anti-Semitic heirs of the Byzantines. Ninety-seven years later, the *500. yıl vakfı* (Quincentennial Foundation), established by the Turkish state and Turkish Jewish elites in 1989, saw itself as the celebration of "five hundred years of friendship" between Turks and Jews. Throughout the nineteenth and twentieth centuries, Jewish accounts in Turkey and abroad of the Ottomans and the Turks offered the same stock figures of tolerant Turks, loyal and useful Jews, and anti-Semitic Christians. It is my contention that to accomplish this staging of five hundred years of harmony, the most significant and influential Jewish historians needed to both deny the Armenian genocide and ignore or deny the existence of Turkish anti-Semitism.

In the 1970s, belief in the power of "world Jewry" was one of the motivating factors that led the Turkish Ministry of Foreign Affairs and the president to turn to Turkish Jews to serve as lobbyists on their behalf, primarily so as to counter international recognition of the Armenian genocide. As part of this effort, in the early 1990s the myth of the Turk as rescuer of Jews during the Holocaust was introduced. The Turkish president and the Ministry of Foreign Affairs, Turkish Jewish elites and their foreign allies, historians of the Ottoman Empire, major American Jewish organizations, and the state of Israel—together they promoted the myth of the virtuous, humanitarian Turk for audiences in Europe and North America. A resurrected version of the 1892 propaganda efforts, this campaign was a brew made of one part Armenian genocide denial and one part stale Jewish tropes of a Muslim-Jewish alliance against the Christian enemy. Promoted by the Quincentennial Foundation, diplomats, politicians, journalists, filmmakers, novelists, and historians, it had all but drowned out critical countervoices in both national and international arenas until the turn of the millennium. This is similar to how fifteenth- and sixteenth-century utopian Sephardic accounts worked to muffle lachrymose fifteenth-century Byzantine Greek (Romaniot) Jewish narratives. Or how the Sephardic 1892 celebrations silenced socialist and Zionist protestations at the turn of the twentieth century. Counternarratives failed to gain traction because they were inconvenient. The dominant narrative succeeded, especially in the modern period, because it allied with the foreign interests of Ottoman and later Turkish Muslims.

Beginning with the turn of the new millennium, major transformations in Turkey have led to new approaches to the past. Among these is the rise of critical Jewish and Muslim voices and the breaking of taboos in Ottoman and Turkish studies, both within and outside of Turkey. These new appraisals demonstrate the continued relevance of the concepts of friend and foe and the triangulated relationship among the three groups, which have in turn contributed to realignments in narrating Muslim-Jewish-Christian relations. What they establish is that the only way for Jews in Turkey or those defending Jews living in Turkey to end old enmities and forge new friendships is to divest themselves of those old affective dispositions in favor of new stances.

To those who would object that Ottoman and Turkish Jews generally enjoyed a better life than their European counterparts, I would point to the consequences of making such a blanket assertion. In my view, the more significant question and the one worthier of analysis is how such a claim has been politicized, instrumentalized, and deployed by Jews and Muslims alike over the past century so as to counter recognition of the Armenian genocide. Without critically engaging with the political uses of history, we cannot hope to compel historians to uphold the ethical standards of the profession. Nor can we aspire to bring about reconciliation between Jew and Armenian, forged when each sees the other as victim of a common experience, rather than competitor in a zero-sum game of recognition.[13]

Beyond Myth and Countermyth

After 1492, the Ottomans allowed as many as one hundred thousand Jews expelled from Spain and Portugal to settle in the empire and to live as Jews with relatively little interference from authorities, rather than as converted Christians as many had been compelled to do in Iberia. Some elite Jewish men and women rose during the same century to great heights of political power, wealth, and influence. This has led to the conventional wisdom that "on balance, the record of the Jewish experience in the Ottoman Empire was exceptionally good."[14] Such an assessment reflects the fact that, as Jonathon Ray has pointed out, in Jewish studies, discussions of comparative tolerance and discrimination have often been reduced to the question of "Was it good for the Jews?" or "Where was it *better* for the Jews?"[15]

These studies typically use a framework locating Muslim treatment of Jews on the spectrum of either utopian or lachrymose extremes—as either a "golden age" of Jewish-Muslim harmony and "an interfaith utopia of tolerance and *convivencia* [coexistence]" or a "countermyth of Islamic persecution." In these accounts, the point of reference is always to compare the experience of Jews in Christendom with their experience in Islamdom.[16] Historians of both schools of thought have used the same method to prove their position, sifting through archives in order to find evidence of either "peaceful coexistence" or "persecution and enmity."[17] Those looking for "a rosy Jewish-Muslim symbiosis" promote an ideological vision of the tenth- and eleventh-century "Spanish golden age" of Jews under Islam, as exemplified by the career of Samuel the Nagid Ibn Naghrela (993–1056), Jewish courtier, vizier of Granada, and general of Muslim armies; and they point out that the expelled Iberian Jews took refuge in Muslim North Africa and the Ottoman Empire. However, those of the opposing view hasten to point out that a decade after the peaceful death of his father, Samuel Ibn Naghrela's son was lynched by a Muslim mob that went on to massacre the Jews of Granada.[18] This history is "the battleground on which we fight over the present," as historians cite examples and counterexamples, quotations and counterquotations, myth and countermyth.[19]

Because the main focus of most studies of Muslim-Jewish relations is the arabophone region,[20] the Israeli-Palestinian struggle casts its long shadow over this historiography, as does the search to contrast "good Muslims" with "bad Muslims." For this reason, many scholars who support Israel focus on the Palestinian mufti of Jerusalem, al-Haj al-Amin Husseini, who collaborated with Hitler during the Holocaust. They seek to smear all Palestinians, the Palestinian movement, and, by extension, all Arabs and all Muslims with constant reference to the iniquitous mufti.[21] Such a figure is then contrasted with the Turkish consul on Rhodes, Selahattin Ülkümen, who during the same years saved Jews from the Nazis.

What then is to be gained by looking at the Ottoman and Turkish case? Why undertake a historiographical study of approaches to Muslim-Jewish relations focusing on turkophone regions from the early encounters of Muslims and Jews in the medieval period to the present?[22] First, consider the utopian tenor of much writing on Ottoman and even Turkish Jews. A common argument offered by an academic is that "Turks and Jews have enjoyed periods of remarkable close ties," as "these relations were always a contrast to the experience of Jews in Western Europe" where anti-Semitism thrived, unlike in Turkish lands where "no trace of it [could] be found," until it was "imported" after World War II.[23] But as Bernard Lewis notes, it is "misleading to compare one's best with the other's worst. If we take the Spanish Inquisition or the German death camps as the term of comparison for Christendom, then it is easy to prove almost any society tolerant."[24]

Second, to have a meaningful debate about the history of Muslim-Jewish relations, one must include studies that focus on areas outside the arabophone region. The Ottoman Empire and Turkey did not follow the historical trajectory of lands that were directly colonized, such as Egypt, Iraq, Morocco, and Tunisia. After gaining independence, these new nations progressively lost their Jewish populations to exile, either to Europe or Israel. Following repeated wars against Israel, the last Jews departed, leaving behind lacunae in the national narratives of their former countries. For some, these lost Jewish communities came to symbolize a nostalgic memory of a vanished world.[25]

Turkey offers a different perspective. Colonization, the struggle for Palestine, and the disappearance of Jewish minorities is not the experience that marks the Muslim-Jewish relationship in modern-era Turkey. The Ottoman Empire annihilated its Armenian population with Jews as eyewitnesses. Although largely depleted, Turkish Jewry survived the transition from empire to nation-state as the Turkish Republic replaced the Ottoman Empire in 1923. Despite the bombast of the current Turkish regime, Turkey has never been at war with Israel, so is one step removed from the bitter conflicts of the Palestinian-Israeli struggle. Here is a land where the Palestine question is one among many, and not the primary one. The Kurdish issue is more important. Despite violence and discrimination, Turkey today still has the second-largest Jewish community in a Muslim-majority country after Iran. Taking these differences into consideration, a detailed study of the historiography of Muslim-Jewish relations in the Ottoman Empire and Turkish Republic can reframe the debate.[26] Focusing on Turkish Muslims and Jews rather than on Arabs and Jews may lead us to reevaluate current interpretative frameworks and address new questions. Freed of the intellectual constraints that bind the study of Muslim-Jewish relations in Middle Eastern studies, especially colonialism and the impact of Zionism, this study utilizes instead the interrelated lenses of messianism, imperial memory, genocide, and anti-Semitism.

Religious impulses, especially messianism, influenced the writing of the history of Muslim-Jewish relations. This can be seen in premodern depictions of the Ottoman sultan as redeemer of the Jews, a benevolent ruler who defeats the Christian enemies and welcomes the Jews exiled from

Europe to settle in the land of Israel in anticipation of the end-time. Imperial memories shaped nation-state narratives as the earlier Jewish trope of the sultan as messianic figure was secularized in the 1892 celebrations of the ingathering of the Andalusian Jews.

Messianism may have been abandoned, but its positive sentiment was retained. As a consequence, Jews began to depict the sultan (and later, by extension, all Turks) as benevolent, tolerant humanitarians who have always treated Jews well. A century later, in 1992, as Turkish Jews marked the five hundredth anniversary of the arrival of the Sephardim in the Ottoman Empire, the trope of the Turkish rescuer motivated only by humanitarianism was extended to the Turkish Republic. This time, Turks had allegedly saved Jews from the Nazis, a historical narrative promoted as proof of the same timeless, humane Turkish nature.

The Armenian genocide and the ethnic cleansing of Greeks in Anatolia shaped Muslim-Jewish relations as well, as Turkish Jews sided with the perpetrators in order to ensure their own survival. Turkish Muslims promoted the view of themselves as tolerant toward Jews so as to deflect attention from their ancestors' past crimes. In this way, Turkey could appeal as an aspiring member state to a European Union in which the litmus test for accession is the manner in which Jews are treated.[27] Denial of genocide and promotion of Turks as rescuers of Jews became prevalent in twentieth-century historiography on the Ottoman Empire and Turkish Republic, as Turkey's alleged rescue of Jews during World War II was added to the concerted effort to counter recognition of the Armenian genocide.

The historiography of the Jews of the Ottoman Empire and Turkey "is so rife with myths that it is tempting to wonder whether they emerged to provide palliatives to the gloomy 'lachrymose' episodes in Jewish history."[28] Scholars have found that the discourse of harmonious relations between Turks (Muslims) and Jews is evident throughout a range of historical accounts: the historiography of early modern Sephardic Jews; the narrative of Ottoman refuge by Ottoman and Turkish Jewish spokesmen since the late nineteenth century; and the histories produced in Turkey in the early 1990s as part of the Turkish state's desire to improve its image and US-Turkish-Israeli efforts to better Turkish-Israeli relations.

It is productive to consider to what extent the myth of harmonious relations between Turks and Jews may be "simply a reaction to negative views of and stereotypes about Turkey."[29] For the myth is not only a reflection on the Jewish experience, but also on the fate of the Armenians. Should a historian aim merely to determine the veracity of a myth, comparing a factual account of the development of Turkish-Jewish relations with "the contents of the discourse of harmony that appeared at the beginning of the 1990s"? Is there an alternative to positivist history writing and to mere fact-checking? In one historian's perceptive formulation, "historians are not accountants, tot[t]ing up the assets and liabilities of this and that society in order to declare a particular tradition more solvent (or in this case, more tolerant) than another. . . . They cannot be translated into a common currency in order to calculate comparative value or be assigned comparative moral worth."[30] My aim here is to move beyond support for choosing either a "golden age" or a "tearful" account of the relations between Jews and Muslims and to avoid what was once labeled "myth, countermyth, and distortion."[31]

Beyond Fact-Checking

Whereas some Ottoman historians would appeal to Leopold von Ranke's dictum to find out "what really happened" and claim that the Sephardic Jews' "accurate historical memory" supports a mournful view, the approach taken here is different. The aim of this book is to connect historical event, historical memory, and the politics of history writing.[32] How did Jews perceive the sultans who ruled them and the Muslim—especially Turkish—population among whom they lived? How have modern historians, especially Ottoman and Turkish Jews, read (or chosen not to read) historical sources that provide answers to these questions? What public narrative have Turkish Jews adopted, and why have Jewish scholars outside Turkey used it so uncritically?

Adopting this approach, this study draws mainly on sources originally written in Ottoman, Turkish, Hebrew, or French, but also texts in Judeo-Spanish, Portuguese, and German. The works analyzed here were selected because they were written by Jewish authors widely recognized as significant; many of these texts were the "best sellers" of their day. The texts are representative because they were written by Jews who lived through the major changes and ruptures that are the critical milestones in the history of their interaction, from their first encounters in the medieval period to the present. An unusually long time span is justified for this historiographical analysis for it is the best means to demonstrate change and continuity over time.[33]

This book examines formal and informal sources and literary, artistic, and archival material. The reader will encounter early modern Jewish epistles and chronicles composed from the fifteenth through the seventeenth centuries; modern Jewish history writing from the mid- to late nineteenth century through the early twentieth century; archival sources from Jewish philanthropic and political organizations; private letters of public Jewish figures; twentieth- and early twenty-first-century Jewish history writing; interviews; newspapers; films; novels; memoirs; and autobiographies. The reader will notice a change in the nature of the sources, with entirely formal sources used at the beginning and a heavy reliance on informal sources by the end. Perhaps surprisingly, she will find that the formal sources are no less passionate than the informal and that both types allow the reader to encounter the subjective feelings and emotional states of their authors.

Historiographical sources do not necessarily reflect reality, but like other narrative sources, their authors project into their writing a version of the desired state of affairs of the time in which they live. It is when Turkish Jews are most vulnerable that they praise Turkish "tolerance" most effusively. Historical works themselves are literary productions intended for religious purposes, moral edification, entertainment, or political ends. They should not be read at face value as repositories of unfiltered facts. They are best read to gain "insight into how elite men and women at that time shaped, formed, and articulated their understanding of the moment in which they lived."[34]

Historians are supposed to relate "true" stories, whereas novelists are allowed to invent characters and events. But as will be demonstrated, when it comes to Muslim-Jewish relations in the Ottoman Empire and Turkey, the boundaries between fact and fiction are not firmly drawn by modern historians. Historical chronicles and modern historical studies sometimes present incredible, unsubstantiated tales as documented fact. An unverified story that passes for "fact" in a historical study can be used in a novel as "fiction." Literary works may use the events, tropes, and characters made familiar in historical works, seeking legitimacy from historical documents that may themselves have been falsified. Novelists, filmmakers, and historians alike play with the boundary separating the two.

Beyond Tolerance, Coexistence, and Conspiracy

The "tolerance" discourse in the Ottoman case operates much as the "convivencia" discourse about al-Andalus: it serves modern political purposes.

Ever since the late nineteenth century, Ottoman Muslims and Jews have promoted the view that Ottoman Muslims/Turks are tolerant, as illustrated by the only example to which they can refer, Turkish treatment of Jews. Since the Hamidian era and the first Ottoman massacres of Armenians, the claim of Turkish tolerance of Jews has gone hand in hand with belief in Jewish conspiracy. While Turkish Muslims deployed the tropes of Turkish Jewish historiography in their presentation of self to the world by drawing on the imaginings of Jews in the Ottoman Empire, they were, paradoxically, also influenced by the ideas of late nineteenth-century European anti-Semitism. They adopted and adapted the European Christian concept of the Jew as the enemy within to form a particularly Turkish anti-Semitic concept of the "crypto-Jew," the Dönme who control Turkey as part of a worldwide Jewish conspiracy.[35] Belief in Jews having extraordinary powers to shape political events tied in with what was later to become genocide denial. It began with an alliance between Zionist leader Theodor Herzl and Ottoman Sultan Abdülhamid II. Playing on Abdülhamid's belief in the undue influence of world Jewry, Herzl and the Zionist leadership offered to silence European condemnation of Ottoman massacres of Armenians; in exchange, Abdülhamid would support the Zionist project to build a Jewish homeland in Palestine. Belief in the power of international Jewry was used again beginning in the 1970s by the Turkish foreign ministry and presidency when they turned to Turkish Jews to promote a positive image of Turkey abroad, this time by scuttling efforts to recognize the Armenian genocide.

This hand-in-hand linkage of history writing and politics has also been evident since the 1980s, articulated by the Turkish and Israeli governments and their mediators—major American Jewish organizations and Turkish Jewish representatives. As illogical as it sounds, commemoration of a medieval event—the welcoming of Sephardim in the Ottoman Empire—is used to counter recognition of a modern event—the genocide of the Armenians by the same empire. Why should anyone assume that the Ottoman regime did nothing wrong to Armenians during World War I just because decades later some Turkish diplomats helped some Turkish Jewish citizens during World War II? Many influential people have made just this incomparable comparison. Turkish presidents Kenan Evren (in office 1980–1989) and Turgut Özal (prime minister, 1983–1989; president, 1989–1993) made the connection explicit in response to US congressional resolutions recognizing the genocide, as did Turkish scholar Mümtaz Soysal, as reported in 1985 in the Turkish Jewish newspaper *Şalom*. "Before accusing the Ottoman Empire, it is first necessary to know the reality that it is the place to which the Jews, fleeing Spain before the Inquisition in 1492, settled and began a new life; the 500th anniversary is about to be celebrated. I absolutely reject the claims that the minorities were ill-treated in Turkey."[36] Because the moral worth of Muslim Turks, Turkey, and the Ottoman Empire vis-à-vis Christian Europe is at stake, "anachronism is not a problem for a discourse about history to which one attributes inviolable values."[37]

All this is not to deny that when compared with their contemporaries, the Ottomans appear to have been far more tolerant of Jews who were persecuted elsewhere but found refuge and thrived in the Ottoman realm. The problem is that "Ottoman treatment of Jews is usually cited when promoting Ottoman models of tolerance and praising the apparent coexistence of Christians, Jews, and Muslims in the early modern empire."[38] Coexistence, however, "is the wrong term for describing inter-group relations in the early modern empire. Coexistence suggests equality between groups. But in the empire certain groups (women, Christians and Jews, and commoners) were legally subordinated to others (men, Muslims, the military class)."[39]

Tolerance is a useful concept only when we consider the power exerted whenever it is exercised. Tolerance is an expression of a power relation in that its presence or absence can be wielded as a threat against a tolerated, and thus vulnerable, group. Tolerance "is based on a state of inequality in which the most powerful party (such as the ruler) decides whether a less powerful group can exist or not and to what extent members of that group are allowed to manifest their difference. A regime can discriminate against certain groups while tolerating their being different." This in fact "was how the Ottoman administration of gender, religious, and class difference normally functioned."[40]

It has been argued that tolerance was an imperial means to "maintain the diversity" of the Ottoman Empire, "to organize the different communities, to establish peace and order."[41] In this analysis, toleration is "a means of rule, of extending, consolidating, and enforcing state power" and cannot be confused with equality or multiculturalism. Unlike the nation-states that succeeded it, the Ottoman Empire was interested in maintaining "difference" and uninterested in transforming difference into "sameness."[42]

In his classic analysis of the Ottoman politics of difference, presented in an interview, Turkish Jewish historian Aron Rodrigue never mentions the genocide.[43] In that interview with historian Nancy Reynolds, he avoids the topic because Reynolds has asked him to consider the empire's approach to Christians and Jews "before the nineteenth century."[44] Excluding consideration of the topic in this way allows her to introduce the empire as "one of the most remarkable historical examples of coexistence among different religious and social groups."[45] The claim is true, perhaps, so long as we continue the conceit that the empire was a premodern entity alone, ignoring the Ottoman annihilation of the Armenians in the modern period. For the interview, Rodrigue agrees to limit the temporal framework in this way, defining Ottoman society according to how it functioned from the sixteenth through eighteenth centuries. He maintains that in that period the Ottomans never sought to "homogenize difference," in Reynolds's words, as "persecution of difference was not acceptable"—an accurate description of Ottoman policies in the early modern era. But he concedes that "the socio-political system of the Ottoman Empire, as I am describing it, *did not exist in the modern period.*"[46]

What replaced the Ottoman Empire's socio-political system? For Rodrigue, the modern period is the era of nation-states that, unlike premodern empires such as the Ottoman Empire, aimed to produce homogenous populations. Crucially, what is left out in his explanation is any accounting for the Ottoman Empire of World War I, which no longer tolerated difference, annihilating groups that stood in the way of efforts to "save" the empire. Was the empire that committed genocide no longer an empire? The Turkish nation-state would not be born until 1923, some eight years after the outbreak of World War I and the Armenian genocide. Who is responsible for the crimes of the empire in the modern era?

The inability of many scholars to deal, intellectually or professionally, with the Armenian genocide is another important factor that weighs against consideration of tolerance as a useful analytical tool.[47] Academic and popular works continue to promote the entire six-century existence of the Ottoman Empire "as a model of tolerance and coexistence for the world to emulate."[48] An influential senior Ottoman historian argues that "the greatness of the Ottoman Empire could be attributed to its policy of religious and ethnic tolerance that allowed a diverse population to peacefully coexist within the borders of a Muslim Empire."[49] How are the events of 1915 encompassed by this sweeping generalization? As this example shows, scholars have failed to integrate the Armenian genocide into Ottoman history. But that event "has to be understood in relation to the long sweep of Ottoman history; it is part of that history. We cannot effectively compare tolerance and religious oppression in the Ottoman Empire to the treatment of minorities in other states or empires until Ottoman historiography itself has greater depth."[50] We will never come to terms with the past by silencing inconvenient aspects of it.

Even the most recent sophisticated analyses of Ottoman tolerance rely on the cliché of utopian relations between Muslim rulers and Jewish subjects to prove their argument, seeking to decouple "Ottoman Empire" and "Armenian genocide." The best example is the important study by Turkish Jewish historical sociologist, Karen Barkey. To provide evidence for Ottoman tolerance, she argues that "as the West banished its Jews, enclosed them in small and filthy ghettos, burned their heretics, unleashed its inquisitors among its own people, and tore apart the fabric of society in religious wars, the realms of the Ottomans were mostly peaceful, accepted diversity, and pursued policies of accommodation."[51] Not only were the Ottomans more tolerant than their Christian European counterparts, as proven by the Jewish case, she claims, but, overall "the centuries of the Pax Ottomanica were relatively calm and free of ethnic or religious strife." Barkey's parenthetical about the intolerance that did occur is characteristic here: "When local incidents occurred, they were not allowed to spiral out of control."[52] To prove this point, she repeatedly cites sultans protecting Jews from Armenian and Greek mobs.

The weakness of this theoretical framework is exposed when Barkey attempts to explain the turn to genocide in the twentieth century. Because "empire" and "tolerance" are linked in her theoretical framework, massacre is only conceivable when the Ottoman Empire no longer acts like an empire.[53] Since the empire is "an expression of tolerance," if genocide occurred, even if administered and organized from the center, it was not the empire that was responsible, for the empire "was no longer fully imperial in its formal structure" at the time it engaged in massacres.[54] The significance of this argument is that it allows Barkey to disassociate "Ottoman Empire" and "Armenian genocide." She places the latter compound noun in quotation marks.[55] We remember the empire, she seems to regret, for its annihilation of one community, rather than what she and generations of Turkish Jews have wanted us to remember—that Jews in the Ottoman Empire "suffered much less persecution than did their brethren" in Europe.[56]

Ironically, Ottoman and Turkish Jews have had a large role to play in the creation of the tolerance discourse. This role is not only of historical interest. It matters to Turkish Jews, who pay the price of tolerance discourse as they are called upon to play the part of an Ottoman living legacy, "to stand symbolically for the Tolerated other."[57] Despite facing daily discrimination and occasional deadly violence, Turkish Jews publicly celebrate the tolerance of the Turkish Republic and its Muslim majority and willingly play the role of the "good" minority promoting the republic's interests to a foreign audience.

This fact of Turkish Jewish collaboration highlights the "other side of tolerance": the tension between public discourse and private conversation that marks the lives of Turkish Jews. Despite what they profess publicly about being secure and happy, Turkish Jews only express their Jewish difference in private. Repeating the trope that they have never experienced anti-Semitism renders it nearly impossible for Turkish Jews to denounce it when it occurs.[58] One cannot discount the fear factor that compels Turkish Jews to present an image of themselves and their relations with Turkish Muslims that is invariably positive. They also want foreigners to promote the same exaggerated narrative so as not to cause them any trouble at home. The Turkish Jewish community has a stake in foreigners repeating the tolerance myth they so keenly promote. Foreigners who do so may be motivated by the feeling that they are being helpful or that they are protecting or "saving" Jews when they emphasize Turkish-Jewish friendship and the enmity of Armenians and Greeks.

Friend and Foe: Muslim-Jewish-Christian Trialogue

Rather than rely on tolerance or coexistence as analytical frameworks for exploring Muslim-Jewish relations in the Ottoman Empire and Turkey, I use the key categories of "friend" and "foe" in order to tease out the ways in which Muslim-Jewish-Christian relations have been narrated. The conventional view focuses on either Jews or Muslims as the essential imagined enemy against which Christendom was constructed.[59] For example, a typical view is that in the eleventh century "Muslims became *the* enemy of Christianity and Christendom: their normative, fundamental, quintessential, universal enemy." After the fall of Constantinople to the Ottomans in 1453, the concept of a united "Christendom" was replaced by the idea of "Europe," and accordingly, the Turkish "Muslim became the enemy of Europe."[60] In fact, Christians thought of Jews and Muslims together. Beginning in the twelfth century, due in part to the Christian encounter with Muslims during the crusades, Christian theologians began to no longer consider Jews as the prime enemy, but to classify Jews together with Muslims, "both groups but subsets in a larger genus of hermeneutically constructed *infideles* who undermined the unity of Christian faith."[61]

For Christian Europe as a whole, the Arab Muslim *and* the Jew, often interchangeable, together stand for the enemy. The Arab is the external military and political enemy; the Jew is the internal religious enemy.[62] In literature, law, theology, and historical chronicles across Europe, Jews were classified together with Muslims as infidels or blasphemers who undermined the unity of Christian faith and territory.[63] Treated as socially inferior, they were prohibited by law from gaining the slightest power over Christians; marriage and sexual relations between Christians and Muslims or Jews was banned.[64] Muslims and Jews were thought of as the "enemies of Europe."[65] We see this in Shakespeare's twin plays, *The Merchant of Venice,* where the Jew is the theological enemy, and *Othello,* known in the author's day as *The Moor of Venice,* where the Muslim is the political and military enemy.[66] In Shakespeare's Venetian imaginary, the two enemies are associated. The conflation is made more explicit in *Titus Andronicus*'s villain Aaron the Moor.[67] But the formulation is stated best by Christopher Marlowe in *The Jew of Malta,* where the evil Jewish character, Barabas, modeled on sixteenth-century Ottoman Jewish courtier Joseph Nasi, "forms a murderous alliance" with his Turkish Muslim slave, Ithamore, named after the biblical Ithamar, the son of Moses's brother Aaron. Barabas declares, "Make account of me as of thy fellow; / we are villains both: / Both circumcised, we hate Christians both."[68]

Marlowe's formulation compels us to consider Edward Said's description of "the Islamic branch" of Orientalism as a "secret sharer of Western anti-Semitism."[69] It also obliges us to think relationally about constructions of Europe and its history, vis-à-vis both Jews and anti-Semitism and Muslims and Orientalism. Viewing the Jewish question together with the Muslim in relation to Christian Europe is to see the three as existing in trialogue. Jews were, after all, identified with Turks in the Christian European imagination, referred to as *Schatze des Sultans* (the darlings of the sultans).[70] This relational approach has been adopted by scholars working on medieval Spain who discourage reference to *dialogue* between two religious communities in favor of the existence of *trialogue*.[71] Particularly relevant for the Ottoman and Turkish Jewish case is the insight in the Spanish context that the "positions Jews and Muslims took vis-à-vis each other" were "very much influenced by what" members of the two minority religions understood to be the interests and ideologies of the majority Christian religion. Their strategy was to adapt to the political views of the dominant group "in an attempt to gain a competitive advantage over their rival minority faith."[72]

The concept of "the enemy" also includes its imagined counterpart, "the friend." As an object of inquiry, politics has been conceived as being "based on the drawing of fundamental distinctions between enemies and friends."[73] Enemies are those imagined to have as their aim the destruction of their "opponent's way of life and therefore must be repulsed or fought in order to preserve one's own form of existence."[74] Moreover, the enemy is "the other, the stranger; and it is sufficient for his nature that he is, in a specially intense way, existentially something different and alien, so that in the extreme case conflicts with him are possible." The enemy is countered by its imagined opposite, the friend, "as a figure identified with the Self, characterized as familiar, and with whom legitimate conflict is not possible." As with the identification of an enemy, identification of and with a friend also has "political costs."[75]

From medieval to modern times, Jews' loyalties were assumed in Christian Europe to be "with Islam against Christendom," for "the friendship of the Jew for the Muslim was taken for granted as fact."[76] As Liberal member of the British parliament T. P. O'Connor declared in 1877, "For many ages—more in the past than in the present, of course—there has been among large sections of the Jews the strongest sympathy with the Mohammedan peoples. A common enemy is a great bond of friendship, and as the Christian was equally the enemy of the Mohammedan and the Jew, they were thereby brought into a certain alliance." It is no coincidence that he was referring to the ethnically Sephardic-Jewish prime minister Benjamin Disraeli's (d. 1881, prime minister 1868; 1874–1880) favorable policy toward the Ottoman Empire in the Russo-Turkish War, for "as a Jew, he [Disraeli] feels bound to make common cause with the Turk against the Christian." O'Connor was correct to argue that Jews in nineteenth-century Europe were largely pro-Turkish and pro-Muslim.[77] Whether we consider such partnerships as the "late Ottoman Muslim-Jewish alliances,"[78] the "strategic alliances"[79] between Turks and Jews that began at the inception of the Turkish Republic and intensified after World War II, or the "Turkish-Israeli entente" promoted as the logical consequence of centuries of allegedly harmonious relations between the two peoples,[80] such affinities are based on shared interests and always involve the exclusion of other non-Muslim groups.

In the case of the Ottoman and Turkish Jewish imagination as articulated by Jewish chroniclers, historians, religious and lay leaders, it is the Christian who stands as the common political enemy. Jews depict themselves as the friend of the Muslim. The "political cost" and ethical consequence of this identification is that Jews must work tirelessly to cover up the crimes of their "friend." Not only in the last century of the Ottoman Empire, but also throughout the entire post-conquest-of-Constantinople period (1453–1922), the external enemy for Jews is depicted—often despite relations at the imperial or individual level—in terms of Christian empires: the Byzantines, the Catholic monarchs of Spain, and the Habsburg Dynasty, and later the independent Kingdom of Greece. In the Turkish period (from 1923), the enemy is embodied in the nation-states of Europe or the European Union. In Jewish narratives and modern Jewish historiography, Ottoman Christians play the role of the "internal enemy." These include Orthodox Christians (Greeks) and Armenians who supposedly bear the traits of Christian Europeans, view Turks (Muslims) as barbarians, and hate Jews; Ottoman Christians also include converts, the Janissaries and viziers who staff the military and administration. The "pure" Turkish sultan always, it is claimed, protects Jews from Armenians, Greeks, and formerly Christian officials. This construction of the Christian enemy shapes the way Jews in these lands have imagined and written about Muslims, from the fifteenth century to the present. With Jews appealing to Muslims and Jews and Muslims appealing to the Christian world, this entangled mutual alliance of interests promotes a common utopian view of their relations, no matter what—and often in spite of what—Muslims think, write, or do about the Jews in their midst.

It is in this framework that the normally sober doyen of Ottoman studies, the "sheikh of historians" Halil Inalcik (1916–2016), the producer of dozens of fact-filled books and hundreds of articles on the administrative, economic, and social history of the Ottoman Empire, finds himself unable to write dispassionately about Jews: "As a historian, I tried to focus on the historical, rational motives and causes for Turkish-Jewish cooperation, setting aside the role of intangible sentiments such as compassion, sympathy, and loyalty."[81] But he cannot. "I think I was mistaken," he confesses. Writing from his affective disposition, the emotional world that motivates an author's work,[82] he continues: "Sometimes human relations are shaped and moved by forces that are deeper and more significant than mere rationality. Shared experiences and positive memories, interwoven through centuries of coexistence, have made Turks and Jews one family united in friendship."[83] If we relocate the European argument that there is no consideration of the "Jewish question" without the "Muslim question" to the Ottoman Empire and Turkey, Christians turn into "enemies of the Turks." In other words, one cannot come to an understanding of Jewish discourse about Ottomans and Turks without also considering the "Christian question."

Although the narratives examined focus on Muslims and Jews, Christians play a large albeit subtextual role in these narratives. As another scholar has noted, interreligious relations in the Ottoman Empire "could best be expressed graphically as a triangle, the vertices of which represent Muslims, Christians, and Jews."[84] Early modern memories of their ancestors having been allowed refuge in the empire, and experience with the fate of Armenians and Greeks in the late Ottoman Empire and early Turkish Republic compelled Ottoman and later Turkish Jews to portray themselves as the friend. Maintaining close, positive relations with the sultan, promoting the mutual alliance of interests between Muslims and Jews, Jews united with Muslims against the common Christian enemy. In modern Jewish historiography, a sharp difference is posited between Jews, Christians, and Muslim Turks: Jews have always been loyal and useful to the state, never rebellious; Christians have been ever disloyal, fifth-column tormentors of Jews and importers of anti-Semitism to the empire and the republic; Muslim Turks and their sultans have been the enduring harbor, the protector of "their" Jews.

Chapter Overview

Adopting the long historical view, the following chapters examine Jewish accounts of Ottomans and Turks from the fifteenth through the twenty-first centuries. After being expelled from Spain and Portugal at the end of the fifteenth century, the Jews who eventually settled in the Ottoman Empire found that its Muslim rulers allowed them to remain Jewish, free from persecution. The *Conversos*, Jews compelled to become Catholic who subsequently joined them in the sixteenth century, were able to return to Judaism. Chapter 1, "Sultans as Saviors," narrates how for this reason Mediterranean Jewish writers of the sixteenth century—those who settled in the Ottoman Empire and those who continued to be expelled from city after city by the Inquisition—extolled the praises of the sultan in messianic terms. As a consequence, their emotional state led them to silence Jewish counternarratives that criticized the sultans. Silence was thus built into the narrative of Turkish Jewish history from its inception in the fifteenth century. The half-dozen myths they promoted about Ottoman treatment of Jews continue to form the basis of utopian claims about Turkish-Jewish relations today.

Chapter 2, "The Empire of Tolerant Turks," addresses how the early modern Jewish affective disposition was repeated in the first Ashkenazi and Sephardi histories of the Ottoman Empire. Reflecting this, in 1892, on the four hundredth anniversary of their ancestors' having taken refuge, Ottoman Jews organized a celebration of Ottoman and Turkish tolerance. From that moment onward, for Ottoman Jews and Muslims alike, historical events and historical memory would be linked to a politics of memory. Both populations saw an advantage in promoting an image of grateful and loyal Jews and tolerant and magnanimous Turks set against the foil of anti-Semitic and traitorous Armenians and Greeks, the other major non-Muslim constituency within Ottoman society. Even as Armenian civilians were massacred in the empire beginning in 1896, Ottoman Jews were joined by foreign Jews, including the leaders of the Zionist movement, who also saw it in their interest to praise Ottoman tolerance and condemn alleged Armenian treachery. Just as earlier Ottoman Jews had silenced the narratives of Byzantine (Romaniot) Jews, so here did the Ottoman Jewish elite promote utopian visions, silencing the voices of the Zionists and socialists among their community. The best example is chief Rabbi Haim Nahum, who privately expressed fears of anti-Semitism and violence against Jews yet publicly sided with the state, even as it annihilated the Armenians.

Chapter 3, "Grateful Jews and Anti-Semitic Armenians and Greeks," examines how, following the Armenian genocide in 1915 and the collapse of the empire within the next decade, Turkish Jews in the new Turkish Republic promoted the same Ottoman-era narrative with the same Ottoman-era stock figures, but with a twist. What is familiar is how the leading Jewish voice, Abraham Galanté, presented Jews responding to Ottoman and Turkish tolerance with loyalty and gratefulness, which he contrasted with treacherous Armenians and Greeks who spread anti-Semitism. What is new is a double silence: he does not mention the Armenian genocide, nor does he choose to remember violence and discriminatory policies directed against Jews in Turkey. One of the reasons he did so is that the absence of Christians left him no one to blame. Despite his own personal experience, he extended the tolerance trope to include all Muslim Turks. Throughout the twentieth century, Galanté was joined by Jewish historians outside Turkey who remained silent about both the Armenian genocide and Turkish anti-Semitism, blaming anti-Jewish sentiment and violence in the empire on Christians. This is important in that unlike Turkish Jews, whose lived experience was both more restricted and their position more precarious,

Jewish historians outside of Turkey were compelled neither by historical memory nor by their own present circumstances.

Chapter 4, "Turkish Jews as Turkish Lobbyists," analyzes the role of leading Turkish Jews as lobbyists for Turkey, a mission they were compelled to undertake beginning in the 1970s, denying genocide on Turkey's behalf in the United States, Europe, and Israel. The turn to Jews as lobbyists on Turkey's behalf was based not only on the old myth of Turkish-Jewish friendship, but also on the anti-Semitic conspiracy theory that Jews control world governments, finance, and media. The Turkish Jewish community leadership, especially Jak Kamhi and Bensiyon Pinto, regularly boasts that it has acted as a special interest group working hand in hand with Turkish presidents, prime ministers, and foreign ministers successfully lobbying foreign Jews to influence their governments to side with Turkey by defeating resolutions to recognize the Armenian genocide, silencing mention of it at international academic conferences, and hindering its commemoration in Holocaust museums. The politicized and governmentalized lobbying had a direct effect on historiography, realized in the works of Turkish Muslim and Turkish Jewish authors alike, as well as foreign Jewish historians, especially Bernard Lewis and Stanford Shaw, enlisted to join the effort pairing a utopian vision of Turkish-Jewish friendship that denied the existence of Turkish anti-Semitism with Armenian genocide denial.

Chapter 5, "Five Hundred Years of Friendship," explores the ways in which the Turkish Jewish lobby became regularized as the Quincentennial Foundation in 1989, which together with Turkish foreign ministers and ambassadors abroad sought to rebrand Turkey's poor international image, unequivocally denying the Armenian genocide by advocating a vision of "500 years of peace and brotherhood" between Turks and Jews. As so many Ottoman and Turkish Jews before them, those leading these efforts omitted their own experiences of anti-Semitic discrimination and violence to present a utopian view of Turkish-Jewish relations. The foundation spent considerable efforts to influence academia, by endowing chairs in Ottoman and Turkish studies, sponsoring conferences, and publishing academic works; and to shape public opinion, including establishing what is billed as a "tolerance Museum" in Istanbul. Despite their efforts, secular Turkish intellectuals undercut the harmony narrative by presenting an unfavorable view of Turkish Jews and of Turkish Muslims' views toward them, confirming the existence of anti-Semitism and utilizing anti-Semitic stereotypes.

Chapter 6, "Whitewashing the Armenian Genocide with Holocaust Heroism," looks at the novel historical claim immediately following the quincentennial that Turkey had played a major role rescuing Jews from the Holocaust, thus squaring the circle of the five-hundred-year claim. The year 1492 was paired with 1942, used following 1992 to illustrate five centuries of Turkey having served as a refuge for Jews persecuted by Christian Europe. This brash claim ignored the fact that Turkish diplomats in Europe had systematically stripped Turkish Jews of their citizenship or refused to recognize them as citizens. Turkey did not take the opportunity to save tens of thousands of Jewish citizens in Europe from the Nazi reign of terror, instead condemning thousands of them to miserable deaths in the camps.[85] Discounting these inconvenient truths, Jews and Muslims promoted the narrative of Turkish rescue of Jews to a separate audience: in the face of persistent anti-Semitism, Jews spoke to a national audience of their loyalty and gratitude in order to be well treated, while representatives of the Turkish state boasted of their good treatment of Jews to an international audience to improve relations with Europe, Israel, and the United States. Whereas the arrival of the Sephardim after 1492 was well documented and initially a memory for Jews alone, 1942 was promoted by the Turkish Foreign Ministry working together with Jewish historians outside of Turkey and was explicitly linked to denying recognition of the Armenian genocide. According to this view, genocide is an if/then proposition: if one accepts the fable that Turks and Jews have lived in peace and brotherhood for five hundred years, as opposed to the historical record, which narrates a completely different story, then one trusts that Turks could not possibly have perpetrated a genocide against the Armenians.

Finally, chapters 7, "The Emergence of Critical Turkish Jewish Voices," and 8, "Living in Peace and Harmony, or in Fear?" relate developments in Turkish and Ottoman historiography at the turn of the new millennium. The most prominent critical Turkish Jewish historian is Rıfat Bali, who was first compelled to take up the pen by a realization that the mantra of the 500 Year Foundation contrasted utterly with what he and fellow Turkish Jews had experienced. Motivated by an affective disposition that makes him take aim at Abraham Galanté, Bali writes not to promote a utopian vision of Turkish-Jewish amity, but to detail the lachrymose state of Jews in the Turkish Republic. Bali redacted and helped publish several mournful memoirs of Turkish Jews who had migrated to Israel, thus providing the Zionist voice in Turkey, which had been long silenced. The works of Avner Levi,

Eli Şaul, and Erol Haker detail Turkish anti-Semitism at the highest levels of government, as well as discrimination and violence against Jews, manifested in the campaign to Turkify the economy and culture, the pogrom in Thrace (1934), the Twentieth Reserve Corps (1942), the Capital Tax (1942–1944), and the Turkish government's World War II–era policies that blocked the large-scale immigration to Turkey of endangered European and Turkish Jews in Europe. Another exemplary Turkish Jewish writer is the novelist Mario Levi, who subverts the utopian view of Turkish-Jewish relations by casting doubt on Turkey's self-serving myths about rescuing Jews during World War II. As a first for a Turkish Jewish author, he does so while linking the Holocaust to the Armenian genocide. Ironically, the novelist creates characters that are far more believable than the stereotypical tolerant Turks, grateful Jews, and anti-Semitic Armenians and Greeks long propagated by historians.

The same emotional state of fear and anxiety, documented also in the memoirs of Beki Bahar, drove the leaders of the Turkish Jewish community, Bensiyon Pinto and Jak Kamhi, however, to insist on propagating the same well-worn myths about Turkish-Jewish relations. Despite their own experiences, which included surviving lynch mobs, assassination attempts, and synagogue bombings, they persisted in claiming the experience of Jews in Turkey is a happy one. In their autobiographies they brag that the Turkish state could rely on them to travel the globe on a moment's notice to work with Jewish allies abroad to deny the existence of Turkish anti-Semitism and thwart attempts at Armenian genocide recognition.

Notes

1. Mevlüt Çavuşoğlu, "Message on International Holocaust Remembrance Day," Republic of Turkey Ministry for EU Affairs, January 27, 2015, https://www.ab.gov.tr/49393_en.html.

2. Ibid.

3. Ibid.

4. See the page at the Internet Archive: https://web.archive.org/web/20140307003335/http://www.turkyahudileri.com/content/view/2883/287/.

5. Turkey does not offer Holocaust education in state schools. The Deutsche Schule Istanbul is one of the only private schools in Turkey that teaches students about the Holocaust. Rifat Bali, "Perceptions of the Holocaust in Turkey," in *Perceptions of the Holocaust in Europe and Muslim Communities: Sources, Comparison, and Educational Challenge*, ed. Günther Jikeli and Joëlle Allouche-Benayoun (London: Springer Science, 2012).

6. The letter is cited in Yair Auron, *The Banality of Denial: Israel and the Armenian Genocide* (London: Transaction, 2003), 106, and in Rifat Bali, *Model Citizens of the State: The*

Jews of Turkey during the Multi-Party Period, trans. Paul Bessemer (Madison, NJ: Fairleigh Dickinson University Press, 2012), 282.

7. This fact has been recognized in modern Jewish studies since its foundation in the mid-nineteenth century. For recent expositions see Laurent-Olivier Mallet, *La Turquie, les Turcs et les Juifs: Histoire, représentations, discours et stratégies* (Istanbul: Les Éditions Isis, 2008), and İ. İzzet Bahar, *Jewish Historiography on the Ottoman Empire and Its Jewry from the Late Fifteenth Century to the Early Decades of the Twentieth Century* (Istanbul: Gorgias Press and Isis Press, 2008).

8. For an overview of this literature, see Fatma Müge Göçek, *Denial of Violence: Ottoman Past, Turkish Present, and Collective Violence against the Armenians, 1789–2009* (Oxford: Oxford University Press, 2014), 4–9.

9. Richard Hovannisian, *Denial of the Armenian Genocide in Comparison with Holocaust Denial* (Yerevan: National Academy of Sciences, 2004), 3, cited in Göçek, *Denial of Violence*, 6.

10. For a concise definition of "affective disposition," see Ronald Grigor Suny, *"They Can Live in the Desert but Nowhere Else": A History of the Armenian Genocide* (Princeton, NJ: Princeton University Press, 2015), 134.

11. Göçek, *Denial of Violence*, 3, 36.

12. William H. Sewell, Jr., *Logics of History: Social Theory and Social Transformation* (Chicago: University of Chicago Press, 2005), 232–262, discussed in Göçek, *Denial of Violence*, 40.

13. Michael Rothberg, *Multidirectional Memory: Remembering the Holocaust in the Age of Decolonization* (Stanford, CA: Stanford University Press, 2009).

14. Avigdor Levy, introduction to *The Jews of the Ottoman Empire*, ed. Avigdor Levy (Princeton, NJ: Darwin, 1994), 124.

15. Jonathan Ray, "Beyond Tolerance and Persecution: Reassessing Our Approach to Medieval Convivencia," *Jewish Social Studies* 11, no. 2 (Winter 2005): 4.

16. Mark R. Cohen, "The 'Golden Age' of Jewish-Muslim Relations: Myth and Reality," in *A History of Jewish-Muslim Relations: From the Origins to the Present Day*, ed. Abdelwahab Meddeb and Benjamin Stora, trans. Jane Marie Todd and Michael B. Smith (Princeton, NJ: Princeton University Press, 2013), 28.

17. David Nirenberg, "What Can Medieval Spain Tell Us about Muslim-Jewish Relations?" *CCAR Journal /A Reform Jewish Quarterly* (Spring/Summer 2002): 18–19.

18. Ibid., 18.

19. Ibid., 19.

20. Mark R. Cohen, "Foreword," in Bernard Lewis, *The Jews of Islam* (Princeton, NJ: Princeton University Press, 2014); Jacob Lassner, *Jews, Christians, and the Abode of Islam: Modern Scholarship, Medieval Realities* (Chicago: University of Chicago Press, 2012); Mark R. Cohen, *Under Crescent & Cross: The Jew in the Middle Ages* (Princeton, NJ: Princeton University Press, 1994, revised edition 2008); Mark R. Cohen, "The Neo-Lachrymose Conception of Jewish-Arab History," *Tikkun* 6, no. 3 (May/June 1991); Norman Stillman, *The Jews of Arab Lands in Modern Times: A History and Source Book* (Philadelphia: Jewish Publication Society of America, 1991); Mark R. Cohen, "Islam and the Jews: Myth, Counter-Myth, History," *Jerusalem Quarterly* 38 (1986); Norman A. Stillman, "History" in *The Jews of Arab Lands: A History and Source Book* (Philadelphia: The Jewish Publication Society of America, 1979); Bernard Lewis, "The Pro-Islamic Jews," *Judaism* 17, no. 4 (Fall 1968); Shlomo Dov Goitein, *A Mediterranean Society: The Jewish Communities of the Arab World*

as Portrayed in the Documents of the Cairo Geniza, 6 vols. (Berkeley, CA: University of California Press, 1967–1993); and Shlomo Dov Goitein, *Jews and Arabs: Their Contacts through the Ages* (New York: Schocken, [1955] 1973).

21. See Marc David Baer, "Muslim Encounters with Nazism and the Holocaust: The Ahmadi of Berlin and German-Jewish Convert to Islam Hugo Marcus," *American Historical Review* 120, no. 1 (February 2015).

22. I do not analyze encounters between Muslims and Jews in the Seljuk Empire as Ottoman (and then Turkish) Jewish accounts of their relations primarily draw meaning from post-1453 Ottoman society.

23. Mehmet Tütüncü, introduction to *Turkish-Jewish Encounters: Studies on Turkish-Jewish Relations through the Ages*, ed. Mehmet Tütüncü (Haarlem, the Netherlands: SOTA Research Centre for Turkestan, Azerbaijan, Crimea, Caucasus and Siberia, 2001), 9. For a similar sentiment, see Benjamin Braude, "Myths and Realities of Turkish-Jewish Contacts," in ibid.

24. Bernard Lewis, *The Jews of Islam* (Princeton: Princeton University Press, 1984), 7.

25. Aomar Boum: *Memories of Absence: How Muslims Remember Jews in Morocco* (Stanford, CA: Stanford University Press, 2014); Abdelkrim Allagui, "The Jews of the Maghreb: Between Memory and History," in *A History of Jewish-Muslim Relations*; Orit Bashkin, *New Babylonians: A History of Jews in Modern Iraq* (Stanford, CA: Stanford University Press, 2012); Mark R. Cohen, "Historical Memory and History in the Memoirs of Iraqi Jews," Ot LeTova: Essays in Honor of Professor Tova Rosen, *Journal for Hebrew and Israeli Literature and Culture Studies, El Prezente, Studies in Sephardic Culture*, ed. Eli Yassif, Haviva Ishay, Uriah Kfir, *Mikan*, 11, *El Prezente*, 6 (June 2012); Lital Levy, "A Republic of Letters Without a Republic?" *AJS Perspectives* (Fall 2010); André Aciman, *Out of Egypt: A Memoir*, reprint edition (New York: Picador, 2007); Sasson Somekh, *Baghdad, Yesterday: The Making of an Arab Jew* (New York: Ibis, 2007); Lital Levy "Self and the City: Literary Representations of Jewish Baghdad," *Prooftexts* 26 (2006); Deborah Starr, "Sensing the City: Representations of Cairo's Harat al-Yahud," *Prooftexts* 26 (2006); Joel Beinin, *The Dispersion of Egyptian Jewry: Culture, Politics, and the Formation of the Modern Diaspora* (Berkeley, CA: University of California Press, 1998); Yoram Bilu and André Levy, "Nostalgia and Ambivalence: The Reconstruction of Jewish-Muslim Relations in Oulad Mansour," in *Sephardi and Middle Eastern Jewries: History & Culture in The Modern Era*, ed. Harvey E. Goldberg (Bloomington, IN: Indiana University Press, 1996); and Abraham Udovitch and Lucette Valensi, *The Last Arab Jews: The Communities of Jerba Tunisia* (New York: Harwood, 1984).

26. The 1,145-page tome, *A History of Jewish-Muslim Relations: From the Origins to the Present Day*, while also primarily concerned with Jews in arabophone regions, from the life of Muhammad to the present, includes thirty-five pages on Muslim-Jewish relations in the Ottoman Empire and in Turkey. Gilles Veinstein offers a thorough historical overview in "Jews and Muslims in Ottoman Territory before the Expulsion from Spain," ibid., 164–169, and "Jews and Muslims in the Ottoman Empire," ibid., 171–195; Nora Şeni presents a summary of more recent events, historiographical trends, and cultural developments in "Survival of the Jewish Community in Turkey," ibid., 490–494. But one-third of the section on Jews in the Ottoman Empire from the fifteenth to nineteenth centuries is devoted to Palestine; the section devoted to the twentieth century, with the exception of Şeni's article and a couple of others on Iran or Central Asia, is almost entirely devoted to Palestine and arabophone regions.

27. Esther Benbassa and Aron Rodrigue, *Sephardi Jewry: A History of the Judeo-Spanish Community, 14ᵗʰ–20th Centuries* (1993; Berkeley: University of California Press, 2000), 194.

28. Benbassa and Rodrigue, *Sephardi Jewry*, 192. They note "first of all the new Ottoman foundation myth, the exceptional welcome given to the Jews," ibid., 194. Five hundred years later, "the last remnant of the Ottoman Empire is appropriating this myth and prolonging it by bringing it up to date." And Turkish Jewry does so in collaboration with the Turks: "Anxious to enter the European Community, with the semivoluntary collaboration of local Jews, Turkey is proclaiming its long tradition of tolerance towards Jews in an attempt to reduce somewhat the ill-effects of its treatment of some minorities in its recent history," namely, Armenians, Greeks, and Kurds. Rodrigue's students, the first an anthropologist, the second a historian, have explored Ottoman or Turkish Jewish propagation of these myths. See Marcy Brink-Danan, *Jewish Life in 21st-Century Turkey: The Other Side of Tolerance* (Bloomington, IN, Indiana University Press, 2012); and Julia Phillips Cohen, *Becoming Ottomans: Sephardi Jews and Imperial Citizenship in the Modern Era* (Oxford: Oxford University Press, 2014). As Rodrigue's student Brink-Danan has written, "Playing their part in international arenas, Jews regularly proclaim Turkey's eternal hospitality and tolerance for difference to a global audience as counterpoint to European politicians' regular criticisms of Turkey's treatment of Armenians" and other persecuted groups. Brink-Danan, *Jewish Life in 21st-Century Turkey*, 33.

29. Mallet, *La Turquie, les Turcs et les Juifs*, 8–9.

30. Nirenberg, "What Can Medieval Spain Tell Us," 19.

31. Norman Stillman, "Myth, Counter-Myth, and Distortion," *Tikkun* 6, no. 3 (May–June 1991).

32. Ibid., 61, 64.

33. Having written the first history of the Dönme, the descendants of the followers of Sabbatai Zevi, from their seventeenth-century origins to the mid-twentieth century, I will not explore the group at length here. See Marc David Baer, *The Dönme: Jewish Converts, Muslim Revolutionaries, and Secular Turks* (Stanford, CA: Stanford University Press, 2010).

34. Marc David Baer, *Honored by the Glory of Islam: Conversion and Conquest in Ottoman Europe* (Oxford: Oxford University Press, 2008), 23.

35. Marc David Baer, "An Enemy Old and New: The Dönme, Anti-Semitism, and Conspiracy Theories in the Ottoman Empire and Turkish Republic," *Jewish Quarterly Review* 103, no. 4 (Fall 2013).

36. "Türkiye'nin tutumu örnek gösterildi," *Şalom*, March 6, 1985, cited in Bali, *Model Citizens of the State*, 320.

37. Mallet, *La Turquie, les Turcs et les Juifs*, 102, 527.

38. "Tolerance and Conversion in the Ottoman Empire: A Conversation with Marc Baer and Ussama Makdisi," *Comparative Studies in Society & History* 51, no. 4 (October 2009): 930. The arguments I cite from this article are my own.

39. Ibid.

40. For a detailed study of Ottoman social hierarchies see Marc David Baer, "Islamic Conversion Narratives of Women: Social Change and Gendered Religious Hierarchy in Early Modern Ottoman Istanbul," *Gender & History* 16, no. 2 (August 2004).

41. Karen Barkey, *Empire of Difference: The Ottomans in Comparative Perspective* (Cambridge: Cambridge University Press, 2008), 115.

42. Aron Rodrigue, "Difference and Tolerance in the Ottoman Empire," *Stanford Humanities Review* 5, no. 1 (1995), quoted in Barkey, *Empire of Difference*, 115, 119–120.

43. Rodrigue, "Difference and Tolerance in the Ottoman Empire."

44. Ibid., 81.

45. Ibid.

46. Emphasis is my own.

47. "Tolerance and Conversion in the Ottoman Empire: A Conversation with Marc Baer and Ussama Makdisi," 936.

48. Ibid., 937.

49. Kemal H. Karpat, *The Ottoman Mosaic: Exploring Models for Peace by Re-Exploring the Past* (Seattle: Cune, 2010). See also Ekmelleddin İhsanoğlu, *A Culture of Peaceful Coexistence: Early Islamic and Ottoman Turkish Examples* (Istanbul: Research Centre for Islamic History, Art, and Culture, 2004), which "focuses on the Islamic culture of peaceful coexistence with particular reference to the history of Islamic civilization and especially the Ottoman world."

50. "Tolerance and Conversion in the Ottoman Empire," 937.

51. Barkey, *Empire of Difference*, 110.

52. Ibid., 146.

53. Ibid., 114.

54. Ibid., 132, 263.

55. Ibid., 278.

56. Ibid., 110.

57. Brink-Danan, *Jewish Life in 21ˢᵗ-Century Turkey*, 33.

58. Mallet, *La Turquie, les Turcs et les Juifs*, 438.

59. Key works that focus on Jews or Judaism as the enemy include David Nirenberg, *Anti-Judaism: The Western Tradition* (New York: Norton, 2013); R. I. Moore, *The Formation of a Persecuting Society: Authority and Deviance in Western Europe, 950–1250*, 3rd ed. (London: Wiley-Blackwell, 2007); Esther Benbassa and Jean-Christophe Attias, *The Jew and the Other*, trans. G. M. Goshgarian (Ithaca, NY: Cornell University Press, 2004); R. I. Moore, *The First European Revolution, c. 970–1215* (Oxford: Blackwells, 2000); James Shapiro, *Shakespeare and the Jews* (New York: Columbia University Press, 1997); Robert Chazan, *Medieval Stereotypes and Modern Antisemitism* (Berkeley, CA: University of California Press, 1997); Gavin Langmuir, *History, Religion, and Antisemitism* (Berkeley, CA: University of California Press, 1990); and Jeremy Cohen, *The Evolution of Medieval Anti-Judaism* (Ithaca, NY: Cornell University Press, 1982). Works focusing on Muslims and Islam include John Tolan, *Sons of Ishmael: Muslims Through European Eyes in the Middle Ages* (Gainesville, FL: University Press of Florida, 2008); Tomaž Mastnak, *Crusading Peace: Christendom, the Muslim World, and Western Political Order* (Berkeley, CA: University of California Press, 2002); John Tolan, *Saracens: Islam in the Medieval European Imagination* (New York: Columbia University Press, 2002); Nabil Matar, *Turks, Moors and Englishmen in the Age of Discovery* (New York: Columbia University Press, 2000); Maxime Rodinson, *Europe and the Mystique of Islam*, trans. Roger Veinus (1980; London: I.B. Tauris, 1988); Edward W. Said, *Orientalism* (New York: Vintage, 1978); Richard W. Southern, *Western Views of Islam in the Middle Ages* (Cambridge, MA: Harvard University Press, 1962); and Norman Daniel, *Islam and the West: The Making of an Image* (Edinburgh: University Press, 1960).

60. Tomaž Mastnak, "Western Hostility toward Muslims: A History of the Present," in *Islamophobia/Islamophilia: Beyond the Politics of Enemy and Friend*, ed. Andrew Shryock (Bloomington, IN: Indiana University Press, 2010), 33, 35.

61. Jeremy Cohen, "The Muslim Connection or on the Changing Role of the Jew in High Medieval Theology," in *From Witness to Witchcraft: Jews and Judaism in Medieval Christian*

Thought, ed. Jeremy Cohen, Wolfenbütteler Mittelalter-Studien Band 11 (Wiesbaden: Harrassowitz Verlag, 1996), 162.

62. Concerned as they are with the Israeli-Palestinian struggle and Jews from arabophone regions in the modern period, Shohat and Anidjar prefer the term "Arab" to "Muslim" or "Turk," even when referring to the early modern era. Ella Shohat, "Rethinking Jews and Muslims: Quincentennial Reflections," *Middle East Report* 178 (1992); Ella Shohat, "Taboo Memories, Diasporic Visions: Columbus, Palestine, and Arab-Jews," in Shohat, *Taboo Memories, Diasporic Voices* (Durham, NC: Duke University Press, 2006); Gil Anidjar, *The Jew, the Arab: A History of the Enemy* (Stanford, CA: Stanford University Press, 2003), ch. 1. Allan Harris Cutler and Helen Elmquist Cutler align the history of anti-Semitism and "antimuslimism" in the context of Christendom's wars with Islamdom. They argue that medieval Christian European anti-Semitism derived from the perception that Jews within Christendom collaborated with Muslims without to undermine Christendom. Allan Harris Cutler and Helen Elmquist Cutler, *The Jew as Ally of the Muslim: Medieval Roots of Anti-Semitism* (Notre Dame, IN: University of Notre Dame Press, 1986).

63. Anidjar, *The Jew, the Arab*, 33–34.

64. For a much more extensive discussion of this topic, see David Nirenberg, *Communities of Violence: Persecution of Minorities in the Middle Age* (Princeton, NJ: Princeton University Press, 1996), esp. ch. 5.

65. Anidjar, *The Jew, the Arab*, xxv.

66. Ibid., ch. 4.

67. Jerry Brotton, *This Orient Isle: Elizabethan England and the Early Modern World* (London: Allen Lane, 2016), 193–196.

68. Christopher Marlowe, *The Jew of Malta*, 2.3.215–8, cited in Anidjar, *The Jew, the Arab*, 102, and Brotton, *This Orient Isle*, 179.

69. Said, *Orientalism*, 27–28; James Pasto, "Islam's 'Strange Secret Sharer': Orientalism, Judaism, and the Jewish Question," *Comparative Studies in Society and History* 40, no. 3 (July 1998); Ivan Davidson Kalmar and Derek Penslar, "Orientalism and the Jews: An Introduction," in *Orientalism and the Jews*, ed. Ivan Davidson Kalmar and Derek Penslar (Lebanon, NH: University Press of New England, 2004).

70. Braude, "Myths and Realities of Turkish-Jewish Contacts," 21.

71. Nirenberg, "What Can Medieval Spain Tell Us," 22. Others have demonstrated how Christians in Spain forged a unified Christian identity based on entanglement with difference within Europe. Jews were designated as this difference, a people seen as problematic because they were internal to Spain and had existed prior to Christians; Muslims also, another circumcised people, seen as both internal to Spain and external in the kingdoms of the Islamic world. See Jonathan Boyarin, *The Unconverted Self: Jews, Indians, and The Identity of Christian Europe* (Chicago: University of Chicago Press, 2009), ch. 1, ch. 2.

72. Nirenberg, "What Can Medieval Spain Tell Us," 26.

73. Andrew Shryock, "Introduction: Islam as an Object of Fear and Affection," in *Islamophobia/Islamophilia: Beyond the Politics of Friend and Enemy*, ed. Andrew Shryock (Bloomington, IN: Indiana University Press, 2010), 8.

74. Carl Schmitt, *The Concept of the Political* (Chicago: University of Chicago Press, 1996), 27, quoted in Shryock, "Introduction," 8.

75. Shryock, "Introduction," 9.

76. Lewis, "The Pro-Islamic Jews," 392.

77. Ibid., 395. In a more recent analysis, Ivan Kalmar concurs that "Disraeli's vision of the Orient informed with remarkable consistency not only his personal identity and his fiction but also his policies as a public figure," including "support for Turkey against Greece and Russia." Ivan Kalmar, "Benjamin Disraeli: Romantic Orientalist," *Comparative Studies in Society & History* 47, no. 2 (April 2005): 353. Disraeli's liberal rival William Gladstone advocated positions on behalf of Armenians; his quote "to serve Armenia is to serve civilization" appeared on the masthead of the New York monthly *Armenia*. Margaret Lavinia Anderson, "'Down in Turkey, Far Away': Human Rights, the Armenian Massacres, and Orientalism in Wilhelmine Germany," *Journal of Modern History* 79, no. 1 (March 2007): 84.

78. Julia Phillips Cohen, "Halal and Kosher: Jews and Muslims as Political and Economic Allies," *AJS Perspectives*, The Muslim Issue (Spring 2012): 41.

79. Bali, *Model Citizens of the State*, 416–417, 446.

80. Mallet, *La Turquie, les Turcs et les Juifs*, 7–8.

81. Halil Inalcik, "Foundations of Ottoman Jewish Cooperation," in *Jews, Turks, Ottomans: A Shared History, Fifteenth through the Twentieth Century*, ed. Avigdor Levy (Syracuse, NY: Syracuse University Press, 2002), 14.

82. Suny, *"They Can Live in the Desert but Nowhere Else,"* 134.

83. Inalcik, "Foundations of Ottoman Jewish Cooperation," 14.

84. Jacob Landau, "Relations Between Jews and Non-Jews in the Late Ottoman Empire: Some Characteristics," in *The Jews of the Ottoman Empire*, ed. with an introduction by Avigdor Levy (Princeton, NJ: Darwin Press, 1994), 539.

85. Marc David Baer, "Turk and Jew in Berlin: The First Turkish Migration to Berlin and the Shoah," *Comparative Studies in Society & History* 55, no. 2 (April 2013).

1

SULTANS AS SAVIORS

JEWS LIVING UNDER MUSLIM RULE IN AL-ANDALUS (CENTRAL and southern Spain) from the tenth through the twelfth centuries have long captured the imagination of modern historians and the public.[1] They seem to
call out to us from the past, for "no other medieval Jewish community had
so many high-ranking personalities in the political and economic spheres;
no other produced a literary culture of such breadth, revealing an intellectual life shared with the Muslims."[2] These Sephardic Jews (*Sefarad*, Hebrew
for "Spain") were remarkable for "the extraordinary cultural vitality of
the elites, combined with their material prosperity, their participation in
public affairs and in the administration of the courts of al-Andalus, their
responsibilities within their communities, and their importance in Jewish history."[3] But due to Christian advances, by the mid-thirteenth century
Muslim Spain was limited to the Kingdom of Granada, which fell to Catholic Isabella and Ferdinand at the beginning of 1492. That same year the
Catholic rulers decreed that Jews would have to convert to Christianity or
be expelled from all their dominions, including Castile, Catalonia, Aragón,
Galicia, Mallorca, the Basque region, Sicily and Sardinia, and Valencia.[4]
Five years later, Jews were expelled from neighboring Portugal.

The masses of Iberian Jews fled first to the Muslim kingdoms of North
Africa, especially Fez in Morocco and the Berber kingdom of Tlemcen
in Algeria, then to Italian cities that still tolerated them, such as Ferr-
ara, Genoa, Naples, and Venice.[5] Eventually, over the course of a century
and following many trials and tribulations, most settled in the Ottoman
Empire. That Muslim-ruled realm already boasted a diverse, tolerated
Jewish population of Greek, Arab, Central European (Ashkenazic), Kurdish, and Sephardic backgrounds. These Jews had either been incorporated
into the empire as it conquered Byzantine and Arab-ruled territories—by
1517, including Jerusalem and Palestine—or had arrived as refugees from

persecution in Central and Western Europe.[6] When Mehmed II (r. 1444–1446, 1451–1481) conquered Constantinople in 1453, he brought Jews from over forty Anatolian and southeastern European towns to repopulate the devastated city and make it flourish. They would constitute 10 percent of the city's population and be the majority in Ottoman Salonica. The sultan gave Jews autonomy to run their own civic and religious affairs under their own leaders. They were joined by many Conversos—Iberian Jews and their descendants forcibly converted to Catholicism, many of whom relished the opportunity to return to Judaism. For incoming Conversos, "emigration to Ottoman territory was a fully affirmed return to the faith of their fathers."[7]

Among the empire's Jews, the Andalusian exiles, whether Jews or Conversos, would soon become "dominant in population and cultural influence," its elites filling many of the same roles they had in the Spanish Muslim kingdoms—as royal physicians, diplomats, courtiers, and merchants; serving in customs, the treasury, and as tax farmers; and playing a larger role than their predecessors had in international trade.[8] Tenth- and eleventh-century al-Andalus boasted Jewish dignitaries such as Córdoban physician, diplomat, and man of Hebrew letters Hasdai ibn Shaprut (ca. 915–ca. 970),[9] and Samuel Ibn Naghrela, head of the Jewish community of Granada, Hebrew poet, and vizier at court,[10] both of whom served the Jewish community and the kingdom. Their fifteenth- and sixteenth-century Ottoman counterparts included the illustrious physicians and diplomatic agents Joseph (b. ca. 1450, Granada) and Moses Hamon (1490–1567); the Portuguese Converso migrants and international merchants Doña Gracia Mendes (1510–1568) and her nephew Don Joseph Nasi (1524–1579); the Duke of Naxos, who also served the Ottoman court as a diplomatic agent; and physician, advisor, diplomatic agent, and international merchant Salomon ben Natan Eskenazi (1520–1602).[11] While in al-Andalus Jews became viziers and even accompanied troops into battle while remaining Jews; in the Ottoman Empire some became viziers only after converting to Islam. The Ottoman sultans Mehmed II and his son Bayezid II (r. 1481–1512) were driven by pragmatism, and the latter, who allowed Iberian Jews to take refuge in his domains, was "interested in these Jews not because they were Jews and because they were persecuted or at risk of persecution, but for what they could contribute to his states, especially if they immigrated with their goods and capital."[12] What interests us in the account that follows is the emotional state of early modern Jews and how it colored their view of the sultans. It is this affect that led early modern Ottoman Jewish authors to silence countervailing narratives in favor of six claims concerning Ottoman treatment of the Jews, claims that persist today within the dominant narrative of Turkish-Muslim relations.

Early Modern Jewish Accounts Make Saviors out of Sultans

The earliest articulation of the myth of Turks as saviors of the Jews comes from Isaac Tzarfati, a French Jew born in Germany who settled in the Ottoman Empire and became the chief rabbi of Edirne (Adrianople).[13] Put "together in collaboration with, if not at the instigation of, Ottoman authorities," Tzarfati's account, composed shortly after the Ottoman conquest of Constantinople in 1453, is "a type of propaganda."[14] Describing the life of Jews in Christian-majority lands, he writes, "I have heard of the afflictions, more bitter than death, that have befallen our brethren in Germany—of the tyrannical laws, the compulsory baptisms and the banishments, which are of daily occurrence. . . . They are driven hither and thither, and they are pursued even unto death." He contrasts this horror with the supposed Jewish utopia in the Ottoman Empire: "I proclaim to you that Turkey is a land wherein nothing is lacking, and where, if you will, all shall yet be well with you. The way to the Holy Land lies open to you through Turkey. Is it not better for you to live under Muslims than under Christians?"[15] Whereas Jews "are allowed to wear the most precious garments" in the Ottoman Empire, "in Christendom, on the contrary, you dare not even venture to clothe your children in red or in blue . . . without exposing them to the insult of being beaten black and blue, or kicked green and red."

Buried within the text is the key line that allows us to understand the mentality of this medieval Jew: "The way to the Holy Land lies open to you through Turkey." Keeping in mind the questions "Where was it good for the Jews?" and "Where was it better?" modern historians focus on Tzarfati's comparison of the torments suffered by Jews in Christian Europe with the purported Muslim Ottoman paradise he describes. But the questions that motivated premodern Jewish history writing revolved around an effort to understand the working of God's plan in human life; Jews were less concerned with the actions of humans in history than with how human actions were signs of God's plan for the Jews.[16] The questions these writers asked were thus "When would God's kingdom on earth be established?" and "When would the Jews return to the Holy Land to witness the rebuilding of the Temple and the end-time?" Tzarfati makes no comment on the Turks' character. The Turks have no agency; God does. The Jews are hapless creatures subject to God's mercy.

More influential than Tzarfati's letter has been the 1523 chronicle of Rabbi Elijah ben Elkanah Capsali (b. ca. 1485–1490; d. ca. 1555), whose ecstatic sentiment, exuberant messianism, and exaggerated claims have dominated Jewish historiography for five centuries.[17] Capsali introduced four claims that have figured prominently in myths regarding Ottoman treatment of Jews: that Mehmed II invited and did not force Jews to settle in Istanbul; that Mehmed II established the chief rabbinate and that Capsali's great-uncle Moses was the first holder of the position; that Bayezid II invited the Iberian Jews to settle in his empire; and that the sultan was a protector of last resort, who always saved Jews from his own officials.[18]

Capsali was a native of Candia (Heráklion) in Venetian Crete and a member of a wealthy family of Greek origin distinguished by its learning.[19] His great-uncle Moses Capsali had been a confidant of the Ottoman sultan Mehmed II.[20] Rabbi Elijah Capsali's famous chronicle *Seder Eliyahu zuta: Toldot ha-'Ot'omanim u-Venitsi'ah ve korot 'am Yisrael be-mamlekhot Turki'yah, Sefarad u-Venitsi'ah* (Minor order of Elijah: History of the Ottomans and Venice, and the people of Israel in Turkey, Spain, and Venice) mainly focuses on the reigns of Mehmed II, Bayezid II, Selim I, and Suleiman I.[21] Capsali deploys the ancient Jewish tropes of the dialectical link between destruction and redemption, the idea that what occurred in earlier ages explains what is transpiring in one's own day. Drawing from the tradition predicted in the Book of Daniel that four world empires would precede the messianic age, Capsali sets the newest, the Ottoman Empire, into the final slot. The final conflict between two world powers, Gog and Magog, Islam and Christianity, was to come before the advent of the messiah.[22] Capsali's chronicle is "saturated with Biblical messianic language and typologies" as he casts the Ottoman sultans "in the redemptive image of Cyrus the Great who restored the Jews to the Land of Israel from their Babylonian captivity."[23]

Capsali comforts Jews with the idea that the Ottoman sultans had gathered together the dispersed Jews in their lands not because of any inherent humanitarianism, but because the sultans were tools of God's plan. "Although we thought the expulsion [from Iberia] was a great evil," he writes, "in fact, 'God designed it for good' [Genesis 50:20]"—in other words, to keep the Jewish population alive. For "'who knows whether at a time like this we will attain the kingdom?' [of the messiah] [Esther 4:14] and salvation may have begun 'When the morning stars sang together, and all the angels of God shouted' [Job 38:7], for the Gatherer of the Dispersed of Israel has gathered us together to be ready for the ingathering of the exiles . . . a sign of the coming of the redeemer."[24]

Reading events in history as divine writ, Capsali composed *Seder Eliyahu zuta* to foretell the salvation of the Jews and the punishment of their enemies—the Christians—at the hands of the Ottomans. Referred to in ecstatic, messianic terms, the sultans are "messengers of God" who punish "wicked" nations and gather together the exiled Jews.[25] Referring to Jeremiah 1:10 ("See, I appoint you this day over nations and kingdoms: to uproot and to pull down, to destroy and to overthrow, to build and to plant") and to Daniel 2:21 (God "removes kings and installs kings"), Capsali claims that God had promised Osman I, the founder of the Ottoman Empire, "a kingdom as hard as iron." This is a reference to the fourth kingdom of the vision of Daniel, the last before the redemption to smite the Jews' oppressors. "'A voice came from heaven, which said' [Daniel 4:28]: Osman, a strong and mighty kingdom will be given to you . . . 'it will be as strong as iron; just as iron crushes and shatters everything—and like iron that smashes—so will it crush and smash all these' [Daniel 2:40]."[26] For Capsali, the Turks are the "rod" with which God will chastise the enemy nations: "See how God, in His wisdom and His intelligence, has made that Turkish nation great and powerful, 'You have blessed his efforts so that his possessions spread out in the land' [Job 1:10].[27] God brought [the Turkish nation] from a distant land and blessed it, and the Turk 'is the rod of His wrath, and His fury is a staff in their hand[s]' [Isaiah 10:5], so that with it God may punish the different nations . . . giving them their full measure [of chastisement]." [28]

Capsali, a kabbalist who believed in the messianic calculations of kabbalistic works, quotes the *Zohar* (The book of splendor), the most important work of Jewish mysticism, and perceives signs of imminent redemption.[29] He subsumes non-Jewish history to serve Jewish messianic purposes, reinterpreting Ottoman history to explain the divine plan that employs the Ottoman sultans as the instruments of redemption. For him, Ottoman history sheds light on the Jewish future.

Capsali sees Mehmed II as the messiah—a new Cyrus and Alexander—and his conquest of Constantinople as a prelude to the collapse of Christendom: "On the 19th day of the month of April of the year 1453 according to [the Christian calendar] when John VIII Paleaologus was the King of Greece,[30] 'the days of punishment have come [for your heavy guilt]; the days of requital have arrived' [Hosea 9:7]—and peace departed from him [the Byzantine Emperor] because God inspired Sultan Mehmed to come [to Constantinople] to dispossess him [of his kingdom], for the measure of the wicked Kingdom of Greece was full, because of all the evil they [the Greeks] had inflicted on Judah and Israel."[31]

Capsali then relates how God spoke to Himself about this messianic role of Constantinople and its conqueror: "'Ruin, an utter ruin I will make it' [Ezekiel 21:32], 'I will blow with the fire of My wrath' [Ezekiel 21:36] upon Constantinople and consume it. 'I will march to battle against it and set it on fire' [Isaiah 27:4]. [God said] 'because of the evils that the Greeks have inflicted upon my people, on my nation, I will give it [Constantinople] into the hand of the executor of my ban, and will pour out my wrath over them.'"[32] Having punished Byzantine Constantinople, God makes Ottoman Constantinople flourish, as a reward to the sultan, who carried out God's will.[33]

In Capsali's account, a rabbi tells Mehmed II that the conquering "King of the North" in Daniel 11:40 is the King of Constantinople, which Mehmed II had now become.[34] Imbued with this view of the sultan, the author is compelled to argue that Jews migrated voluntarily to Constantinople, ignoring "the mass population transfers" noted in Karaite, Rabbanite, Greek, and Italian sources, as well as later Ottoman archival material. These sources designated some Istanbul Jews as *sürgün* (forcibly deported, comprising many Romaniot and all Anatolian and southeastern European communities) and others as *kendi gelen* (voluntary immigrants, consisting mainly of Sephardic communities).[35] Capsali has to overlook these facts in order to argue that Mehmed II invited Jews to Constantinople, just as King Cyrus of Persia had brought the Jews back to Jerusalem to build their temple. He makes this explicit by describing Mehmed II's "invitation" using the language of the decree of Cyrus.[36]

Capsali praises the next ruler, Bayezid II, for welcoming the expelled Sephardim and likens him to Cyrus. Bayezid "heard of all the misfortune that the King of Spain had inflicted on the Jews, and that they were seeking 'a resting place for their feet' [Deuteronomy 28:65], and he took pity on them." Accordingly, "he sent messengers 'and he issued a proclamation throughout his realm by word of mouth and in writing' [Ezra 1:1][37] to prevent any governor of his towns from turning the Jews away and driving them out; they were ordered instead to welcome them warmly, kindly, and hospitably, and whoever did not would be put to death."[38]

Capsali claims that the Ottoman officials welcomed all the Jews in this fashion, such that "'they were a wall about them both by night and by day all the time that they were with them' [I Samuel 25:16]; 'they were not harmed, nor did they miss anything' [I Samuel 25:15]. Myriads of the expelled [Iberian] Jews came to Turkey, and they filled the country."[39] For Capsali, this was a sign that deliverance for the Jews was near:

> From that day on God began to gather together the dispersed of his people, that they may be ready in one place for the coming of the redeemer; and the troubles that passed over the Jews in those times are (according to) the word of the prophet [Daniel 12:1]: "and there shall be a time of trouble, such as never was since there was a nation even to that same time." Happy is he that waits and he will attain the time of the end; "An end is come, the end is come" [Ezekiel 7:6]; the redeemer is near to come, "and his days shall not be prolonged" [Isaiah 13:22].[40]

God punished Spain and rewarded the sultan for welcoming its Jews, "blessing Turkey [the Ottoman Empire]" as a result.[41]

Selim I (r. 1512–1520) was the next act in Capsali's drama, for he conquered Jerusalem. He was a messianic figure whose conquest of the Land of Israel was another sign that the time of redemption was near: "God spoke to Himself: 'Behold, I summon my servant Selim to set up his throne in Egypt,'. . . 'and he will gain control over treasures of gold and silver and over all the precious things of Egypt' [Daniel 11:43]"; the verse describes the King of the North.[42] Capsali continues: "'[And I will set fire to the temples of the gods of Egypt]; he will burn them down and carry them off. He shall wrap himself up in the land of Egypt, as a shepherd wraps himself up in his garment. And he shall depart from there in safety' [Jeremiah 43:12]." As God is sovereign over the realm of humanity, "'He gives it to whom He wishes' [Daniel 4:29]." Furthermore, Capsali continues, what God says comes to pass (Isaiah 55:11). Moreover, after Sultan Selim begins to rule in Egypt, "'as for idols, they shall vanish completely' [Isaiah 2:18] and the idols in [Egypt] will be cut off and this will be in the time of redemption . . . for the messiah will come to us very quickly because since the expulsion [of the Jews from Spain] God began to 'assemble the banished of Israel, and gather the dispersed of Judah from the four corners of the earth.' [Isaiah 11: 12]."[43] He compares Selim not only to Cyrus and Alexander, as his predecessors had done, but also to David, who, because he had blood on his hands, was not permitted to build the Temple; that duty was for his son, Solomon, the Ottoman Suleiman I (r. 1520–1566), in whose day Capsali expected the messiah to come.[44]

Capsali writes ecstatically of Suleiman's conquest of Rhodes, which would lead Rome to fall, thereby eliciting the advent of the messiah.[45] The text ends with this hope in 1523: "'Everyone's eyes looked to him with hope' [Psalms 145:15] and he dwelled in peace and without fear, for he is the tenth king [sultan] of the Turks, and 'every tenth one shall be holy to God' [Leviticus 27:32] and 'in his days Judah shall be delivered and Israel shall dwell secure' [Jeremiah 23:6] and 'a redeemer shall come to Zion' [Isaiah 59:20]."[46]

Along with his messianic role, Suleiman is also praised by Capsali for having saved Jews from persecution by one of his own officials, in this case the governor of Egypt, Ahmed Shaitan ("Satan").[47] The trope of the blameless sultan would become standard in Jewish historiography on the Ottomans.

Also in the sixteenth century, Samuel Usque (ca. 1500–after 1555) composed *Consolação ás tribulações de Israel* (The consolation of the tribulations of Israel, 1553) in Portuguese for the Converso, or new Christian, diaspora. Expelled from Spain, Usque's family settled in Portugal, where he was born as a Converso. After the Inquisition was installed in Portugal in 1531, he moved to Italy. He argued that the greatest human consolation for the persecuted Iberian Jewry, in particular for Portuguese Conversos like himself, was "the great nation of Turkey [the Ottoman Empire]. This country is like a broad and expansive sea which our Lord has opened with the rod of His mercy, as Moses did for you in the Exodus from Egypt, so that the swells of your present misfortunes, which relentlessly pursue you in all the kingdoms of Europe like the infinite multitude of Egyptians, might cease and be consumed by it," for "here the gates of liberty are always wide open for you that you may fully practice your Judaism."[48] While the western Mediterranean was a sea of slavery, death, and expulsion, the eastern Mediterranean was a sea of salvation and freedom. "Here," he argues, "you may restore your true character, transform your nature, change your ways, and banish false and erring opinions . . . embrace your true ancient faith and abandon the practices opposed to God's will, which you have adopted under the pressures of the nations in which you have wandered."[49] For it is only in the Ottoman Empire where former Jews "may come to terms" with their souls, "unafraid that pressures will remove it from His law, as has happened in other kingdoms."

Usque, an "ardent follower" of the Portuguese Converso and messianic claimant Diego Pires / Solomon Molho (burned at the stake in 1530), believed his group's suffering marked the end of history. The great comfort was that all these sufferings were foretold by the prophets, and that as the prophecies of evil were verified, so Jews should trust that the prophecies of good would also be fulfilled. Writing to fellow exiles, he argued that Conversos suffered because the millennium was at hand, after which a new age would dawn in which their misfortunes would end.[50] Jews, he argued, had sinned and become idolatrous like the nations around them. For this they had been punished by God: if they repented, God would forgive them; if they returned to Judaism and God, their misfortunes would end. Usque interpreted the expulsions as fulfillments of biblical prophecies, which meant that once all the Conversos returned to Judaism, redemption of the Jews would be at hand.[51]

Usque, like Tzarfati, also countered a lachrymose depiction of Christendom with utopia in Islamdom: "Among the riches and pleasures of joyous Asia I find myself a poor and weary traveler . . . Now Europe, O Europe, my hell on earth, what shall I say of you?"[52]

Usque's *Consolação* was a main source for the physician Joseph ben Joshua ha-Kohen (1496–after 1577), who was born in France, the son of expelled Castilian Spanish Jews. The latter's family was subsequently expelled from Provence, and he spent most of his life in Genoa, where he also faced expulsion decrees.[53] Ha-Kohen's *Sefer divre ha-yamim le-malkhey Tzarefat u-malkhey beyt Ottoman ha-Togar* (History of the kings of France and the kings of the dynasty of Othman, the Turk) (1554–1577) is the only Jewish historical work of the sixteenth century to have as its primary focus gentile empires.[54] When Jews are mentioned, it is to record persecution.[55] Ha-Kohen claims that the main impetus for writing the chronicle was the expulsions of the Jews from Spain, Portugal, and France. His aim in doing so is to prove that Christians would be punished by the Ottomans for the afflictions to which they subjected Jews, and that redemption was at hand: "The expulsions from France as well as this exceedingly bitter exile [i.e., from Spain] have aroused me to compose this book, so that the Children of Israel may know what [the Christians] have done to us in their lands, their courts and their castles, for behold the days approach."[56]

Ha-Kohen focuses on the exploits of Ottoman sultans. He describes Mehmed II as "a scourge and breaker of the uncircumcised."[57] Suleiman I is one of the central figures of ha-Kohen's text. In narrating his reign, ha-Kohen presents the main theme that the end-time is approaching and asserts that it is important to write a universal history of the struggle between Gog and Magog, Islam and Christianity.[58] Writing in the first three decades of the sixteenth century, ha-Kohen understood Gog and Magog to be represented by the Ottoman and Habsburg dynasties respectively. He interpreted the fact of these empires contending to mean that one should expect to hear the footsteps of the messiah and the advent of the messianic age, as depicted in Ezekiel 38:1–29 where the enemies of the Jews were to be defeated and the Temple restored. As in Capsali's history, ha-Kohen understood the Ottomans and their sultan, Suleiman I, to be prophesied in Daniel's dream, where "the fourth beast shall be the fourth kingdom upon earth, which shall be different from all kingdoms, and shall devour the whole earth, and shall trample it down, and break it in pieces," and from which "ten kings shall arise." For ha-Kohen, "God aroused the spirit of [the tenth king] Suleiman to conquer Rhodes" and "aroused his spirit to set out to rebuild the walls of Jerusalem," to which he appended the prayer that Jerusalem might be rebuilt and the messiah come in his lifetime.[59] He expressed a similar sentiment in his popular, lachrymose work, *Emek ha-bacha* (The vale of tears, 1575), which begins: "I have entitled the work *Emek ha-bacha* because that title corresponds to its very content. Everyone who reads in it will be astounded and will gasp, with tears welling down from his eyes; and putting his hands to his loins, he will ask; 'How long, Oh God?' God, may the days of our mourning come to an end and may He send us the Just Messiah, and he will redeem us, soon, for His Mercy's sake. Amen, Amen."[60]

Though scholars debate both the extent to which these works are apocalyptic and messianic and the intensity of their messianism, all agree that Capsali, Usque, and ha-Kohen narrate Ottoman history with the aim of revealing God's plan in the world, which will end with the messianic age of redemption. Capsali did not treat the Ottoman sultans "as political and historical figures but as messianic figures according to a Jewish messianic interpretation."[61] These historians were not expressing gratitude for benevolent treatment by the Ottoman dynasty; rather, they expressed belief that the Ottoman sultans were the instruments of God's will.[62] They "are merely a *figura*" performing a divine plan that has Jews at its center.[63]

Writers throughout the sixteenth century echoed Capsali's assessment of the sultan as savior and the Ottoman Empire as the place where Jews would fulfill their religious hopes and expectations. The most influential sixteenth-century Ottoman rabbi, Samuel de Medina of Salonica (1506–1589), scion of an eminent Castilian family, depicted Mehmed II as fulfilling the divine plan: "God awakened the spirit of the king and he came and besieged this great city of Constantinople, and God gave it into his hand and he captured it."[64] Echoing earlier writers, de Medina claimed that whereas in Christendom Jews could not live as Jews and at times could not even live, in the Ottoman Empire they lived as Jews "under the wings of the Divine Presence."[65] Other sixteenth-century Jewish writers, such as Samuel ben Joseph Algazi, of Crete, author of *Toledot Adam* (The generations of Adam) also expressed longing for the messiah, who by his calculations was to arrive in 1583 as part of a divine plan that encompassed the rise of the Muslims as the avengers of the Jews on their Christian tormentors—in other words, the Ottoman conquerors of Constantinople.[66] The title pages of Hebrew books published in Istanbul throughout the sixteenth century included dedications to "the great king sultan, may he live forever, may the Lord be his helper, and his kingdom be exalted forever, amen" as well as messianic hopes, including "in his times and in ours Judea will be redeemed and Israel shall live peacefully." A dedication from a collection of rabbinic responsa published in 1556 declared the sultan to be "a faithful shepherd (Moses), our master the Sultan Suleiman, may his splendor be exalted, and his honor grow, and in his times and ours may Judea and Israel be redeemed and may the redeemer come to Zion." Scholars relate that "in Jewish tradition the faithful shepherd is Moses, who led his people in the wilderness for forty years and finally brought them to the gates of the Promised Land."[67]

In the early seventeenth century, yet another, a fifth, myth was added to the enduring Sephardic narrative of the legendary Ottoman reception of the Jews involving an alleged statement by the then sultan, Bayezid II. Spanish Converso Immanuel Aboab (c. 1555–1628), who returned to Judaism in Italy and died in Jerusalem, claimed that Bayezid II, upon hearing of the expulsion of Iberian Jewry, said of the Spanish King Ferdinand, "Can you call such a king wise and intelligent? He is impoverishing his country and enriching my kingdom!"[68]

The Sephardic narrative as related by Aboab, ha-Kohen, Usque, Capsali, and others has prevailed in Jewish historiography at the expense of counternarratives articulated by other Jews in the Ottoman Empire. Byzantine (Greek, Romaniot) Jews reacted negatively to the Ottoman conquest of the city. "Jews in Crete and Rhodes wrote laments on the fall of Constantinople and the fate of its Jewish community," describing how Jews were killed or sold into slavery.[69] Their writings were filled with open anti-Ottoman sentiment incited by forced deportation. Between 1453 and 1470, Byzantine Jews, whether Karaite or Rabbinate, expressed anti-Ottoman views. But while Byzantine Jews tended to view the Ottomans as "despots," Iberian

Jews who arrived two generations later considered them "saviors."[70] From the sixteenth century onward, Jewish writers "disregarded these facts and attitudes," failing to mention what had befallen Byzantine Jews in Constantinople. These writers instead praised the conquerors, who enacted divine retribution on the oppressors of Jewry, the Byzantines.[71] With an eye toward interpreting contemporary events in terms of God's plan for the Jews, proponents of the Sephardic narrative found most appealing the voices of Jewish writers that spoke ecstatically and in messianic terms of the fall of evil Byzantium, which had inherited the mantle of evil Rome. These Jewish writers were most receptive to texts such as Spanish rabbi Isaac Abravanel's *Mayane yeshua* (The well springs of salvation, 1496), which uses biblical verse to explain how "God brought His vengeance" upon Byzantium, again taken as a sign of the Jews' imminent redemption.[72]

In addition to the conquest of Byzantium, the subsequent Ottoman reception of Spanish Jewry in the Ottoman Empire "resulted in the widespread Jewish sympathy toward Ottoman authorities" and silence about their misdeeds: the "friendly policies of Mehmed on the one hand, and the good reception by Bayezid of Spanish Jewry on the other, caused the Jewish writers of the sixteenth century to overlook both the destruction which Byzantine Jewry suffered during the Ottoman conquests and the later outbursts of repression."[73] Indeed, "the Romaniot exiles were bitter over their forced dislocation by the Ottomans, a sentiment that persisted at least until the 1480s. . . . In contrast, the Iberian Jews, realizing that the Ottomans had given them something that nobody else would, felt grateful; this led to the myth that the expellees had been invited by the Ottomans."[74] The prevailing historiography of Ottoman Jewry contrasts a lachrymose view of experience under Christian rule that mourns the Byzantine "yoke" and the Spanish "expulsion" with a distinctly Sephardic utopian view of Muslim sovereignty that celebrates Ottoman "liberation" and "welcome."[75]

A Pivotal Jewish Savior Replaces the Sultan

In 1665 and 1666, Sabbatai Zevi (Hebrew, Shabbetai Tzevi, 1626–1676) of Smyrna (Izmir) launched the second-greatest messianic movement in the history of the Jewish people after that of Jesus of Nazareth. In the wake of this upheaval, Ottoman Jews essentially replaced successive Muslim redeemers (the Ottoman sultans Mehmed II, Bayezid II, Selim I, and Suleiman I) with a Jewish messiah. Following Sabbatai Zevi's failure to be crowned emperor, however, early modern Ottoman Jewish writers dropped messianic claims altogether.

By the mid-seventeenth century, Jews had fallen from favor in the eyes of the ruling Ottoman elite. They had lost their former privileged position in the economy and in the palace, a position they would never recover. The reasons had as much to do with material changes such as worldwide economic trends in the cloth trade in which they were heavily invested and the 1660 fire in the heart of the main Jewish quarter in Istanbul, as with attitudes toward Jews held by Mehmed IV (r. 1648–1687, d. 1693), his mother, and the pietist religious movement and its preachers, whom they supported. In contrast with previous centuries, Jews lost possession of their homes after the fire—the multistoried "Jewish apartments" that marked the skyline of the port. Nor were they allowed to rebuild their synagogues, even that of the Aragón Sephardic community. Instead, they were expelled upon pain of death from their destroyed neighborhood so that it could be converted into a Muslim quarter abutting the walls of the palace with an imperial mosque at its heart. Whereas Mehmed II had "welcomed Jews expelled from Central Europe and brought Anatolian and Rumelian Jews to repopulate Istanbul after it was conquered," and his successor, Bayezid II, had "allowed Iberian Jews to settle in the city following their expulsion from Spain and Portugal," in the mid-seventeenth century, "Mehmed IV's court confiscated the synagogue properties of the descendants of these Jews and expelled their congregants from the heart of the city."[76]

Several years later, the upheaval accompanying the messianic movement of Sabbatai Zevi in 1665–1666 convinced the palace that Jews were disloyal, even seditious; by the end of the 1660s, Jewish physicians serving and residing in the palace—the most influential of Ottoman Jews, many of whom were Sephardic—were compelled to convert to Islam in order to retain their positions.[77] The sultan's court lost its sixteenth-century attitude, which, as in al-Andalus, had allowed Jews to rise to high positions and play an active role at court while remaining practicing Jews. Thereafter the Ottomans briefly preferred converted Jews as physicians and then turned to the Greek Christian community to provide the leading physicians, diplomats, and courtiers. Whereas at the beginning of the decade, "Jews had a privileged position with the royal family and resided mainly in the heart of the city, by the end of the decade the geographic position of the Jews reflected their fall from importance." This geographic move and loss of social status contributed in turn to conversion. "Most Jews in Istanbul resided on the Golden Horn and the Bosporus, and those who remained in the most important palace positions were compelled to convert to Islam."[78] The large-scale dispersion of Jews to areas in the city in which they had previously not resided led to tension with their new Muslim neighbors, who sought to expel the new arrivals. In one such neighborhood, a married Muslim woman was accused of committing adultery with a Jewish man, which led in 1680 to Istanbul witnessing what would turn out to be the only public stoning of an accused Muslim adulteress during 465 years of Ottoman rule in the city.[79] Rather than serving as the rescuer of last resort, the sultan allowed the Jew, too, to be killed, offering him the chance to convert to Islam, thereby permitting him to die swiftly and with dignity by decapitation. Whereas in the sixteenth century, "Jews had been so privileged at court" that Sultan Suleiman "had intervened on behalf of converted Jews condemned to the stake in the papal states, a century later, there was no Jew of any stature who could intervene to save the life of a single Jew who had dared to commit adultery with a Muslim."[80]

A turning point for Jewish accounts of the Ottomans accompanied Sabbatai Zevi's messianic movement. In the fall of 1665, Sabbatai Zevi's "prophet" Nathan of Gaza sent an epistle to Raphael Joseph Çelebi in Egypt in which he predicted Sabbatai Zevi "will take dominion from the Turkish sultan without any warfare. Through the hymns and praises he will utter, all the nations will be brought into submission. Wherever he turns to conquer, he will take with him the Turkish sultan alone. All the kings will become his tributaries; the Turkish sultan alone will be his personal slave."[81] Sabbatai Zevi was to be the "sultan of sultans" ruling from Istanbul; he ordained thirty-eight followers to be the kings of the thirty-eight kingdoms of the world.[82] The Muslim messiah, the rod of God, would be replaced by a Jewish messiah. Unfortunately for Sabbatai Zevi and the Jews who believed in him, however, he became sultan only in their imagination. In 1666, faced with the choice of conversion or death, he became a Muslim and served the sultan as honorary gatekeeper prior to being exiled to spend the remainder of his days in remote Montenegro. Hundreds of his devotees followed his example and converted to Islam; while ostensibly Muslim, they secretly practiced a hidden culture centered on Sabbatai Zevi's beliefs and rituals. In later centuries, their descendants would become known as Dönme, Turkish for "convert."[83]

Whereas Jewish writers outside the Ottoman Empire wrote extensively on the movement after its end, within the empire not a single history of the movement was printed. Deeming Sabbatai Zevi the messiah was viewed by Ottoman authorities as politically subversive. Likewise, his enemies were wise not to attack him, for as a Muslim, he had an elevated status above them in the religious hierarchy of the empire. Accusing him of blasphemy could lead to their own punishment and not his; Jews were wary of appearing to insult Islam. They preferred to be silent, ignoring "the whole matter as far as possible, and hoping that time and oblivion would heal the wound."[84]

This self-censorship is apparent in a significant late seventeenth-century Jewish chronicle. The Ottoman Egyptian Cairene rabbi Joseph Sambari (ca. 1630s–after 1673) composed *Sefer divre Yosef* (The book of Joseph's sayings) in 1673.[85] Sambari, a man well connected to the leading Jews of Egypt—in the 1660s he was secretary to Raphael Yosef Çelebi, chief financier of the Ottoman governor of Egypt—used Capsali's chronicle as one of his most important sources, as well as Joseph ha-Kohen's *Divre ha-yamim*, for his narration of the Ottoman era.[86] What is new in his account of the Ottomans is the lack of messianic attribution: depicting the sultan in positive, yet not messianic fashion.[87] Another departure is that one of the major themes of the book is "the social marginalization and humiliation of the Jews under Muslim rule."[88] Approaching the history of Jews in Ottoman Egypt from a socioeconomic perspective, a contemporary Israeli scholar attributes such sentiment to the fact that in his estimation, "the history of the Jews of Egypt during the Ottoman period is not a happy affair," as they faced Janissary extortion, hostile Greeks fomenting blood libels (which to the great disappointment of Jews, Muslim religious authorities failed to refute), avaricious Muslim soldiers, and the occasional execution of prominent Jews to serve as an example to those engaging in illegal practices such as coin clipping.[89] But what was eating Sambari, for whom Muslim rule was no liberation? He perceived the subjection of Jews to Muslim rule as punishment for their sins.[90]

Sambari wrote in a dark vein not as a reflection of socioeconomic conditions, but because he exhibited the "agony" of a disillusioned follower of Sabbatai Zevi.[91] God was punishing Jews for having followed a messiah; the bursting of the bubble of messianic intoxication allowed them to understand that their true state was as slaves to another people. Sambari's patron, Raphael Yosef Çelebi, was Sabbatai Zevi's main advocate in Egypt; through him Sambari met Sabbatai Zevi, becoming an early follower.[92] He composed his work after Sabbatai Zevi and his followers converted to Islam and their works were banned by the rabbis.

Sambari's account of the movement was ripped out of the manuscripts of his *Divre Yosef*.[93] Yet, there are hints in surviving parts of the text to his disillusionment. Sambari's purpose in writing the work in part is to remind Jews that God always saves them from persecution at the hands of their enemies and that everything that happens in human history is part of divine plan, yet he still asks God to send the true messiah during his lifetime.[94]

What modern scholarship has retained from Sambari is yet another sixth core pillar in the myth of Ottoman treatment of Jews. Especially indebted to Capsali for his narration of the reign of Mehmed II, Sambari repeats the claim that Mehmed II invited Jews to settle in the city. But he also exaggerates Capsali's already-exaggerated claims regarding the close relationship between his uncle Moses Capsali and the sultan. Sambari embellishes the relationship by stating that the chief rabbi was given a permanent seat in the imperial council, for he "sat with the Mufti and Patriarch in the Divan of the sultan."[95] This false claim entered modern Jewish scholarship in the nineteenth century and is repeated today.[96] Basing himself on Capsali, Sambari also wrote that Sultan Bayezid "took in the unfortunate, wandering Jews, . . . those expelled from Spain . . . into his land."[97] As has been noted, "all Jewish historiography would be influenced by this idyllic vision, putting the Ottoman sovereigns on a pedestal and mythifying the welcome given the Sephardim," while ironically, as another has argued, failing to mention the messianic-apocalyptic motivation of the original authors to whom we owe this view.[98]

Conclusion

Messianic impulses at the core of early modern Jewish accounts form together an affective disposition compelling the authors of this period to be grateful to the rulers of the kingdom that allowed them to live as Jews. Such messianism shaped a utopian image of the Ottomans and their sultan. In the fifteenth and sixteenth centuries, Jews such as Isaac Tzarfati, Elijah ben Elkanah Capsali, Samuel Usque, Joshua ha-Kohen, and Samuel de Medina focus on the Ottoman sultan as a personification of the empire, depicting him in messianic terms as the one who fulfills God's plan in the world by punishing the Jews' Christian oppressors, both Byzantine and Catholic. They also credit him for ingathering the Jewish exiles from newly Christian Spain, conquering Jerusalem, and allowing Jews to settle in the Holy Land. In their view, all serve as portents of the dawning of the messianic age. In seventeenth-century accounts, such as that of Joseph Sambari, the Ottoman savior is replaced by a Jewish one, the messianic claimant Sabbatai Zevi.

Modern historiography has retained six important claims from these early modern accounts: that Mehmed II invited Jews to settle in Constantinople; that he established the position of the chief rabbi; that this rabbi was seated in the imperial divan closer to the sultan than the Orthodox patriarch; that Bayezid II invited the Iberian Jews to settle in his empire; that he quipped, "You call Ferdinand a wise king, he who has made his country poor and enriched ours!"; and that the sultan always saved Jews from his own officials.

What is striking is how Ottoman Armenian and Orthodox Christian (Greek) chronicles mirror the accounts of Ottoman Jews. Armenian writers blamed their subjugation to the Ottomans on their "immense sins."[99] A sixteenth-century Armenian chronicler declared that "because my sins have become so great, the Ottomans have conquered the Armenian provinces, destroying and laying low all the villages and settlements."[100] There were more Greeks in the Ottoman Empire than Armenians, and many more Greeks than Jews, who were the smallest of the non-Muslim ethnoreligious communities, never surpassing half a million people, vastly outnumbered by Christians. Greeks not only formed a majority of the population in the empire's first two centuries, serving as Christians in the military and the administration; for longer than that, converted Greeks predominated in the Ottoman military and administration, as Greek princesses and slave girls filled the harem. Despite the two very different experiences of Ottoman rule, we see some of the same themes expressed in Jewish and Greek history writing: how the sultans on the one hand protect the community (here Greeks) from their internal enemy (here Muslims), love them, and treat them with justice; yet, on the other hand, how the Ottomans are the scourge of the Christians. In fifteenth- and sixteenth-century Greek-language chronicles, "almost all authors considered the Ottomans to be a punishment from God for Christians' sins."[101] For example, George Sprantzes, eyewitness to the fall of Constantinople, "accepted the Ottomans as part of the divine order as such a punishment. He even likened the Ottoman sultan to God's executioner, writing that '. . . even he [the sultan] has a place and post [in the eyes of] God, like his executioners . . . who fulfill His will and command.'"[102] Jewish chroniclers and some of their modern historians would have agreed.

Greek chronicles written outside the Ottoman Empire tended to be anti-Ottoman, whereas those composed within the empire tended to favor

Ottoman rule; for the Jews, the most ecstatic pro-Ottoman tracts were written outside of the empire by Jews persecuted in Christian empires and kingdoms.[103] But overall, Greek writers from the fifteenth through the seventeenth centuries displayed a wide range of opinion on Ottoman rule and the legitimacy of its rule, ranging from affirmation and apologia to lachrymose accounts, whereas modern Jewish historiography has largely promoted apologia through reference to utopian premodern accounts, reflecting early modern Jewish messianism.[104]

Not only were these narratives exaggerated, overstated, and embellished, they also depended on silencing other countervailing voices, especially those of Byzantine Jews. Dominant narratives by their very nature depend on silencing critical narratives. When Sabbatai Zevi and his followers are censored and made to go underground as the Dönme, another silence enters into the creation of these hegemonic Sephardic narratives. They can only allow the sultan, and not a treacherous rabbi, to be the savior of the Jews.

Notes

1. See Alex Novikoff, "Between Tolerance and Intolerance in Medieval Spain: The Historiographic Enigma," *Medieval Encounters* 11, nos. 1–2 (2005); Ross Brann, *Power in the Portrayal: Representations of Jews and Muslims in Eleventh- and Twelfth-Century Spain* (Princeton, NJ: Princeton University Press, 2009); David Nirenberg, *Communities of Violence: Persecution of Minorities in the Middle Ages* (Princeton, NJ: Princeton University Press, 1998); Nirenberg, "What Can Medieval Spain Teach Us"; David Nirenberg, "Love Between Muslims and Jews in Medieval Spain: A Triangular Affair," in *Jews, Muslims, and Christians in and Around the Crown of Aragon: Essays in Honor of Professor Elena Lourie*, ed. Harvey Hames (Leiden: Brill, 2004); Jane Gerber, *The Jews of Spain: A History of the Sephardic Experience* (New York: New York University, 1992); Howard Sachar, *Farewell España: The World of the Sephardim Remembered* (New York: Vintage, 1995); Maria Menocal, *The Ornament of the World: How Muslims, Christians, and Jews Created a Culture of Tolerance in Medieval Spain* (New York: Back Bay Books, 2003); Jonathan Ray, "Beyond Tolerance and Persecution: Reassessing Our Approach to Medieval *Convivencia*," *Jewish Social Studies* 11, no. 2 (Winter 2005); Kenneth Wolf, "*Convivencia* in Medieval Spain: A Brief History of an Idea," *Religion Compass* 3, no. 1 (2009); Maya Soifer, "Beyond *Convivencia*: Critical Reflections on the Historiography of Interfaith Relations in Christian Spain," *Journal of Medieval Iberian Studies* 1, no. 1 (2009); Jonathan Shannon, "Performing al-Andalus, Remembering al-Andalus: Mediterranean Soundings from Mashriq and Maghrib," *Journal of American Folklore* 120, no. 477 (2007).

2. Mercedes García-Arenal, "The Jews of Al-Andalus," in *A History of Jewish-Muslim Relations*, 111.

3. Ibid.

4. Ibid., 119. See Anonymous, "Jewish Account of the Expulsion" (Italy, 1495), trans. from the Hebrew by Jacob Marcus, in Jacob Marcus, *The Jew in the Medieval World: A Source Book, 315–1791* (New York: Atheneum, 1979).

5. Gilles Veinstein, "Jews and Muslims in the Ottoman Empire," in *A History of Jewish-Muslim Relations*, 174.

6. Gilles Veinstein, "Jews and Muslims in Ottoman Territory before the Expulsion from Spain," in *A History of Jewish-Muslim Relations*, 164–165.

7. Veinstein, "Jews and Muslims in the Ottoman Empire," 172.

8. Ibid., 171.

9. For a synopsis of his life and career, see Raymond Scheindlin, "Hasdai ibn Shaprut," in *A History of Jewish-Muslim Relations*.

10. For a synopsis of his life and career, see Raymond Scheindlin, "Samuel ibn Naghrela," in *A History of Jewish-Muslim Relations*.

11. For brief accounts of their lives and careers, see Stanford Shaw, *The Jews of the Ottoman Empire and the Turkish Republic* (New York: New York University Press, 1991), 86–90.

12. Veinstein, "Jews and Muslims in the Ottoman Empire," 178.

13. Salo Wittmayer Baron, *A Social and Religious History of the Jews*, 2nd revised ed., 18 volumes (New York: Columbia University Press, 1952–1983) 18:453n32.

14. Veinstein, "Jews and Muslims in Ottoman Territory," 166.

15. Quoted in Lewis, *The Jews of Islam*, 135–136; and in Baron, *Social and Religious History*, 18:21.

16. Yosef Hayim Yerushalmi, *Zakhor: Jewish History & Jewish Memory* (Seattle, WA: University of Washington Press, 1982).

17. Aryeh Shmuelevitz, "Jewish-Muslim Relations in the Writings of Rabbi Eliyahu Capsali," (in Hebrew) *Pe'amim* 61 (Fall 1994): 81; Joseph Hacker, "Ottoman Policy toward the Jews and Jewish Attitudes toward the Ottomans during the Fifteenth Century," in *Christians and Jews in the Ottoman Empire: The Functioning of a Plural Society*, 2 vols., ed. Benjamin Braude and Bernard Lewis (New York: Holmes & Meier, 1982), 1:118–119.

18. Bahar claims incorrectly that Capsali is the source of the apocryphal quote attributed to Bayezid II: "You call Ferdinand [of Spain] a wise king; him, who by expelling the Jews has impoverished his country and enriched mine!" Bahar, *Jewish Historiography on the Ottoman Empire*, 47. For the correct attribution, see below.

19. For background on Capsali's life, see Meir Benayahu, *Rabi Eliyahu Kapsali, ish Kandiah: Rav manhig ve historyon* (Tel Aviv: Tel Aviv University Press, 1983).

20. Rabbi Moses Capsali was brother of Rabbi David Capsali, the grandfather of Rabbi Elijah Capsali. Benayahu, *Rabi Eliyahu Kapsali*, 20; Martin Jacobs, *Islamische Geschichte in jüdischen Chroniken: Hebräische Historiographie des 16. und 17. Jahrhunderts*, Texts and Studies in Medieval and Early Modern Judaism 18 (Tübingen: Mohr Siebeck, 2004), 58, 61; Aleida Paudice, *Between Several Worlds: The Life and Writings of Elia Capsali: The Historical Works of a 16th-Century Cretan Rabbi*, Forum Europäische Geschichte 7 (Munich: Martin Meidenbauer, 2010), 60–63.

21. Eliyahu Capsali, *Seder Eliyahu zuta*, 3 vols. (1975–1983), ed. Aryeh Shmuelevitz, Shlomo Simonsohn, and Meier Benayahu (Jerusalem: Mekhon Ben-Tsvi, 1975).

22. Yerushalmi, *Zakhor*, 23, 34, 36–37

23. Ibid., 65.

24. Capsali, *Seder Eliyahu zuta*, 1:240. Also quoted in Charles Berlin, "A Sixteenth-Century Hebrew Chronicle of the Ottoman Empire: The Seder Eliyahu Zuta of Elijah Capsali

and its Message," *Studies in Jewish Bibliography, History, and Literature in Honor of I. Edward Kiev*, ed. Charles Berlin (New York: KTAV, 1971), 31; and Paudice, *Between Several Worlds*, 158–159.

25. Aryeh Shmuelevitz, "Capsali as a Source for Ottoman History 1450–1523," *International Journal of Middle East Studies* 9 (1978): 339–340; Paudice, *Between Several Worlds*, 87, 92–93.

26. Capsali, *Seder Eliyahu zuta*, 1:43. Also quoted in Benjamin Lellouch, "Eliyahu Capsali, Jewish Cantor of the Ottomans," in *A History of Jewish-Muslim Relations*, 201; Jacobs, *Islamische Geschichte in jüdischen Chroniken*, 141–142; and Jacobs, "Exposed to All the Currents of the Mediterranean: A Sixteenth-Century Venetian Rabbi on Muslim History," *AJS Review* 29, no. 1 (April 2005): 42–43.

27. Capsali, *Seder Eliyahu zuta*, 1:10.

28. Ibid.; also quoted in Jacobs, *Islamische Geschichte in jüdischen Chroniken*, 66; Lellouch, "Eliyahu Capsali," 200; and Jacobs, "Exposed to all the Currents," 40. The original text in Isaiah reads, "Assyria, rod of My anger, in whose hand, as a staff, is My fury! I send him against a people that provokes Me, to take its spoil and to seize its booty and to make it a thing trampled like the mire of the streets." *JPS Tanakh*.

29. For an emphasis on his kabbalistic leanings, see Benayahu, *Rabbi Eliyahu Capsali*; see also Berlin, "Sixteenth-Century Hebrew Chronicle."

30. The Ottoman siege of Constantinople began April 6, 1453, and the city fell on May 29; the last Byzantine emperor was actually Constantine XI, John VIII's successor.

31. Capsali, *Seder Eliyahu zuta*, 1:65. Also quoted in Jacobs, *Islamische Geschichte in jüdischen Chroniken*, 153; Jacobs, "Exposed to all the Currents," 41; Paudice, *Between Several Worlds*, 114–115.

32. Ibid.

33. Henriette-Rika Benveniste, "The Idea of Exile: Jewish Accounts and the Historiography of Salonika Revisited," in *Jewish Communities Between the East and West, 15th-20th Centuries: Economy, Society, Politics, Culture*, ed. L. Papastefanaki and A. Machaira (Ioannina: Isnafi, 2016), 39.

34. Cited in Berlin, "Sixteenth-Century Hebrew Chronicle," 27.

35. Steven Bowman, *The Jews of Byzantium, 1204–1453* (University: University of Alabama Press, 1985), 188. For a detailed study of how the *sürgün* affected Jews, see Joseph Hacker, "The *Sürgün* System and Jewish Society in the Ottoman Empire during the Fifteenth to Seventeenth Centuries," in *Ottoman and Turkish Jewry: Community and Leadership*, ed. Aron Rodrigue (Bloomington: Indiana University Turkish Studies Department, 1992).

36. Berlin, "Sixteenth-Century Hebrew Chronicle," 28.

37. The first chapter of the Book of Ezra refers to how God "roused the spirit" of King Cyrus of Persia to allow the Jews exiled to Babylon by King Nebuchadnezzar to resettle in Jerusalem and rebuild their temple.

38. Capsali, *Seder Eliyahu zuta*, 1:218. Quoted also in Shaw, *Jews of the Ottoman Empire*, 33; Benbassa and Rodrigue, *Sephardi Jewry*, 7; and Lellouch, "Eliyahu Capsali," 201–202.

39. Capsali, *Seder Eliyahu zuta*, 1:219.

40. Cited in Berlin, "Sixteenth-Century Hebrew Chronicle," 31.

41. Benveniste, "Idea of Exile," 40.

42. Capsali, *Seder Eliyahu zuta*, 1:314. Also quoted in Berlin, "Sixteenth-Century Hebrew Chronicle," 35; Jacobs, *Islamische Geschichte in jüdischen Chroniken*, 171–172; and Jacobs, "Exposed to all the Currents," 43.

43. Cited in Berlin, "Sixteenth-Century Hebrew Chronicle," 34.

44. Berlin, "Sixteenth-Century Hebrew Chronicle," 35; Jacobs, *Islamische Geschichte in jüdischen Chroniken*, 178.

45. Berlin, "Sixteenth-Century Hebrew Chronicle," 38–39.

46. Capsali, *Seder Eliyahu zuta*, 2:7. Also quoted in Berlin, "Sixteenth-Century Hebrew Chronicle," 38; Jacobs, *Islamische Geschichte in jüdischen Chroniken*, 183; and Jacobs, "Exposed to all the Currents," 49.

47. The Egyptian Purim, based on the alleged events which occurred in 1524, is discussed in Yerushalmi, *Zakhor*, 47–48.

48. *Samuel Usque's Consolation for the Tribulations of Israel (Consolaçam às tribulaçoes de Israel)*, trans. Martin A. Cohen (Philadelphia: Jewish Publication Society of America, 1964), 231.

49. Ibid.

50. Heinrich Graetz, *History of the Jews*, 11 vols., trans. B. Löwy (Philadelphia: Jewish Publication Society of America, 1891–1898), 4:559–561.

51. Yerushalmi, *Zakhor*, 64.

52. Cited in Yerushalmi, *Zakhor*, 55.

53. Harry S. May, "Introduction," in Joseph Hacohen and The Anonymous Corrector, *The Vale of Tears (Emek Habacha)*, trans. plus critical commentary by Harry S. May (The Hague: Martinus Nijhoff, 1971), viii; Jacobs, *Islamische Geschichte in jüdischen Chroniken*, 82–85, 99; Martin Jacobs, "Joseph ha-Kohen, Paolo Giovio, and Sixteenth-Century Historiography," in *Cultural Intermediaries: Jewish Intellectuals in Early-Modern Italy*, ed. David B. Ruderman and Giuseppe Veltri (Philadelphia: University of Pennsylvania Press, 2004), 68.

54. Jacobs, *Islamische Geschichte in jüdischen Chroniken*, 88–91.

55. Jacobs, "Joseph ha-Kohen," 69.

56. Joseph ha-Kohen, *Sefer divrei ha-yamim le-malkhei Tzarefat u-malkhei beit Otman ha-Togar* (Sabionetta 1554), 113a, quoted in Yerushalmi, *Zakhor*, 64; and Jacobs, *Islamische Geschichte in jüdischen Chroniken*, 94.

57. Joseph ha-Kohen, *The Chronicles of Rabbi Joseph ben Joshua ben Meir the Sephardi*, trans. C. H. F. Bialloblotzky (London 1835), 273, quoted in Paudice, *Between Several Worlds*, 141.

58. Yerushalmi, *Zakhor*, 65.

59. Ha-Kohen, *Sefer divrei ha-yamim le-malkhei Tzarefat u-malkhei beit Otman ha-Togar*, 163b, quoted in Jacobs, *Islamische Geschichte in jüdischen Chroniken*, 208; ha-Kohen, ibid., 261a–262b, quoted in Jacobs, *Islamische Geschichte in jüdischen Chroniken*, 219–220; and in Bahar, *Jewish Historiography*, 63.

60. Hacohen and Anonymous Corrector, *Vale of Tears*, 1.

61. Paudice, *Between Several Worlds*, 157.

62. Jan Schmidt, review of Martin Jacobs, *Islamische Geschichte in jüdischen Chroniken*, *Journal of Early Modern History* 8, no. 3–4 (2004): 447.

63. Paudice, *Between Several Worlds*, 157.

64. Ibid., 553. On the life and work of Medina, see Morris Goodblatt, *Jewish Life in Turkey in the XVIth Century as Reflected in the Legal Writings of Samuel De Medina* (New York: Jewish Theological Seminary of America, 1952). Goodblatt offers many subjective statements that are not based on any evidence. For example, he claims that "The Sultans looked with suspicion upon their Greek and Armenian subjects and placed no trust in their faithfulness to the state." Ibid., 118. This is a doubtful claim for the sixteenth century; most likely, Goodblatt shows the influence not of the sixteenth-century sources used for his study,

but that of modern historiography, which he cites elsewhere. He asserts, in contrast with the disloyal Christians, that the sultans were "soon impressed by the devotion and reliability of the Jewish immigrants."

65. Benveniste, "Idea of Exile," 40.

66. Bahar, *Jewish Historiography*, 57.

67. Minna Rozen, *A History of the Jewish Community in the Istanbul: The Formative Years, 1453–1566* (Brill: Leiden, 2002), 43.

68. Immanuel Aboab, *Nomologia o discursos legales* (Amsterdam, 1629), 195. See Benbassa and Rodrigue, *Sephardi Jewry*, 7; "Aboab, Immanuel," *Encyclopaedia Judaica Jerusalem*, 16 vols. (Keter: Jerusalem, 1971), 2:90; and "Ottoman Empire," *Encyclopaedia Judaica Jerusalem*, 16 vols. (Keter: Jerusalem, 1971), 16:1532–1533.

69. Joseph Hacker, "Ottoman Policy toward the Jews," 1:120. See also Bowman, *Jews of Byzantium*, 177–195.

70. Paudice, *Between Several Worlds*, 108–109.

71. Hacker, "Ottoman Policy toward the Jews," 1:121.

72. Bowman, *Jews of Byzantium*, 180.

73. Hacker, "Ottoman Policy toward the Jews," 1:123–124.

74. Rozen, *History of the Jewish Community*, 44.

75. Mallet, *La Turquie, les Turcs et les Juifs*, 20–21.

76. Baer, *Honored by the Glory of Islam*, 90–91. See chapter 4, "Islamizing Istanbul," 81–104.

77. For these events, see Baer, *Honored by the Glory of Islam*, chapter 6, "Converting the Jewish Prophet and Jewish Physician," 121–138.

78. Ibid., 122.

79. Marc David Baer, "Death in the Hippodrome: Sexual Politics and Legal Culture in the Reign of Mehmet IV," *Past & Present* 210, no. 1 (February 2011): 61–91.

80. Ibid., 87–88.

81. "Nathan of Gaza, A Letter to Raphael Joseph," trans. David Halperin, in *Sabbatian Heresy: Writings on Mysticism, Messianism, & the Origins of Jewish Modernity*, ed. Paweł Maciejko (Waltham, MA: Brandeis University Press, 2017), 6. The letter is also quoted in Gershom Scholem, *Sabbatai Sevi: The Mystical Messiah*, trans. R. J. Zwi Werblowsky (Princeton, NJ: Princeton University Press, 1973); and Matt Goldish, *Sabbatean Prophets* (Cambridge, MA: Harvard University Press, 2004). Another version of the letter appears in Abraham Galanté, *Nouveaux documents sur Sabbetaï Sevi: Organisation et us et coutumes de ses adeptes* (Istanbul: Fratelli Haim, 1935), 110–111.

82. Galanté, *Nouveaux documents sur Sabbetaï Sevi*, 113–118.

83. See Baer, *Honored by the Glory of Islam*, 126–129, 255–256, and Baer, *The Dönme*, 1–24.

84. Gershom Scholem, *Sabbatai Sevi*, 704; Bahar, *Jewish Historiography on the Ottoman Empire*, 101–104.

85. See Shimon Shtober, introduction to *Sefer divre Yosef le-Rabbi Yosef Sambari* (Jerusalem: Ben-Tzvi Institute, 1994), (English abstract, ii–ix); Jacob Lassner, "Joseph Sambari on Muhammad and the Origins of Islam: A Learned Rabbi Confronts Muslim Apologetics and a Christian Polemical Tradition," in Jacob Lassner, *The Middle East Remembered: Forged Identities, Competing Narratives, Contested Spaces* (Ann Arbor, MI: University of Michigan Press, 2000); Martin Jacobs, "An Ex-Sabbatean's Remorse? Sambari's Polemics against Islam," *Jewish Quarterly Review* 97, no. 3 (2007); and Shimon Shtober, "Islam and Sabbateanism in the Chronicle Sefer Divrei Yosef," in *Jews and Muslims in the*

Islamic World, ed. Bernard Dov Cooperman and Zvi Zohar (Bethesda, MD: University Press of Maryland, 2013); Jacobs, *Islamische Geschichte in jüdischen Chroniken*, 114–115.

86. Jacobs, *Islamische Geschichte in jüdischen Chroniken*, 80, 103, 110–111, 124.

87. Ibid., 255.

88. Jacobs, "An Ex-Sabbatean's Remorse?," 357.

89. Michael Winter, "The Relations of Egyptian Jews with the Authorities and with the Non-Jewish Society," in *The Jews of Ottoman Egypt (1517–1914)*, ed. Jacob Landau (Jerusalem: Misgav Yerushalayim, 1988), 418 (in Hebrew).

90. Jacobs, "An Ex-Sabbatean's Remorse?" 361.

91. Shtober, "Islam and Sabbateanism," 324.

92. Jacobs, *Islamische Geschichte in jüdischen Chroniken*, 111, 116.

93. Ibid., 112.

94. Sambari, *Sefer divre Yosef*, 312, 24f, quoted in Jacobs, *Islamische Geschichte in jüdischen Chroniken*, 112; Sambari, *Sefer divre Yosef*, 77, 10–14, quoted in Jacobs, *Islamische Geschichte in jüdischen Chroniken*, 118. In one passage Sambari relates how the prophet Elijah intervened with Sultan Suleiman to foil a ruse by a jealous grand vizier to massacre all the Jews of the empire. Related in Moïse Franco, *Essai sur l'histoire des Israélites de l'Empire ottoman depuis les origenes jusqu'à nos jours* (Paris: A. Durlacher, 1897), 61–62.

95. Sambari, *Sefer divre Yosef*, 248: 9–13, quoted in Jacobs, *Islamische Geschichte in jüdischen Chroniken*, 250.

96. Bahar, *Jewish Historiography on the Ottoman Empire*, 55, note 2.

97. Sambari, *Sefer divre Yosef*, 252: 65–253, 70, quoted in Jacobs, *Islamische Geschichte in jüdischen Chroniken*, 251.

98. Esther Benbassa and Aron Rodrigue, *The Jews of the Balkans: The Judeo-Spanish Community, 15th to 20th Centuries* (Oxford: Blackwell, 1995), 8; Bahar, *Jewish Historiography on the Ottoman Empire*, 60–69.

99. Manuel of Karahisar cited in Suny, *"They Can Live in the Desert but Nowhere Else"*, 43.

100. Hovhannes Tsaretsi cited in Ibid.

101. Henry Shapiro, "Legitimizing the Ottoman Sultanate in Early Modern Greek," *Journal of Turkish Studies* 40 (2013): 331.

102. Georgios Sphrantzes, *Memorii: 1401–1477*, ed. Vasile Grecu (Bucharest: Editio Academiae Rei Publicae Socialistae Romaniae, 1966), 114, quoted in Shapiro, "Legitimizing the Ottoman Sultanate."

103. Shapiro, "Legitimizing the Ottoman Sultanate in Early Modern Greek," 330.

104. See Benbassa and Rodrigue, *Sephardi Jewry*, 1–10; Mallet, *La Turquie, les Turcs et les Juifs*; and Bahar, *Jewish Historiography on the Ottoman Empire*.

2

THE EMPIRE OF TOLERANT TURKS

THE EMOTIONAL WORLD OF NINETEENTH-CENTURY ASHKENAZIC AUTHORS OF both influential historical fiction and authoritative academic histories was shaped by the need to confront anti-Semitism. Frustrated by the barriers they faced to integration in their own societies, despite the promise of emancipation, they "exploited the tolerance they ascribed to Islam to chastise their Christian neighbors for failing to rise to the standards set by non-Christian society hundreds of years earlier."[1] Criticism of the majority society went hand in hand with self-criticism. German Jewish elites used the Sephardic model to promote their own self-transformation. Tolerant Muslim al-Andalus, they realized, had allowed Jews to be free. Granted equality, they flourished, leading, they believed, to their having become refined, cultured, "proud, dignified, respectable, and, indeed, physically beautiful."[2] These were traits that German Jewish elites found lacking in their own people of the time, their "decayed" spiritual and even physical condition less a fault of their own than a state to be blamed on their having been persecuted and restricted for so long. If only contemporary Germany had as open a cultural and political environment as the *convivencia* in medieval Muslim Spain, so they argued, would German Jewry be transformed. In its absence, they would make themselves worthy of emancipation by emulating Sephardic manners and the Sephardic model of acculturation: Jews who were fully Jewish and fully immersed in the majority culture. Their idea of a "golden age" for Jews in medieval al-Andalus and their adulation of the Sephardim remains influential to this day in both popular and academic accounts.

One finds the best articulation of this view in the influential work of the greatest of these pro-Islamic, pro-Turkish, and pro-Sephardic Ashkenazic Jews, Heinrich Graetz (1817–1891), embittered because his religion disqualified him for a professorship at a German university.[3] Graetz was simply imposing the view of the cultural assimilation of German Jews that he wished German Christians to adopt when he declared of the Jews of al-Andalus, "The Jewish inhabitants of this happy peninsula [Iberia] contributed by their hearty interest to the greatness of the country, which they loved as only a fatherland can be loved."[4] What he envisioned was Jewish self-transformation in a tolerant Germany leading to "a harmonious *Volksgemeinschaft* (national community), with Germans and Jews united in mutual respect, admiration, and service to the Fatherland."[5] He turned to history writing as the means of making this happen, emphasizing Islamic tolerance as a "foil" for his "hostile feelings about Christianity and the contemporary anti-Semitic movement."[6]

While it is true that "to a great extent, our own perception of medieval Sephardic Jewry is a cultural legacy bequeathed to us by nineteenth-century German Jews," it is not the case that romantic images of that age were "first crafted" by them.[7] In Graetz's magnum opus, *Geschichte der Juden* (Leipzig, 1853–1874, eleven volumes) we see echoes of early modern Sephardic Jewish messianic views. *Geschichte der Juden* provides the first iteration of premodern Sephardic claims about the Ottoman sultans in modern Jewish historiography. To Graetz—who cited Tzarfati and was influenced by the work of Capsali ("a good historian" who "aimed at relating the truth"), ha-Kohen ("a careful historian," "an impartial narrator," whose "work is a trustworthy source of information"), Usque, and Sambari—the Ottomans were the "heavy but deserved judgement [that] descended on Christendom."[8] As part of the divine plan, "heavy vengeance had been exacted" when Mehmed II conquered Byzantium and subsequent sultans threatened the Catholic powers. To Graetz, who believed alongside his early modern predecessors that "history is not ruled by chance, but that a higher hand guides it," it seemed "almost providential that, at a moment when the persecutions in Europe were increasing in number and virulence, the new Turkish empire should have arisen to offer an hospitable asylum to the hunted Jews."[9] Graetz was aware that the early modern historians he quotes were motivated by messianic fervor, and he did not merely convey their views, as a recent historian claims.[10] Graetz did share in some of their convictions, but not all. What was supposedly new about modern Jewish history writing at the time was its scientific approach to the past, which entailed the abandonment of the "belief that divine providence is not only an ultimate but an active causal factor in Jewish history."[11] It is significant, therefore, that we find traces of this very belief in the work of one of its greatest masters.

Graetz faithfully transmitted five of the six main myths of the early modern Sephardic narrative. The first four are that Mehmed II had invited Jews to settle in newly conquered Constantinople; that he established the chief rabbinate; that the "most humane monarch" Bayezid II invited fleeing Iberian Jewry to take refuge in his empire; and that he exclaimed, "'You call Ferdinand a wise king, he who has made his country poor and enriched ours!'"[12] The latter statement, a kind of proof text for Ottoman benevolent attitudes toward Jews, has been repeated by almost every modern Jewish historian writing on Ottoman Jewry from the nineteenth century to the present.[13] From Sambari, Graetz transmitted the specious claim that Mehmed II "even summoned this [chief] rabbi to the divan, and singled him out for special distinction, giving him a seat next to the mufti . . . and precedence over the patriarch."[14] Many have correctly argued that Graetz used the "overstated assertions of medieval Jewish historians, and it was via his popular history that the exaggerated and rose-colored version of Ottoman Jewish history found its way into" modern Ottoman Jewish, Turkish Jewish, European, and North American historiography.[15]

To illustrate the "happy condition" of the Jews in the Ottoman Empire, Graetz quotes Isaac Tzarfati's circular letter, as well as extensively from other early modern Jewish writers.[16] In his view, Jewish life in Christendom "was an unremitting *Leidensgeschichte*, a history of suffering."[17] He contrasts "the happy lot of Jews under the crescent"—agreeing with Tzarfati's rapturous claim that the Ottoman Empire was "a land 'in which nothing, absolutely nothing, is wanting'"—with "their hard fate under the shadow of the cross," where they "were savagely hunted," facing "relentless persecution."[18] Because the Ottoman sultans received them so warmly, he contends, the Jews at first enjoyed very happy days in Turkey. They were a godsend to this comparatively new state, which "could depend on the fidelity and usefulness of the Jews," as tradesmen, craftsmen who supplied new weapons and weapons technology to the Ottomans, artists, physicians, and interpreters.[19] In sum, considering the rise of Jews at court in the sixteenth century, when "a Jew, who would have been burned at the stake without ceremony in the countries of the cross, occupied a very influential position in the land of the crescent, rose to the rank of duke, and ruled over many Christians." Because "all the Jews in Turkey, amounting to millions in number, rose with and by him to a free and honorable station, the envy of their despised and less numerous brethren in Christian Europe," the Ottoman Empire became "a kind of Eastern Spain."[20] Retaining the early modern Jewish view that Christians were the Jews' enemy and Muslims the rod of his punishment, Graetz blamed any problems faced in the empire on Christians, whose hatred "followed the Jews even into Turkey. If there were neither Roman Catholics nor Protestants, there were Greek Catholic Christians," who "persecuted the Jews."[21] When they leveled the blood libel against Jews, however, "the sultan issued a decree that such malicious calumnies should be brought before him and not ordinary judges" such that "hatred against Jews" was "restrained in Turkey" while it "raged the more openly in Christian countries."[22]

At the same time that it conveyed the core myths and sentiments of the early modern Sephardic writers, pro-Islamic, pro-Sephardic Ashkenazic history writing such as Graetz's would have an influence on modern Ottoman Jewish history writing. French Jewish Enlightenment thought also contributed to modern Sephardic historiography. Yet both were preceded by earlier intellectual developments in the eighteenth-century Ottoman Empire. A network of Istanbul-based emissaries charged with raising money for contemporary Jews in the Holy Land stimulated Jews to imagine themselves "as part of an intertwined community that could act collectively in the present" rather than primarily "through a common mythical, biblical past, or a common utopian, messianic future."[23] The Sabbatian denouement also played a role in this transformation.

The emissaries "prepared the ground for the more far-reaching, pan-Jewish international philanthropy of the nineteenth century, in particular in the guise of the Alliance Israélite Universelle" founded in 1860.[24] The alliance, based in Paris, stimulated by the realization in the wake of the Damascus Affair of 1840 that Western European Jews could intervene on behalf of Jews in the Ottoman Empire, was created at the instigation of Adolphe Crémieux (1796–1880).[25] Crémieux had played a role during the Damascus Affair and would serve as alliance president, as well as vice president of the central governing body of French Jewry, and the minister of justice. He is most famous for issuing the decree granting citizenship to the Jewish minority in French Algeria, but denying the same right to the Muslim majority.[26] The alliance created hundreds of schools throughout Muslim-majority lands, especially the Ottoman Empire, which aimed to make Jews into "modern," francophone, useful citizens by educating them in modern schools and modern trades.[27] The "militantly westernizing" teachers, mainly Ottoman Jews trained in Paris, "returned to spread their newly adopted culture with all the zeal of neophytes."[28] The introduction and success of these schools, in turn, was facilitated by a francophone Ottoman Muslim elite promoting administrative reforms in the general context of the *Tanzimat* (1839–1876), which abolished slavery and granted equality to Ottoman Christians and Jews, including the ability to serve in the military, followed by citizenship.

Like their German Jewish counterparts, Ottoman Jewish elites of the nineteenth century sought acceptance from the majority in order to remake their community. They aimed to fashion a new, modern Jewish self, stripped of superstition and religious obscurantism, one that served the fatherland, spoke the majority language, and remained true to the faith.[29] They also turned to history writing. Reflecting the secularizing French Enlightenment and its offshoot in the alliance, we see among nineteenth-century Ottoman Jewish historians a new, secular spin on Ottoman Jewish history that downplays or ignores the messianic content of early modern scholarship and castigates the beliefs of their Jewish ancestors, while retaining the ecstatic emotions of their predecessors. Rather than appearing as messiahs or the tools of God's plan, Ottoman sultans are tolerant rulers who treat the Jews well. First Ottoman and then Turkish Jews began to write again about the messianic movement of Sabbatai Zevi. In contrast to two centuries earlier, however, they approached the topic critically and scientifically, rather than out of conviction or despair. Moïse Franco (1864–1907) wrote of the "unbelievable audacity" of the "strange man" who attracted a following not due to his intellect, but due to his good looks and beautiful voice. He acknowledged that of all the Jewish messiahs (except Jesus), Sabbatai Zevi is the only one who left behind a sect, the Dönme, which even two centuries after his death in Franco's day had six to seven thousand followers, "half-Jewish, half-Muslim," in Ottoman Salonica.[30] To analyze the movement, Edirne rabbi Abraham Danon (1857–1925) used Ottoman chronicles and European travelers' accounts and explored the socioeconomic conditions of Ottoman Jews at the time of the Sabbatian movement's outbreak.[31] Istanbul historian Abraham Galanté (later Avram Galanti, Bodrumlu, 1873–1961) offered a "scientific" account based on translations of many "authentic" documents—in Ottoman, Turkish, Armenian, Greek, and Hebrew.[32] His aim was to explain the "factors which contributed to the stubbornness of a great part of world Jewry" that believed that Sabbatai Zevi was the awaited messiah.[33] Salonican Joseph Néhama (1881–1971) condemned Sabbatai Zevi, Natan of Gaza, and subsequent leaders of the Dönme for being mad, depraved, and sexually perverted.[34] Rather than be concerned with divine plans and redemption, these first Ottoman Jewish historians adapted, alongside the Jewish elite, the integrationist aims of the *Wissenschaft des Judentums* (Academic study of Judaism) scholars, utilizing history as a tool to project an image of rational and educated Jews who were patriotic, loyal, and useful.

Tolerant Sultans and the Four-Hundredth-Anniversary Celebrations of 1892

In 1888, Danon established *El Progreso*, the first Jewish journal in the Ottoman Empire to include Ottoman Jewish history. Its series, "La istoria Israelita en Turkiya" (The history of the Jews of Turkey) consists largely of translations of Graetz's work.[35] Most significantly, while several passages in Graetz refer to Iberian Jews who settled in the Ottoman Empire as Spanish "fugitives," "exiles," or "emigrants," which places the emphasis on *Spain* as their homeland, Danon consistently changes the phrase to "Spanish refugees." This subtle change allows him, speaking on behalf of Ottoman Jewry, to emphasize the Jews' new *Ottoman* homeland and to give voice to his gratitude and loyalty to the dynasty.[36]

Mercado Joseph Covo (1874–1940), a teacher at an alliance school, played a crucial role in presenting to the Judeo-Spanish reader the vision of Ottoman Jewry as the most loyal and most useful Jews in Europe.[37] Claiming to be a descendant of Joseph ha-Kohen, he presented a utopian view that relied on Graetz, Danon, and others, arguing that the Ottoman Empire was the first "open land to receive all the oppressed who desired tranquility."[38] Covo deployed Enlightenment vocabulary to reinforce this image of the Ottoman Empire as a "refuge" where Jews "benefited from the freedom of religion." He even referred to the attribution of an apocryphal statement to the sultan, traceable through Danon back to Graetz, so as to emphasize the sultan's intelligence in recognizing the Jews as "true citizens" capable of "making the country flourish." He omitted all accounts of Ottoman sultans as messiahs. Covo concludes, "Are we Jews, all across the world, not indebted to this government, which was the first to love us? . . . We must forever recognize [the Ottoman Empire] and express the most profound respect for everything bearing the name 'Ottoman.'"[39]

Following Danon and Covo's lead, late Ottoman Jews promoted a carefully crafted image of Jews' unswerving loyalty to the sultan. In the late nineteenth century, Ottoman Jews fostered the myth of themselves as patriotic, "a model community with a special relationship to the state," which led to competition with Ottoman Christians seeking the same position[40]—and, one might add, involvement in state projects that favored Jews and punished others, especially Armenians and Greeks. The claim of a special Ottoman-Jewish relationship, which depicts tolerant Ottomans opening their gates to grateful, persecuted Jews, is a myth promoted as a public political performance by Jewish elites of model citizenship in response to the political reforms and ensuing crises of their age.[41] Wishing to create a public image of Jews as the most useful, esteemed, and loyal of government allies caused Jewish elites to willfully forget and suppress commemoration of dark episodes such as Sultan Mahmud II's execution of leading members of the Jewish community in 1826.[42]

In 1892, this vision culminated in Ottoman Jews celebrating the anniversary of the arrival of Iberian Jewry in the empire for the first time. Reading special prayers in synagogues across the empire and sending telegrams to the sultan expressing their gratitude, a tradition was invented that invoked the myth of the Ottomans as humane rescuers of Jews.[43] These myths, which set European Christian persecution against the foil of Ottoman Muslim tolerance, dovetailed with Ottoman government efforts to manage and improve their international image. The Smyrna (Izmir) journalist and Jewish community leader Aron de Joseph Hazan invented the centenary holiday that would also encourage the Ottoman government to accept Jewish refugees fleeing blood libels and pogroms in his day.[44] In the words of Ottoman Jewish journalists, the Ottoman dynasty gave Jews refuge from "the tyranny of the Spanish government and European barbarism," obliging them to declare their gratitude publicly.[45] More was at stake. According to Hazan, "Not only will doing so offer absolute proof of the profound gratitude we feel towards the Ottoman government, it will also constitute a direct response to those [Ottoman Muslim] anti-Semites who accuse us of being ingrates and who claim that we are not true patriots."[46]

Forging a Jewish-Muslim Mutual Alliance of Interests beyond the Ottoman Empire

The message was also transmitted to Europe and North America. The 1893 annual report of the alliance on the status of Jews in the Ottoman Empire declares "there are but few countries, even among those which are considered the most enlightened and the most civilized, where Jews enjoy a more complete equality than in Turkey [the Ottoman Empire]." They praise the sultan and government for displaying "towards Jews a spirit of largest toleration . . . In every respect, Abdul-Hamid proves to be a generous sovereign and protector of his Israelite subjects." In response, "the unflinching attachment of Jews to His Person and to the Empire is the only way in which they can express their gratitude. Thus, the Sultan, as well as his officials know that Jews are among the most obedient, faithful and devoted subjects of Turkey."[47]

Ottoman Jews led the effort to promote a positive image of the Ottomans at the Columbian Exhibition in Chicago the same year.[48] Its Jewish representatives lectured audiences and journalists, giving the Ottoman government's perspective.[49] Such celebrations of Ottoman tolerance also highlighted differences between Jews and Ottoman Christians.[50] It is therefore no coincidence that Jews promoted a Muslim-Jewish alliance in a period when tensions between the Ottoman government and Armenians and Greeks were high. Scholars have argued that while the nineteenth-century Ottoman Empire witnessed the rise of Muslim-Christian sectarianism, Muslim-Jewish relations escaped the trend of worsening intercommunal relations, with the exception of Palestine beginning in the twentieth century.[51] At the same time, Christian-Jewish relations, already poor, "became worse than ever before under Ottoman rule."[52] The reason for "the traditional pattern" of Muslim-Jewish relations continuing but Christian-Jewish relations worsening can be explained by the fact that Jews "continued their prolonged efforts to win the goodwill and sympathy of the Muslims also by demonstrating their loyalty to the Ottoman state and by siding with Muslims at times of Muslim-Christian tensions."[53] Ottoman Jews continued to express their solidarity with Muslims and the Ottoman government and to distance themselves from Christians during the massacres of Armenians in Jewish neighborhoods in Istanbul in 1896 and during the Greco-Ottoman war of 1897.

In 1896, as Armenians were massacred in the capital and elsewhere in the empire, Jewish claims of "special affinity with Muslims . . . helped solidify Jews' image as a model" religious minority precisely as the relationship between the Ottoman regime and Christians worsened.[54] And being a model minority meant siding with the Muslim majority. Jewish involvement in violence against Armenians contributed to lasting tensions between Jews and Christians. As thousands of Armenians in Hasköy, Istanbul—home also to many Jews—were massacred in August, some Jews participated in the violence, attacking Armenians and looting their homes. Many Jews were eyewitnesses to what befell their Armenian neighbors and their goods at the hands of Turks and Kurds. Some blamed the victims for bringing it upon themselves as they sought to overthrow the government. Jewish archival documentation—namely that of the alliance in Paris—confirms that Jews participated in the murder of Armenians at that time.[55] In 1908, Ottoman chief rabbi Haim Nahum reported to the alliance his visit to the former Armenian patriarch where he more or less apologized for Jews "helping the Kurds to search out the hiding places of victims."[56]

Yet other Jews had saved Armenians, some by letting them borrow prayer books and prayer shawls so they could pretend they were Jews.[57] Jewish leaders in Istanbul debated publicizing the fact that Jews had actually endangered their own lives to save Armenians. But elite Jews decided to suppress reports that Jews had aided Armenians, worrying about what it would mean for their alliance with Muslims against a common enemy.[58] Reflecting this sentiment, in September 1896, a man named V. Gerson wrote to the alliance noting that "it would be reckless to publicize that the Jews had helped the Armenians whom the Ottomans view, perhaps justifiably, as traitors, dishonest, anarchists. To assist such traitors and rebels is not patriotic and may incur the anger or even the vengeance of the Ottomans. If the Jews publish a defense of acts we are accused of but did not commit, who knows what may happen to us during the new massacres."[59]

Ottoman Jews' propaganda efforts were echoed by those of Theodor Herzl (1860–1904), the founder of political Zionism. The leaders of the Zionist movement offered a pro-Ottoman view as they wished to gain the support of Sultan Abdülhamid II (r. 1876–1909) for their cause of establishing a Jewish homeland in Ottoman Palestine. This included "helping the Sultan in his battle over public opinion" regarding the Armenian problem.[60] Herzl believed that if the Zionists assisted the sultan on the Armenian issue, the sultan would support the Zionists; and he acted accordingly during the 1890s and the Armenian massacres. In 1896, an agent of the sultan suggested to Herzl that he marshal "Jewish power" on the Ottoman Empire's behalf so as to temper international outrage regarding the massacres of Armenians. Herzl gave a one-word response: "Excellent!"[61]

In that year, "when European sympathy for the Armenians was at its height and pressure on the Ottoman padishah was intense, Herzl used all his contacts, as Zionist leader and as newspaperman, to turn the tide." In a journal entry from June 1896, Herzl wrote that "this is the service he demands of me: that I prevail upon the newspapers of Europe (in London, Paris, Berlin and Vienna), to present the Armenian question in a fashion friendly to Turkey [the Ottoman Empire], and that I convince the Armenian leaders themselves to surrender to him, whereupon he will be willing to meet all sorts of their demands."[62] When interviewed in the English press that July and asked whether he had gained the sultan's support of his program at the price of Jewish support against the Armenians, he rejected this claim, but added that "people in England have not been entirely fair towards the sultan. He personally abhors brutality, and he honestly yearns to live in peace with all of his subjects."[63] In August 1896, as Armenians were massacred in Istanbul, Herzl feared this would lead to the deposition of Sultan Abdülhamid II, which would mean the end of the Zionist dream.[64] Accordingly, Herzl "attempted to rouse public opinion to support the Sultan despite the worsening of atrocities against the Armenians."

Herzl and the sultan imagined "the Jews" could silence negative opinion about the Ottomans and hinder Christian rebellion. Both Herzl and the sultan were using each other to fulfill their own aims; both lived in a world of fantasy. In Herzl's view, "the sultan gives us the piece of land, and for that we will put everything in order for him, regulate his finances, and determine public opinion of the entire world in his favor."[65] Sultan Abdülhamid II turned to the Jews as a friend to cease hostile activities of the Christian enemy while invoking an anti-Semitic fantasy, imagining a Europe controlled by Jews.

Friends and Enemies in the First Ever History of Ottoman Jewry

During the Greco-Ottoman war of 1897, Ottoman Jews continued to express their solidarity with Ottoman Muslims and the Ottoman government and to distance themselves from Christian communities. Ottoman Jewish journalists promoted the common interests of Jews and Muslims, portraying them equally as the victims of Christians. Jews aided the war effort, promoting patriotic acts including raising funds, sewing uniforms, volunteering as soldiers, praying for victory, and even attacking Greek prisoners and circulating stories of martyrdom at the hands of Greeks.[66] Accordingly, Jewish journalists and leaders wrote more often of "the hardening line between those they portrayed as the friends and enemies of the empire."

That year, Moïse Franco published the first monograph ever devoted to a history of Ottoman Jewry, *Essai sur l'histoire des Israélites de l'Empire*

Ottoman depuis les origines jusqu'à nos jours (Essay on the history of the Jews of the Ottoman Empire from the origins to the present day). Trained by the alliance in Paris at its École normale israélite orientale, he had served as headmaster in several alliance schools in the empire. He based the groundbreaking work on French, Hebrew, and Judeo-Spanish sources, in part on Tzarfati, Capsali, Usque, and especially Sambari. The book was heavily indebted in tone and content to Danon, and thus to Graetz.[67] At the beginning of his study, Franco mentions the sufferings of those Jews unfortunate enough to have "fallen under the iron yoke of the Byzantine tyrants."[68] As a foil, he contrasts their plight with a rosy narrative of Ottoman sultans as tolerant and Ottoman Jews as satisfied, for they live well and free, especially in comparison with their religious brethren in Christian Europe, citing Tzarfati's letter, which he claims inspired "a multitude" of Central European Jews to immigrate to the empire.[69] But there is no messianic praise, let alone biblical quotation; he refers disparagingly to the kabbalist precursors of Sabbatai Zevi as "cranks, fiends, conjurers of spirits, workers of miracles, and wonders."[70]

Franco's history progresses from sultan to sultan, painting a utopian tableau where Jews and Muslims lived in amity. The empire's second sultan, Orhan, allowed Jews to build a new synagogue and to practice their religion "in complete freedom" at the first Ottoman capital of Bursa.[71] The Jews of Adrianople (Edirne), the second Ottoman capital, "enthusiastically" rushed to welcome the Muslim conquerors as "justice and tolerance reigned under the banner of the crescent."[72] Murad II acted very favorably toward the Jews.[73] He repeats Capsali's claim that Mehmed II appointed Moses Capsali as "chief rabbi" and gave him a seat in the divan along with government ministers, the mufti, and the Greek patriarch, and then follows it with Sambari's claim that Capsali was seated closer to the sultan than the patriarch.[74] He makes no mention of the sufferings of Romaniot Jews but repeats Capsali's claims that Bayezid II "eagerly" received the Iberian exiles, ordering his provincial governors "to affably welcome them." He also attributes to the sultan the famous apocryphal saying, "You call Ferdinand a wise king, he who impoverishes his kingdom and enriches my own."[75] The Spanish Jews, he asserts, quickly "gained the confidence of the Turks [Ottoman Muslims], making themselves useful to their new fatherland" in industry and trade, and weapons technology.[76] Thus, by his account, the "Christian persecutors, by expelling Jews from their countries, literally put their weapons into the hands of the Ottomans, their enemies."[77] About Selim I, whom early modern Jews had proclaimed the messiah and the instrument of God for conquering Jerusalem, Franco says only that "there is nothing remarkable to mention," other than that he too had a Jewish physician.[78] About Suleiman I, whose reign ushered in the messianic age according to Capsali, Franco mentions that Jews were "grateful" that he rebuilt the walls of Jerusalem but does not add to this any eschatological comment.[79] He is more interested in narrating the lives of Jews who served the palace and other Jewish dignitaries.

What also catches Franco's attention are the blood libels he attributes primarily to Greeks, who blamed Jews for murdering Christian children in order to bake matzo for Passover, a subject to which he devotes considerable space throughout the volume, including an entire section of the work. He condemns as "anti-Semitic" late nineteenth-century Greek newspapers that promoted the claim that Jews engaged in ritual murder and incited the "hatred of the Greek populace" to exact vengeance.[80] Reflecting on the sixteen blood libel accusations between 1861 and 1876 he asks rhetorically what would have happened if the imperial government had not protected the Jews; he doubts whether a single Jew would have remained alive had it not.[81] "The prejudice" that Jews use Christian blood in their rituals "is still firmly entrenched in the hearts of the Christians of the East, especially the Christians of the Orthodox Church" he concludes.[82] Even when faced with the counterfactual of blood libels fomented by Muslims, Franco claims that Christians are to blame. He alleges that the Janissaries responsible for a 1633 blood libel were "recently converted" from among the Greeks.[83] His placing the blame for misfortune suffered by Jews in the Ottoman Empire on Christians is another example of the secularization of earlier accounts: the Greek minority of modern histories has been added to the Byzantine Greeks of premodern chronicles. Franco's history was popular and was republished several times, even as late as the end of the twentieth century.

The Last Ottoman Chief Rabbi Haim Nahum, Utopian but Fearful

The year Franco's book was published, Haim Nahum (1873–1960) was ordained a rabbi at the progressive seminary in Paris connected with the alliance.[84] An important late Ottoman and early republican Jewish public figure who promoted utopian views in public but privately voiced darker concerns about Muslim attitudes to Jews, Nahum served as the last Ottoman chief rabbi from 1909 to 1920. No Jewish religious leader had enjoyed "as powerful a status" in the empire since Moses Capsali.[85] Nahum observed how in his era Ottoman Muslims praised Jews for their devotion and loyalty, while expressing anti-Semitism. In a letter he wrote to the secretary general of the alliance in Paris in 1898, Nahum quotes from an article in the Turkish-language press, "The Jews and the Turkish Language," published in *Tercüman-i hakikat* (Interpreter of truth), whose Muslim author praises Ottoman Jews for introducing Ottoman Turkish in their schools, making them "true Ottomans."[86] According to this author, "all Ottomans have an imperative duty to appreciate this devotion and this loyalty on the part of the Jews . . . How many good and useful consequences are there for us in our relationships with the Jews!" The author praises the alliance, which "has seen that the Jews have lived in security under the efficient protection of the Empire for long years, and it has always appreciated this imperial kindness and justice." According to Nahum, the author of the article ends section two by writing, "We congratulate all our Jewish co-citizens on their efforts; and thank them once again for their love of our homeland, our government, and our language." Nahum recounts that the author then "adds a long postscript to this article in which he censures and attacks anti-Semites."[87]

In Istanbul, Nahum taught for the alliance and assisted Abraham Danon, into whose family he would marry. He was appointed French teacher at the École supérieure du génie et de l'artillerie, where he met many of the revolutionary military men who would foment the 1908 revolution that would successfully depose Abdülhamid II.[88] But he again had to contend with anti-Semitism. In a letter to the president of the alliance in 1904, Nahum explains how "since I began teaching there, I have tried to banish the anti-Semitic spirit that prevails in the military corps of this high school."[89]

Nahum was appointed acting chief rabbi shortly after the revolution and at the beginning of 1909 was elected chief rabbi over his father-in-law.[90] The speech given by the grand vizier Ahmed Riza Bey at the chief rabbi's induction ceremony in 1909 presents Jews as the ally of the Muslims. "The Jews have hitherto been outstanding by their attachment and their sincere friendship for the great Muslim Ottoman nation, with which they have always lived in a very good relationship, like a single body and a single soul. The loyal Jewish nation has always been an active and useful element. We hope that it will render many more services to the government and the country."[91] But two months later Nahum was reporting on the counterrevolution, as Armenians were massacred in Adana and the Jews feared that they would be next. "We have escaped a terrible massacre. The reactionary movement was going to 'attack the Jews' first. The population did not repudiate it. We are still not completely out of danger despite the state of siege and the harsh measures the present government is taking to repress any reactionary initiative."[92]

Nahum felt a threat from among his own flock as well, as support for Jewish nationalism in the empire was increasing, and as opponents of the Young Turks debated Zionism in parliament in the prewar years.[93] Nahum was concerned that Zionism would turn authorities against the Jews, a community that "had hitherto been considered loyal to the central power and enjoyed relative tranquility, for which it paid by remaining silent."[94] For their part, the Zionists continued to praise Sultan Abdülhamid II. Only a few months after the latest massacres of Armenians in 1901, the Fifth Zionist Congress held in Basel offered "a public expression of admiration" for the sultan; the Congress sent Abdülhamid II a telegram expressing "dedication and gratitude which all of the Jews feel regarding the benevolence which His Highness the Sultan has always shown them."[95] This is not out of keeping with how Ottoman Jews publicly viewed the sultan. Nahum ensured that an anti-Zionist pamphlet written by Ottoman Jewish journalist David Fresco was distributed "to all the ministers, senators, deputies, and newspaper editors," confirming Ottoman Jewry's rejection of Zionism, as had been publicly voiced by the communities of Salonica and Izmir.[96] To fight "the rising tide of Zionism," Nahum came up with a plan in autumn 1909: a declaration in the Ottoman parliament by a friend of the Jews who would ask in part, "Does the government not think that this movement is of a nature to damage the unity of the Ottoman homeland?" Nahum envisaged the minister of the interior rising to "speak of the loyalty of the Ottoman Jews, which has been demonstrated in ways that are known in memorable circumstances, of the patriotism with which they welcomed the military law that now makes them the equals of their co-citizens. . . . He would denounce the creation of a separatist nationalist movement as a very grave danger to the Jews, which could alienate the sympathies of their co-citizens." [97]

Nahum was assisted in his efforts by passionate Ottomanist Moiz Kohen/Munis Tekinalp (1883–1961). Speaking at the Ninth World Zionist Congress in Hamburg in 1909, Tekinalp contrasted a lachrymose vision of life for Jews in Christian lands with a utopian account of Muslim rule. He declared that "Turkey [the Ottoman Empire] is the only land that has been spared from the plague of antisemitism, appearing to us as a modern Canaan, the promised land for today's Jews, who flee from the modern Egypts, the lands of slavery and grief" [Romania and Russia].[98] Tekinalp mentions how "the legendary tolerance of the Turks" is so well known it has become a truism.[99] The "tolerance of the Ottomans and strong bonds of friendship between Muslims and Jews," moreover, serve as the most "alluring incentive" for Jews to immigrate to the empire. Anti-Semitism and intolerance are not only "unknown" in the empire, but "for the Jews, Turkey [the Ottoman Empire] was more than tolerant, it was their guardian angel during the critical moments in our history," including the Inquisition and the frequent charges of ritual murder, "inconceivable" in an Islamic empire.[100] He asserted that Ottoman Jews were "true Ottoman patriots" committed to Ottomanism. Arguing against Zionism, he supported Jewish immigration into the empire on condition that the Jewish immigrants became Ottoman patriots and were distributed across the empire (i.e., not concentrated in Palestine alone). He contended that loyal Jews would serve to offset disloyal (Christian) groups because "the respective interests of the Jews" and the empire coincided.[101] He ended his speech by citing his early modern ancestors, quoting Bayezid II inviting the Jews to his land and Isaac Tzarfati declaring, "Here every man may dwell at peace under his own vine and fig tree."[102]

Conclusion

Over the course of the nineteenth century, Ottoman Jews, having been gradually secularized, likewise secularized their approach to the Ottoman Muslim deliverer. They nevertheless retained the emotional fervor of their predecessors, converting the sultans into rescuers of the Jewish people, tolerant and benevolent rulers who saved Jews from harm. In the second half of the nineteenth century, German Jewish historian Heinrich Graetz claimed that the sultans Bayezid II, Selim I, and Suleiman I "not only tolerated the fugitive Jews, but gave them a hearty welcome."[103] Graetz's idealization of the Ottoman rulers was taken up later in the nineteenth century by the Ottoman Jewish historian Abraham Danon, by Mercado Joseph Covo and Aron de Joseph Hazan, who in 1892 launched the first commemoration of the arrival of the Sephardim in the Ottoman Empire, and by Moïse Franco, author of the first history of Ottoman Jews, as well as Theodor Herzl, leader of the Zionist movement. Each of these writers aligned themselves publicly with the Muslim rulers of the empire against Ottoman Armenians and Greeks. Just as their early modern counterparts had, for religious reasons, avowed an alliance between Muslims and Jews against their common Christian enemies (Byzantines, Catholic monarchs, Habsburgs), for political reasons late Ottoman writers explicitly articulated a mutual alliance of interests between Jews and Muslims against their common enemies—Greece and Russia (uncoincidentally Christian-ruled empires), and the rebellious Christian populations within the empire itself. Whether driven by religious or political motives—or even by fear in the case of the chief rabbi Haim Nahum—what was common was an affective disposition compelling Ottoman Jews to praise and side with Ottoman Muslims.

This utopian vision succeeded as the dominant narrative because of a common alliance with Ottoman Muslims; it was useful to both communities concerned. Jews took sides, taking the part of the Muslims against the Christians. They understood that power would remain in the hands of the former, and they wished to associate with that power in a politics of alignment that would best serve their interests. They chose to invest in empire, by demonstrating their patriotism and loyalty, expressing absolute devotion to the sultan. Just as with lachrymose Byzantine Jewish accounts of the Ottomans in the fifteenth century that had been overlooked by their coreligionists and then forgotten, Jewish counternarratives also existed at the turn of the twentieth century. The Zionist narrative, which claimed that the future of the Jews lay not in a multicultural empire that tolerated them, but rather in a Jewish state of their own, was not popular in the late nineteenth century among Ottoman Jews. It could not gain traction among an elite that bound itself with the fortunes of the empire. Another competing narrative was offered by socialist revolutionaries, whose movement was led by Jews or Dönme, the descendants of the converted followers of Sabbatai Zevi. Yet such an ideology, which aimed to overturn the existing order, was frowned upon by Jewish intellectual elites who sought the state as an anchor in stormy seas not to be jettisoned in favor of the unknown. In 1911, when Sultan Mehmed V (r. 1909–1918) visited Salonica, Ottoman Jewish socialists—representatives from the Socialist Workers' Federation, an organization primarily made up of Jews—were arrested for being a public menace and for threatening disorder. Their leader, Abraham Benaroya was exiled for encouraging a boycott of the sultan's visit, which threatened to damage the carefully crafted image of Jews as loyal subjects. Zionists were jailed for antipatriotic activities. Nonetheless, chief rabbi Jacob Meier told the sultan, "I am pleased to report that nowhere in your vast empire does there live one single Jew who does not love and venerate his beloved homeland."[104]

Notes

1. Cohen, "The 'Golden Age' of Jewish-Muslim Relations," 28. Cohen credits Bernard Lewis, "The Pro-Islamic Jews," for recognizing that Graetz used the medieval model of Islamic tolerance of Jews to criticize his own modern society. For detailed studies analyzing how nineteenth-century German Jewish intellectuals perceived medieval Sephardim as cultural mediators offering a model for successful integration, see *Sephardism: Spanish Jewish History and the Modern Literary Imagination*, ed. Yael Halevi-Wise (Stanford, CA: Stanford University Press, 2012); Jonathan Skolnik, *Jewish Pasts, German Fictions: History, Memory, and Minority Culture in Germany, 1824–1955* (Stanford, CA: Stanford University Press, 2014); John Efron, *German Jewry and the Allure of the Sephardic* (Princeton, NJ: Princeton University Press, 2015); and Carsten Schapkow, *Role Model and Countermodel: The Golden Age of Iberian Jewry and German Jewish Culture During the Era of Emancipation*, trans. Corey Twitchell (London: Lexington Books, 2016).

2. Efron, *German Jewry and the Allure of the Sephardic*, 16.

3. Bernard Lewis appears to be the first scholar to coin these phrases. See Lewis, "The Pro-Islamic Jews," 391.

4. Graetz, *History of the Jews*, 3:41, cited in Norman A. Stillman, "History" in Norman A. Stillman, *The Jews of Arab Lands: A History and Source Book*, 54.

5. Efron, *German Jewry and the Allure of the Sephardic*, 231.

6. Ibid., 19.

7. Ibid., 2.

8. Graetz, *History of the Jews*, 4:267, 406, 511, 556.

9. Ibid., 4:268, 554. Elsewhere Graetz writes, "He who believes that Providence manifests itself in history, that sins, crimes, and follies on the whole serve to elevate mankind, finds in the French Revolution complete confirmation of this faith. Could this eventful reaction, which the whole of the civilized world gradually experienced, have happened without the long chain of revolting crimes and abominations which the nobility, the monarchy, and the Church committed? . . . The Revolution was a judgment which in one day atoned for the sins of a thousand years." Ibid., 5:428.

10. Bahar, *Jewish Historiography on the Ottoman Empire*, 155.

11. Yerushalmi, *Zakhor*, 89.

12. Graetz, *History of the Jews*, 4:268, 356, 364, 406.

13. Bahar, *Jewish Historiography of the Ottoman Empire*, 70; note 3 lists specific references to these authors.

14. Graetz, *History of the Jews*, 4:268.

15. Bahar, *Jewish Historiography of the Ottoman Empire*, 117.

16. Graetz, *History of the Jews*, 4:271.

17. Efron, *German Jewry and the Allure of the Sephardic*, 207, Graetz, *History of the Jews*, 4:271.

18. Graetz, *History of the Jews*, 4:271

19. Ibid., 400–401.

20. Ibid., 4:364, 593.

21. Ibid., 4:552.

22. Ibid., 4:553.

23. Matthias Lehmann, *Emissaries from the Holy Land: The Sephardic Diaspora and the Practice of Pan-Judaism in the Eighteenth Century* (Stanford, CA: Stanford University Press, 2014), 2.

24. Ibid., 5.

25. The Damascus Affair refers to the event where Jews were libeled by Christians, and the alleged perpetrators of an alleged ritual murder of a French citizen were tortured by local Muslim officials, some being killed. But thanks to the intervention of Western European Jews, the remaining prisoners were freed and the sultan issued an edict condemning blood libel.

26. Benjamin Stora, "The Crémieux Decree," in *A History of Jewish-Muslim Relations*.

27. Aron Rodrigue, *French Jews, Turkish Jews: The Alliance Israélite Universelle and the Politics of Jewish Schooling, 1860–1925* (Bloomington, IN: Indiana University Press, 1990).

28. Aron Rodrigue, *Jews and Muslims: Images of Sephardi and Eastern Jewries in Modern Times* (Seattle, WA: University of Washington Press, 2003), 5.

29. John Efron and Julia Phillips Cohen both refer to W. E. B Dubois's theory of "double consciousness" to describe the difficult position of the respective community elites in the same era, although they deploy the concept in diametrically opposing ways. Efron, *German Jewry and the Allure of the Sephardic*, 6–7; Cohen, *Becoming Ottomans*, xi.

30. Franco, *Essai sur l'histoire des Israélites de l'Empire Ottoman*, 94, 108, 113.

31. Abraham Danon, "Sur Sabbatai Cevi et sa secte," *Revue des études Juives* 37 (1898).

32. Abraham Galanté, *Nouveaux documents sur Sabbataï Sevi: Organisation et us et coutumes de ses adeptes* (Istanbul: Fratelli Haim, 1935), 4.

33. Ibid.

34. Joseph Néhama, "Sabbataï Sevi et les Sabbatéens de Salonique," *Revue des Écoles de l'Alliance Israélite* 3 (1902); Mihalis Daskalakis-Giontis, "Defining Neighbours: Greeks and Dönme in Joseph Nehama's *History of the Israelites of Salonica*" (MA thesis in Hebrew and Jewish Studies, University College London, 2015), 34–37.

35. Devin Naar, "Fashioning the "Mother of Israel": The Ottoman Jewish Historical Narrative and the Image of Jewish Salonica," *Jewish History* 28, no. 3 (2014): 351–352.

36. See Graetz, *History of the Jews*, 4:383, 392, 399, 400, 402; Naar, "Fashioning the "Mother of Israel," 351.

37. Naar, "Fashioning the "Mother of Israel," 360–362.

38. Ibid., 363.

39. Ibid., 366.

40. Cohen, *Becoming Ottomans*, xiii.

41. Ibid., 4.

42. Ibid., 6–7.

43. Ibid., 56–57.

44. Ibid., 47.

45. Ibid., 49.

46. Quoted in Ibid., 54.

47. *Bulletin de l' Alliance Israélite Universelle*, no. 18 (1893): 38–39, quoted in Paul Dumont, "Jewish Communities in Turkey during the Last Decades of the Nineteenth Century in the

Light of the Archives of the Alliance Israélite Universelle," in *Christians and Jews in the Ottoman Empire*, 1:221, and in Shaw, *The Jews of the Ottoman Empire*, 210.

48. Cohen, *Becoming Ottomans*, 63.

49. Ibid., 64.

50. Ibid., 71–72.

51. Bruce Masters, *Christians and Jews in the Ottoman Arab World: The Roots of Sectarianism* (Cambridge: Cambridge University Press, 2001), ch. 5, "Intercommunal Dissonance in the Nineteenth Century," 130–168.

52. Moshe Ma'oz, "Communal Conflicts in Ottoman Syria during the Reform Era: The Role of Political and Economic Factors," in *Christians and Jews in the Ottoman Empire*, 2:91.

53. Ibid., 100.

54. Cohen, *Becoming Ottomans*, 16.

55. Yair Auron, *Zionism and the Armenian Genocide: The Banality of Indifference* (London: Transaction, 2000), 150.

56. Ibid., 151.

57. "Eyewitness to Massacres of Armenians in Istanbul (1896)," in *Sephardi Lives: A Documentary History, 1700–1950*, ed. Sarah Stein and Julia Cohen (Stanford, CA: Stanford University Press, 2014).

58. Ibid., 74. The Hebrew-language paper *Hamelitz*, published in St. Petersburg, praised the Ottomans and their treatment of Jews and blamed the Armenians for the riots: "And among the Jews there is no outburst nor outcry; the Jews are serene and quiet, praying for the wellbeing of the state. . . . The High Authority in Turkey has taken note of this and will always extend to the Jews its covenant of peace; it has given them protection and refuge from the wrath of the Greeks and many other Christian peoples who were hostile to the Jews and full of murderous thoughts of death and destruction. But Turkey has preserved its covenant and its mercy toward the Jews to this very day." Issue 214, October 4, 1895, quoted in Auron, *Zionism and the Armenian Genocide*, 145. The same article turns to the Armenians: "The Jews are grateful to the Sultan and his government and to his Muslim people . . . their hands will be forever joined together. When the Armenians conspired to rise up several days ago in riots in the streets of Constantinople, the Sephardic Jews stood together with the Muslims and the policemen and their assistance helped them to carry the day against those who had risen up against them. The Armenians who seek greatness and freedom for themselves have shown that they are no longer worthy of this honor, since they almost allowed themselves to raise the banner of rebellion, to spill the blood of innocent people including several Jews whom they had injured and would have murdered." Jews and Muslims together "pursued them to the end." Ibid., 146.

59. Letter in the archive of the alliance, quoted in Auron, *Zionism and the Armenian Genocide*, 152.

60. Ibid., 112.

61. Anderson, "'Down in Turkey, Far Away,'" 87.

62. Auron, *Zionism and the Armenian Genocide*, 116.

63. Ibid., 117.

64. Ibid., 119.

65. Anderson, "'Down in Turkey, Far Away,'" 89.

66. Cohen, *Becoming Ottomans*, 81.

67. Bahar correctly claims that the only premodern Jewish historian to which Franco refers in the footnotes is Sambari, whose manuscript he read at the alliance library in Paris; however, he refers to the other historians in the text. Bahar, *Jewish Historiography on the Ottoman Empire*, 147.

68. Franco, *Essai sur l'histoire des Israélites de l'Empire Ottoman*, 2, also cited in Mallet, *La Turquie, les Turcs et les Juifs*, 27.

69. Franco, *Essai sur l'histoire des Israélites de l'Empire Ottoman*, 34–35.

70. Ibid., 82.

71. Ibid., 28.

72. Ibid., 29.

73. Ibid., 30.

74. Ibid., 32.

75. Ibid., 37, also quoted in Veinstein, "Jews and Muslims in the Ottoman Empire," 177.

76. Franco, *Essai sur l'histoire des Israélites de l'Empire Ottoman*, 38–39.

77. Ibid., 39.

78. Ibid., 46.

79. Ibid., 47.

80. Ibid., 158–159, 185, 220–233 (for the period 1861–1876); 229–230.

81. Ibid., 232.

82. Ibid., 233.

83. Ibid., 87–88.

84. *Haim Nahum: A Sephardic Chief Rabbi in Politics, 1892–1923*, ed. with an introduction by Esther Benbassa, trans. from the French by Miriam Kochan (Tuscaloosa, AL: University of Alabama Press, 1995), 5–6.

85. Rozen, *A History of the Jewish Community in the Istanbul*, 201.

86. *Haim Nahum*, 55.

87. Ibid., 56.

88. Ibid., 8.

89. Ibid., 86.

90. Ibid., 11–13.

91. Letter, Haim Nahum, Istanbul, to Jacques Bigart, Secretary-General of the Alliance, Paris, March 29, 1909 in ibid., 158.

92. May 17, 1909, in ibid., 159.

93. Ibid., 15.

94. Ibid., 17.

95. Auron, *Zionism and the Armenian Genocide*, 104; Anderson, "'Down in Turkey, Far Away,'" 90.

96. *Haim Nahum*, 19; letter from January 3, 1910, in ibid., 162.

97. Ibid., 161.

98. Jacob M. Landau, *Tekinalp: Turkish Patriot, 1883–1961* (Istanbul: Nederlands Historisch-Archaeologisch Instituut, 1984), 21. The original speech in German appears in 45–54; here 45–46.

99. Ibid., 46.

100. Ibid., 47.

101. Ibid., 21.

102. Ibid., 54. He repeats many of these themes and claims Tzarfati referred to the empire as an "earthly paradise for the world's persecuted Jews" in "Die Juden in den Balkanländern," *Monatsschrift der österreichisch-israelitischen Union* 25, no. 9–10 (September-October 1913): 17, in Landau, *Tekinalp*, 92.

103. Graetz, *History of the Jews*, 4:400.

104. Cohen, *Becoming Ottomans*, 122–123.

3

GRATEFUL JEWS AND ANTI-SEMITIC ARMENIANS AND GREEKS

ACCORDING TO THE OFFICIAL OTTOMAN CENSUS, THE OTTOMAN Jewish population grew from 184,000 in 1883 to 215,000 in 1897.[1] In 1908, the empire counted 256,000 Jewish subjects within its borders, but the number decreased to 187,000 in 1914. Most of that decrease can be accounted for by the loss of Ottoman Salonica, perhaps the only Jewish-majority city in the world.[2] In 1912–1913, four southeastern European powers (Bulgaria, Greece, Montenegro, and Serbia) defeated the Ottomans in the First Balkan War, leading to the Ottoman loss of Salonica. Salonican Jews urged the Great Powers to either return their city to Ottoman sovereignty or allow it to become an independent city-state. As friends of the Ottomans, Salonican Jews feared the Greek enemy.[3] The Ottomans managed to defeat Bulgaria in the Second Balkan War in 1913, but it had already lost the majority of its territory in the region, which it had held for over five centuries. The wars were accompanied by massacres of Christians and Muslims and a great influx of Muslims into the ever-shrinking Ottoman Empire.

Haim Nahum, "A Man for All Governments"

As the wars broke out, Haim Nahum voiced some doubt about the Jewish friend, the Muslim, hinting again about the rise of anti-Semitism. After the war, he promoted recognition of Jewish patriotism. In 1912, Nahum wrote to his contacts at the French embassy. "The measures taken might give the impression that the international fleet only came to safeguard the life and property of the European colony and the Christians, because people like to believe that Jews and Muslims fraternize and that we have nothing to fear. Nevertheless, despite the measures for any contingency adopted by the government, which has strengthened the patrols that move through the whole town night and day," Nahum asked the French to ensure "a French ship anchored on the Golden Horn, between Hasköy and Balat, which are inhabited mainly by our poor coreligionists."[4] At the end of the Balkan Wars, Nahum declared that "large numbers of our coreligionists fought in the ranks of the Ottoman army; the least little communities sent contingents; many are missing, dead, or wounded." He also mentions "a commission, which has just been set up for the erection of a monument to the memory of Jewish soldiers who fell in battle."[5]

When World War I broke out in 1914, the Ottomans sided with Germany, their long-standing military and economic partner. During World War I, Nahum told the Germans that he favored Jewish integration and identification with the majority society and "emphasized that it was in the Ottoman Jews' interest to keep their distance from Zionism in order to preserve their good relations with the authorities."[6] Yet at the same time, he played down the Zionist threat to the Ottoman authorities. During the war, he denied the fact that in 1917 the minister of the navy, commander of the Fourth Army, and military governor of Syria Cemal Pasha (assassinated in 1922) had expelled Jews from Jaffa, Palestine.[7] But writing in the Judeo-Spanish and Ottoman press after the war, he claimed "that he had intervened with his Ottoman political friends in Istanbul in order to end the 1917 deportations."[8] Writing in the Judeo-Spanish press to the president of the alliance in Paris, he wrote that "thanks to the policy I followed, I prevented the Jews of Turkey and Palestine from sharing the fate of the Armenians and Greeks (and the Greek papers themselves have proclaimed this loud and clear)."[9]

For Jews, Cemal Pasha became the bogeyman for having expelled Jews from Palestine, and Talat Pasha (interior minister 1913–1917; grand vizier, 1917–1918; assassinated in 1921), who had close relations with Nahum, was their friend. For the Armenians, it was the opposite: they were targeted for destruction by Talat Pasha. The Armenians were subject to annihilation by the Ottoman regime during the war.[10] When the Ottomans lost most of their remaining territory in southeastern Europe in the Balkan Wars, including Salonica, the homeland of many of the Committee of Union and Progress (CUP) leaders, persecuted Muslims of southeastern Europe streamed into the empire by the millions seeking vengeance. This fueled hostility against Christians in the empire. A humiliated Ottoman minister of war and commander in chief, İsmail Enver Pasha (in office 1914–1918; death in battle, 1922), wrote, "Revenge, revenge, revenge, there could be no other word."[11] One of the reasons for the Ottomans joining the war on the side of Germany was the opportunity to fight against archenemy Russia, long seen as having meddled in Ottoman affairs on behalf of the Armenians. That some Ottoman Armenians joined the Russians was enough to confirm to the Ottoman regime that all Armenians were traitors, no matter the fact that "far more Ottoman Armenians joined the Ottoman army and fought against Russia until they were disarmed," sent to labor battalions, and subsequently executed.[12] This occurred after the battle of Sarıkamış on the Caucasus frontier against Russia (December 1914–January 1915), which resulted in the destruction of the Ottoman Third Army, a disaster that Enver Pasha blamed on Armenians. Between the defeat at Sarıkamış and the landings at Gallipoli, which the regime feared would lead to a Bulgarian or British occupation of Istanbul, the regime decided to deport all the Armenian civilians of the eastern provinces.

The emotional state of the perpetrators—their affective disposition— explains the motivation of the Ottoman regime. They had a state of mind that convinced them that it was necessary to annihilate the Armenians.[13] Panic, despair, and a desire for revenge caused the regime to see a hidden Armenian hand, an Armenian terrorist, everywhere; to first engage in sporadic deportations and massacres, and then in mass murder and pillage. In February, the Ottomans failed to take the Suez Canal from the British. In February and March, Enver Pasha ordered tens of thousands of Armenian men serving in the Ottoman military to turn in their weapons. They were then put into labor battalions, suffering a high death rate. Those who survived were shot. On the evening of April 24, 1915, in the wake of the Armenian uprising in the eastern city of Van, the interior minister, Talat Pasha, ordered three hundred Armenian political leaders, educators, writers, clergy, and dignitaries in Istanbul to be jailed and tortured, then hanged or shot. Next, as the Ottomans were bogged down defending Gallipoli over the ensuing nine months, there were mass arrests of Armenian men throughout the empire. The men were tied together with ropes in small groups, taken to the outskirts of their towns, and shot dead or bayoneted. Talat Pasha issued written orders to provincial governors in western, central, and eastern Anatolia to deport Armenian women, children, and the elderly to Deir ez-Zor in the Syrian Desert and other camps, under the oversight of Cemal Pasha. These "were not intended to be places of refuge. They were way stations toward extermination."[14] At the same time, Enver Pasha gave oral commands to Bahaettin Şakir (assassinated in 1922), head of the "Special Organization," to have irregular Muslim forces, Turks and Kurds, annihilate the caravans as they moved out of the towns. Tens of thousands of Armenian girls and women were adopted into Muslim families as daughters or brides, thereby escaping deportation. While they managed to survive, albeit as Muslims, up to one million Armenians were murdered.

Jews served as eyewitnesses to the genocide. In autumn 1915, alliance teacher Léon Sémach recounted the "dreadful and indescribable scenes" of mass expulsion, confiscation of possessions, torture, hunger, thirst, disease, murder, fatigue and deprivation, and the hanging of local Armenians because "the Turkish [Ottoman] government decided to finish" them off. He declared "this community is destined for complete destruction if the war lasts a few months longer." [15] But by then it was already over for the Armenians. At the end of August 1915, Talat Pasha wrote in a telegraph to authorities in Ankara, "The Armenian question in the eastern provinces has been resolved. There is no need to sully the nation and the government with further atrocities."[16] Indeed, by 1917 the millennia-long Armenian presence in Anatolia had been put to an end.

During the genocide, Jewish American US ambassador to the Ottoman Empire Henry Morgenthau (in office 1913–1916) reports that when he attempted to intervene on the Armenians' behalf, Talat Pasha referred instead to Ottoman tolerance of Jews and the long-standing Muslim-Jewish friendship. "Why are you so interested in the Armenians, anyway?" Talat Pasha reportedly asked. "You are a Jew; these people are Christians. The Muslims and the Jews always get on harmoniously. We are treating the Jews here all right. What have you to complain of?"[17] Morgenthau was so worried that the Ottomans would do to the Jews what they were doing to the Armenians, however, that he warned local Jews not to do anything that would provoke an attack, especially Zionist activities. Writing to his friend, prominent US rabbi and Zionist leader Stephen S. Wise on October 19, 1915, the ambassador noted, "Fortunately the American public are sending large sums for the Armenians. . . . It is going to be a most difficult task to persuade the Turks [Ottoman Muslims] to permit me to assist the Armenians whom they do not wish helped by any foreigners. They do not want the Armenians to feel that they have any friends outside of Turkey [the Ottoman Empire]." But instead of being "contented" to merely "punish" the Armenians, the Ottomans "think that they must annihilate the entire race. This should be a lesson to the Zionists. I positively fear that if any of the Zionists would do anything against the Turkish [Ottoman] authorities in Palestine, there may be a wholesale persecution and attempted annihilation of all the Jews in Turkey [the Ottoman Empire]. These men do not distinguish between guilty and innocent."[18]

The memoirs of Zionists—members of the Zionist Executive in Germany, their representatives in Istanbul, and those living in Palestine—reveal that they were terrified by the annihilation of the Armenians. As Alexander Aaronsohn recounted in 1916, Jews in Palestine "were in a state of great excitement because an order had recently come from Turkish [Ottoman] authorities bidding them surrender whatever firearms or weapons they had in their possession . . . we knew that similar measures had been taken before the terrible Armenian massacres, and we felt that some such fate might be in preparation for our people."[19] But their private fears were not matched by public intervention, as they sided with Germany and their ally, the Ottoman Empire. Their good relations with the Ottoman authorities, the Jewish US ambassadors in Istanbul, and the German government enabled them to hinder the persecution of Jews in Palestine.

When faced with persecution, Sephardi Jews responded in their time-worn fashion. When Albert Antebi, an Ottoman Sephardi in Palestine, was told he and dozens of other notables were soon to be deported to Bursa, he reminded Cemal Pasha how his family "was distinguished for its loyalty to the Ottoman cause," and that "the Jews had always been grateful to Turkey and remembered the hospitality given to the Spanish exiles during the fifteenth and sixteenth centuries."[20] It worked. They were spared deportation to Anatolia.

In 1916, US Ambassador Abraham Elkus (in office 1916–1917, d. 1947)—who like his predecessor, Morgenthau, and their predecessor, Oscar Straus (in office 1909–1910; envoy 1887–1889 and 1898–1899, d. 1926), was also Jewish—expressed how he was profoundly disturbed by "the unchecked [Ottoman] policy of extermination" of the Armenians, but he was unable to hinder it.[21] When he reached out to Zionist officials for their assistance, as the World Zionist Organization was based in Germany and was on excellent terms with the Ottoman ally, they were reluctant to help US efforts. Elkus asked World Zionist Organization representative in Istanbul Richard Lichtheim (in office 1913–1917) to help him coordinate efforts with the German embassy to prevent persecution of both Armenians and Jews, but Lichtheim demurred.[22]

The Americans and Germans were successful in their efforts to protect Jews, however: the Germans in particular "emerged as the saviors of the Jews and chief protectors of their enterprise in Palestine;" indeed, "had it not been for Germany's persistent interventions" with the Ottoman government, "the Jewish community in Palestine would not have survived."[23] The German government and the US government exerted utmost efforts to protect them from local officials and Cemal Pasha, who planned to deport all the Jews of Palestine to Anatolia to replace the Armenian population.[24] Although Germany followed the principle of not interfering in the internal affairs of the Ottoman Empire regarding the Armenians, German officials made an exception to this rule in order to save the Jews of Palestine because they believed that Jews had a strong influence over US public opinion, expecting that saving Jews would help Germany's war effort.[25]

When hundreds of Jews were deported from Jaffa in December 1914, German and US officials intervened and local Ottoman officials were dismissed.[26] In 1917, when the ten thousand Jews of Jaffa were deported, and the Jews of Jerusalem and the rest of Palestine faced the same policy, Germany intervened again on their behalf.[27] As Colonel (later General) Friedrich Freiherr Kress von Kressenstein, chief of staff of the Eighth Corps of Cemal Pasha's Fourth Army recalled, "Dislocation of so large a population would have led to unimaginable consequences. The terrible incidents of the Armenian exodus would have been repeated. . .The evacuation of a town in Turkey [the Ottoman Empire] is tantamount to its complete annihilation."[28] The deportation order was cancelled. The German ambassador to Washington, Count Johan Heinrich Bernstorff, urging Ottoman officials to treat Jews mildly, reports that in 1917 Talat Pasha assured him, "We have done much harm to the Armenians but we shall do nothing to the Jews."[29] The reason was that he expected Zionists and Jews to suppress critical reports of his regime in the press and promote its propaganda instead.

Germany and the Central Powers, including the Ottoman Empire, were defeated at the end of World War I. Shortly before the war ended, the leaders of the Ottoman regime—Talat Pasha, Enver Pasha, Cemal Pasha and other prominent Ottoman officials, including Bahaettin Şakir—fled to Germany, where they were offered asylum. Britain, France, and the United States demanded that Germany send the members of the regime home to stand trial. The requests were denied.

As the Allies occupied Istanbul, Ottoman military tribunals were held in 1919 and 1920. Ahmed Riza declared in the Ottoman parliament how Armenians "were savagely murdered" as part of "an official" policy carried out by the state.[30] In 1919, military tribunals arrested hundreds of CUP members, military officers, and government officials, and there were over a dozen trials. The postwar government acknowledged what had happened and acted to punish the perpetrators: the lieutenant governor of Yozgat was hanged, but his funeral turned into a demonstration as he was seen as a hero and martyr.[31] Two other perpetrators were executed, fifteen others condemned to death in absentia, including those who had fled to Berlin. The press printed accounts of the atrocities, including the statement of Vehib Pasha, which asserted that "the killing and liquidation of the Armenians, as well as the plundering and seizure of their property," was "the result of the decisions of the CUP Central Committee and . . . the person who outfitted, commanded, and brought into service these butchers of humanity within the Third Army's zone was Bahaettin Şakir."[32]

But the Ottoman government gave up on the prosecution, and most defendants were set free. Nationalists came to power, whose leader, Mustafa Kemal (Atatürk, 1881–1938, the future first president of Turkey, 1923–1938), blamed the victims. Mustafa Kemal had declared already in 1919 that "whatever has befallen the non-Muslim elements living in our country is the result of the policies of separatism they pursued in a savage manner when they allowed themselves to be made tools of foreign intrigues and abused their privileges. There are probably many reasons and excuses for the undesired events that have taken place in Turkey [Ottoman Empire]. And I want definitely to say that these events are on a level far removed from the many forms of oppression which are committed in the states of Europe without any excuse."[33] As one scholar observes, "all the classic elements in the defense of violent aggression are here: they asked for it, it was not really so bad and anyway, others have done the same and worse."[34] He might have added that Mustafa Kemal used Christian persecution of Jews in Europe to silence charges of Ottoman Muslim persecution of Armenians.

In 1921 and 1922, members of an Armenian revenge organization assassinated the members of the genocidal regime who had taken refuge outside the Ottoman Empire. They shot Talat Pasha, Bahaettin Şakir, and Cemal Azmi, former governor of Trabzon province, in Berlin; they killed Cemal Pasha in Tbilisi. During these years, from 1919 to 1922, the world's first memorial to the Armenian genocide stood in the heart of occupied Istanbul in Taksim Square.[35]

The Jewish leadership in Istanbul had nothing to say about these crimes. Morgenthau mentions how Talat Pasha had close relations with Chief Rabbi Haim Nahum. Nahum was "a man for all governments" who "was in turn the Young Turks' man . . . the man of the ephemeral government of İzzet

Pasha in 1918, and the man of Mustafa Kemal in 1919," the man who would found the Turkish Republic.[36] Nahum never held a government position but was always expected to mediate between the Ottoman Empire and foreign powers: he was "the only chief rabbi ever invested with such a broad political role." In 1915, he failed in his task to negotiate a separate peace between France, Britain, and the Ottomans. In 1918, his second unsuccessful mission was to turn Western Jewry in favor of the Ottomans and to gain the support of neutral countries as well.[37] Later that year he was sent on a third mission, as an intermediary between Grand Vizier İzzet Pasha and the Entente Powers. But the French and British distrusted him, as he had supported the pro-German policies of the CUP during the war.[38] He returned to Istanbul, only to be sent back to Paris in 1919 by the Kemalists hoping to make contacts in Western Europe.[39] He spoke favorably of the Turkish nationalist movement to the French press. "Nahum did his best to rectify the unflattering image that the Western press painted of the Kemalists and conducted a veritable campaign to explain the policy of the movement and its leaders."[40] In 1922, he was sent on a mission by the provisional nationalist government to promote pro-Kemalist propaganda in Western Europe. Speaking in the name of Turkey, "he had become Ankara's man."[41] In 1922 and 1923, he served as advisor to the Turkish delegations to the Lausanne conference, headed by his former pupil at the École du génie et de l'artillerie, İsmet Pasha (İnönü, the future Turkish president, 1938–1950). The Turkish press lauded his efforts, although in the mid-1960s, after his death, anti-Semitic attacks were launched against him in Turkish publications calling him a traitor, which could not be further from the truth. Nahum always loyally served the "masters of the country."[42]

Ottoman Myths in the Turkish Republic

The period from 1912 to 1922 witnessed the massacres and mass population movements of Christians and Muslims during the Balkan Wars; the devastation of World War I, in which the Ottoman Empire suffered casualties at a proportionally higher rate even than France and implemented the genocide of approximately one million Armenians; and a five-year civil war between Greece and the Orthodox Christians of Anatolia against Muslims—Turkish and Kurdish, but also Balkan and Caucasian—which ended in the ethnic cleansing of the Orthodox Christians of Anatolia, an action legalized in 1923–1924 in the population exchange between Greece and the newly established Turkish Republic. As a result of all this bloodshed, the Christian and Jewish population of Anatolia was reduced from one-fifth (20%) of the population at the start of World War I to one-fortieth of the population (2.5%) by 1927. The Turkish census that year recorded 82,000 Jewish citizens, a decrease of 105,000 since the 1914 census.[43]

Along with these demographic changes, in its first decade the new republic engaged in a centralized process of ethnocultural homogenization, secularization, and Turkification. One result was that former Muslim allies in war and genocide—notably the Kurds—were victimized by their former Turkish allies. Another outcome was the loss of whatever vestiges remained of centuries of Ottoman tolerance of difference, pluralism, communal religious autonomy, and political pragmatism and flexibility. These were replaced with the pursuit of sameness, monoculturalism, and monolingualism; individual rather than communal rights; the disestablishment of religious communities and the stripping of their powers; and single-party, single-ruler authoritarianism.[44]

How would Turkish Jewry—whose population had decreased by nearly two-thirds in a little more than a decade—make a place for themselves in the new nation-state? Could they rely on the same myths as they had in the past, despite the end of the age of empire?

Mustafa Kemal, who would name himself Atatürk, "the father of the Turks," and who would lead the Turkish Republic from its founding in 1923 to his death as its first president and leader of its ruling *Cumhuriyet Halk Partisi* (CHP, Republican People's Party), declared that on the one hand, "Jews are one of our loyal elements," who "share a common fate with the sovereign element, the Turks [Muslims], because they have proven their devotion to the nation and homeland."[45] Yet on the other hand, "Armenians do not have a share whatsoever" in Turkey.[46] The "Christian minorities" [Armenian and Greek] are the enemy, for they "strive to destroy the state as quickly as possible in order to obtain their aims."[47] In his 1928 Ottoman-language work, *Türkler ve Yahudiler: Tarihî, siyasî tetkik* (Turks and Jews: A historical and political investigation), Turkish Jew Abraham Galanté invokes the same binary between Jewish friend/Christian enemy as he imagines relations among Christians, Jews, and Muslims in the Ottoman Empire and Turkish Republic. The Jews' "attachment" to Turks and "siding with" Turkey is well known to Christians, who accordingly "view Jews as the enemy," he argues.[48] Galanté presents Turks as tolerant, benevolent protectors and Jews as their loyal, grateful, and useful guests. He passes over the inconvenient counterexample of the messianic movement of Sabbatai Zevi, who Jews expected would overthrow the sultan and make him his personal slave.[49] Ignoring the episode he contrasts loyal Jews with treacherous Armenians and Greeks, who spread anti-Semitism within the empire and sided with the occupying powers after World War I.

In 1941, less than a decade after the anti-Jewish pogroms in Thrace and a more recent sustained anti-Semitic campaign in the press, Galanté declared that "anti-Semitism does not exist in Turkey," and that "the Turks' spirit of justice and tolerance, their sense of morality and humanity render them incapable" of understanding Nazism.[50] He maintained his silence about the Ottoman genocide of the Armenians and the massacres and expulsion of the Greeks between 1918 and 1924, as had Mustafa Kemal Atatürk. Their silence illustrates how "the Turkish Republic was originally based on forgetting," as "organized amnesia" was "self-administered by the Republican reformers"[51] including Atatürk and Galanté.[52]

This amnesia is best illustrated by the way the Turkish Republic responded to the Armenian genocide perpetuated by its predecessor. Already in 1922, Mustafa Kemal declared that "the new Turkey has absolutely no relation with the old Turkey. The Ottoman state has gone down in history. Now, a new Turkey is born."[53] This approach became official Turkish historical narrative in accordance with Atatürk's 1927 six-day speech given before the general congress of the single ruling party, the CHP. Known simply as *Nutuk* (The speech), it is to this day "narrated in all textbooks from elementary school to universities" in the centralized Turkish education system.[54] The main themes of the speech—and of the official discourse on the Armenian genocide—are silence, denial of the genocide, general amnesia about past violence (unless presenting Turks as the real victims), identifying with the perpetrators, never questioning the great prophetic and infallible leader (Atatürk), and promoting the racial purification of the land in the face of a life-or-death Darwinian struggle with minorities.

Atatürk "conceived of himself as an 'I-nation.'" As a historian, "dictating the only legitimate and authorized historical reading of the Turkish past," the "I-nation incarnated a war declared on many different kinds of internal enemies," including the Ottoman past and the Christians of Anatolia.[55] In the very first sentence of the *Nutuk*, Atatürk begins his narrative of Turkish history following the Armenian genocide on May 19, 1919, with his own phoenix-like emergence at Samsun out of the ruins of the Ottoman Empire, when, as he would have it, Christians from every direction sought to destroy the nation. He declares May 19, 1919, to be his own and the nation's birthday, the day that Turkey and its father, Atatürk, were born. The Armenian genocide is passed over in silence, expunged from history. Quite the reverse, Atatürk argues that it is the Muslims of Anatolia and not the Christians who are the victims. Later in the text, he speaks of "Armenian massacres," by which he means Armenian massacres of Muslims, not the Armenian genocide. He claims that it was the Turkish nation that was the guiltless and oppressed victim, subject to massacres by murderous, evil Armenians. Focusing on the "Armenian atrocities" in his seminal work framing republican Turkish history allows him to argue that it is the Armenians, and not the Turks, who are guilty of a policy of extermination.

Perpetrators of the genocide were honored by the new republic. One of these was Dr. Mehmed Reşid (suicide in 1919), who as governor of Diyarbekir was responsible for the death of 120,000 Armenians. He justified their murder with these words: "There are two alternatives: Either the Armenians will liquidate the Turks, or the Turks will liquidate them!" As a physician, he utilized a medicalized language concerning the body politic. "The Armenian bandits were a load of harmful microbes that had afflicted the body of the fatherland. Was it not the duty of the doctor to kill the microbes?"[56] Many of the people in central positions of power in Atatürk's early republic had been involved in the genocide and other atrocities. Celal Bayar, responsible for atrocities committed against Greeks in the Aegean region, became prime minister (1937–1939) and later president (1950–1960). Şükrü Kaya, who had overseen most of the deportations of Armenians while serving as the general director of the Department of Nomadic Tribes and Immigrants, became foreign minister (1924–1925) and interior minister (1927–1938). Abdülhalik Renda, who as governor had deported the Armenians of Bitlis and Aleppo to their deaths, became minister of finance (1924–1934 discontinuous), minister of defense (1927–1930), speaker of the Grand National Assembly (1935–1946), and acting president for one day upon Atatürk's death in 1938.[57] In 1943, the remains of Talat Pasha, the main architect of the Armenian genocide, were reburied in a monumental tomb in Istanbul.

Abraham Galanté, The Unofficial Spokesman for Turkish Jewry

In the early Turkish Republic (1923–1950), Jews found the old story articulated by a new voice—that of Abraham Galanté. Like Nahum, Galanté always followed the prevailing trend in late Ottoman and early republican Turkish politics: working first as a censor for Abdülhamid II's regime, "screening foreign printed material to weed out publications critical of the Sultan and his policies"; then joining a secret cell of the CUP and founding a Jewish committee that supported the CUP-led 1908 revolution that toppled the sultan the following year; speaking out later against the Allied occupation of Istanbul; joining the nationalist movement; and finally serving as a parliamentarian in the new republic.[58]

Beginning as a teacher at an Ottoman imperial lycée, Galanté became professor and chair of Ancient History of Oriental Peoples at the predecessor to Istanbul University after World War I, serving as the only Jewish professor.[59] He was dismissed at the end of the 1920s for not accepting the language reforms from Ottoman to modern Turkish, which entailed the replacement of the Arabic alphabet with the Latin, however. But according to his biographer, Galanté's main mission in the early republic was to act as "the unofficial spokesman for the Jewish community, trying hard to redress the slipping status of the Jews in the eyes of the Turks," behaving "more as a public relations man than a historian, at times confusing by necessity each respective role."[60] We see evidence of this in his scholarly work.

Galanté is the author of sixty books and approximately one hundred articles on Turkish Jewry. The most significant for our purposes is *Türkler ve Yahudiler*, which originally appeared in Ottoman Turkish in 1928, five years after the founding of the republic; it was later published in French in 1932 and in a revised second version in modern Turkish in 1947.[61] When it first appeared in 1928, the Turkish Jewish population of the nation-state had decreased marginally over the previous two decades, and numbered 77,000.[62] *Türkler ve Yahudiler* takes as its model Franco's and thus Danon's and Graetz's history. Galanté aimed to demonstrate that despite what the Turkish public might think following recent events—including a telegram allegedly sent on behalf of Turkish Jewry to Spain declaring its loyalty, and a mass Jewish demonstration in Istanbul—Jews were loyal to the republic. He wished to prove that the history the Ottomans and Turks had shared with Jews had been peaceful and mutually beneficial. Considering the context in which he was writing—in a land that had witnessed the Armenian genocide and civil war with and then expulsion of the Greeks, and where the position of Jews was delicate at best—it is understandable why he would have published an apologia narrowly focusing on any evidence he could find demonstrating the loyalty and usefulness of Ottoman and Turkish

Jews. Perhaps given new urgency by recent traumatic events, his retelling of Turkish Jewish history repeats what Ottoman Jews had been writing since 1892. Placing Atatürk's slogan "Don't be afraid to tell the truth" on the book's cover, Galanté tells the "truth" (even when it counters his own lived experience) that Turkish Jews wished Turkish Muslims to hear—and that both Jewish and Muslim Turks wished Christian Europeans to hear. It is no coincidence that this utopian approach to Muslim-Jewish relations in Ottoman and Turkish history was also articulated by the Turkish nation's leader, Atatürk—yet another example of the Muslim-Jewish alliance of interests in narrating the same perspective on the past.

Echoing both the official republican historiography's silence on the Armenian genocide as part of a general amnesia about past violence (unless Turks are the victims and Christians the perpetrators) and the older Jewish historiographical tradition of utopian Muslim-Jewish relations, Galanté repeats all the platitudes of the 1892 centenary celebrations, with no mention of the cataclysmic affairs of recent years. In the 1947 version, he ignores anti-Semitism in the Turkish press, overlooks the anti-Jewish pogrom in Thrace in 1934, and barely mentions the fate of Turkish Jews in Europe. He fails to relate how the Capital Tax imposed between 1942 and 1944 stripped the patriotic and loyal author of his own wealth and property.[63] As he was unable or unwilling to note events that acutely affected his own social and economic position, one cannot expect him to have written of the Armenian genocide of 1915, the expulsion of Greeks in 1923 and 1924, or the 1936 law stripping Christians and Jews of their charitable foundations. Remaining silent on these events while at the same time emphasizing the alleged disloyalty and anti-Semitism of Armenians and Greeks served to justify key episodes of state violence against Christians. It also served to align both Jewish interests with Muslim interests and Jewish approaches to the past with the official history of the new republic.

Rather than focusing on lachrymose events, Galanté's history promotes the familiar utopian vision of Muslim-Jewish relations. He quotes his own 1921 letter to the editor published in an Ottoman Turkish–language newspaper during the Allied occupation of Istanbul after World War I.[64] Incited by reports in the Istanbul Christian (most likely Greek-language) press defending the foreign occupation as necessary and just because it meant the "rescuing" of "unfree" peoples including Jews, Galanté argues instead that Jews had no need to be "saved" by outsiders; Turkey already served as a refuge for Jews oppressed by Christians elsewhere. Galanté offers a dozen historical examples proving that Jews had lived in comfort in Turkey, and that Jews outside of Turkey had always seen it as a place of refuge. The monograph is an expanded version of that letter, aiming to prove the symbiotic relationship between Muslims and Jews. In it, he cites the "services (*hizmetler*) the two component parts (*unsurlar*) of the nation rendered each other," and, linking the Jews' fate with that of Muslim Turks, he asserts that "the Jews will share in the Turks' rise and advancement in the future." No mention is made of the other constituent elements of the Ottoman Empire that did not make it into the Turkish nation-state, for they have no future, it is implied; unlike the Jews, they did not side with the Turks.

Two events compelled Galanté to expand his 1921 letter into a book-length apologia in 1928: the first, occurring in 1926, involved reports in the Turkish press that several hundred Turkish Jews sent a telegram to Spain declaring their loyalty; the second, following in 1927, was the Elza Niyego affair.[65] Niyego was a young Jewish woman murdered by a married Muslim man whom she had spurned. At her funeral procession in Istanbul, tens of thousands of Jews marched through the streets shouting, "We want justice!" The event culminated in the arrest of scores of Jews charged with unlawful assembly, disturbing the peace, inciting the public to malice, insulting the police, and insulting Turkishness. The Elza Niyego affair caused the Turkish press again to question Jews' loyalty and label them "ungrateful." In response, an embarrassed Galanté declared counterfactually that "never mind *planning* a demonstration against Turkey, even the *thought* of demonstrating against Turkey would never cross the mind of Turkish Jewry."[66] This was because "Turkish Jews, and the entire Jewish world, always remember the goodness shown to them by the fatherland with gratefulness and indebtedness." The positive emotional weight of the past renders Jews tongue-tied when faced with negative experiences in the present.

For this reason, the main sources Galanté uses for the study, "written with the desire to serve my fatherland, Turkey," are Hebrew- and Portuguese-language sources including Tzarfati, Capsali, Usque, and ha-Kohen, and the works of other Ottoman and Turkish Jews, especially Franco, whose book serves as a model for his book's content and structure. When he discusses sixteenth-century Jewish texts that speak of Ottoman sultans in messianic terms, he strips them of their apocalyptic imagery and biblical references, focusing instead on their embrace of Jews. Referring to Bayezid II, he cites Capsali: "Sultan Bayezid, the King of Turkey, heard of all the misfortune that the King of Spain had inflicted on the Jews, and hearing that they were seeking a resting place for their feet, took pity on them. He issued a proclamation to prevent any official from turning the Jews away and driving them out; they were ordered instead to welcome them in a friendly manner, and hospitably, and commanded that whoever did not would be put to death."[67] Galanté does the same regarding Samuel Usque. He notes that Usque believes the empire to be a model of tolerance, adding a few choice lines. "You will find that you are free to practice Judaism in Turkey where the gates of liberty are open unconditionally. *These gates will never close [to you].* There you may renew your faith, change your ways, and save yourself from foreign usage and customs . . . embrace your true ancient faith and abandon the practices opposed to God's will, which you have adopted under the pressures of the nations in which you have wandered, *you will receive great favors from the sultan.*"[68] Although Galanté is the first Ottoman or Turkish Jewish author to quote extensively from archival sources, he does so selectively. Nor does his work in the archives change in any way his thesis or hinder him from repeating the earlier myths, including Bayezid II's apocryphal line, "You call Ferdinand a wise king, he who impoverishes his kingdom and enriches my own?"[69]

While Galanté eschews a personification of the empire in the sultan, like Franco, he retains a chronological, sultan-by-sultan account interwoven with thematic sections. The book takes up the subject of Turkish (Muslim) benevolence to Jews and Jewish service to Turks (Ottoman and Turkish Muslims) in the fields of science and technology (printing, medicine, weapons technology), politics (diplomacy), the economy (trade and industrialization), the arts (music); and, from the nineteenth century, public service (government ministries, parliament), the press, and education. In his 1941 work on the Jews of Istanbul, he mentions that "several" of the foreign professors employed at the university were Jewish, "proving that Turkish borders were not closed" to Jews, and he places this in the context of the alleged absence of anti-Semitism in Turkey and the "spirit of tolerance" and "humanity" of the Turks.[70] In the 1947 version of *Türkler ve Yahudiler,* he changes the scale of the "welcome" to claim that when mostly Jewish scholars fled Hitler's Germany, the countries that benefited the most included Turkey, which took in forty professors and sixteen assistants.[71] This is in accordance with his thesis that from the fourteenth through the nineteenth centuries, the Ottoman Empire allowed Jews escaping persecution at the hands of Christians to immigrate; moreover, the Turks protected the Jews—the "loyal *millet*" (ethnoreligious community)—from attacks and blood libels by Ottoman Christians, Armenian and Greek, a topic to which he devotes dozens of pages across many of his works.[72] Jews had most to fear from Ottoman Christians; Muslims were innocent of anti-Semitism. "No Jews in the world have ever been protected as well by their state as has Turkish Jewry. Jews know this, and write Jewish history expressing this in golden letters," as does he.[73] Galanté leaves the reader of the postwar version with the line, "As is known, during the war, Turkey took the lead among nations in helping and assisting [German] Jewish refugees fleeing Europe."[74] He makes no mention of the fate of the tens of thousands of Turkish Jews in Nazi-occupied Europe.

Türkler ve Yahudiler is "a cumulative index of deeds and accomplishments of Turkish Jews throughout history, ranging from the most insignificant facts; such as recording a dinner of appreciation given to the beauty queen of Turkey by the Turkish Jews established in Brazil; to a more important court decision clearing certain Jews in Bursa accused of collaboration with the Greek occupation forces; including a most complete who's who of Jewish names at the service of Turkey."[75] It uses the same method employed in all his works, all of which fulfill the same function: to recount the benefit of Jews to Turkish society. His book, *Medicins Juifs au service de la Turquie* (Jewish physicians in service to Turkey), an exhaustive case in point, records the 178 Jewish physicians who served the Ottoman Empire and Turkey between 1453 and 1938.[76]

Despite promoting such a perspective, Galanté encountered anti-Semitism in the late Ottoman Empire and early Turkish Republic. His responses differed according to who was articulating it—Greeks or Muslims. In the case of Greek anti-Semitism, he was outspoken in refuting it; but with Muslims he preferred silence, that is until after World War II, when much of his family was murdered by the Nazis. Fluent in Greek, as was Franco before him, already at the turn of the twentieth century he had published journalistic pieces in Judeo-Spanish, French, and Turkish condemning Greek anti-Jewish sentiment, especially in relation to blood libels. From 1918 to 1923, he reported on Greek atrocities against Jews.[77] Although he served as a member of parliament representing Ankara during World War II, a time when the most explicit anti-Jewish measures were passed, including the Capital Tax, Galanté chose silence. He preferred not to use his seat in the Grand National Assembly to oppose such laws, or to condemn anti-Semitic speeches by his colleagues.[78] Ironically, as a member of the government, he was least effective as a spokesperson for his people. According to his biographer, it may well be that his publication in 1942 of one chapter from his history published the previous year, *The Jews of Istanbul* (1941), as a separate monograph, *Rôle économique des Juifs d'Istanbul* (The economic role of the Jews of Istanbul, 1942), was his way of protesting the Capital Tax.[79] In it, he presents the important role Jews played in the economic development of the city.[80]

The Holocaust seems to have compelled Galanté to change his approach. The Nazis murdered three of his sisters, a brother-in-law, and many nieces and nephews on the island of Rhodes. He collected testimony from the survivors and in 1948 published a memorial book in French to the martyred Jews, where he mentions those saved by the Turkish consul, Selahattin Ülkümen.[81] Perhaps this was what finally compelled him, at the age of seventy-five, to publish a study in Turkish the same year refuting "two forgeries," *The Protocols of the Elders of Zion* and Henry Ford's *International Jew*, recently published in Turkish translation.[82] On the whole, considering the sum of his long and prolific career, one can conclude that Galanté consistently praised "Turkish hospitality to the Jews of five centuries ago, in spite of the constant assaults by the mother country to the Jews of his time," generally electing to remain silent on lachrymose events.[83]

Jewish Historians outside Turkey Promote Galanté's Thesis

Prior to the war, Zionism had not attracted the loyalty of many Ottoman Jews. After having faced two and a half decades marred by anti-Semitism, discrimination, and violence, however, after 1948 nearly half the Turkish Jewish population emigrated to the newly established Jewish state of Israel. As a result, the Jewish population in Turkey had decreased from 77,000 in 1945 to 46,000 a decade later.[84] In the post-World War II era, Galanté was practically the only Jewish historian remaining in Turkey; the rest had either passed away or emigrated. While it is fairly accurate to state that "the dramatic geopolitical shifts rocking the Balkans and Turkey changed the texture of scholarly communities and of scholarship itself, influencing not only what was to be written thereafter but also which topics and collegial relationships were possible to remember, and which were better left forgotten,"[85] outside of Turkey, Jewish historians retained the romantic utopian vision from the earliest Jewish accounts.

One can understand the strategic interest of Turkish Jews like Galanté and his successors in promoting an idealized vision of the past and fantasies of harmonious contemporary relations between Muslims and Jews. They were representatives of a beleaguered, dwindling religious minority struggling to survive, their population having gradually shrunk throughout the course of the early republic. Turkish Jews faced discrimination in an authoritarian, homogenizing state that was the successor to an empire which, in its waning years, had annihilated one of its constituent minorities and expelled another. Turkish Jews were fully aware of what could befall them; they pined for better days and hoped to compel their return by invoking the past. The position its spokesmen take is understandable. What is unjustifiable, because it is both unethical and unprincipled, however, is the way independent scholars outside of Turkey not subject to the same economic, intellectual, and political constraints and therefore under no inducement to adopt Turkish Jewish self-censorship, have promoted Galanté's one-sided vision of the Ottoman and Jewish past. For in doing so, they have sided with the Turkish state, denied the Armenian genocide, and shielded Turkish Muslims from the tar of anti-Semitism.

Jewish historians born in the Ottoman Empire, Russia and the Soviet Union, the United Kingdom, the United States, France, and Israel regularly counter lachrymose accounts of life for Jews in Christian Europe—which they portrayed in dystopian terms as being unique in its unrelenting intolerance, forced conversions, expulsions, and massacres—with utopian accounts of the Ottoman Empire. None mention the Armenian genocide. Galanté is the linchpin connecting earlier Jewish historians with later ones. He published articles in Aaron de Joseph Hazan's periodical *La buena esperansa* (Good hope); Salamon Rosanes and Galanté worked together, "exchanging documents and information more than once"; he "borrowed, at times heavily" from Franco.[86] His 1913 work on the Nasi family was used by Cecil Roth, who described him "as the sole member of an elusive Society of Turkish Jewish Studies."[87] Galanté opened the gates for Western scholars by translating and publishing many Ottoman documents relating to Ottoman Jews.[88]

The Russian scholar Simon Dubnow (1860–1941, murdered in Riga) was greatly influenced by Graetz. Although approaching history from a social rather than intellectual perspective, he modeled his *A General History of the Jews* (1896) and *World History of the Jewish People* (1925–1929, ten volumes) on Graetz's history.[89] He restates Graetz's claims about the Ottomans: "The deep-rooted anti-Semitism of the Greek [Byzantine] rulers made the Jews friends of the conquerors; and the Turks [Ottomans], for their part, treated the Jews as allies."[90] Facing the counterfactual example of Torlak Kemal—a Jew who converted to Islam, served as a leader in the 1416 Sufi uprising of Sheikh Bedreddin, and was hanged for it—Dubnow notes, "A Jewish revolutionary was naturally a rarity among Jews, who generally were loyal."[91] For him, Capsali was "always loyal to the government authority."[92] Quoting Capsali, he repeats his claims that Mehmed II invited the Jews to settle in Constantinople after the conquest and established the chief rabbinate. "And the sultan placed chairs [the Ottoman council members did not sit on chairs, they sat on settees!] in the royal divan [government council]: one for the Ishmaelite mufti, another for the Greek *patrik* [patriarch], and a third for the Jewish rabbi, so that each nation may be ruled by its leader." Capsali's "chair was in the royal divan beside that of the mufti, and he was a favorite of the sultan."[93] Dubnow contrasts discrimination against Jews in Byzantine Constantinople and persecution of Jews in Christian Europe with the Ottomans' granting "freedom to the enslaved Jews," and provides a lengthy quote from Isaac Tzarfati's letter, recognizing its "hint" of messianism.[94] Relying on Usque and ha-Kohen, he notes that Jewish chroniclers "envisioned the sign of Providence in the fact that, shortly before the expulsion of the Jews" from Spain and Portugal, "a place of asylum for the Jews opened up," namely, the Ottoman Empire. Dubnow also hints at belief in the workings of a divine plan. When the Ottomans conquered Constantinople, "a change occurred in the destiny of the Diaspora, which was entirely different from that of eleven centuries before," when "the banner of the cross of Constantine the Great, was raised in the same city. At that time, the groundwork was laid in the city of Constantinople for that medieval regime that had oppressed Jews for a thousand years;" but "now the Turkish [Ottoman] Stambul was destined to offer asylum to the victims of that regime, who were expelled from the arch-Catholic Spain."[95] Its ruler, Bayezid II, remarked, "I don't consider this king (Ferdinand of Spain), who impoverishes his own country and enriches ours, as wise."

Salamon Abraham Rosanes (1862–1938) of Ottoman Bulgaria, who immigrated to Palestine, authored the six-volume *Korot ha-Yehudim be-Turkiyah ve-artsot ha-kedem* (History of the Jews of Turkey and the Jews of the East, 1907–1945) based principally on Jewish sources including the letter of Tzarfati.[96] The work has been described as "essentially a monument to Turkish Jewish learning and the benevolent Ottoman regime that made it possible."[97] From the history's first page, Rosanes presents a roseate view of the Ottomans, whom he depicts as agents of divine providence, as had his early modern forebears. Setting the scene with a lugubrious tone, he writes, "The Middle Ages had not yet concluded, the Congregation of Israel had not yet drained the cup of bitterness, the hardships had not yet abated, the horrible persecutions were still to come upon the Jews in all of the lands of their dispersion, and from every direction." Jews would be expelled from France and Germany, and in the Iberian Peninsula "the [Christian population] was beginning to turn away from the Islamic believers, to the great detriment of both the Arabs and the Jews together. The crescent moon had begun to dim in *Sepharad* (Spain)." He then switches to a joyful mood, exclaiming, "Yet, divine providence would have it—as if to prepare a sanctuary and path of escape for the Dispersed Remnant—that the crescent would now begin to radiate the first rays of light from the edges of the Ottoman Empire."[98] The situation of the Jews "had been bitterly evil in the last period under Byzantine rule" where they "were persecuted and reviled by the masses."[99] Accordingly, "the coming of the Turks [Ottomans] was for them not only a change of masters, but also a great change in their status: they emerged from darkness to bright light, from bondage to freedom." Rosanes also deploys the friend/enemy binary. The Jews "loved the victors not only as Lords of the land but as brothers and as adherents of a religion close in content to their own. From the other side, the Turks [Ottomans] also appeared to show signs of affection for the Children of Israel [the Jews]. In their opinion, the hatred of the local, defeated Christian inhabitants toward them and their faith made the Jews a safer bet, and among them they saw greater affection toward the Muslims." The fact that "many more of their traditions and customs were either identical or very similar among both Jews and Muslims," heightened "the level of affection between the victors and the nation of Israel."[100]

For Rosanes, the "affection" between Jews and Muslims in the Ottoman Empire reached its apogee in the sixteenth century; citing Rabbi David Massir Leon, he claims that this was a time when Jews "rejoiced greatly at the news that Sultan Selim I had come to power and they prophesized a future for him in which 'the kingdom shall be established—blessed be the Name—and a new king shall arise, a king who shall bring [righteous] judgments to the land, in whom the spirit of the Lord is present, and His Glory shall be exalted.'" In response, "rightly so did the Jews show signs of their affection toward the new sultan, for their situation would be greatly improved under the staff of his rule." Contrasting a sad depiction of Jews under the cross with a cheerful vision of life under Muslim, especially Ottoman, sovereignty, he narrates how "the miserable wanderers" who had come from the Iberian Peninsula "were able to escape their debasement and poverty, and no longer bore upon their countenances the signs of that awful travail." Especially during the reign of Sultan Selim I, the Jews "began to ascend to the heights of joy, of wealth, and enlightenment, until finally reaching the pinnacle of happiness that awaited them during the days of his successor, Sultan Suleiman I."[101]

When conditions for Jews in the Ottoman Empire were less than ideal, Rosanes, like the others, blamed the difficulties on converted Christians, the Janissaries, who "treated the Jews dreadfully, by and large, and regularly fell upon them and their households, defiling them and mistreating them greatly."[102] Even in the author's own day, the Janissaries were "spoken of in curses among the Jews [of Turkey], when the old days are recalled with fear and trembling and bitterness. Even eighty years after they were utterly extirpated from the face of the earth [i.e., in 1906; the Janissaries were annihilated in 1826], Jewish mothers in the East, when they wish to scare their children, say 'The Janissaries are coming!'"

Joseph Néhama of Ottoman Salonica and then Greek Thessaloniki was Galanté's contemporary. Néhama studied, like Galanté, at the École normale israélite orientale, the teacher training school of the alliance in Paris. He returned to Salonica to teach and serve as principal of the local alliance school, and he served as a general inspector for alliance schools in the Middle East. Following the Balkan Wars and the Ottoman loss of his hometown, Néhama remained in Greece rather than migrating to the remaining territories of the Ottoman Empire. At the same time as Galanté was publishing microhistories of the Jews of Istanbul, Néhama wrote a seven-volume account of the Jews of Salonica, the first two volumes appearing in 1935 and the next two a year later.[103] An anti-Zionist, he urged Jews to remain in Greece despite a rising wave of anti-Semitism. When the Nazis occupied Salonica, he escaped to Athens but was finally caught and deported to Bergen-Belsen in 1944. He managed to survive the camp and returned to Salonica where he devoted himself to documenting the Holocaust and the distinguished Sephardic past that it had destroyed, editing a memorial book to the sixty-five thousand murdered Jews of Salonica in 1949.[104]

Néhama used a vast array of sources to compose his history of Salonican Jewry, including Graetz, Danon, Covo, Franco, and Galanté. He states that his greatest debt is to Rosanes's Hebrew-language *History of the Jews of Turkey*. It is not surprising that his approach to Muslim-Jewish relations in the Ottoman Empire is quite similar to his predecessors'. He depicts the sixteenth century (1536–1593) as "the Golden Age of Salonican Sephardism."

Néhama contrasts Byzantine persecutions of Jews with Ottoman rule, giving many examples of the "kindly attitude of the Turks [Ottoman Muslims]," and how the Turks could count on the Jews' "loyalty" in return.[105] The sultans stand in for the entire Turkish people, and each sultan's kindnesses are listed in turn. Mehmed II is credited with establishing the position of chief rabbi and with appointing Moses Capsali to office.[106] Néhama quotes Tzarfati's letter and contrasts the prosperity and peace in Ottoman lands with the persecution of Jews in Christian Europe.[107] Compared with North Africa, Italy, France, and Flanders, the other regions to which expelled Iberian Jewry fled, the Ottoman Empire offered "the friendliest welcome."[108] He singles out Bayezid II for being "helpful" and the Jews' protector. In this "hospitable land ruled by tolerance and liberty, they could openly practice their faith." And in return the Jews introduced to the Ottoman army the latest weaponry; many served the court as physicians, advisors, and diplomats.[109] The Ottomans "could count on their loyalty," and—unlike the Greeks and Armenians, "probable allies" of the Christian powers against whom the sultans were constantly at war—could trust them.

Néhama argues that Bayezid II "generously opened the gates of his empire," where, relying on Sambari, he claims that Jews benefited from the fact that the chief rabbi "had a seat at the divan next to the mufti and the Orthodox patriarch."[110] According to him, when the destitute Jewish refugees arrived in Ottoman Salonica, they became joyous, able at last to breathe the air of liberty, to live without oppression or restriction, to flourish, even though the Janissaries could ruin their peace.[111] While all non-Muslims could face insecurity at the hands of these soldiers, the Jews had a better position in society (than Armenians or Greeks), he claims, because the Ottomans (Muslims) "gave them special consideration, a marked kindness, a favor which often manifested itself."[112] The Ottomans "could count on the Jew's loyalty." This brought about the emotional world of Salonican Jews, as "joy reigned, a profound and intense joy of a people who, after having known the agony of exile, felt themselves on firm ground, in a welcoming country, where they could feel a sense of relief."[113] The Jews, Néhama declared, experienced happy times, became joyous and prosperous, because in Salonica they "had recovered the peace and quiet, safety and wealth that the fanaticism and the intolerance of the Catholic church had taken" from them.[114]

Given that he lived in Greece rather than, like Galanté, in Turkey, it is perhaps not surprising that Néhama describes amicable relations between Jews and the Greeks and Muslims of the city. The "exiles of Spain, Sicily, Calabria, and later Portugal, welcomed by the Turkish authorities," settled throughout the city, "mixing with Greeks and Turks in daily life smoothly, without discord."[115] But again, we cannot but note that his emotional disposition leads him to repeat the trope of the tolerant Turk and the grateful Jew.

Néhama declares that in the sixteenth century the Sephardic Jews of Salonica experienced their most glorious period, "a real golden age."[116] The sixteenth century was an era of forced migration for Sephardic Jews.[117] Chased out of Europe, they preferred the East "where their faith was not a crime" and they could practice their religion.[118] From this point of view, Salonica was a "blessed place" that offered them life, liberty, and the pursuit of happiness, "commercial prosperity, security of life and property, and complete tolerance granted by the Ottoman ruler to practice their religion."[119] They were fortunate that "Salonica was the great refuge of the survivors. It offered all the persecuted, expelled, and desperate Jews of Europe and Africa" the "possibility to rebuild their lost homes."[120] As evidence, he quotes Samuel Usque's enthusiastic account of Salonica, a little Jerusalem, after visiting around 1552.[121] "God has raised the sceptre of his pity and devoured the river of your misfortune, o Jacob . . . Salonica is solidly established as the foundation of the faith. The Jews of Europe, especially those who are persecuted and banished, take shelter under its shade and are warmly received, as if this city were our respectable mother Jerusalem herself. The land which surrounds it is watered by numerous rivers. Its plants are excellent and nowhere else does one see such lovely trees. Their fruit is exquisite."[122] He thus encourages his fellow Conversos to settle in Ottoman lands, giving them comfort, courage, and hope.

Néhama discusses the danger to Jews of lawless Janissaries, but he asserts neither that they targeted Jews in particular nor that they did so because they were converted Christians.[123] Instead of promoting a Turkish-Jewish symbiosis, as did Galanté before him, he describes the functioning of Ottoman pluralism. He contends that in Salonica Turks and Turkish authorities did not enter the Jewish quarter; to them, it was a foreign country. The Turks had their own part of the city and did not mix with

Jews. So too did Jews keep to themselves, as if in a city of their own. Keeping to their own realms, Turks and Jews did not encounter each other very often.[124]

Ottoman Jews in Greek Thessaloniki were compelled by their circumstances to change and expand on the older utopian narrative proclaiming five centuries of Ottoman-Jewish symbiosis since the arrival of the Iberian exiles after 1492 and create a new mythology promoting a supposed Hellenic-Jewish synergy that began in antiquity.[125] Typical is the apologetics of Mercado Covo, a teacher in Jewish schools, who during the Ottoman era was an advocate of Ottomanism and Ottoman-Jewish romance, but after the city fell to Greece, became an outspoken voice of Hellenism and Jewish-Greek symbiosis. Whereas at the time of the four hundredth anniversary celebrations of the arrival of the Sephardim in the Ottoman Empire he had asked rhetorically, "Are we Jews, all across the world, not indebted to this government, which was the first to love us? . . . We must forever recognize [the Ottoman Empire] and express the most profound respect for everything bearing the name 'Ottoman,'" forty years later in Greek Thessaloniki he would argue, "The Jews have been in Salonica since the most ancient times. They are as ancient as the Greeks." Together "they trembled before the Bulgarian advance and the invasion of the Lombards, Normans, Romans, and Epirotes; they suffered from threats from the Catalans, Turks [Ottomans], and Serbs . . . and the capture of the city by the Turks [Ottomans]. Greeks and Jews together witnessed all the triumphs and all the miseries. Following successes and failures, they now work together for the grandeur and happiness of this two-thousand-year-old city."[126]

Joseph Néhama smoothly converted "staunch Ottomanism into Hellenism."[127] The transformation is evident when we compare two works. His 1914 study published in Paris, *La Ville convoitée* (The coveted city), emphasizes Salonica as a post-1492 Sephardic and Jewish metropolis—"it is a parcel of medieval Judaic Iberia," simultaneously "Jewish and Spanish," a "lost canton of Judea and a makeshift district of Castile"[128]—and argues that the best political future for the city is its internationalization. In that work he depicts the diverse ethno-religious groups of the city living without any connection to the others, lost in their own national dreams, lacking unity and common purpose, each building a future in their own way; divided, they do not even communicate with the other. They are inscrutable to one another and do not understand each other. But two decades later, he would write of Jews and Greeks united in common purpose since ancient times.

In his magnum opus, the seven-volume *History of the Jews of Salonica* pub-lished in Salonica in the 1930s, the city is depicted as a Macedonian (Greek) metropolis and part of Hellenic history, dating back to ancient times when Greek pagans converted to Judaism and the two elements mixed together in the city. Thereby could Jews in his day claim Greek descent.

The cost of this ideological change was having to downplay or remain silent about Greek anti-Semitic violence. Rather than include nineteenth- and twentieth-century Greek atrocities against Jews, he chose to focus on Greek-Jewish solidarity in the revolutionary era and the first decades of Greek rule in Salonica. Committed to the Hellenization of Salonica's Jews, in his multivolume history he celebrated the Greek army's conquest of the city in 1912, although when the Greeks took the city he had informed the AIU in Paris that the Jews were not jubilant but lamented the violence already committed against them and worried about impending massacre and mass expulsion.[129] By minimizing anti-Semitic violence that he and his read-ers had experienced from the beginning of Greek rule through the 1930s, and by promoting the positive aspects of anti-Jewish measures, including expropriation of properties after the great fire of 1917 and the destruction of the largest Jewish cemetery in the world, Néhama "projected his hope of a bright Greco-Jewish future" hoping to "predispose the educated Salonican youth into viewing its host society in a more favorable light and thus facili-tate its assimilation."[130] Like Galanté, only after the Holocaust did he openly write about anti-Jewish violence and discrimination in Greece.

In the United Kingdom, Cecil Roth (1899–1970) was the most sig-nificant academic and popular historian of the Jews. He served often as president of the Jewish Historical Society of England, was reader (associate professor) in postbiblical Jewish studies at Oxford University from 1939 to 1964, and served as editor in chief of the new edition of the *Encyclopaedia Judaica*, published in sixteen volumes in 1971.[131] His social history, *A Short History of the Jewish People* (first edition 1936; revised and enlarged edition 1948) is indebted to Dubnow and Graetz. Believing in "the Providence that guides the process of history," Roth finds the Islamic empires to be more tolerant than Christendom.[132] Treated well, the Iberian Jewish "refugees" offered their tolerant new rulers their services "as financial agents, diplo-mats, physicians, interpreters and (particularly in Egypt) mint-masters."[133] Because most found refuge in the Ottoman Empire "the Jewish people must always recall the Turkish [Ottoman] Empire with gratitude because, at one of the darkest hours of their history, when no alternative place of refuge was open and there seemed no chance of succour, it flung open its doors widely and generously for the reception of the fugitives, and kept them open."[134] Roth repeats the main themes of the early modern chroniclers and thus the narrative of the Ottoman utopia in a single paragraph. The chief rabbi "was given a seat at the Divan next to the Mufti himself. Immigrants arrived from all over Europe, to take advantage of the new conditions. The exiles from Spain found a warm welcome . . . 'What! Call ye this Ferdinand "wise"—he who depopulates his own dominions in order to enrich mine?' Sultan Bajazet is reported to have said, and he encouraged the immigration by every means which lay in his power."[135]

In his postwar volume devoted to the sixteenth-century Portuguese Conversa turned Ottoman Jewish patroness Doña Gracia Mendes Nasi, we also find all the by now familiar themes and quotations.[136] This is no coincidence, since Roth relies on Galanté, Franco, Capsali, Usque, and Tzarfati. He does counter their seamless and roseate picture with a list of oppressions, but he places responsibility with former Christians—Janissaries and viziers—and Greek blood libels.[137] On the whole, he emphasizes the sultans' tolerance and benevolence and the Turks' humanity; Christian Europe was crueler, more bloodthirsty, more intolerant in his view.

In the United States, Salo Wittmayer Baron (1895–1989) held "the first chair in Jewish history at a secular university in the Western world," established at Columbia University in 1930.[138] His monumental *A Social and Religious History of the Jews* (1937, three volumes; 1952–1983, second edition, eighteen volumes), which relies on Tzarfati, Capsali, ha-Kohen, Usque, and Sambari, as well as Rosanes, provides little discussion of messianism and no mention of Sabbatai Zevi, as he conveniently ends his narrative nearly two decades before the messianic outburst. The work—written in the same spirit as Roth's to challenge the lachrymose version of premodern Jewish history then prevalent—retains the long-established idealistic depiction of the Ottoman rulers and their treatment of Jews, characterizing the Ottoman Empire as a land where persecuted Jewry found "friendly treatment" in a "haven of refuge." Experiencing "another Jewish Golden Age," they responded with "loyalty."[139] Echoing Graetz, Baron argues that "for most Turkish Jews the contrast between the tolerant Ottoman regime and that of the Western Christian powers, from whose lands their ancestors had fled or been expelled, remained a permanent recollection. It nurtured a sense of patriotism and allegiance to the sultan."[140] This impression was also bolstered by his use of Galanté's works. In February 1936, prior to the publication of the first version of his history, he wrote a letter to Galanté in Istanbul asking for "a complete list" of his publications, their prices, and the name of a bookseller from whom they could be obtained so that a library in New York could "acquire the whole set." In a second letter sent in April, he thanked Galanté for sending the books, claiming "I have already had the opportunity to make use of some of the extensive information assembled" by the Turkish Jewish author, asking him to send him any forthcoming publications and hoping they would have a chance to meet the following year when Baron traveled through Turkey.[141]

Baron echoes Graetz when he argues that the rise of the Ottomans was a good omen for the Jews of the Mediterranean: "The emergence of the Ottoman Empire could not have come at a more propitious moment for the European Jews, whose position in the fourteenth and fifteenth centuries had reached a new low point" following expulsions, massacres, banishment, and forced conversions—all of which caused these Jews "to seek new shelters."[142] Using the same functionalist logic, he explains how "the far-sighted" Ottoman sultans "realized the great benefits their country could derive from these culturally and economically advanced" Iberian and Italian Jews; the sultans "were also convinced that as sufferers from Christian intolerance these new immigrants would become more loyal servants" than their Christian subjects. The Jews, in turn, "greatly benefited" to such an extent that, in the early centuries of the empire, the Jews "must have been grateful to a government which enabled them to live a fairly secure life with relatively little discrimination and ample opportunities for making a living."[143] He quotes Isaac Tzarfati to prove the point. "Far-sighted" Mehmed the Conqueror, who "invited" Jews to settle in Constantinople,[144] was "aided" by the Italian Jewish physician, financier, and advisor Giacomo of Gaeta (Italy).[145] The Venetians tried to convince him to poison Mehmed, in return for great financial reward, but in vain. As Baron states again and again, the Jews' loyalty was not to be doubted.

Relying on Capsali's chronicle, yet casting doubt on the veracity of his claims,[146] he records how Mehmed II appointed Moses b. Elijah Capsali to a position "somewhat similar" to that of the Orthodox patriarch. "Later Jewish tradition claimed that the rabbi's position was placed ahead of that of the patriarch which, though unsupported by any Turkish documentary evidence, may have taken place when, in later generations, the Jews had become a large, affluent, and highly influential part of the ethnoreligious structure of the empire."[147] This is because, as he repeatedly asserts, the regime "could rely on Jewish loyalty much more unequivocally and permanently" than on that of the Armenians and Greeks who were "subject to blandishments from their powerful coreligionists outside the country."[148]

Baron explains the saying attributed to Bayezid II in the same fashion, for the Catholic monarchs "must have perceived the incongruity of providing an enemy with enterprising new settlers equipped with considerable skills and capital" which "undoubtedly accrued to the benefit of the Ottoman economy and armed forces."[149] Baron refers to the empire as a "new haven of refuge"[150] repeating his earlier statement, again echoing Graetz, that "Ottoman expansion could not have come at a more propitious moment for medieval Jewry" following centuries "of growing intolerance toward Jews and Judaism among the Christian nations," and accordingly, "many pious Jews may well have seen in these new developments an encouraging omen that, to quote an old rabbinic saying, God often 'provides a remedy before the affliction.' For generations thereafter the Ottoman Empire became the main haven of refuge for the persecuted Western Jews." He argues that a motivating factor compelling Ottoman tolerance of Jews from that era to the end of empire was the fact that Jewish "loyalty appeared much more dependable than that of some other ethnic groups with brethren living as free nations across the borders."[151] Here again is an anachronism, for the Kingdom of Greece was not founded until 1832; the First Republic of Armenia was established in 1918.

Following Jewish historiographical tradition, Baron blames any problems faced by the Jews in the empire to Janissaries and Ottoman officials who had converted from Christianity, and to Christians in general. Baron notes how "remarkably, we have but few data about the reaction of the general public to the Jewish mass immigration."[152] What data he does mention mainly concerns backlash against their arrival by Ottoman Greeks,[153] allowing him to then segue into a section regarding Christian accusations of Jewish ritual murders, beginning with a sixteenth-century accusation by Armenians and then citing others by Greeks down through the nineteenth century. While the Ottoman sultans, thanks to influential Jews at court such as Moses Hamon, were induced to ensure that such cases were heard before the imperial divan, when it came to Ottoman Christians, "although most of the accusations arose from suspicious or willful distortions by Greeks rather than Muslims, the Greek Church did little to stem their reappearance."[154] Baron also credits Moses Hamon with another alleged intervention together with Suleiman I, this time against Grand Vizier Ibrahim

Pasha, who "evinced deep-seated anti-Jewish feelings doubtless stemming from his original Greek ancestry" and allegedly tried to convince the sultan to expel the Jews.

Baron devotes the longest section to "Doctors, Merchants, Diplomats," the highly influential and well-placed Jews at court in the sixteenth century, allowing him to illustrate the theme of Jewish loyalty and benefit to the sultans.[155] Regarding court physician Isaac Hamon, for example, his "incorruptibility was recorded in connection with a Spanish envoy's futile effort to bribe him to intervene with the sultan in favor of a truce between Spain and the Ottoman Empire. Isaac emphatically declined."[156] He devotes a long section to Joseph Nasi, merchant, banker, courtier, and diplomat, who rendered "important services" to the sultan.[157] Baron contrasts Jewish loyalty with Ottoman Christian perfidy in the persons of Joseph Nasi and the Greek Orthodox patriarch. Nasi, he asserts, hated Spain, the Ottoman Empire's greatest enemy, for he was a courtier loyally performing "his patriotic duty"[158] to his government and its imperial ambitions. This required undermining the Habsburgs to such an extent that Phillip II declared Nasi "the person most responsible for inspiring the machinations being conducted to the detriment of all Christendom and of our kingdoms. He has great intelligence into what goes on at this court and in other parts of my kingdoms."[159] The Greek Orthodox patriarch, in contrast, who worked for the Spanish intelligence network, "committed treasonable acts against his own country."[160]

Deploying one anachronism after another, Baron concludes that as the Ottoman Empire granted "basic protection of human rights" to the Jews, the Jews "reciprocated with a growing sense of Turkish patriotism,"[161] notwithstanding the fact that there was no such concept as Turkish patriotism in the sixteenth-century Ottoman Empire, let alone human rights anywhere before the twentieth century. Such a claim brings to mind Graetz's statement about Iberian Jewry: "The Jewish inhabitants of this happy peninsula [Iberia] contributed by their hearty interest to the greatness of the country, which they loved as only a fatherland can be loved."[162]

In 1984, just one year after the publication of Baron's final volume covering Jewish life in the Ottoman Empire, Princeton University-based English Jewish historian Bernard Lewis (1916–2018) published *The Jews of Islam*, in which he argues that, comparatively speaking, the Ottoman Empire was a "paradise" for Jews.[163] Lewis, unlike Baron able to read Ottoman-language sources, could have offered a more complicated, nuanced account of the

Jewish experience in that empire; yet on balance he offers nearly the same positive Jewish account of the Ottomans, with the addition only of Ottoman archival and demographic data. Lewis relies on Baron, as well as Franco, Rosanes, Galanté—to whom he is especially indebted—Capsali, and Joseph ha-Kohen, and he notes that Graetz's history "is still of value."[164] It is not surprising that he describes Jews in the empire as friends of the Muslims, with Christians as their enemies.

After long excursuses on terminology, sources, and demographic data regarding Ottoman Jewry, Lewis debunks the myth of Mehmed II's alleged establishment of the chief rabbinate.[165] But, like Galanté, he then pivots so as to emphasize aspects of Ottoman Jewish history that Ottoman and Turkish Jews had long promoted—principally the Jews' usefulness and loyalty to the empire. He describes the significance of Jewish contributions in "medicine, the performing arts, and printing," as well as Jewish economic contributions in commerce, trade, and manufacturing, as tax farmers, in the customs service and mint, as merchants to the Janissary corps and pashas, and in the transfer of weapons technology.[166] He notes that Jewish accounts of the Ottomans are "almost uniformly favorable," citing the choicest passages in Tzarfati and Usque.[167] After tempering these accounts with counterfactual incidents, Lewis then repeats the conventional argument that "one reason for Jewish well-being under Ottoman rule is that Jews were seen as a useful and productive element."[168] Jews were not merely permitted to live in Ottoman domains, he argues; "they were encouraged, assisted, and sometimes compelled." Moreover, "the Ottomans did not merely admit Jewish refugees. They often provided transport for them and decided where they should go."[169] Is Lewis implying, as Turkish Jews would later claim, that Bayezid II sent ships to Spain to ease their voyage? Lewis describes how "the Jews developed a sort of symbiotic relationship with the Turks [Ottoman Muslims], who needed the services they were able to provide and preferred them to their competitors" or enemies, whom Lewis names, not surprisingly, as "mostly Christians—at first Greeks and Italians, later joined by Arabic-speaking Christians from the Levant, and finally, to an increasing extent, by Armenians." Along with their "capital" and "useful knowledge," the Jews appealed to the Ottomans, Lewis argues, because they were the friend, just as the Armenians and Greeks were the enemy. "They had, from the Turkish [Ottoman Muslim] viewpoint, the great advantage of not being Christian and therefore not being suspect of treasonable sympathies with the major enemy of the Ottomans, which of course meant European Christendom."

French scholar Paul Dumont (b. 1945), coeditor with Gilles Veinstein (1945–2013) of the Turkish studies annual, *Turcica*, promoted the
same views as his predecessors. Writing when Baron was finishing his
last volume, Dumont begins a section of an article concerning "Relations
between Communities" in the nineteenth-century Ottoman Empire by
quoting French Jewish praise of Ottoman tolerance and their description
of Ottoman Jewry's loyalty to the sultan, compares it to the Jews' plight in
contemporary Russia and Romania, and then devotes two pages to Armenian and Greek anti-Semitism.[170] Turning to Muslims, he argues that relations "were, on the whole, much more satisfactory" as "there is no doubt"
that Muslims "were much more tolerant than Christians."[171] He tempers
this assessment by admitting that Muslims, even Sultan Abdülhamid II
himself, believed to some extent in the blood libel, and that there were
occasionally anti-Jewish riots in Muslim neighborhoods. But he asserts
that within the boundaries of the present Turkish Republic, it was "only
in eastern Anatolia" where Jews and Muslims had "problems," which he
blames on Kurds, not Turks, a claim that would be repeated by later Jewish
historians.[172]

Downplaying Ottoman Muslim Anti-Jewish Sentiment, Blaming Violence on Christians

To maintain rosy accounts of Turkish-Jewish relations down the centuries,
Jewish historians of the Ottoman Empire went out of their way to minimize
anti-Jewish sentiment held by Ottoman Muslims, as well as blame acts of
violence against Jews on Ottoman Christians rather than Muslims.

The first mention of a Jew in an Ottoman chronicle occurs in the
Tevārīḫ-i Āl-i ʿOsmān (Chronicles of the House of Osman) written in the
early 1480s by Aşıkpaşazade (1400–1484) at the behest of Sultan Bayezid II,
a ruler remembered in Jewish chronicles and modern Jewish scholarship
for proffering a warm embrace to Iberian Jews.[173] Aşıkpaşazade cast asper-
sion on Mehmed II's converted Jewish physician and vizier, Giacomo of
Gaeta, whose Muslim name after conversion was Hekim Yakub Pasha
(ca. 1430–1484). Aşıkpaşazade remarked that "prior to Hekim Yakub, they
never assigned public office to Jews because they are considered *müfsidler*
[corrupters of morals]. But thanks to Hekim Yakub when he became vizier,
however many greedy and ill-omened Jews there are, they all meddled in
the sultan's business."[174] Even after converting to Islam, Hekim Yakub was

referred to as a Jew whose appointment to government office opened the floodgate for interference in imperial politics by other Jews. According to Aşıkpaşazade, Jews were invariably sources of moral corruption. As Bernard Lewis pointed out in the 1950s, Aşıkpaşazade referred in one recension of the text to the Jewish tax farmer "Yakub son of Israel," executed in 1472, thusly: "Until he came, financial administrators were not hanged."[175] Comfortable with sharing this snippet of anti-Jewish sentiment with fellow Orientalists, Lewis shied away from exposing it to a wider lay audience. Over thirty years after including the comment in a specialist journal, Lewis failed to mention it in his 1984 book intended for a popular audience, *The Jews of Islam*.

Haim Gerber (b. 1945) dismisses the "declarative, philosophical and theoretical hatred" found in literary texts such as Aşıkpaşazade, or the seventeenth-century travelogue of Evliya Çelebi (1611–ca. 1683), a Muslim Istanbulite and companion of Sultan Murad IV (r. 1623–1640). Evliya propagated the libel involving Jewish ritual murder, slaveholding, and abuse of Muslim boys;[176] imagined Jews were driven by an evil desire, since "all their deeds are calculated to treachery and the killing of Muslims, especially anyone named Muhammad";[177] and expressed both elite and popular Muslim antipathy to Jews.[178] Gerber views these sentiments as "not convincing" and not "represent[ing] the view of the wider masses."[179] Instead, he argues Jews and Muslims had "basically friendly relations, even a close symbiosis" as determined by their economic relations.[180] This is an indefensible assertion, for in lending, selling, and buying, the distaste for the economic other can be uncoupled from the choice of a beneficial economic transaction. A historian's perspective is shaped as much by how he or she reads historical sources as by which sources the scholar selects for reading. Gerber's chapter entitled "Jewish Tax-Farmers in the 16th and 17th Centuries" is a case in point.[181] Because Gerber chooses to ignore literary sources in his summary of nearly four decades of research in the archives, he fails to acknowledge incidents of violence recounted elsewhere. Ottoman chronicles from the period of his study record incidents located across the empire, from southeastern Europe to Egypt, in which a variety of Jewish financial officials, both tax farmer and keeper of the mint alike, were executed or lynched by angry mobs.[182] Gerber's work is as political and ideological as the accounts he criticizes, but mentioning such inconvenient incidents would detract from the rosy depiction of relations between Jews and Muslims he seeks to assemble.[183]

The most notorious case of mob violence against a prominent Jew was the lynching of a Jewish *kira* (Greek: lady-in-waiting) to the harem in Istanbul in 1600 by Muslim soldiers.[184] In the early twentieth century, Galanté narrated the kira's rise to power and its end with her "stabbing." Importantly, he did so without reconciling the story against his idealized portrayal of Muslim-Jewish relations in the Ottoman Empire.[185] He did this by substituting in an early 1926 publication the term "janissaries"—infantry troops of Christian origin recruited as children through the *devshirme* (child levy) and converted to Islam—for the term *"sipahi,"* conventionally understood as Turkish Muslim cavalry.[186] While Galanté corrected this in a 1941 publication, Stanford Shaw (1930–2006), author of the most widely read history of Ottoman and Turkish Jewry, chose to follow Galanté's earlier version, also transforming the sipahi into janissaries and blaming the kira's death on Christians: "She finally fell from power and was killed by the Janissaries," due in part to the "hatred of several recently converted Christian devshirme men, who were particularly unhappy at such Jewish influence on the court."[187] Gilles Veinstein made the same switch, blaming the janissaries for her downfall.[188] The cumulative effect of these elisions allows modern Jewish historians writing for popular audiences to promulgate a rosy picture of relations between Ottoman Muslims/Turks and Jews.

While the Ottoman texts use the term "sipahi" and not "janissary," in this case it is possible that the sipahi in question were actually *kapıkulu sipahi,* who drew salaries like janissaries as opposed to relying on fiefdoms, and who were mostly of Christian origin. Nevertheless, no matter their origins, Muslims lynched the kira. Bearing in mind the polemics of their published works and public advocacy, the most likely reason Galanté, Shaw, and Veinstein chose the definitive term "janissary" and not the more ambiguous term "sipahi" is due to the conventional distinction between the two terms—"janissary" are Christian converts, "sipahi" born Turkish Muslims. The unambiguous choice of "janissary" would prevent the reader imagining any anti-Jewish act to originate with Muslims. For this reason Shaw's index to *The History of the Jews of the Ottoman Empire and Turkish Republic* has no entry for "sipahi," but under "janissaries" over a dozen citations of "attacks on and persecution of Jews by" are listed.[189] In the English version of his history of Turkish Jewry, historian of the Turkish chief rabbinate Naim Güleryüz mentions how "Jewish women such as" the kira "exercised considerable influence in the Court," but cannot bring himself to mention her brutal end. [190]

Conclusion

The trend of depicting the Ottoman past in utopian terms was continued in the early and mid-twentieth century in the Turkish Republic by the only remaining Jewish historian Abraham Galanté, who expanded the claim about Ottoman sultans to characterize all Turkish Muslims as exemplars of human virtues, all the while railing against treacherous Christians, especially Greeks, and expunging from memory the Armenian genocide and episodes of violence directed against Jews. Pairing grateful Jews with their opposite, Armenian and Greek traitors, and impugning their reputation by blaming them for anti-Semitism became motifs in studies published outside Turkey. In the mid- and late twentieth century, this tendency was propagated in Europe, North America, and Israel into the 1980s by the towering figures of Jewish and Ottoman history, including Simon Dubnow, Salamon Rosanes, Joseph Néhama, Cecil Roth, Salo Wittmayer Baron, and Bernard Lewis, and into the 1990s and 2000s by Haim Gerber, Stanford Shaw, and Gilles Veinstein, who dismissed anti-Jewish sentiment held by Muslims and blamed anti-Jewish violence on Ottoman Christians, even when the Ottoman sources they use label the perpetrators as Muslims. The view became conventional wisdom in histories of the Ottoman Empire and the Turkish Republic.

Modern historians of the Ottoman Empire who rely on Galanté's work when depicting the "united destinies" and interests of Turks and Jews in the face of anti-Semitic Christian enemies who "persecuted Jews in the empire"[191] tend to ignore lachrymose events, even if they are readily available in Jewish accounts. Those historians able to read Ottoman Turkish passed over violent episodes narrated in popular, published, easily accessible Ottoman chronicles: the execution of the head of a delegation of Jews in Istanbul in the seventeenth century;[192] the execution of a Jew convicted of adultery with a married Muslim woman, also in the seventeenth century;[193] the beheading of a Jewish convert to Islam who apostatized in the eighteenth century; the threat of a sultan or grand vizier to expel or convert all the Jews of the empire or put them to death.[194] Some scholars, especially those based in Israel, have discussed early modern Ottoman Jewish responsa, sermons, poetry, and correspondence that contain "harsh and explicit statements" expressing "hatred, expectations of Divine retribution, and even actual acts of revenge" against Muslim officials who humiliated and exploited them and extorted funds from them.[195] Other Israeli scholars find Jewish sources relating occasions where Jews were beaten and robbed, taunted, abused, or murdered by Muslims, who desecrated their bodies.[196] One finds few mentions of such violent episodes, in place of the overwhelmingly utopian visions, in the most influential modern studies.

Notes

1. Figures given in Shaw, *The Jews of the Ottoman Empire and the Turkish Republic*, Appendix 2, 273.

2. Ibid., 274.

3. Aron Rodrigue, "The Mass Destruction of Armenians and Jews in the 20th Century in Historical Perspective," in *Der Völkermord an den Armeniern und die Shoah/The Armenian Genocide and the Shoah*, ed. Hans-Lukas Kieser, Dominik Schaller (Zurich: Chronos Verlag, 2002), 308.

4. November 14, 1912, to president of Alliance, in *Haim Nahum*, 172–173.

5. May 4, 1914, in ibid., 172–173.

6. Ibid., 20.

7. Ibid., 21.

8. One of the leaders of the Zionists in Palestine, Meir Dizengoff, reports in his memoirs that when Cemal Pasha and Enver Pasha visited Palestine, they declared, "Zionists beware! If you oppose us we will do to you what we have done to the Armenians!" Auron, *Banality of Indifference*, 71. In the spring of 1917, orders were issued to deport the five thousand Jews from Tel Aviv, arousing great fear that the rest of the Jews of the country would also be deported and later killed, as they had killed the Armenians; this led to international condemnation, and Cemal Pasha cancelled the order. Ibid., 73. Then in autumn 1917, the Nili intelligence organization (a pro-British spy ring) was discovered, leading Jews in Palestine to again express the fear that the Jewish community would suffer the fate of the Armenians, impending expulsion and massacre. Ibid., 83. In fact, according to Auron, what had motivated the Nili in their pro-British orientation was a desire to avoid the fate of the Armenians—which their activities the Yishuv saw as threatening to cause that which the Nili had sought to avoid. Ibid., 85.

9. *Haim Nahum*, 182.

10. This narrative of the genocide is based on the following studies: Suny, *"They Can Live in the Desert but Nowhere Else"*; Göcek, *Denial of Violence*; Taner Akçam, *The Young Turks' Crime Against Humanity: The Armenian Genocide and Ethnic Cleansing in the Ottoman Empire* (Princeton, NJ: Princeton University Press, 2012); Uğur Ümit Üngür, *The Making of Modern Turkey: Nation and State in Eastern Anatolia, 1913–1950* (Oxford: Oxford University Press, 2012); *A Question of Genocide: Armenian and Turks at the End of the Ottoman Empire*, ed. Ronald Suny and Fatma Müge Göçek (Oxford: Oxford University Press, 2011); Donald Bloxham, *The Great Game of Genocide: Imperialism, Nationalism, and the Destruction of the Ottoman Armenians* (Oxford: Oxford University Press, 2007); and Robert Melson, *Revolution and Genocide: On the Origins of the Armenian Genocide and Holocaust* (Chicago: University of Chicago Press, 1996).

11. Letter of May 8, 1913, from Enver Pasha to his wife, cited in Suny, *"They Can Live in the Desert but Nowhere Else,"* 187.

12. Suny, *"They Can Live in the Desert but Nowhere Else,"* 231.

13. Ibid., xx.

14. Ibid., 314.

15. Letter from Léon Sémach, Bursa, to the central office of the Alliance Israélite Universelle, Paris, October 11, 1915, translated from French into English as "A Report on the Deportation of Armenians from Bursa (1915)," in *Sephardi Lives*, 158–160.

16. Coded telegram from Interior Minister Talat to the province of Ankara, August 29, 1915, cited in Suny, *"They Can Live in the Desert but Nowhere Else,"* 317.

17. Henry Morgenthau, *Ambassador Morgenthau's Story* (New York: Doubleday, 1918), 124.

18. Box 14–15, Reel 13–14, Correspondence with Wise, Stephen S. (Stephen Samuel), 1874–1949, Special Correspondence, Henry Morgenthau Papers, Manuscript Division, Library of Congress, Washington, DC.

19. Isaiah Friedman, *Germany, Turkey, Zionism: 1897–1918* (Oxford: Oxford University Press, 1977; new edition, London: Transaction, 1998), 198–199.

20. Ibid., 223.

21. Ibid., 285.

22. Richard Lichtheim, *Rückkehr: Lebenserinnerungen aus der Frühzeit des deutschen Zionismus* (Stuttgart: Deutsche Verlags-Anstalt, 1970), 353. He emigrated to Palestine in 1934, and during World War II served as the WZO representative in Geneva, from where in 1942 he published some of the first reports of the Holocaust as it unfolded.

23. Friedman, *Germany, Turkey, Zionism*, ix.

24. See especially Friedman, *Germany, Turkey, Zionism*, chapter 11, "Germany Protects the Zionists in Palestine," 191–227; and Lichtheim, *Rückkehr*, chapter 15, "Deutschland und Amerika schützen die Juden Palästinas," 263–286.

25. Lichtheim, *Rückkehr*, 341–342.

26. Friedman, *Germany, Turkey, Zionism*, 226.

27. Ibid., 346.

28. Ibid., 352.

29. Ibid., 370.

30. Cited in Vahakn Dadrian and Taner Akçam, *Judgement at Istanbul: The Armenian Genocide Trials* (New York: Berghahn Books, 2011), 46.

31. Suny, *"They Can Live in the Desert but Nowhere Else,"* 337.

32. *Takvim-i vekayi*, April 12, 1919, cited in Dadrian and Akçam, *Judgement at Istanbul*, 280.

33. *Atatürk'ün söylev ve demeçleri, vol. 2 (1906–1938)*, ed. Nimet Unan (Ankara: Türk Tarih Kurumu, 1959), 12, cited in Erik Zürcher, "Renewal and Silence: Postwar Unionist and Kemalist Rhetoric on the Armenian Genocide," in *A Question of Genocide*, 312.

34. Zürcher, "Renewal and Silence," 312.

35. Emily Greenhouse, "The Armenian Past of Taksim Square," *New Yorker*, June 28, 2013.

36. *Haim Nahum*, 27. The reference to the Young Turks refers to the period from 1909 to 1918.

37. Ibid., 29.

38. Ibid., 30.

39. Ibid., 31.

40. Ibid.

41. Ibid., 32.

42. Ibid. In 1925 he left Turkey, however, and became chief rabbi in Cairo, a position he held until his death in 1960.

43. Figures given in Shaw, *The Jews of the Ottoman Empire and the Turkish Republic*, Appendix 3, 285.

44. See Marc David Baer, "The Double Bind of Race and Religion: The Conversion of the Dönme to Turkish Secular Nationalism," *Comparative Studies in Society & History* 46, no. 4 (October 2004).
45. Mustafa Kemal Atatürk, speech in Izmir, February 2, 1923, quoted in Abraham Galanté, *Histoire des Juifs d'Istanbul: Depuis la prise de cette ville, en 1453, par Fatih Mehmed II, jusqu'à nos jours*, (Istanbul: Imprimerie Hüsnütabiat, 1941), 1:40, and in Avram Galanti, *Türkler ve Yahudiler: Tarihî, siyasî tetkik*, rev. 2nd ed. (Istanbul: Tan Matbaası, 1947), 86. The quote also appears as the dedication in Shaw, *The Jews of the Ottoman Empire and the Turkish Republic*.
46. "Adana esnaflariyle konuşma," *Hakimiyeti milliye*, March 21, 1923, in Gazi Mustafa Kemal (Atatürk), *Atatürk'ün söylev ve demçeleri I-III* (Ankara: Atatürk Kültür Dil ve Tarih Yüksek Kurumu, 1997), 2:129–132, cited in Rıfat N. Bali, *Cumhuriyet yıllarında Türkiye Yahudileri: Bir Türkleştirme serüveni, 1923–1945* (Istanbul: İletişim, 1999), 234.
47. He made these claims at the very beginning of his six-day speech before the general congress of the single ruling party, the CHP, in 1927, which became the official narrative of the founding of the republic. The Turkish text is available on the website of the Turkish Ministry for Culture and Tourism, http://ekitap.kulturturizm.gov.tr/TR,81464/nutuk.html. For analyses of the speech, see Taha Parla, *Türkiye'de siyasal kültürün resmi kaynakları, Cilt I: Atatürk'ün nutuk'u* (Istanbul: İletişim, 1994); Fatma Müge Göçek, "Defining the Parameters of a Post-Nationalist Turkish Historiography through the Case of the Anatolian Armenians," in *Turkey Beyond Nationalism: Towards Post-Nationalist Identities*, ed. Hans-Lukas Kieser (London: I.B. Tauris, 2006); Hülya Adak, "National Myths and Self-Na(rra)tions: Mustafa Kemal's *Nutuk* and Halide Edib's *Memoirs* and the *Turkish Ordeal*," *South Atlantic Quarterly* 102, no. 2/3 (2003); and Toni Alaranta, "Mustafa Kemal Atatürk's Six-Day Speech of 1927: Defining the Official Historical View of the Foundation of the Turkish Republic," *Turkish Studies* 9, no. 1 (2008). For his approach to the Armenian genocide, see especially Fatma Ulgen, "Reading Mustafa Kemal Ataturk on the Armenian genocide of 1915," *Patterns of Prejudice* 44, no. 4 (2010).
48. Galanti, *Türkler ve Yahudiler*, 75.
49. Despite later publishing a monograph in French about the Sabbatian movement, *Nouveaux documents sur Sabbataï Sevi: Organisation et us et coutumes de ses adeptes* (Istanbul: Fratelli Haim, 1935), Galanté did not mention Sabbatai Zevi in the 1935 French version of *Turks and Jews*, nor in the 1947 modern Turkish version.
50. Galanté, *Histoire des Juifs d'Istanbul*, 46–47.
51. Esra Özyürek, introduction to *The Politics of Public Memory in Turkey*, ed. Esra Özyürek (Syracuse, NY: Syracuse University Press, 2007), 3.
52. The other significant Jewish reformer was Moiz Kohen/Munis Tekinalp. Galanté's *Vatandaş, Türkçe konuş!* (Citizen, speak Turkish!) campaign was mirrored by Tekinalp's "Ten Commandments" for Turkifying the Jews. Loyal Ottomanist and then devoted Kemalist, Tekinalp was also devastated by the Capital Tax. On his life and work, see Jacob M. Landau, *Tekinalp: Turkish Patriot, 1883–1961* (Istanbul: Nederlands Historisch-Archaeologisch Instituut, 1984).
53. Quoted in Üngür, *The Making of Modern Turkey*, 225.
54. Fatma Müge Göçek, *The Transformation of Turkey: Redefining State and Society from the Ottoman Empire to the Modern Era* (London: I.B. Tauris, 2011), 24.
55. Adak, "National Myths and Self-Na(rra)tions"; Hamit Bozarslan, "Kemalism, Westernization, and Anti-Liberalism," in *Turkey Beyond Nationalism*, 30.
56. Quoted in Hans-Lukas Kieser, "Dr. Mehmed Reshid (1873–1919): A Political Doctor," in *Der Völkermord an die Armeniern und die Shoah*, 262.

57. According to Mithat Şükrü Bleda, secretary general of the CUP from 1916 to 1918, Dr. Mehmet Reshid had served the fatherland, understanding the cure it needed: "Either to destroy the illness and the ill, or to see the entire Turkish people and its country perish at the hands of maniacs." He meant the Armenians, perceived as mentally ill. According to Bleda, he was wrongly hanged for it, as were Mr. Kemal, kaymakam of Boğazlıyan, Nusret, mutassarif of Yozgat, and Dr. Mehmed Reshid. But because "Reshid Bey's [and the others'] behavior was sanctioned by the National Assembly of Turkey by according his children an annuity in return for his services to the fatherland and recognized by Atatürk," the verdict passed on these men was a historic error that punished the Turkish nation. Mithat Şükrü Bleda, *İmparatorluğun çöküşü* (Istanbul: Remzi, 1979), 61–62, quoted in Kieser, "Dr. Mehmed Reshid," 270.

58. Albert Kalderon, *Abraham Galante: A Biography* (New York: Sepher-Hermon, 1983), 17, 31, 48–49.

59. Ibid., 47.

60. Ibid., 52.

61. Galanti, *Türkler ve Yahudiler.*

62. Shaw, *The Jews of the Ottoman Empire and the Turkish Republic*, Appendix 3, 285.

63. Bali, *Cumhuriyet yıllarında Türkiye Yahudileri*, 456.

64. Galanti, *Türkler ve Yahudiler*, 3. The letter was published in *Vakit*, no. 118, March 21, 1921.

65. Ibid., 3–4; Bali, *Cumhuriyet yıllarında Türkiye Yahudileri*, 149.

66. Ibid., 5. Emphasis added. On the affair, see Bali, *Cumhuriyet yıllarında Türkiye Yahudileri*, 109–131, esp. 115–116, and Mallet, *La Turquie, les Turcs et les Juifs*, 221–232.

67. Galanti, *Türkler ve Yahudiler*, 35.

68. Ibid. Italics mine.

69. He does the same in *Histoire des Juifs d'Istanbul*, 7.

70. Ibid., 46–47.

71. Galanti, *Türkler ve Yahudiler*, 135–136.

72. For example, see ibid., 26–30, where he discusses Christian accusations of child murder in the Ottoman Empire from the sixteenth through the nineteenth centuries.

73. Ibid., 23.

74. Ibid., 189.

75. Kalderon, *Abraham Galante*, 54.

76. Ibid., 58. Abraham Galanté, *Medicins Juifs au service de la Turquie* (Istanbul: M. Babok, 1938).

77. Kalderon, *Abraham Galante*, 22, 28, 48.

78. Ibid., 59.

79. Abraham Galanté, *Rôle économique des Juifs d'Istanbul* (Istanbul, Impr. Hüsnütabiat, 1942).

80. Kalderon, *Abraham Galante*, 60.

81. Abraham Galanté, *Appendice à l'Histoire des Juifs de Rhodes, Chio, Cos etc., fin tragique des communautés Juives de Rhodes et de Cos oeuvre du brigandage Hitlerien* (Istanbul: Kağıt ve Basım İşleri, 1948).

82. Avram Galanti, *Iki uydurma eser: I. Siyon önderlerinin protokoları, II. Beynelmilel Yahudi: Tarihi, siyasi, tenkidi tetkik* (Istanbul: Kağıt ve Basım İşleri, 1948). Ford's original work is Henry Ford, *The International Jew: The World's Foremost Problem*, vol. 1 (Dearborn, MI: Dearborn, 1920).

83. Kalderon, *Abraham Galante*, 73.

84. Shaw, *The Jews of the Ottoman Empire and the Turkish Republic*, Appendix 3, 285.

85. Julia Phillips Cohen and Sarah Abrevaya Stein, "Sephardic Scholarly Worlds: Toward a Novel Geography of Modern Jewish History," *Jewish Quarterly Review* 100, no. 3 (2010): 380.

86. Kalderon, *Abraham Galante*, 25, 51, 69.

87. Ibid., 70. Abraham Galanté, *Don Joseph Nassi, Duc de Naxos, d'après de nouveaux documents*, Conférence faite à la Société Bene B'rith le Samedi 15 Fevrier 1913, Constantinople, J & A Fratelli Haim.

88. Bernard Lewis, *Notes and Documents from the Turkish Archives, A Contribution to the History of the Jews in the Ottoman Empire*, Oriental Notes and Studies (Jerusalem 1952), 2, where he mentions Galanté's *Documents officiels Turcs concernant les Juifs de Turquie* (Istanbul: Haim Rozio, 1931), an annotation, translation, and historical description of 114 official documents.

89. Robert M. Seltzer, "Dubnow, Simon," *The YIVO Encyclopaedia of Jews in Eastern Europe*, http://www.yivoencyclopedia.org/article.aspx/Dubnow_Simon.

90. Simon Dubnow, *History of the Jews*, trans. Moshe Spiegel, 5 vols. (South Brunswick, NJ: Thomas Yoseloff, 1967–1973), 3:394.

91. Ibid., 3:394–395.

92. Ibid., 3:397.

93. Ibid., 3:395. Cited in Bahar, *Jewish Historiography on the Ottoman Empire*, 119–120.

94. Ibid., 3:396.

95. Ibid., 3:471.

96. Salamon Abraham Rosanes, *Korot ha-Yehudim be-Turkiyah ve-artsot ha-kedem* (vol. 1–3, Husitin, 1907, 1910–1911, 1913–1914; vol. 4–5, Sofia, 1933–1934, 1936–1937; and vol. 6, Jerusalem, 1945) (in Hebrew).

97. Mark Cohen, "The Jews under Islam: From the Rise of Islam to Sabbatai Zevi," in *Bibliographical Essays in Medieval Jewish Studies* (New York, 1976), reprinted with a supplement as Princeton Near East Paper Number 32, Princeton, 1981, 200.

98. Shlomo (Salomon) Rosanes, *Divrei yamei Israel be-Togarma ('al-pi mekorot rishonim), Helek rishon: Yamei ha-gerushim ve ha-nedurim ve hityashvut ha-plitim be-Togarma (1300–1520)* (History of the Jews of Turkey according to the earliest sources, Part I: The Period of the [Spanish & other] expulsions, migrations and settlement of the refugees in Turkey, 1300–1520), 2nd revised ed. (Tel Aviv: Dvir, 1930) (in Hebrew), 1:1.

99. Ibid., 1:5.

100. Ibid.; also cited in Galanti, *Türkler ve Yahudiler*, 9; and cited in Naim Güleryüz, *Türk Yahudileri tarihi I: 20. yüzyılın başına kadar* (Istanbul: Gözlem, 1993), 52.

101. Rosanes, *Divrei yamei Israel be-Togarma*, 1: 91.

102. Ibid., 1:4.

103. Joseph Néhama, *Histoire des Israélites de Salonique*, Tome I, *La communauté Romaniote, Les Sefardis et leur dispersion* (Paris: Librairie Durlacher/Salonique: Librairie Molho, 1935); Joseph Néhama, *Histoire des Israélites de Salonique*, Tome II, *La communauté Sefaradite, période d'installation (1492–1536)* (Paris: Librairie Durlacher/Salonique: Librairie Molho, 1935); Joseph Néhama, *Histoire des Israélites de Salonique*, Tome III. *L'age d'or du Sefaradisme Salonicien (1536–1593)* (first volume) (Paris: Librairie Durlacher/Salonique: Librairie Molho, 1936); Joseph Néhama, *Histoire des Israélites de Salonique*, Tome IV, *L'age d'or du Sefaradisme Salonicien (1536–1593)* (second volume) (Paris: Librairie Durlacher/Salonique: Librairie Molho, 1936).

104. *In Memoriam: Hommage aux victimes Juives des Nazis en Grèce*, Tome II, ed. Joseph Néhama (Salonique: Communauté Israélite de Thessalonique, 1949). He also published a Judeo-Spanish-French dictionary: Joseph Néhama, *Dictionnaire du judéo-espagnol* (Madrid: Consejo Superior de Investigaciones Científicas, 1977). The last volumes of his history of Salonican Jewry, completed in 1940, were published posthumously in 1978.

105. Néhama, *Histoire des Israélites de Salonique*, 1:113–114.

106. Ibid., 115.

107. Ibid., 116–117.

108. Ibid., 168.

109. Ibid., 169.

110. Néhama, *Histoire des Israélites de Salonique*, 2:11, 13.

111. Ibid., 35–36.

112. Ibid., 38.

113. Ibid., 135.

114. Ibid., 138.

115. Ibid., 167.

116. Joseph Néhama, *Histoire des Israélites de Salonique*, Tome III. *L'age d'or du Sefaradisme Salonicien (1536–1593)* (first volume) (Paris: Librairie Durlacher/Salonique: Librairie Molho, 1936), 7.

117. Ibid., 8.

118. Ibid., 17.

119. Ibid., 18.

120. Ibid., 42.

121. Ibid., 47–48; *Consolacaos*, 3:34.

122. Ibid., 48.

123. Joseph Néhama, *Histoire des Israélites de Salonique*, Tome IV, *L'age d'or du Sefaradisme Salonicien (1536–1593)* (second volume) (Paris: Librairie Durlacher/Salonique: Librairie Molho, 1936), 124–126.

124. Ibid., 126.

125. Devin Naar, *Jewish Salonica: Between the Ottoman Empire and Modern Greece*, Stanford Studies in Jewish History and Culture, ed. David Biale and Sara Abrevaya Stein (Stanford, CA: Stanford University Press, 2016), chapter 4, "Paving the Way for Better Days: The Historians," 189–238.

126. Cited in ibid., 200–201.

127. Cited in ibid., 210.

128. Ibid., 212–213.

129. Rodrigue, *Jews and Muslims*, 236–238; Daskalakis-Giontis, "Defining Neighbours," 23–29.

130. Daskalakis-Giontis, "Defining Neighbours," 33.

131. See http://www.oxfordjewishheritage.co.uk/resources/further-reading/170-cecil-roth -1899–1970.

132. Cecil Roth, *A Short History of the Jewish People*, illustrated edition revised and enlarged (London: East and West Library, 1948), 271, 444.

133. Ibid., 274.

134. Ibid., 279.

135. Ibid., 275.

136. Cecil Roth, *Dona Gracia of the House of Nasi: A Jewish Renaissance Woman* (Philadelphia: Jewish Publication Society of America, 1948).

137. Ibid., 97–98, 100.
138. Yerushalmi, *Zakhor*, 81; Michael Stanislawski, "Salo Wittmayer Baron: Demystifying Jewish History," *Columbia University Alumi Magazine* (Winter 2005), http://www.columbia.edu/cu/alumni/Magazine/Winter2005/llbaron.html.
139. Salo Wittmayer Baron, *A Social and Religious History of the Jews*, 18 volumes, second edition, revised and enlarged, vol. 18, *The Ottoman Empire, Persia, Ethiopia, India, and China* (New York: Columbia University Press, 1983), 6–7, 43–44.
140. Ibid., 293.
141. Letters of Salo Baron in New York to Abraham Galanté in Istanbul, February 13 and April 24, 1936. The Central Archives for the History of the Jewish People (Jerusalem), Galanté Papers, P-112/45, reproduced in *Sephardi Lives*, 411–413.
142. Baron, *A Social and Religious History of the Jews*, 18: 6–7.
143. Ibid., 20.
144. Ibid., 22.
145. Ibid., 25, 32–35.
146. Ibid., 453, footnote 32.
147. Ibid., 28; Capsali, *Seder Eliyahu zuta*, 1:81.
148. Baron, *A Social and Religious History of the Jews*, 18:29.
149. Ibid., 37.
150. Ibid., 43.
151. Ibid., 44.
152. Ibid., 71.
153. Ibid., 72.
154. Ibid., 73.
155. Ibid., 74–118.
156. Ibid., 77.
157. Ibid., 87.
158. Ibid., 90.
159. Ibid., 94.
160. Ibid., 91.
161. Ibid., 120.
162. Graetz, *History of the Jews*, 3:41, cited in Stillman, "History," 54.
163. Lewis, *The Jews of Islam*, 166.
164. Ibid., 209, note 2.
165. Ibid., 126–128.
166. Ibid., 129–135.
167. Ibid., 135–136.
168. Ibid., 138.
169. Ibid., 138–139.
170. Dumont, "Jewish Communities in Turkey during the Last Decades of the Nineteenth Century," 221–225. The same alliance quote would be cited as evidence for positive relations between Muslims and Jews in Donald Quataert, *The Ottoman Empire, 1700–1922* (Cambridge: Cambridge University Press, 2000), 176–177.
171. Dumont, "Jewish Communities in Turkey during the Last Decades of the Nineteenth Century," 224.
172. Ibid; Shaw, *The Jews of the Ottoman Empire and the Turkish Republic*, 85.
173. *Âşıkpaşazade, Osmanoğulları'nın tarihi*, ed. Kemal Yavuz and M. A. Yekta Saraç (Istanbul: K, 2003); Halil Inalcik, "How to Read 'Ashık Pasha-zade's History," *Studies*

in Ottoman History in Honour of Professor V.L. Ménage, ed. C. Heywood and C. lmber, (Istanbul: Isis, 1994), 139–156.

174. *Âşıkpaşaoğlu tarihi*, ed. H. Nihal Atsız (Istanbul: Milli Eğitim, 1970), 229; *Âşıkpaşazâde tarihi (Osmanlı tarihi 1285–1502)*, ed. Necdet Öztürk (Istanbul: Bilge, 2013), 297–298.

175. The text that includes this line is cited in Öztürk, *Âşıkpaşazâde tarihi*, 298n5512. Lewis refers to "the Istanbul edition, (1332), 192," quoted in Bernard Lewis, "The Privilege Granted by Mehmed II to his Physician," *Bulletin of the School of Oriental and African Studies* 14, no. 3 (1952): 562n5, which also refers to a citation of the line in M. Tayyib Gökbilgin, *XV–XVI asırlarda Edirne ve Paşa livası* (Istanbul, 1952), 148.

176. *Seyahatname* II, 253b13, quoted in Robert Dankoff, *An Ottoman Mentality: The World of Evliya Çelebi* (Leiden: Brill, 2006), 68–69.

177. *Seyahatname* I, 215a35, quoted in Dankoff, *An Ottoman Mentality*, 68. As proof, he relates that in the mid-sixteenth century a Jewish physician in Ottoman Budapest confessed "I have poisoned forty men named Muhammad," including a vizier, by lacing a fruit drink with deadly poison." *Evliya Çelebi seyahatnâmesi*, ed. Orhan Şaik Gökyay, Topkapı Sarayı Bağdat 304 Yazmasının Transkripsiyonu-Dizini, 1. Kitap: İstanbul (Istanbul: Yapı Kredi, 1996), 68–69. The citation in the original is 1:47b20.

178. See his description of the 1638 festive procession of guilds before Sultan Murad IV in Istanbul, narrating how "because they were Jews" the "accursed" guild of Jewish tavernkeepers "were treated with contempt by being made to go very last." *Evliya Çelebi Seyahatnâmesi*, 316. The citation in the original is 1:215a20.

179. Haim Gerber, introduction to *Crossing Borders: Jews and Muslims in Ottoman Law, Economy and Society* (Istanbul: Isis, 2008), 8.

180. Ibid., 26.

181. Gerber, *Crossing Borders*, 127–142.

182. For example, eighteenth-century chronicler Defterdar records the lynching of Yasef, Jewish master of the mint of Egypt, by Janissaries in Cairo in 1697. Defterdâr Sarı Mehmed Paşa, *Zübde-i vekayiât* (Ankara: Türk Tarih Kurumu, 1995), 611.

183. Gerber, *Crossing Borders*, 20.

184. Johannes H. Mordtmann, "Die jüdischen Kira im Serai der Sultane," *Mitteilungen des Seminars für orientalische Sprachen: Westasiatische Studien* 32, no. 2 (1929); Abraham Galanté, *Esther Kyra d'après de nouveaux documents: Contribution a l'Histoire des Juifs de Turquie* (Istanbul: Fratelli Haim, 1926); Selânikî Mustafa Efendi, *Tarih-i Selânikî*, ed. Mehmed İpşirli, 2 vols. (Istanbul: Istanbul Üniversitesi Edebiyat Fakültesi, 1989), 2:854–855. See also Mehmed İpşirli, "Mustafa Selânikî and his history," *Tarih Enstitüsü Dergisi* 9 (January 1978). Selaniki's account of the event is discussed in Baki Tezcan, *The Second Ottoman Empire: Political and Social Transformation in the Early Modern World* (Cambridge: Cambridge University Press, 2010), 65, 107, and 188; and Leslie Peirce, *The Imperial Harem: Women and Sovereignty in the Ottoman Empire* (Oxford: Oxford University Press, 1993), 243. The narrative of the fall of the kira reappears later in four seventeenth-century chronicles: Katip Çelebi (1609–1657), *Fezleke*, 2 vols. (Istanbul: Ceride-i Havadis, 1286/1869), 1:128; Mehmed Hemdemî Çelebi, *Solakzâde tarihi*, ed. Dr. Vahid Çabuk, 2 vols. (Ankara: Türk Kültür Bakanlığı, 1989), 2:406; Shaykh al-Islâm Karaçelebizade Abdül Aziz Efendi (1592–1658), *Ravzat ül-ebrar el-mübeyyin bi-hakaik il-ahbar* (Cairo: Bulak, 1248/1832), 489; and Kürd Hatib Mustafa, *Risâle-i Kürd Hatib*, Eski Hazine 1400, Topkapı Palace Museum Library, Istanbul, 18a; then again in an early printed Ottoman chronicle, the eighteenth-century

Tarih-i Naima (Naima's history) or *Ravdat-ül-Hüseyn fî hülâsâ-i ahbâr-il-hâfikayn* (The garden of al-Huseyin, or, choicest news of east and west; ca. 1697–1704), by the *vakanüvis* (official chronicler) Mustafa Naima (1655–1716), Na'ima, *Tarîh-i Naîmâ*, 6 vols. (Istanbul, 1281–1283/1864–1867), 1:231, 247; Naîmâ Mustafa Efendi, *Târih-i Na'îmâ (Ravzatü'l-Hüseyn fî hulâsati ahbâri'l-hâfikayn)*, ed. Mehmed İpşirli, 4 vols. (Ankara: Türk Tarih Kurumu, 2007), 1:162–163.

185. Galanté, *Esther Kyra, d'après de nouveaux documents*, 7, 8–14.

186. For his changing Selaniki's "sipahi" to "janissary" see *Esther Kyra, d'après de nouveaux documents*, 8–9. He corrects this in Abraham Galanté, *Histoire des Juifs d'Istanbul: Depuis la prise de cette ville, en 1453, par Fatih Mehmed II, jusqu'à nos jours*, vol. 1 (Istanbul: Fratelli Haim, 1941), 14–15.

187. Shaw, *The Jews of the Ottoman Empire and the Turkish Republic*, 91.

188. Veinstein, "Jews and Muslims in the Ottoman Empire," 185.

189. Shaw, *The Jews of the Ottoman Empire and the Turkish Republic*, 361.

190. Naim Güleryüz, *The History of the Turkish Jews*, condensed from a lecture by the author, revised 2nd ed. (Istanbul: Rekor, 1992), 11.

191. See Feroz Ahmad, "Unionist Relations with the Greek, Armenian, and Jewish Communities of the Ottoman Empire," in *Christians and Jews in the Ottoman Empire: The Functioning of a Plural Society*, ed. Benjamin Braude and Bernard Lewis, 2 vols. (New York: Holmes & Meier, 1982), 1:425–426, which refers to Galanté; and Feroz Ahmad, *The Making of Modern Turkey* (London: Routledge, 1993), 44, where he claims "the non-Muslims, with the exception of Ottoman Jews, did not regard the post-1908 state as their state, through which they could further their interests. On the contrary, their interests were better served while the state was weak and dominated by the Powers."

192. Baron, *A Social and Religious History of the Jews*, 18: 230; Yaron Ben-Naeh, *Jews in the Realm of the Sultans: Ottoman Jewish Society in the Seventeenth Century*, trans. Yohai Goell, Texts and Studies in Medieval and Early Modern Judaism 22 (Tübingen: Mohr Siebeck, 2008), 75, 110.

193. Baer, "Death in the Hippodrome."

194. In the eighteenth century, this Jew had apparently converted to Christianity, then to Islam, and reverted to Christianity. Avraham Meyuhas, *Bnei Avraham*, 2 vols. (Istanbul 1773), Even ha'ezer, fol. 21a (in Hebrew), cited in Ben-Naeh, *Jews in the Realm of the Sultans*, 145n143. For examples of threats to force Jews to convert or be put to death, see the eighteenth-century account in Rabbi David ben Eliezer Lehno, *Devar sefatayim*, 174–176, cited in Ben-Naeh, *Jews in the Realm of the Sultans*, 149n152.

195. See Ben-Naeh, *Jews in the Realm of the Sultans*, 140–142.

196. Jacob M. Landau, "Hebrew Sources for the Socio-Economic History of the Ottoman Empire," *Der Islam* 54, no. 2 (1977): 208; Leah Bornstein-Makovetsky, "Non-Urban Social Encounters between Jews and Muslims in the Ottoman Empire during the 16th through 18th Centuries," in *Jews and Muslims in the Islamic World*, ed. Zvi Zohar (Bethesda, MD: University of Maryland Press, 2012), 3.

4

TURKISH JEWS AS TURKISH LOBBYISTS

IN THE EARLY 1970S, THE TURKISH PUBLIC AND state were abruptly and brutally shocked out of their amnesia regarding the Armenian genocide by two revenge murders of Turkish diplomats. On January 27, 1973, an elderly Armenian survivor assassinated the Turkish general consul and deputy consul of Los Angeles at a hotel in Santa Barbara, on the pretext of giving them a watercolor painting of Sultan Abdülhamid II.[1] Two years later, the Armenian Secret Army for the Liberation of Armenia (ASALA), founded by leftist Armenian descendants of genocide survivors in Lebanon, began to attack Turkish embassy personnel around the world. As part of a campaign launched between 1975 and 1986 to force Turkey to acknowledge the genocide, they and similar groups—for example, the Justice Commandos of the Armenian Genocide and the Armenian Revolutionary Army—killed over three dozen Turkish diplomats in Europe, the Middle East, and the United States, as well as Turkish and non-Turkish civilians in Turkey and Europe.

At that time, the Turkish Foreign Ministry had only one brochure in English depicting its side of the story.[2] Turkish officials initially believed the terrorists were either Greeks avenging the 1974 Turkish occupation of Northern Cyprus, or, befitting the Cold War context, Turkish leftists. By 1980, as the attacks continued, it finally dawned on them that the assassins were Armenians, and that Turkey had to respond to the events of sixty-five years prior.[3] As a result, beginning in 1980, "denial was institutionalized and professionalized: a special agency . . . was founded within the Foreign Ministry to coordinate all issues" related to the Armenian genocide.[4] The main strategy was to "frame the 'Armenian question' as a problem of *contemporary* terrorism rather than an outcome of Turkey's genocidal past."[5] It was mainly retired Turkish diplomats who went into action, without any professional historical training or concern for professional standards, let alone an understanding of the ethics regarding the reading, use, and citation of historical documents. They were instead driven by an affective disposition of having seen their friends in the diplomatic service murdered and fearing the same fate for themselves. They published book after book promoting a provocation thesis, blaming the deaths of Armenians in 1915 on the seditious activities of traitorous Armenian terrorists.

The most representative book of this genre is career diplomat Kâmuran Gürün's (1924–2004) nearly five-hundred-page tome, *Ermeni dosyası* (The Armenian file, 1983), "the definitive work illustrating the official Turkish stand," published by Turkey's History Foundation, translated into English and French.[6] It argues that Armenian subversive activities justified their deportation. Rather than focus on Armenians as the victims of Ottoman policies, this narrative instead promotes the counterthesis that it was the Armenians—puppets of European imperial powers (especially Russia and England); tools of a worldwide conspiracy—who were the perpetrators, massacring thousands of Turks. The dust jacket of the English translation gives a sense of the book's aim and argument: "The myth that the Ottoman Empire's Armenian subjects were the innocent victims of wanton massacre has had a powerful hold." This "myth" has "served the interests of those countries who wanted to carve up the sick man of Europe especially after the end of the First World War." In contrast, Gürün claims, *Ermeni dosyası* "presents the first objective account of this subject available in English." Its author "has had full access to foreign and Ottoman national archives and has sifted through the relevant documents from every available source," allowing him to provide "the evidence, which gives the English-speaking world its first opportunity to see Armenian terrorism in perspective, from the time of the First World War up to the present day. At the same time, the author examines the links between today's Armenian terrorists and other international terrorist organizations." Gürün, an employee of the Turkish Foreign Ministry for thirty-four years from 1948 to 1982, "had full access" to primary sources that have to this day not been made available to others. It was Gürün who proposed a task force to organize Turkish lobbying efforts abroad to counter Armenian genocide recognition, which depended on Jewish participation.

He recounts how in a report to the Turkish National Security Council and the prime minister's office at the end of 1981, he emphasized "the possibility of using the Jewish communities . . . as a counterbalancing element" against "the Armenian terrorists."[7] It was at that moment that Turkish Jews, including Jak Kamhi (b. 1925, Tepebaşı, Istanbul), were first allowed to participate in meetings of international Jewish organizations, where, in the words of another prominent Turkish Jew at the time, they eagerly "strove to help Turkey and the present government in its attempts and efforts to make [their] country better and more favorably known" to Western public opinion.[8] What Turkish and American Jews expected in return for supporting Turkey's efforts was improved relations between Turkey and Israel. As Gürün recalls in his memoirs, he advised the government that while publishing books with the Turkish view was necessary, to be successful in the international arena, Turkey had to form a lobby abroad "that will oppose the Armenian claims at every forum." He argued further that Turkey's "natural ally on this matter is still the Jewish lobby," so much so, in fact, that "we must look into the possibility of employing the Jewish lobby as a matter of national interest."[9]

Bilâl Şimşir (b. 1933), another career diplomat who served in the Turkish Foreign Ministry from 1960 to 1998, published books in a similar vein. He edited the four-volume English-language series, *British Documents on Ottoman Armenians*, published by the Turkish Historical Society, a foundation established in 1931 by Atatürk, who recognized that "writing history is as important as making history."[10] The Turkish State Archives did their bit by publishing a series of books beginning with the bilingual *Arşiv belgelerine göre Kafkaslaräda ve Anadolu'da Ermeni mezâlimi I: 1906–1918/Armenian Violence and Massacre in the Caucasus and Anatolia Based on Archives* (Ankara 1995), under the direction of its general director. It argues the Ottoman Empire was the most tolerant state in history, as illustrated by a single example, the fact that Jews took refuge in the empire after 1492.[11] In contrast to the Jews' assumed loyalty, Ottoman Armenians "betrayed" the state.[12] In his preface, the prime ministry undersecretary Ali Naci Tuncer argues that the Armenians "first caused rebellions which they later turned to massacres by which they deliberately exterminated the Muslim-Turkish people living in East Anatolia and the Caucasus . . . These published records clearly reveal that the Turks have not violated and massacred the Armenians, as the latter claim, in contrary [*sic*] it shows how the Armenians exterminated the Turks."[13] In keeping with this view, in 1999, a forty-three-meter-tall building housing the Memorial and Museum of the Turkish Martyrs Murdered by Armenians (*Ermeniler tarafından katledilen şehit Türkler anıt ve müzesi*) was erected, towering above Iğdir on the Turkish-Armenian border. The remains of İsmail Enver Pasha, the former minister of war and commander in chief who had played a key role in the annihilation of the Armenians, were brought from near Dushanbe, Tajikistan, where he had been killed by the Soviet Army in 1922, to Istanbul and reburied at the time the memorial was being constructed.

That same year of 1999, the Turkish ambassador to Washington, DC, wrote a letter, sent to all 535 congresspeople, criticizing plans to create a collection of all US records pertaining to the Armenian genocide.[14] In his letter, he claims that "the Ottoman Armenians of Eastern Anatolia became subject to a relocation only after as many as 1.1 million Muslims and 100,000 Jews, the overwhelming proportion civilians, were killed in massacres conducted by disloyal Ottoman Armenians fighting alongside Russian forces in Eastern Ottoman Anatolia." This is a fantastical claim; according to the official Ottoman census, there were less than one third that number of Jews in eastern Anatolia at the time.[15] Facts appear to matter less to such propagandists than does reaffirming the Muslim-Jewish alliance so as to spur Jewish members of the US Congress to defend their putative Muslim allies.

Following these developments, Bilâl Şimşir turned to prose narratives, including *Şehit diplomatlarımız* (Our martyred diplomats) concerning the Turkish diplomats murdered by Armenian terrorists in the 1970s and 1980s, and *Ermeni meselesi 1774–2005* (The Armenian question, 2005).[16] The blood-curdling argument of the latter book shamelessly borrows its tropes from anti-Semitic conspiracy theories. According to Şimşir, the cause of the "Armenian problem" is that "the Armenians betrayed the Ottoman Empire; they served the enemy; they stabbed the Turkish soldiers in the back." They did this, he contends, because "it is an Armenian tradition to kill Turks," as "Armenians raise their children to be assassins, instilling in them a desire to kill innocent Turks, their culture passing the assassin tradition from generation to generation." Even today, he states, "Armenia refuses to recognize Turkey's borders and has set its gaze on Turkey . . . which is to say that Turkey faces people who are unstable, pathologic, incorrigible, and shameless." If we substitute "Jew" for "Armenian" and "Germans and Germany" for "Turks and Turkey" in these sentences, we immediately understand the dangerous and irrational nature of such thinking. Şimşir's claims of Armenians stabbing Turks in the back was echoed by the minister of justice Cemil Çiçek the same year, who labeled the attempts to hold the first public conference recognizing the Armenian genocide at a Turkish university "treason" and a "stab in the back of the Turkish nation."[17] Şimşir has long cooperated with genocide deniers outside Turkey, including US historians of the Ottoman Empire Justin McCarthy (b. 1945) and Heath Lowry (b. 1942), who have both published works with him and used his work extensively.[18]

Gürün did not write about Jews, as he was active in the 1980s, before the turn to the World War II rescue myth discussed in chapter 6. Şimşir, on the other hand, exploits the Jewish rescue myth to the full, claiming not only that Turks cannot be anti-Semitic, despite his deployment of anti-Semitic-styled conspiracy tropes regarding Armenians, but that the heroic Turks were the only nation to stand up against the Nazis. In his two-volume study, *Türk Yahudiler: Avrupa ırkçılarına karşı Türkiye'nin mücadelesi* (Turkish Jews: Turkey's battle against European racists), Şimşir asserts that (unlike the Armenians) the Turkish Jews were "always loyal to Turkey, and never betrayed the Turks." Because of this, when the Turkish Jews in France were threatened, Turkey "took them under its protection," and the Turkish embassy and consular staff in France "waged an honorable legal battle to protect and save them and largely succeeded," as it "fought the good fight against European racists."[19] In addition to being written to serve an explicit political aim—that of whitewashing Turkey—*Türk Yahudiler* is an untrustworthy historical source; it consists of excerpts from purported official Turkish documents whose contents and existence cannot be verified, as no independent-minded scholar has been allowed access to them.

Enlisting Turkish Jews as Lobbyists for Turkey

In 2007, the Turkish Foreign Ministry awarded Jak Kamhi the "Extraordinary Service Award" for his decades-long role promoting denial of the Armenian genocide in Europe and for having lobbied members of the US Congress to reject draft resolutions recognizing the annihilation of the Armenians.[20] A wealthy industrialist, Kamhi is founder of the construction and electronics company Profilo Holding, which began as Profilo Steel Factory Collective Company in 1954. His list of professional affiliations is long: he has served as board member of the Istanbul Chamber of Industry (since 1960, as the first Jewish member); as president of the Economic Development Foundation, the Turkey-France Business Council, and the Quincentennial Foundation (1989–2008, and honorary president thereafter); as member of the European Round Table of Industrialists and, the Prime Ministry's foreign promotion advisory board; and as chief advisor to the Prime Ministry on external lobbying and promotion.[21] As Heathy Lowry, the editor of the English translation of Kamhi's autobiography writes on the book's dustjacket, "It would not be an exaggeration to state that Jak Kamhi has been one of the key players in the shaping and implementation of Turkish foreign policy and international relations throughout the past half century. He continues to put his heart and soul into serving as one of his country's foremost champions in the international arena."[22]

To understand the role of Jak Kamhi, we must return to the early 1970s, for it was at that point in time, when the Jewish community had shrunk to less than thirty-eight thousand members,[23] that Turkish Jews were first given an opportunity by the republic to prove themselves, in contrast to the Armenians and Greeks, as "model citizens." Turkish Armenians were seen to have been "compromised" by the terrorist organization ASALA's attacks on Turkish diplomats and, soon thereafter, international calls for recognition of the Armenian genocide, including in the US Congress. Turkish Greeks were seen to have been "tainted" by Turkey's invasion and occupation of Northern Cyprus and the ensuing US arms embargo.[24] As they had a century before during the Ottoman-Greek war of 1897, Turkish Jewish community leaders enthusiastically supported the Turkish invasion and occupation of Cyprus in 1974.[25]

As Jak Kamhi relates in his autobiography, the Cyprus campaign "marked the beginning of my political life."[26] He joined a ten-man diplomatic delegation led by a Turkish ambassador "appointed by the [Bülent] Ecevit government to explain the reasons for the intervention [invasion and occupation] to political leaders in Europe and the U.S." Kamhi recognizes that one of the reasons he was included "was to gain the support of" Jews in the countries they visited, having first obtained names of "influential" Jews from the Israeli consul general in Istanbul.[27]

Turkey realized it needed an effective lobby.[28] Praising his own community's efforts, a Turkish Jew argued that "the way to end the influence of the enemy lobbies was to work together with the other powerful lobby, the American Jewish lobby," using it as a vessel to convince members of Congress to change their views and policies concerning Turkey.[29] Major American Jewish organizations represented the only constituency in the United States that Turkey believed would be both sympathetic and powerful, and after the first successful post-Cyprus mission, it again gave Kamhi the nod to head the effort. The Turkish Jewish community regularly boasts that it identified itself as fit for that job and dutifully stepped in as a special interest group to successfully lobby the American Jewish community to come over to Turkey's side.

The turn to Jews as lobbyists on Turkey's behalf was based not only on the long-standing perception of centuries of friendship between Turks and Jews, but also on the anti-Semitic conspiracy tropes that Jews are powerful beyond their numbers, that they hold the keys to Washington and indeed all world capitals, and that they control world finance and media. As advisor to the Ministry of Foreign Affairs, Gürün recounts his role in convincing President Evren to establish international lobbies for Turkey in the 1980s. "Before us stands the possibility of making use of world Jewry. . . . The ones who are working to block [anti-Turkish] rumors and who speak out openly against Armenian terror are the Jewish members of Congress." For Gürün, the reason was that "the day that we have the American Jewish lobby against us . . . no decision in Turkey's favor will make it through Congress. We will not be able to obtain any assistance whatsoever from financial circles in America . . . Whatever we do, it is incumbent upon us not to underestimate the power of the world Jewish lobby." He argues that Jews make and unmake world leaders. "Every single person who enters the office of [Jewish lobbyist] M. Squadron in New York is met with the photographs on his desk of every single American presidential candidate. The Jewish lobby can bring the German government to its knees, it can cause the French government to fall into worry and concern, it can do battle with the Russian government." In sum, "it is not Israel that does this—it is the world Jewish lobby . . . a powerful ally in our struggle, not just against the Armenians, but against the Greeks as well."[30] Gürün also quipped that "there should also be publications about how the Jews were helped by the Turks . . . as it should not be forgotten that there are 5 million Jews in the United States as opposed to 500,000 Armenians."[31] As President Özal (prime minister, 1983–1989; president, 1989–1993) told a Turkish Jewish journalist, "The strength of the Israeli [*sic*, Jewish] lobby in the United States is well known."[32]

Israeli diplomats were well aware that "the Turks believe in *The Protocols of the Elders of Zion* and other conspiracy theories of an anti-Semitic nature, which make them believe that Israel has vast powers at its disposal," and they made the most of it.[33] Instead of unburdening the Turkish government of these beliefs, they informed their Turkish counterparts that American Jews were extremely powerful, and that if relations with Israel were upgraded, the American Jewish lobby would serve Turkey's interests and defeat US congressional proposals to recognize the Armenian genocide.

In their lobbying efforts, Turkish Jews regularly leveraged such anti-Semitic motifs as the alleged Jewish control of the media and the extraordinary ability of world Jewry to influence political decisions. Narrating "how the media was silenced in a day," Kamhi explains the diplomatic delegation's operations in France in 1975: he met Elie Rothschild, the president of the Representative Council of Jewish Institutions, briefing him "on the realities of our Turkey, and stressed how we had helped oppressed and persecuted communities over the centuries."[34] The Jewish leader summoned his communications director and told him to "put an end to the campaign of negative propaganda against Turkey in the media." Subsequently, "as if by miracle, that evening the televisions fell silent [not reporting on Turkey] and the next morning Turkey was also forgotten by the newspapers." The same leader "was also influential in England, and that country likewise changed its stance upon his recommendation."[35] Kamhi's accounts mirror conspiracy theories that grant sweeping national and international influence to Jews in general and the Rothschild family in particular. In Washington, DC, they contacted B'nai B'rith and the Israeli embassy, and met congressmen. "We briefed them on the Jews living in Turkey and how we had shared the same land and destiny as Turkish Muslims for 500 years."[36] As a result, he claims that "our delegation played a very important role in the lifting of the arms embargo that had been imposed on Turkey."

Relationships forged on that first trip lobbying on Turkey's behalf would prove important for later efforts with American congresspeople, senators, and administrations. Turkish Jews served as the intermediaries between Turkey, Israel, and major American Jewish organizations. The reason for their assuming this role was another correct assumption. Jews, whose success in business and industry relied on government licenses and support, would do their bidding because they had no other option. They were not in a position to turn the government down. As Kamhi recalled, the first lobbying assignment in 1975 was "a chance to prove myself both at home and abroad."[37]

Kamhi's work with American Jewish organizations continued after that first effort, and he returned to the United States in 1977, thereafter visiting frequently, working together with Jak Veissid, Naim Güleryüz, and the leaders of the Turkish Jewish community. But "we received our greatest support from the Ministry of Foreign Affairs and Turkish ambassadors," he admits, as "the Ministry of Foreign Affairs' undersecretaries also took a close interest in the matter and joined in our [lobbying] effort."[38] He singles out Kâmuran Gürün as one of these.

Lobbying against the Genocide

After constant lobbying had produced the desired effect and the US embargo on arms shipments to Turkey was lifted in 1978,[39] the efforts of Turkish Jews would then be turned to deny the Armenian genocide. As Kamhi relates during the late 1970s, "With Prime Minister [Süleyman] Demirel's [1924–2015; prime minister, 1965–1971, 1975–1977, 1977–1978, 1979–1980, 1991–1993; president, 1993–2000]) permission, contributions from members of the Jewish community, and interventions by the Israeli government, we were able to hinder such negative initiatives as the so-called [Armenian] genocide claims."[40] In 1978, a US presidential executive order was signed to begin the process of establishing a Holocaust memorial in Washington, DC, and from the beginning Turkey was concerned that the Armenian genocide would be included.[41] Astonishingly, President Jimmy Carter's Jewish aide, Stuart Eizenstat, reported that Turkish ambassador Şükrü Elekdağ (in office 1979–1989) told him that although Turkey had treated its Jews well for centuries and had taken in Jewish refugees from Nazi Germany, if the Armenian genocide were included in the new museum, "Turkey could no longer guarantee the safety of the Jews in Turkey."[42] Elekdağ was also reported making a similar comment to another member of the Holocaust Memorial Museum Committee. Israel also weighed in, pressuring Washington not to include the Armenian genocide. As did Turkish Jewish leaders who wrote a letter to the World Jewish Congress "pleading that their future was at stake" over the decision to include the genocide or not.[43] With the assistance of Kamhi and Turkish chief rabbi David Asseo (b. 1914, in office 1961–2002), Holocaust Memorial Museum Committee chairman Monroe Freedman and another committee member, Hyman Bookbinder, both of whom were Jewish, told the Turkish press that the Armenian genocide would not be included in the museum.[44] Gürün recorded with great satisfaction at that time that "although the efforts on the issue of including the Armenians in the Holocaust Memorial Museum appeared successful at one point, the actions we took on a governmental level and the actions of those leading members of the Jewish community in Turkey succeeded in turning the American Jewish community against this idea."[45]

Although Turkey had recognized Israel in 1948, it established diplomatic relations at the ministerial, not ambassadorial level. When Israel declared Jerusalem its capital in 1980, Turkey withdrew its minister and downgraded relations to a level just one step removed from ending them.[46] Israel and Turkish Jews were interested in improving relations between the two countries, as was the United States. Working together to deny the Armenian genocide by promoting utopian visions of Turkish-Jewish harmony instead was a means to reach this goal.

In his autobiography, fashion designer Vitali Hakko (1913–2007) recounts his efforts to promote a positive vision of Muslim-Jewish relations in the Ottoman Empire and Turkey at that time. He narrates these events without any sense of irony and barely one hundred pages after describing the discriminatory policies Turkish Jews faced during the early republican era, policies that had a profound effect on his own life. Hakko started out as a hat maker, finding fame in 1934 with the creation of Şen Şapka (Happy Hat). He became a renowned fashion designer, the "Pierre Cardin of Turkey," and established the Vakko brand scarf and flagship clothing store in the heart of Beyoğlu, Istanbul (1962) offering ready-to-wear fashion. In 1981, on the occasion of the one hundredth anniversary of the birth of Atatürk, Hakko was given the task of staging fashion shows in several European capitals showcasing Turks as "the heirs of all of the cultures and civilizations of Anatolia—Hittite, Greek, Roman, Byzantine, Seljuk, Ottoman, and modern Turkey."[47] What of the Armenians? He mentions Armenians only as terrorists, members of ASALA who assassinate Turkish diplomats; Hakko feared that his shows would become their target as well.[48] He fails to mention the reasons Armenians were attacking Turkish missions abroad. Did he wonder whether the absence of Armenian culture and civilization from his "Anatolian Sun" shows had anything to do with Armenian terrorism? Hakko's efforts were his first efforts lobbying for Turkey, and they occurred only one year after Turkey's brutal 1980 coup. The shows were a great propaganda success for Turkey and its military regime, with whom he was on good terms, and he met with coup leader Kenan Evren and Bülend Ulusu (in office 1980–1983), who was a figurehead, postcoup prime minister. Ulusu and Hakko discussed the necessity of creating a foundation to promote a positive Turkey brand abroad, and the prime minister promised his full support. Hakko boasts how "the birth of the Türk Tanıtma Vakfı (Turk Promotion Board) is indebted to his 1981 traveling fashion show."[49]

In 1982, the three most prominent Turkish Jewish leaders were Jak Kamhi, Chief Rabbi David Asseo, and Jak Veissid. As a prominent and influential businessman and informal ambassador to the US Jewish community, Kamhi had close relations with Israeli politicians such as Shimon Peres (1923–2016; prime minister, 1977, 1984–1986, 1995–1996; president, 2007–2014).[50] Asseo had served as chief rabbi since the early 1960s, when the interior minister told him "that there were no problems between Turkey and its Jews that could not be solved in a spirit of . . . deep friendship," a situation that "does not resemble that existing between Turkey and its Greek population."[51] Asseo responded in kind, stating that his community had no complaints about the government, "and that relations between the two were quite good, certainly in comparison with those of the Armenian and Greek communities."[52] In the mid-1960s, Asseo publicly refuted "the unjust" and "untrue" charges that Turkey discriminated against Greeks, asserting in an editorial that Turkey "has provided examples of true humanity and civilization to the entire world," as proven by its treatment of Jews.[53] Jak Veissid, attorney and chairman of the lay council,[54] came from a family that had provided the Jewish community's secular leaders since the seventeenth century.[55]

When the Israeli Holocaust Memorial and Museum in Jerusalem, Yad Vashem, organized the First International Conference on the Holocaust and Genocide in 1982, Kamhi, Asseo, and Veissid recognized that another chance for lobbying against international recognition of the Armenian genocide had presented itself to the Turkish Jewish community. Turkey sprang into action to ensure that no papers on the Armenian genocide would be presented, and it turned to Turkish Jews for assistance. As reported in the US and Israeli press, a delegation of Turkish Jews visited Israel to warn that should the conference proceed, there would be reprisals against Turkish Jewry. This message was passed on to planned conference participants, including Holocaust survivor and Nobel Peace Prize winner Elie Wiesel (1928–2016), who withdrew and reported his reasons to the *New York Times*.[56] Spokesmen for the Israeli Foreign Ministry conceded that they had worked to cancel the meeting or to ensure that there would be no official Israeli participation "out of concern for the interests of Jews." The Turkish ambassador to the United States felt compelled to write a letter to the editor of the *New York Times* denying the allegations, entitled, "Turkey's Jews are Under No Threat."[57] He also felt it necessary to mention that Armenian terrorists had recently murdered twenty-two Turkish ambassadors and their family members.[58] This compelled the counselor for the US Holocaust Memorial Council, a US official, to report that in 1981 a Turkish diplomat had threatened that if the Armenian genocide were included in the museum, "the safety of the Jews in Turkey would be threatened."[59] That year, when it looked as if the Armenian genocide would be included in the planned museum, a spokesman for the Turkish Foreign Ministry stated that Turkey had "always behaved in a positive manner toward the Jews" and "if the Jews wish to distort historical truths by giving the Armenians a place in the museum, they would be providing an example of profound ingratitude."[60] Writing in the Turkish daily newspaper, *Tercüman*, a Turkish journalist mingled tolerance discourse and anti-Semitism, declaring, "We opened our arms to every Jew fleeing Nazi oppression, and we embraced them as if they were our own countrymen. At that time, we even left them to monopolize our economy. . . . We have no bad blood, no conflicts . . . the first reaction should come from them, the first voice of protest should be raised from this sector."[61]

Kamhi and Rabbi Asseo quickly responded. "This matter," wrote Kamhi in *Tercüman* four days later, "was closed three months ago, the necessary initiatives were taken and the Armenian game came to naught, so why is it coming out again? I spoke with America by telephone. I spoke with the necessary places . . . rest easy . . . we are again going into action with all our strength. We will foil this plan."[62] In an interview shortly thereafter, Asseo stated that "both the Jewish community of Turkey and the Jewish individuals and institutions throughout the world will come out against this exploitation against the noble Turkish nation. Naturally we will expend every ounce of effort that we possess, just as has always been the case up to now."[63] Kamhi and Asseo sent cables to the American Jewish Conference and World Jewish Conference asserting that Jews had lived peacefully in Turkey for five hundred years and they should not include the Armenian genocide in the new museum.[64]

Israel Charney, one of the 1982 genocide conference organizers, narrated how he encountered a man waiting for him outside his home near Tel Aviv University. "He introduced himself as Jack [*sic*] Veissid, president of the Jewish community of Istanbul. . . . He explained in a very explicit tone that the Israeli Ministry of Foreign Affairs was very concerned about my conference, and that Jewish lives were in jeopardy. Veissid then said that Iranian and Syrian Jews were fleeing through Turkey's borders, and the Turks would close the borders if the conference took place."[65] Charney's account is verified by a cable sent from the Israeli consulate in Istanbul to the Israeli Ministry of Foreign Affairs in June. "The main reason for our reckless attempts to cancel the conference was the hint that we received about Jewish refugees from Iran and Syria crossing into Turkey. . . . Veissid found that all the arguments he prepared against the conference were insignificant compared to the issue of the refugees. . . . Veissid used this argument out of a sense of urgency and responsibility to our Jewish brothers and used it to convince Charny and his other partners to cancel the conference."[66] The consul also added, "We invested significant effort in order to reduce damages to Turkey from the Armenian participants." In August, the consul noted in a cable that Kâmuran Gürün, then counselor to Turkey's Ministry of Foreign Affairs, "thinks that our help to the Turkish Ministry of Foreign Affairs in preventing the Armenians from attending the conference primarily served us, the Jews. He argued that if Armenian participants had attended the conference, they would have helped to reinforce the anti-Semitic elements who attempt to blur the Holocaust and the existence of extermination camps with a scientific approach."[67] Gürün had again played on the traditional friend/enemy dichotomy that had so long animated Muslim-Jewish relations in Turkey and the Ottoman Empire.

According to discussions regarding Israeli-Turkish relations conducted within the Israeli Foreign Ministry at the time, Turkish Jews "had an advantage over other minorities there. Because the Turkish authorities were extremely concerned about their negative public image with respect to treatment of minorities (especially the Armenians and Kurds), they resolved to make an example of their treatment of the Jews."[68] According to a recent Israeli ambassador to Ankara, when Israeli actions spark Turkish criticism, and when the Armenian issue rises to the fore, Turkish Jews are anxious of backlash and publicly side with Turkey. As he observes, "This is not the Jewish community in Australia or the United States, which enjoys freedom of speech." Turkish Jews are not free to criticize Turkey or appear to be disloyal for fear of being persecuted if they do.

As they occupied West Beirut in June 1982, Israeli military forces destroyed the Armenian terrorist organization ASALA's headquarters, perceiving the group as an ally of Palestinian guerrilla organizations and an enemy of its friend, Turkey.[69] It is likely that Israel passed on intelligence gathered during its occupation to Turkish authorities, who then dispatched paramilitary teams to Europe and the Middle East, tracking down and killing ASALA members.[70] Depriving the Armenian militants of their base, the Israeli military operation contributed to their decreased ability to launch attacks against Turkish missions.[71]

In 1983, the Turkish cultural attaché in Washington invited members of the Holocaust museum committee to his office. Also present were several non-Jewish American historians of the Ottoman Empire including Justin McCarthy and Heath Lowry, referred to earlier as the editor of the English-language version of Kamhi's autobiography. McCarthy, whose monographs have been translated into Turkish by the Turkish military chiefs of staff and the Turkish Historical Society, would earn the Order of Merit from Turkey for promoting the official Turkish denialist position, such as when he represented the "Turkish view" on a panel discussion following the screening of the film, *The Armenian Genocide* on PBS in 2006.[72] Lowry was the head of the newly founded Institute of Turkish Studies (Washington, DC, established 1982), an organization created with assistance and financing from the Turkish government to combat recognition of the Armenian genocide; he would serve in the position for a decade.[73] As a veteran Turkish Jewish denialist lobbyist, Kamhi notes in his autobiography that Lowry "always assisted us" in such efforts.[74] A photo of a tuxedo-wearing Lowry along with Kamhi's wife and the then Ambassador Nüzhet Kandemir (in office 1989–1998) graces Kamhi's autobiography. It is important to note here that after heading the Institute of Turkish Studies, Lowry served as Bernard Lewis's successor at Princeton University, both in terms of teaching Ottoman history, and in playing a leading public and lobbying role in genocide denial as holder of the Atatürk Chair from 1993 to 2010. Both McCarthy and Lowry earned their doctorates under Stanford Shaw at the University of California, Los Angeles (UCLA) in 1978 and 1977 respectively. At that meeting in 1983, both men lectured the committee members for an hour denying that a genocide had occurred, arguing there had been an armed struggle between equal sides, and that the Turks had had to defend themselves from the Armenians. At lunch, echoing his 1978 words to President Carter, the then Turkish ambassador to the United States Şükrü Elekdağ declared to the American Jews that "if the Armenians are so much as mentioned in your Holocaust Memorial Museum it will go badly for the Jews of Turkey. Also for Jewish refugees from Iran. We permit them to cross into our territory, even without passports. This could stop."[75] Soon after, advertisements paid for by "Jewish members of the Assembly of Turkish American Associations" appeared in a dozen Jewish American newspapers urging readers to write to the Holocaust Memorial Museum Council demanding that the Armenian genocide not be mentioned in the museum, for among other reasons the Ottoman Empire and Turkey had always tolerated the Jews and during World War II, as Turkey had taken in German Jewish refugees, Armenians were busy signing up to join the Waffen SS. The organization was established in 1979 to counter Greek and Armenian lobbying in the US and was aided in this effort by American Jewish organizations who denied the genocide had occurred and accused Armenians of being anti-Semites.[76]

Turkey again swung into action in 1985, as another US congressional resolution recognizing the Armenian genocide was being proposed. Turkish Jewish religious and lay leaders intervened to ensure that US Jewish organizations would rescind invitations to Armenian genocide scholars to speak and cease the publication of material mentioning the genocide. The Assembly of Turkish American Associations paid for the publication of a letter of petition in the *New York Times* and the *Washington Post*, calling on the US Congress not to recognize the Armenian massacres as a genocide.[77] The letter, signed by sixty-nine US-based academics only five of whom were from Turkey (mainly historians of the Ottoman Empire, the most prominent being Bernard Lewis, discussed below), promotes the view that what occurred in Anatolia was a civil war in which Christians and Muslims suffered equally. "Serious inter-communal warfare (perpetrated by Muslim and Christian irregular forces), complicated by disease, famine, suffering, and massacres" leading to an "immense death toll" among "both Muslim and Christian communities."[78] Lowry crafted the petition, for which he received the Foundation for the Promotion and Recognition of Turkey Prize the following year. As part of its aim to hinder recognition of the Armenian genocide, Turkey proceeded over the course of a decade to establish six chairs in Ottoman and Turkish history throughout the United States: at Princeton, Harvard, Indiana, Chicago, Portland State, and Georgetown. One of them went to Lowry; when he was given Princeton's chair in 1996, it became the center of the Turkish government's denialist activities in the United States.[79]

When the European Parliament passed a resolution recognizing the Armenian genocide in 1987, it also censured Turkey's refusal to do so in the resolution's text. The Union of Turkish Immigrants in Israel protested by sending a letter to the Turkish press as well as the European Union and United States congresses, stating that "hospitality and tolerance are among the virtues of the Turkish people. Some five hundred years ago, when the Jews were expelled from Spain, after the Inquisition, it was the Ottoman Empire and the Turkish people who opened their doors to us."[80] Tolerance of Jews was again used to counter genocide recognition. Also by Muslim writers, such as journalist Mehmet Ali Birand, who, aware of "the power of the Jews in the American media," worried that mention of the genocide in the museum would be publicized far and wide. Another Turkish journalist mentioned that although "our Jews," whether of Sephardic or German origin, were treated well for five hundred years by Ottomans and Turks, but that if "these same Jews" presented Turks as "perpetrators of genocide," they would be guilty of "ingratitude and shameful behavior."[81] The Turkish Immigrants Union in Israel shared this sentiment, urging Israeli politicians to act. "It should never be forgotten that it was the Turks who welcomed the Jews who departed from Spain some five hundred years ago. Constructing a shared memorial with the Armenians is not a suitable response to the hospitality that Turkey has shown; on the contrary, it runs in direct contradiction to it."[82] Birand observed with delight that Armenian Americans had characterized the antigenocide campaign in the United States as a "love-in between the Turks and the Jews."[83]

That same year, a new US congressional resolution was introduced and then defeated, as Turkish Jewish leaders joined Israeli diplomats in lobbying and pressure.[84] This time, Jewish Americans were split. Reform Jewish organizations supported genocide recognition and the inclusion of the Armenian genocide at the new United States Holocaust Memorial and Museum in Washington, DC, as did their Liberal Jewish counterparts in the United Kingdom and Israel.[85] But those congressmen who supported the resolution faced the public relations firm hired to promote the upcoming five hundredth anniversary of the arrival of the Sephardim in Turkey, which sent a letter written by Jak Kamhi denying the claims of genocide. The chief rabbi of Turkey also sent a personal letter to every member of the US Senate denying the genocide and promoting recognition of eternal Ottoman and Turkish tolerance of Jews.[86]

In 1989, the Israeli press reported that "Turkey was ready to raise the level of diplomatic representation in Israel if Jewish organizations in the United States became active against an Armenian memorial day."[87] Turkish foreign minister and later prime minister Mesut Yılmaz (prime minister in 1991, 1996, and 1997–1999) told his Israeli counterpart that Turkey was ready to begin normal diplomatic relations. Of the leaders of nine American Jewish organizations, he demanded their help in defeating the genocide resolution and ensuring that the genocide was not included in the new Holocaust museum, and their support for Turkey's bid for membership in the European Union. The reason American Jews should support Turkey in these efforts, he argued, was to be found in their historical relationship: Turkey had always been a haven for Jews, whether they came from Spain after 1492, from Germany during the Nazi era, or from then present-day Iran and Syria.[88] When the resolution was defeated, the chief rabbi sent a letter of congratulations to Orthodox Jewish Senator Joe Lieberman, who played an important role in its defeat.[89] In a lead article, the main media organ of the Turkish Jewish community, Şalom, celebrated the result. Declaring that Turkish Jews have "for centuries led an existence on Ottoman/Turkish soil that has been the envy" of Jews in other countries, it rejects "this 'black stain' with which others wish to smear our country," thus countering Armenian genocide recognition with a utopian vision of Muslim-Jewish relations.[90] Turkey and Israel exchanged ambassadors for the first time in 1992.

With the opening of the new United States Holocaust Memorial and Museum in 1993, Turkey worked together with Israel and a number of major American Jewish organizations to ensure that the Armenian genocide would not be mentioned in the permanent exhibition. One month before its opening, the Turkish chief rabbi sent a fax to the museum's directors criticizing even minimal mention of Armenians, demanding that the museum include Turkish ambassadors in Europe who had allegedly rescued Jews from the Holocaust.[91] Kamhi would later boast about it in his autobiography: "As Kâmuran Gürün mentions in his memoirs, we worked to ensure that no other claims would be included in the museum." Accordingly, "Our Jewish community Presidents Jak Veissid and Naim Güleryüz and I, as well as Nedim Yahya and many other community members worked tirelessly on this issue." And "with the help of certain Israeli and American Jewish organizations, we were able to prevent the inclusion of the 'so-called Armenian genocide' in the Washington Holocaust Museum."[92]

The Los Angeles Museum of Tolerance opened the same year. Unlike its counterpart in Washington, it included the Armenian genocide as part of its permanent exhibition. The Turkish Foreign Ministry and the Turkish Jewish leadership were outraged. Using anti-Semitic tropes, the spokesman of the Foreign Ministry accused the director of the museum of having been bought off. A Turkish journalist echoed the argument, writing that although Turkish Jews had "performed an essential service both for their homeland, Turkey, and for their race" by ensuring that the genocide would not be mentioned at the museum in Washington, "world Jewry" should think about its "failure" to prevent the genocide's mention in Los Angeles. This "failure" by "world Jewry," he suggested, could be explained by it having been bribed into collaboration with funds given it by the state of California and its Armenian American governor.[93] An outraged Jak Kamhi sent a scathing fax from the Turkish Foreign Ministry offices to the director of the Museum of Tolerance. After decrying the museum's neglect of Ottoman and Turkish tolerance of Jews fleeing the Inquisition in 1492 and the Nazis in 1942, Kamhi leveraged anti-Semitic motifs and genocide denial in support of his complaint. "You deserve the highest award for ungratefulness and it is disgusting to think that all these were willfully made for money paid by others." He asks, "How can a Jew put on the same level the loss of millions of lives with those who perished in an act of rebellion? Did German Jews who lost their lives in concentration camps try to establish a separate sovereign state on German territory? Did they form armed bands and kill their German neighbors? How can you compare our innocent brethren who did not have a bare knife to defend themselves with pitiless bandits? How did you accept to denigrate the holiness of the Shoah for petty cash?" Then he pivots, contrasting the Jewish and Armenian experiences. "I, as a Turkish Jew, did not suffer from the Holocaust because my country protected me from it." He condemns the museum director's "criminal action" of having destroyed "the fruits of many constructive efforts" between the two allies (Turks and Jews), as well as "the amelioration of relations between Israel and Turkey . . . to the rank of embassies." He ends with the same anti-Semitic refrain: "How do you think Turks will judge your unwarranted action, as the whole world knows that you did these for money."[94]

Kamhi boasts about the campaign in his autobiography. "We have persistently worked for the removal" of the exhibition on the Armenian genocide from the Museum of Tolerance "since the 1990s."[95] He invited the director of the museum foundation to Turkey and "consequently received a positive response from officials at the museum; as a result, documents on the Armenian genocide were removed from the museum to be replaced with documents on the painful events [the genocide of Muslims] that had occurred in Bosnia."[96] He mentions how "I was able to come to an understanding" with the museum "regarding changing an anti-Turkish film, and had the chance to explain Turkey and 500 years of Jewish life in Turkey."[97] Indeed, in subsequent years the museum ceased showing a brief film that mentioned the Armenian genocide. In its place, a new film, sponsored by Kamhi, addressed the genocide of Muslims in Bosnia instead.[98]

Bensiyon Pinto, Three Decades a Lobbyist for Turkey

Businessman Bensiyon Pinto (b. 1936) has served the Turkish Jewish community since the 1970s: as Jak Veissid's deputy from 1980 to 1983; as an executive board member in 1989–1990 when the Quincentennial Foundation was established; from 1994 to 2004 as president of the community; and thereafter as its honorary chairman. The back cover of his autobiography, published by Turkey's largest publishing house, offers praise from then prime minister Recep Tayyip Erdoğan (prime minister, 2007–2014; president, 2014–present), former justice minister Cemil Çiçek, Turkish chief rabbi İsak Haleva, and then Israeli president Moshe Katsav.[99] Pinto boasts how he has always "fought on behalf of Turkey against the lobby" in the United States to prevent sanctions against Turkey.[100] Already in 1982, after meeting with European representatives in Turkey, Pinto made up his mind to "dedicate" his "entire life to change" the negative image foreigners held of Turkey.[101] He set a personal goal for himself: "Wherever I am and whatever platform I am on, I will promote Turkey." He fulfilled his vow by contacting Turkey's ambassadors to European nations and the United States, offering his services, mainly consisting of putting them in touch with leading Jews in their respective countries. In turn, the Turkish state regularly asked him to accompany prime ministers, presidents, and foreign ministers abroad, and when foreign dignitaries visited Turkey.[102] As he mentions repeatedly in his autobiography, he has been on very good terms with Israeli and Turkish prime ministers and presidents since the 1980s.[103] He credits Turgut Özal with instilling in him the importance of lobbying when the then prime minister asked Turkish Jews as a community to do some things for Turkey—namely, maintain communications with influential people in the United States to improve Turkey's image.[104] He told Özal, "You taught me what lobbying means."[105]

Pinto's autobiography contains letters from prominent people praising him for his tireless devotion to Turkey's international interests. In it, Erdoğan thanks him for "the services that you have rendered our country" and believes that he will "continue to defend Turkey's interests both at home and abroad."[106] Then deputy prime minister and foreign minister and future president Abdullah Gül (president, 2007–2014) also notes that Pinto "promoted Turkey abroad and made a leading contribution to Turkey's foreign relations."[107] General Necdet Timur stated that "his name came to the forefront in the context of international initiatives he undertook during difficult periods that caused serious problems for Turkey. . . . [S]tate and government officials who knew him well expected and believed that he would do something to help."[108] Implying the Armenian genocide, former foreign minister and prime minister Mesut Yılmaz notes, "In defending our country's interests" relating to the Ottoman past, the Turkish Jewish community has "made an important contribution."[109] Above all others, he maintains, Pinto "played a very important role as an intermediary who managed to get prominent members of the foreign Jewish lobbies [*sic*, communities] to come to Turkey and meet with us . . . and participated in some foreign visits getting these lobbies to act in Turkey's favor." A Turkish member of parliament is more explicit: "He mobilized all his friends to ensure that the draft resolution on the so-called Armenian genocide in the US House of Representatives was shelved, proving that he is a man who loves Turkey."[110]

Pinto boasts of his international lobbying efforts to deny the Armenian genocide, which he refers to as "the so-called Armenian genocide."[111] Pinto states that he has "been speaking loudly on this issue," trying "to explain to those around me, to the wider society and to state officials on several occasions that more comprehensive team work is needed to promote our [denialist] point of view." He fears the genocide will be recognized. He argues that when the US Congress threatens to pass a resolution recognizing genocide "it is not enough to say: 'Ahmet Bey, Mehmet Bey, Jak [Kamhi] Bey, and Bensiyon [Pinto] Bey, pack your bags, go and talk to the relevant people and sort out this business,'" and he proceeds to give a concrete example of how Turkish Jewish leaders play a role in lobbying on behalf of Turkey.

In 2003, during a dinner honoring the then Israeli head of state, Moshe Katzav, then Turkish prime minister Tayyip Erdoğan asked Pinto whether he could talk to the Israeli president about "the problems we are facing about the so-called genocide. We need to do something about America, and we need a helping hand." When he met with the Israeli president the following day, Pinto "explained the difficulties the Turkish state was experiencing with the so-called genocide." Pinto sat next to Katzav and explained Turkey's concerns, asking him to get in touch with his contacts in the United States. Katzav promised that he would "sort out this business"[112] and called him the next day. "Tell your prime minister that the matter has been settled." Pinto relayed the message to the prime minister in person.

Pinto uses this example to criticize Turkey's approach to genocide denial. Calling them "short-term solutions," Pinto advocated "more permanent measures," an argument he made to Erdoğan "whenever a suitable opportunity arose." He suggested the establishment of "a ministry or a directorate" staffed by well-trained people that would conduct lobbying activities "in a professional manner, not left to amateurs' goodwill." Pinto describes his other personal efforts in some detail. "I have tried my best recently. At a cocktail party given for the newly arrived US consul general in Istanbul, I explained to very important people how crucial it was to resolve the issue of [efforts to recognize] the so-called genocide."[113] "Let's claim ownership of our nation's history," he declares, by denying genocide and promoting a vision of Turkish tolerance of Jews, rather than coming to terms with the violent past.

Pinto notes that "during my time as chairman [of the Turkish Jewish community], we managed to achieve some results in our relations with the U.S. through our lobbying activities."[114] Lobbying, as he defines it, "is a form of public relations." Its essence is not "to deceive people," but to "find a clever way to inform your interlocutors. When there is a situation that is unpleasant from your nation's point of view, it is necessary never to remain silent, but to immediately intervene." He meets as many people as he can, and if he thinks someone "can be useful for my country, I try to strengthen the connection." For this purpose, he is "always asking myself: 'How can I be useful to my country?'" He tries always to explain Turkey to foreigners, consulting regularly with Veissid and Kamhi. He recounts having convinced the Israeli ambassador to Turkey to write a favorable opinion piece on Turkey, meeting with *New York Times* journalists critical of Turkey—as did Kamhi[115]—as well as the executive director of the American Jewish Committee, denying he was "Turkey's lawyer."[116] He boasts that he was able to convince the committee leader of his view, so that instead of condemning Turkey, it began to "defend Turkey's interests in America. This is called lobbying."[117]

Foreign Jewish Historians of the Ottoman Empire as Lobbyists for Turkey

The systematic effort to promote a utopian vision of Ottoman-Jewish and Turkish-Jewish harmony concomitant with Armenian genocide denial included recruiting foreign historians of the Ottoman Empire to join the effort. The two most prominent scholars to serve this role were Bernard Lewis and Stanford Shaw. Until the 1990s, one was hard pressed to find a single foreign historian of the Ottoman Empire who utilized Ottoman-language sources, conducted research in Turkey, and recognized the Armenian genocide. Lewis and Shaw are typical of such non-Turkish historians who identified with Turks (as opposed to Arabs, and more specifically, Palestinians) and taught at elite European and American universities from the 1950s to the 1990s.

Lewis was an immensely influential historian, shaping opinion about Islam and Muslims in academia, popular culture, and politics for much of the twentieth century and the first decade of the twenty-first century, especially in the United Kingdom and United States.[118] A linguistically gifted Jewish *Wunderkind* from North London, Lewis earned a BA in 1936 and PhD in 1939 at the School of Oriental and African Studies (SOAS), becoming fluent in all the major languages of the Middle East. During World War II, he served in British intelligence and the Foreign Office, largely due to his linguistic skills. Others outside the UK were impressed by his abilities: Lewis became the first foreigner given access to the Ottoman archives in Turkey, conducting research there at the end of the 1940s. At that time, he began a lifelong relationship with the Turkish state and academia. He taught at SOAS until the early 1970s, when he took a position at Princeton University, retiring in the mid-1980s. At Princeton, he joined a department whose members had long condoned Ottoman violence against Armenians. Ottoman historian of Jewish background, Norman Itzkowitz (who first conducted research in Turkey in the mid-1950s, and who taught at Princeton from 1958 to his death in 2019), denied the Armenian genocide by promoting the view of "mutual hostilities" between Armenians and Turks. Itzkowitz's mentor, Lewis V. Thomas (who taught Turkish at Princeton from 1947 to his death in 1958, when Itkowitz took over his position), reflecting the Cold War context, justified Ottoman atrocities against Armenians in the name of "progress."[119]

Lewis served as an editor of the *Encyclopedia of Islam* from 1960 to 1991. He published nearly three dozen books, some of which, such as *The Arabs in History* (1950, sixth edition, 1993) and *The Emergence of Modern Turkey* (1961, 1968, new edition 2001), have been used as standard university textbooks and required reading in government offices, including the US State Department. Others of his writings have been popular with nonspecialists, including "The Roots of Muslim Rage" (*Atlantic Monthly*, 1990), which introduced the clash of civilizations thesis; "The Revolt of Islam" (*New Yorker*, November 2001); and his two best sellers, *What Went Wrong? Western Impact and Middle Eastern Response*, which appeared shortly after the September 11, 2001, attacks, and *The Crisis of Islam: Holy War and Unholy Terror*, published a year later.[120] His books and articles have been translated into dozens of languages. He was interviewed and often cited in the international press.

Remarkable for a scholar were the breadth and depth of Lewis's government connections. From World War II, when he served in British intelligence, to the era of the Gulf War (1990–1991) and US invasion of Iraq (2003) he had sustained and intimate connections with ruling governments in Europe, the Middle East, and the United States, serving in an advisory role, explaining Muslims and Islam to parliaments, prime ministers, presidents, royalty, and even the pope. His influence in the George W. Bush White House and Pentagon is well known. One cannot overestimate his impact.

In his autobiography, *Notes on a Century: Reflections of a Middle East Historian*, Lewis relies on old Jewish tropes by referring to the Muslim as the friend of the Jew and the Christian as the enemy. He explains how, as a Jew, he is aware of the "affinities," especially religious affinities, between Judaism and Islam, Jews and Muslims. "These affinities, and my growing awareness of them, certainly helped me achieve some understanding, even a sympathetic understanding, of Islam."[121] He mentions how "the great majority" of the Jews of Spain "found refuge in the Ottoman Empire."[122] After discussing how Christians persecuted Jews in medieval Europe, he explains that anti-Semitism, a hostility that "attributes a quality of innate and cosmic evil to the Jews" is "distinctively Christian."[123] In the Muslim-majority world, by contrast, "in most of medieval and early modern Islamic history, Jews seemed to have fared rather better than Christians."[124] This is because "after the death of the Prophet, Christendom was the main rival and enemy, and Jews were unimportant and at times even useful. So the attitude to Jews was different. I wouldn't say it was friendly but it was more tolerant than toward Christians. This continued into the Ottoman period, when Jews were found to be extremely useful—a valuable, revenue-producing asset."[125]

Positive views of Muslim-Jewish relations go together with his denial of the Armenian genocide. Lewis mentions how in the 1961 version of *The Emergence of Modern Turkey* he used the term "holocaust" (uncapitalized) to describe the massacres of Armenians by Turks in 1915.[126] He claims falsely that in the third edition, "published a year later," after which Adolf Eichmann had been tried and executed in Israel, he "replaced the word 'holocaust' with 'slaughter'—not to question or minimize what happened, but to avoid a comparison with the destruction of six million Jews in Nazi-ruled Europe, for which 'holocaust' had by then become almost a technical term." However, the third edition of his book was not published until 2002. The first edition (1961) and second edition (1968) both use the term "holocaust." As he states in the preface to *The Emergence of Modern Turkey*, he began the book in the academic year 1949–1950, which he spent mostly in Istanbul. At that time, just after the (Jewish) Holocaust (capitalized), Lewis chose the same word as an accurate description of what the Armenians experienced in the Ottoman Empire. When he revised the book in the 1960s he also felt the term "holocaust" described the fate of the Armenians, as well as that of the Turks. It was not until his reworking of the book in the late 1990s that he dispensed with the term altogether. The timing is significant.

In *The Emergence of Modern Turkey*, Lewis uses the provocation thesis to blame the Armenians for their own demise.[127] Lewis argues that whereas the Armenians had once been loyal and trusted by Ottoman Muslims, the creation of Russian Armenia "on the eastern border of Turkey [Ottoman Empire]" where "Armenian governors and generals ruled provinces and commanded armies," led to the creation of an Armenian nationalist movement that "was the deadliest of all threats."[128] This was because the Armenians "lay in the very heart of the Turkish homeland," and "to renounce these lands would have meant . . . the dissolution of the Turkish state." The problem with this assertion is that a Turkish state did not yet exist. It is important to note that Lewis does not entertain the notion that it could also have been the homeland of the Armenians (or the Greeks or Jews or Kurds for that matter). This is an "implied rationale" for genocide:[129] "In this transparent paragraph Lewis subtly rewrote the history of Anatolia from a land in which Armenians and Kurds were the earlier inhabitants into one in which they become an obstacle to the national aspirations of the Turks." Moreover, his "reading of a notion of ethnic homogeneity as the basis for a national republic of the Kemalist type, which lay in the future, into the moment of Armenian annihilation is ahistorical and anachronistic." [130] In *The Jews of Islam*, Lewis also consistently referred anachronistically to Ottoman Muslims as Turks, further evidence that his concerns are with the modern era and the present.

Lewis argues that the placement of the Armenians in the "Turkish" heartland led to a struggle "between two nations for the possession of a single homeland," which he believes belongs rightfully to the Turks. This struggle "ended with the terrible holocaust of 1915, when a million and a half Armenians perished."[131] The "holocaust" destroyed Armenians alone. The second edition published in 1968 retains the same term—"holocaust"— but adds doubt about the total number of Armenians killed, and mentions that potentially more Turks were killed in the same holocaust: the struggle "ended with the terrible *holocaust* [emphasis added] of 1915, when, according to some estimates, up to a million and a half Armenians perished, as well as an unknown number of Turks."[132] In the third edition published in 2001, Lewis edits the text so that the struggle "ended with the terrible *slaughter* [emphasis added] of 1915, when, according to estimates, more than a million Armenians perished, as well as an unknown number of Turks."[133] The common noun "holocaust" is changed to "slaughter," and the number of Armenian victims decreases from "a million and a half" to "more than a million." The victims of the "slaughter" include Turks. Why had he changed his view? Could it be related to his being named an honorary member of the Turkish Historical Society (1972), being awarded the Citation of Honor by the Turkish Ministry of Culture (1973), being named an honorary member of the Atatürk Academy of History, Language, and Culture (1984), or being awarded the Annual Education Award for Outstanding Achievement in the Promotion of American-Turkish Studies (1985)? What had happened during the 1980s?

In his autobiography, Lewis notes that in 1985 the Armenians and their supporters attempted to get the US Congress to recognize the massacres as a genocide. Such efforts, presumably, caused him to change his own view on historical events. Lewis was the most prominent academic to have signed a letter of protest against the effort.[134] In 1993, he gave a number of interviews in the French press regarding that year's US congressional bill to recognize the Armenian genocide, which, like all other bills before and after, was defeated. Lewis again argued that "the Armenians posed a problem for the Turks because of the advance of the Russians and anti-Ottoman population in Turkey."[135] Note here the use of the word *Turkey* in place of *Ottoman Empire*, an odd "mistake" for a historian to make. For the "Turks [Ottomans]," he continues, "it was necessary to take punitive and preventative measures against an unstable population in a region that was menaced by an alien invasion." He concedes that "terrible things took place and that numerous Armenians—and also Turks—perished." However, he expresses strong doubt that "that there was a systematic decision to annihilate the Armenian nation."[136]

He narrates the event by proffering the provocation thesis that "while the Armenians suffered appalling losses, the comparison with the Holocaust was misleading. The one arose from an armed rebellion. . . . The Armenians, seizing the opportunity presented by World War I, rose in rebellion against their Turkish [Ottoman] overlords in alliance with Britain and Russia, the two powers with which Turkey [the Ottoman Empire] was at war." After the "rebellions of the Armenians" were "suppressed," the "surviving Armenians" were sent into exile. During the "struggle" and deportation, "great numbers of Armenians were killed."[137] In other words, the Armenians, supported by Turkey's eternal enemies, are responsible for their grim fate.

It should be noted here that Lewis's argument is similar to how Atatürk had explained away the genocide. In his first public speech after establishing his rebel government in Ankara in 1919, Atatürk had declared, "Whatever has befallen the non-Muslim elements living in our country is the result of the policies of separatism they pursued in a savage manner, when they allowed themselves to be made tools of foreign intrigues and abused their privileges.... And I want definitely to say that these events are on a level far removed from the many forms of oppression which are committed in the states of Europe without any excuse."[138]

Lewis compares these events, and the Armenians, unfavorably with the Holocaust, and the Jews. "The slaughter of the Jews, first in Germany and then in German-occupied Europe, was a different matter. There was no rebellion, armed or otherwise. On the contrary, the German Jews were intensely loyal to their country."[139] The Armenians, as Lewis has established, were traitors. In sum, according to Lewis, the Armenians deserved their fate and the Jews did not: the Armenians "were involved in an armed rebellion; the Jews were not, but were attacked solely because of their identity."[140] According to Ronald Suny's perceptive formulation of Lewis's argument, "There was no genocide, and the Armenians are to blame for it."[141] Lewis's "statement distinguishing the Armenian case from the Holocaust" may be downloaded from the website of the Assembly of Turkish American Associations.

In 1995, Lewis was held liable on civil charges, brought against him in Paris by the Forum of Armenian Associations and the Ligue internationale contre le racisme et l'antisémitisme (LICRA), for "inflicting emotional damage upon another party because of his dereliction of responsibility as a scholar."[142] He claims that the Turkish embassy in Paris had offered to pay all his legal bills, but he turned them down.[143] Lewis mentions how "a number of distinguished French Turcologists" signed a letter "rebutting the slurs leveled by the plaintiffs against their entire profession."[144] Lewis was defended by his colleague, Jewish historian of the Ottoman Empire Gilles Veinstein, who in an article that relies on the work of genocide deniers and non-Jewish students of Stanford Shaw, Justin McCarthy, and Heath Lowry, and the Ministry of Foreign Affairs official Gürün, denies that the

Ottomans committed genocide against the Armenians.[145] Finally, adding insult to injury, Lewis compares his Armenian opponents to Nazis. "Five plaintiffs in four lawsuits had a battery of lawyers against my single, valiant defender. Against such odds, I had about as much chance as the Polish cavalry confronting the German tanks in 1939."[146]

Stanford Shaw, a native of the American Midwest, was more extreme than either his mentor, Lewis, or his dissertation advisor, Lewis V. Thomas. Shaw earned an MA in Near Eastern history at Princeton University in 1955 and then traveled to London to study under Lewis at SOAS. He pursued PhD research in Cairo and Istanbul from 1955 to 1957. It was not a good time to be a Jew with a British surname in Egypt. A cohort of army officers had overthrown the British- and Jewish-friendly monarch, King Farouk, in 1952. Two years later, after uncovering an Israeli spy ring made up of Egyptian Jews, they choreographed show trials and hanged the Jews in public. In 1956, the same revolutionary officers nationalized the Suez Canal, leading to the withdrawal of the British. In the wake of a joint Anglo-French-Israeli attack, Egypt expelled tens of thousands of European and Egyptian Jews, along with Armenians and Greeks. Nor was Turkey free of anti-Christian and anti-Jewish violence during this period, the time when Shaw first resided there. The pogrom of September 6–7, 1955, in Istanbul mainly targeted Greeks, but Armenian and Jewish businesses, homes, and houses of worship were also looted, and individuals from all three groups were beaten, raped, and killed. Although there at the time, Shaw does not mention the 1955 pogrom in his opus, *The Jews of the Ottoman Empire and the Turkish Republic*, published over three decades later. Indeed, in preference to listing Jews alongside Greeks and Armenians as victims of violence at the hands of Turkish Muslims, Shaw alleges that in the late 1960s and early 1970s, Greeks attacked "Jews and Jewish property in Istanbul, Izmir, and Cyprus as part of the attacks on Turks which accompanied Greece's efforts to annex independent Cyprus following the British withdrawal" in 1960.[147] After completing his degree in 1958, Shaw taught at Harvard University for a decade, then at UCLA for three decades, and finally at a private Turkish university until the end of his life.

What matters most to a historian is access to sources. If she cannot access original archival and literary material, she cannot produce original research. Shaw received a very warm welcome in Turkey from its officials and Jewish establishment. When I met him in the late 1990s at his home in lovely Bebek, Istanbul, I found him to be friendly, affable, helpful, generous, and modest. No wonder Turks liked him so much. I was surprised when he warned me, however, not to wear a Star of David necklace in religious neighborhoods of the city or at the office of the Istanbul mufti where I conducted dissertation research. I did not, nor would I have. Shaw was given access to sources that to this day none others have seen. When a historian receives access to materials in such circumstances, he can cherry-pick his selections, presenting what he finds as the sum total of what exists; given that his claims are made based upon original material unseen by others, no one will be able to verify or refute them. Forever indebted to this preferential treatment and the accompanying exclusive access, the historian adopts the views of his friends as his own. Should he have an epiphany and shed these views, access to VIP treatment and culled sources would be lost.

With the publication in 1977 of what was to become the standard textbook on Ottoman history, *History of the Ottoman Empire and Modern Turkey*, Shaw and his non-Jewish Turkish wife, Ezel Kural Shaw, gained notoriety. In the second of their two-volume study, Shaw and Shaw repeatedly deny the Armenian genocide, accuse Armenians of slaughtering Turks, and characterize Armenians as disloyal.[148] Perhaps for this reason, after Shaw's Los Angeles home was bombed, the permanent Turkish representative to the United Nations referred to it as "a good history."[149] Referring to the 1896 massacres, Shaw and Shaw note that the sultan ordered "the government to crack down on the Armenian merchants of Istanbul to lessen their substantial economic power," thus appearing to justify the massacres. But "imagine if a historian wrote that Hitler's government had decided to 'crack down' on Berlin's Jews," thus justifying the Holocaust?[150] Referring to the slaughter of Armenians in Adana in 1909 as an Armenian "uprising," they deny that Armenians were specifically targeted in massacres,[151] deploying instead the provocation thesis in order to blame the Armenians for their own deaths. But by referring to the deaths of "people of all religions" they convert tens of thousands of Armenian victims into people without ethnoreligious identity. They repeatedly refer to all Ottoman Armenians as terrorists, as tyrants who oppress Muslims and Jews, and as traitors siding with Russia.[152]

Shaw and Shaw justify the deportation of Armenians from the eastern provinces in 1915, arguing that it was undertaken "to get them away from all areas where they might undermine the Ottoman campaign against Russia." They claim that the Ottoman army was ordered to protect them, "to make certain that neither the Kurds nor any other Muslims used the situation to

gain vengeance for the long years of Armenian terrorism." Despite these pre-
cautions, Shaw and Shaw conclude that "about 300,000 died if one accepts
the Ottoman census reports, or 1.3 million if the Armenian sources are utilized."[153] The reader has no doubts as to which figure they should trust. They
then deny that the Armenian genocide occurred. "The Armenians also feel
that the deaths resulted from a planned policy of genocide by the Ottoman
government. This accusation was repeated by several European commis-
sions during and after the war." Postwar official Ottoman statements, trials,
and executions of perpetrators, as well as eyewitness accounts of perpetrators, their allies, and survivors—all these facts are ignored. Against Armenian "feelings," which the reader is led to understand as subjective and
untrustworthy, and European "accusations," which can only be false, Shaw
and Shaw counter with Ottoman archival sources they portray as objective
and reliable. "The Ottoman cabinet records, however, do not confirm this,
but, rather, manifest numerous efforts to investigate and correct a situation
in which some 6 million people—Turks, Greeks, Arabs, Armenians, Jews,
and others—were being killed by a combination of revolts, bandit attacks,
massacres and counter massacres, and famine and disease, compounded
by destructive and brutal foreign invasions in which all the people of the
empire, Muslim and non-Muslim alike, had their victims and criminals."[154]
Rather than the Ottomans being responsible, they blame Armenian and
Greek revolts, bandit attacks, and massacres, and "foreign invasions," leaving the reader with the impression there was a civil war rather than genocide. Notably, the choice of the figure "6 million" is neither arbitrary, nor
based on any data; the highly symbolic number is chosen to draw a parallel
not between Armenian and Jewish victims of genocide, as one would expect
from a serious historian, but between the Ottomans and the Holocaust. All
Ottoman peoples suffered alike, they claim, but they focus on Armenian
"slaughter" of Muslims. They conclude that genocide claims are little more
than European propaganda, and they refer to the "so-called crimes" of the
wartime Ottoman regime.[155]

A recipient of the Medal of Honor from the president of the Turkish
Republic, Shaw chose to be buried at a Jewish cemetery in Istanbul. In
recognition of Shaw's decades-long efforts at promoting a positive international reputation for Turkey based on a utopian vision of Jewish-Turkish
harmony on the one hand, and Armenian genocide denial on the other
hand, his funeral was attended by the leaders of Turkey's Jewish community, including the chief rabbi İsaak Haleva and leading Turkish Jewish

lobbyist on behalf of Turkey Jak Kamhi, as well as the then deputy prime minister and foreign minister, and future president, Abdullah Gül.[156]

Conclusion

Anti-Semitism and denial of the Armenian genocide go hand in hand. Motivated by the anti-Semitic idea that Jews are powerful beyond their numbers and have the power to influence the decisions of all European and North American governments, the Turkish foreign ministry turned to Turkish Jews to serve as the "friend," in the guise of a Turkish lobby abroad. Driven by an affective disposition of gratefulness, as well as fear and anxiety, leading Turkish Jewish industrialists accepted the call and promoted a positive image of Turkey to foreigners, by opposing the aims of Turkey's "enemies," the Greek and Armenian lobbies, which included hindering recognition of the Armenian genocide.

Following the invasion and occupation of Cyprus in 1974, Turkey desired an improved international image, an end to an arms embargo, access to international markets, and more sophisticated weapons.[157] Improved relations with the United States and Israel would satisfy these aims, but at the time Turkey had no effective lobby. Accordingly, it turned to Turkish Jews to serve as intermediaries with US Jewry and Israel to promote Turkey's foreign policy goals. Leading Turkish Jews, such as Jak Kamhi, readily served Turkish government aims, from which they, too, would benefit. Notably, "the single most important factor in successfully concluding the process of normalization between Israel and Turkey" was denial of the Armenian genocide.[158] Kamhi's company hired a public relations firm in the US to promote a positive image of Turkey in general, and specifically "to oppose any resolutions regarding remembrance of the Armenian 'genocide.'"[159] It was largely thanks to the efforts of Kamhi and the Turkish Jewish community that during the 1980s the leadership of the various American Jewish organizations were "eventually brought around" to genocide denial, thereby helping to block it from being included in the US Holocaust museum and in school curricula. The American Jewish organizations agreed to genocide denial in order to support Israel's aims and to prevent any harm coming to Turkish and Middle Eastern Jewry.[160] Their efforts led to improved and then full diplomatic relations between Turkey and Israel.

These diplomatic events and political lobbying campaigns formed the background to the recruitment of foreign Jewish scholars, especially

Bernard Lewis and Stanford Shaw, to promote the same views: the loyal Jew as the friend of the Turks and the treacherous Christian (Armenian and Greek) as their common enemy; the blaming of anti-Semitism in Turkey on Christians, even as it was articulated by leading Turkish foreign ministry officials and Turkish presidents working with Turkish Jews in pursuance of their foreign policy aims; and the denial of the Armenian genocide. The Turkish Jewish lobby would be institutionalized as the Quincentennial Foundation, led by Kamhi, which worked in concert with the Ministry of Foreign Affairs to improve Turkey's international image, explicitly countering efforts to recognize the Armenian genocide by promoting a vision of "500 years of peace and brotherhood" between Turks and Jews.

Notes

1. Göçek, *Denial of Violence*, 600n87.
2. Ibid., 429.
3. Ibid., 438–439.
4. Seyhan Bayraktar, "The Grammar of Denial: State, Society, and Turkish-Armenian Relations," Roundtable, One Hundred Years of Denial: The Armenian Genocide, *International Journal of Middle East Studies* 47, no. 4 (2015): 802. Bayraktar is based in Switzerland.
5. Ibid., 803.
6. Kâmuran Gürün, *Ermeni dosyası* (Ankara: Türk Tarih Kurumu, 1983); Göçek, *Denial of Violence*, 443.
7. Kâmuran Gürün, *Fırtınalı yıllar dışişleri müsteşarlığı anıları* (Istanbul: Milliyet, 1995), 351–352, quoted in Bali, *Model Citizens of the State*, 239.
8. Bali, *Model Citizens of the State*, 241.
9. Gürün, *Fırtınalı yıllar dışişleri müsteşarlığı anıları*, 428–429, quoted in Bali, *Model Citizens of the State*, 243–244.
10. See the no-longer-active website of the Turkish Historical Society, https://web.archive.org/web/20080725080032/http://www.ttk.org.tr/index.php?Page=Sayfa&No=1.
11. *Arşiv belgelerine göre Kafkaslaräda ve Anadolu'da Ermeni mezâlimi I: 1906–1918/ Armenian Violence and Massacre in the Caucasus and Anatolia Based on Archives* (Ankara: T. C. Başbakanlık Devlet Arşivleri Genel Müdürlüğü, 1995), 24.
12. Ibid., 25.
13. Ibid., 7–8.
14. Letter of the Turkish Ambassador in Washington, Baki Ilkin, May 27, 1999, in Vahakn N. Dadrian, *Key Elements in the Turkish Denial of the Armenian Genocide* (Cambridge, MA: Zoryan Institute, 1999), Appendix 1, 59–74, quoted in Auron, *The Banality of Denial*, 256.
15. According to the official Ottoman census of 1914 the number of Jews in eastern Anatolia amounted to 31,650, broken down by region as follows: Bitlis province, 0; Adana province, 66; Aleppo province, which included Antep, 12,193; Diyarbekir province, which included Diyarbekir and Mardin, 2,085; Mamuretulaziz province, which included Malatya,

Harput, and Dersim, 14,807; Van province, 1,383; Urfa sancak, 865; and Maraş sancak, 251. Shaw, *The Jews of the Ottoman Empire and the Turkish Republic*, Appendix 2: Population of the Ottoman Empire in the Late Nineteenth and Early Twentieth Centuries According to Official Ottoman Census Reports, 273–285. The next official census, the first in the Turkish Republic, which was conducted in 1927, counted 2,546 Jews in these same provinces: Adana, 159; Diyarbekir, 392; Gaziantep, 742; Hakkari, 43; Malatya, 8; Maraş, 265; Mardin, 490; Urfa, 318; Van, 129. Ibid., Appendix 3: Jewish Population in the Turkish Republic, 1927–1965, 285–286.

16. *British Documents on Ottoman Armenians*, ed. Bilâl Şimşir (Ankara: Türk Tarih Kurumu Basimevi, 1989); Bilâl Şimşir, *Şehit diplomatlarımız* (Ankara: Bilgi, 2001); Bilâl Şimşir, *Ermeni meselesi 1774–2005* (Ankara: Bilgi, 2005).

17. The conference at public Boğaziçi University was canceled by court order but subsequently held at private Bilgi University. Sebnem Arsu, "Seminar on 1915 Massacre of Armenians to Go Ahead," *New York Times*, September 24, 2005.

18. See *Armenians in the Ottoman Empire and Modern Turkey, 1912–1926*, ed. Justin McCarthy, Bilâl Şimşir, Heath Lowry, and Mim Kemal Öke (Istanbul: Boğaziçi University Press, 1984); Guenter Lewy, *The Armenian Massacres in Ottoman Turkey: A Disputed Genocide* (Salt Lake City: University of Utah Press, 2005). Lewy argues "no authentic documentary evidence exists to prove the culpability of the central government of Turkey for the massacre of the 1915–6." Ibid., 206, cited in Marc A. Mamigonian, "Academic Denial of the Armenian Genocide in American Scholarship: Denialism as Manufactured Controversy," *Genocide Studies International* 9, no. 1 (2015): 68. While denying genocide, he does blame Armenian actions for their fate: "Armenians can hardly claim that they suffered for no reason at all." Lewy, *The Armenian Massacres in Ottoman Turkey*, 109, cited in Mamigonian, "Academic Denial of the Armenian Genocide in American Scholarship."

19. Bilâl Şimşir, *Türk Yahudiler: Avrupa ırkçılarına karşı Türkiye'nin mücadelesi*, 2 vols. (Ankara: Bilgi, 2010).

20. Gül Demir and Niki Gamm, "Jak Kamhi: A Man of Exemplary Character and Determination," *Hürriyet Daily News*, August 18, 2007.

21. Jak Kamhi is the father of businessman and Turkish MP Cefi Kamhi (in office, True Path Party, 1995–1999), subsequently Turkey's representative to the European Jewish Parliament; and of Hayati Kamhi, owner of a world-leading boat-building company.

22. The same blurb appears both on the original Turkish version and on the English translation. Jak Kamhi, *Gördüklerim yaşadıklarım* (Istanbul: Remzi, 2013); and Jak V. Kamhi, *What I've Seen What I've Experienced*, edited by Heath Lowry (Istanbul: Bahçeşehir University Press, 2013).

23. Shaw, *The Jews of the Ottoman Empire and the Turkish Republic*, Appendix 3, 285. The last Turkish census to identify citizens by religion was taken in 1965, from which the 38,000 figure is derived.

24. Bali, *Model Citizens of the State*, 176.

25. Ibid., 191–192.

26. Kamhi, *Gördüklerim yaşadıklarım*, 169.

27. Ibid., 230–231.

28. Bali, *Model Citizens of the State*, 196.

29. Denis Ojalvo, "Le Lobbysme juif en Turquie" (MA thesis, Galatasaray University, 2005). A Turkish summary is available on the Turkish chief rabbinate's home page as "Türk Yahudileri lobiciliği," http://www.turkyahudileri.com/index.php/tr/makale-ve-tezler/114-turk -yahudi-lobiciligi-1.

30. Gürün, *Fırtınalı yıllar dışişleri müsteşarlığı anıları*, 430–431, quoted in Bali, *Model Citizens of the State*, 245.

31. Gürün, *Fırtınalı yıllar dışişleri müsteşarlığı anıları*, 433, quoted in Göçek, *Denial of Violence*, 448.

32. Sami Kohen, "Dispatch from Istanbul," *Jewish Chronicle* (London), March 2, 1984, cited in Mallet, *La Turquie, les Turcs et les Juifs*, 395.

33. Mallet, *La Turquie, les Turcs et les Juifs*, 408.

34. Kamhi, *Gördüklerim yaşadıklarım*, 231.

35. Ibid., 231–232.

36. Ibid., 233.

37. Ibid., 227.

38. Ibid., 239.

39. Bali, *Model Citizens of the State*, 201.

40. Kamhi, *Gördüklerim yaşadıklarım*, 259–260.

41. Bali, *Model Citizens of the State*, 205.

42. Judith Miller, *One by One, by One: Facing the Holocaust* (New York: Simon and Schuster, 1990), 259, quoted in ibid., 206.

43. Ibid., 207.

44. Bali, *Model Citizens of the State*, 254.

45. Gürün, *Fırtınalı günler*, 345–346, quoted in Bali, *Model Citizens of the State*, 254.

46. Auron, *The Banality of Denial*, 63.

47. Vitali Hakko, *Hayatım. Vakko.* (Istanbul: Şedele, 1997), 190.

48. Ibid., 189–190, 193, 194.

49. Ibid., 197.

50. Nineteen years later, during an official visit to Turkey in 2001, Peres would declare to the Turkish press that the Armenian "allegations" of genocide are "absurd." Cited in Mallet, *La Turquie, les Turcs et les Juifs*, 421.

51. Asseo reported his conversations with Turkish government officials to the Israeli consul in Istanbul. Report of the consul general Yehuda Levitt to Moshe Sasson, chargé d'affaires at Israel's Ankara embassy, quoted in Bali, *Model Citizens of the State*, 98.

52. Ibid., 101.

53. "Türkiye hahambaşılığının açıklaması, *Şalom*, June 1, 1966, quoted in ibid., 110–111.

54. Eldad Ben Aharon, "A Unique Denial: Israel's Foreign Policy and the Armenian Genocide," *British Journal of Middle East Studies* 42, no. 4 (2015): 649.

55. Rozen, *A History of the Jewish Community in the Istanbul*, xi–xii.

56. "Israelis Said to Oppose Parley after Threat to Turkish Jews," *New York Times*, June 3, 1982, quoted in Auron, *The Banality of Denial*, 220.

57. Published June 10, 1982. The director of the American Jewish Committee's Middle Eastern Affairs department George Gruen clarifies the matter, explaining that the ambassador was correct in that Turkish Jews were not in danger, but that Turkey had still engaged in a sort of blackmail. Those whose lives were in danger were the Iraqi and Syrian Jews secretly being helped by Turkey. According to Gruen, "officials in Ankara told Israeli and American Jewish contacts that Turkey might have to reconsider its humanitarian and compassionate policy in illegally helping Jewish refugees . . . if the Israeli and Jewish communities engaged in blackening Turkey's name . . . by raising the World War I Armenian issue." Bali, *Model Citizens of the State*, 248–249.

58. Quoted in Auron, *The Banality of Denial*, 221.

59. "Turkish Threats to U.S. Reported," *New York Times*, June 22, 1982, quoted in ibid., 221.
60. Bali, *Model Citizens of the State*, 251–252.
61. Rauf Tamer, "Ateşle oynamak," *Tercüman*, August 19, 1981, quoted in ibid., 252.
62. Rauf Tamer, "Bu haftadan kalan," *Tercüman*, August 23, 1981, quoted in ibid., 252.
63. Quoted in ibid., 252–253. The statement was published in three Turkish newspapers.
64. Cited in ibid., 253.
65. Ben Aharon, "A Unique Denial," 646–647.
66. Ibid., 647.
67. Ibid., 648.
68. Ibid., 649.
69. Göçek, *Denial of Violence*, 447.
70. Ibid., 451.
71. Ibid., 453.
72. "Armenian Genocide PBS debate," YouTube video, 26:27, from a debate panel televised by PBS on April 17, 2006, posted by "Ellen Salmonson," February 11, 2017, https://www.you tube.com/watch?v=dOo3QlxWZ5Q.
73. Concerning the Institute of Turkish Studies, Kamhi notes, "On the instigation of Ambassador Şükrü Elekdağ, our Turkish American compatriots were encouraged to organize institutions, and as a result, a number of influential foundations and associations were established." Kamhi, *Gördüklerim yaşadıklarım*, 347. Like most scholars in Ottoman and Turkish studies, I, too, benefited from a grant from the Institute of Turkish Studies at the beginning of my career.
74. Kamhi, *Gördüklerim yaşadıklarım*, 348.
75. Sachar, *Farewell España*, 110.
76. Bali, *Model Citizens of the State*, 235–236.
77. Auron, *The Banality of Denial*, 216, 227; Bali, *Model Citizens of the State*, 274; Howard Eissenstat, "Children of Özal: The New Face of Turkish Studies," *Journal of the Ottoman and Turkish Studies Association* 1, no. 1–2 (2014): 28; Mamigonian, "Academic Denial of the Armenian Genocide in American Scholarship," 67.
78. Quoted in Eissenstat, "Children of Özal," 24–25.
79. William Honon, "Princeton Is Accused of Fronting for the Turkish Government," *New York Times*, May 22, 1996.
80. Quoted in Bali, *Model Citizens of the State*, 275.
81. M. Ali Birand, "ABD ile ilişkilerde büyük bir kriz yaklaşıyor," *Milliyet*, December 19, 1987, and Melih Aşk, "Yahudi ve Ermeni ayıbı," *Milliyet*, December 20, 1987, quoted in ibid., 287.
82. Cited in Bali, *Model Citizens of the State*, 289.
83. Ibid., 290.
84. Auron, *The Banality of Denial*, 103–104.
85. Ibid., 105–106.
86. Bali, *Model Citizens of the State*, 282.
87. Auron, *The Banality of Denial*, 109.
88. Bali, *Model Citizens of the State*, 277–278.
89. Ibid., 284.
90. "Red ediyoruz," *Şalom*, May 2, 1990, quoted in Bali, *Model Citizens of the State*, 284.
91. Bali, *Model Citizens of the State*, 293.
92. Kamhi, *Gördüklerim yaşadıklarım*, 345.

93. "Ermeni vali Ankara'ya kızdırdı," *Milliyet*, August 8, 1985, and Metin Toker, "Bunu biz değil dünya Yahudileri düşünsün," *Milliyet*, August 11, 1985, cited in Bali, *Model Citizens of the State*, 295.

94. Cited in Bali, *Model Citizens of the State*, 296–297.

95. Kamhi, *Gördüklerim yaşadıklarım*, 345.

96. Ibid., 346.

97. Ibid., 244.

98. Letter from Jak Kamhi to Rıfat Bali, cited in Bali, *Model Citizens of the State*, 299. In recent years the museum has commemorated the genocide by hosting events on April 24.

99. Bensiyon Pinto, *Anlatmasam olmazdı: Geniş toplumda Yahudi olmak* (I had to tell it: To be Jewish in Turkish society) (Istanbul: Doğan, 2008); Bensiyon Pinto, *Jude sein in der Türkei: Erinnerungen des Ehrenvorsitzenden der jüdischen Gemeinde der Türkei Bensiyon Pinto*, trans. Richard Wittman (Würzburg: Ergon, 2010); Bensiyon Pinto, *My Life as a Turkish Jew: Memoirs of the President of the Turkish-Jewish Community, 1989–2004*, interviewed by Tülay Güler, ed. Leyla Engin Arık, trans. Nicole Pope (Kindle edition, 2011).

100. Pinto, *Anlatmasam olmazdı*, 165.

101. Ibid., 286.

102. Ibid., 287.

103. Ibid., 291.

104. Ibid., 292.

105. Ibid., 293.

106. Ibid., 307.

107. Ibid., 309.

108. Ibid., 318.

109. Ibid., 321.

110. Ibid., 314.

111. Ibid., 166.

112. Ibid., 167.

113. Ibid., 168.

114. Ibid., 272.

115. In his autobiography, Kamhi also mentions how he has persuaded American journalists to change their view. In 1999, the Turkish ambassador to the United States was not pleased with William Safire's writing. The ambassador asked Kamhi to host him when he visited Turkey. Kamhi introduced him to the Israeli ambassador and leaders of the Turkish Jewish community. Kamhi boasts about how Safire had written an article after the visit in which he stated, "People in Istanbul explained that in 1492, when Ferdinand and Isabella expelled the Jews from Spain, Ottoman Sultan Bayezid II welcomed the refugees to his country." Kamhi, *Gördüklerim yaşadıklarım*, 280.

116. Pinto, *Anlatmasam olmazdı*, 279.

117. Ibid., 280.

118. His post as assistant lecturer in "the History of the Near and Middle East," established in 1938 at the School of Oriental and African Studies, University of London, was the first in the United Kingdom (located in a history department) and second in Western Europe (after Claude Cahen in Paris). In 1949, as full professor, he was appointed the first chair of "the History of the Near and Middle East" at the same institution, serving until 1974. Bernard Lewis, with Buntzie Ellis Churchill, *Notes on a Century: Reflections of a Middle East Historian* (New York: Viking, 2012), 86–88.

119. Itzkowitz denied the Armenian genocide in a 1968 book review, where he prefers the term "Armenian problem" to genocide or persecution, arguing that "it is undeniable that the Armenians suffered, but their suffering has to be seen against the background of their own atrocities committed against the Turks wherever Armenians had the opportunity." He accuses the author of the book he reviews of being biased against Turks and a poor historian because he "condemns the Turks . . . for what he believes to have been a decided attempt at genocide." Itzkowitz finds such an account "most disappointing and regrettable." Norman Itzkowitz, review of *Germany and the Ottoman Empire 1914–1918* by Ulrich Trumpener, *Middle East Journal* 22, no. 4 (1968): 516; also quoted in Mamigonian, "Academic Denial of the Armenian Genocide in American Scholarship," 64–65. Referring to the genocide, Thomas had argued that "had Turkification and Moslemization not been accelerated there by the use of force, there certainly would not today exist a Turkish Republic, a Republic owing its strength and stability in no small measure to the homogeneity of its population, a state that is now a valued associate of the United States." Lewis V. Thomas and Richard N. Frye, *The United States and Turkey and Iran* (Cambridge, MA: Harvard University Press, 1951), 61. According to Richard Hovanissian, Thomas "confused historical scholarship with a subjective assessment of American national interest and unwittingly provided a license to exclusivist regimes prepared to employ stringent policies to achieve uniformity and homogeneity." Richard Hovannisian, "The Critic's View: Beyond Revisionism," *International Journal of Middle East Studies* 9, no. 3 (1978): 380.

120. Bernard Lewis, "The Roots of Muslim Rage" *Atlantic Monthly*, September, 1990; Bernard Lewis, "The Revolt of Islam," *New Yorker*, November 19, 2001; Bernard Lewis, *What Went Wrong? Western Impact and Middle Eastern Response* (New York: Oxford University Press, 2002); Bernard Lewis, *The Crisis of Islam: Holy War and Unholy Terror* (New York: Random House, 2003).

121. Lewis, *Notes on a Century*, 240–241.

122. Ibid., 242.

123. Ibid., 243.

124. Ibid., 243–244.

125. Ibid., 244.

126. Ibid., 286.

127. Robert Melson, *Revolution and Genocide: On the Origins of the Armenian Genocide and the Holocaust* (Chicago: University of Chicago Press, 1992). For a good example of this thesis, see Lewy, *The Armenian Massacres in Ottoman Turkey*. The same series published two more examples of the provocation thesis: Justin McCarthy et al., *The Armenian Rebellion at Van* (Salt Lake City: University of Utah Press, 2006), and McCarthy, Turan, and Taşkıran, *Sasun: The History of an 1890s Armenian Revolt* (Salt Lake City: University of Utah Press, 2014). On these works, which blame the Armenians for their fate, see David Gutman, "Review: Ottoman Historiography and the End of the Genocide Taboo: Writing the Armenian Genocide into Late Ottoman History," *Journal of the Ottoman and Turkish Studies Association* 2, no. 1 (2015): 173–174, 176–177. See also Dikran Kaligian, "Anatomy of Denial: Manipulating Sources and Manufacturing a Rebellion," *Genocide Studies International* 8, no. 2 (2014), who argues that such studies are heavily indebted to the work of Esat Uras. Uras played a role in the Armenian genocide as a senior official in the Ottoman Ministry of the Interior, serving as director of the Directorate for Public Security's Intelligence Department. Although "based on these experiences," his account is full of "distortions as well as key omissions" and has created "the template for Turkish genocide denial." Ibid., 210, 220.

128. Bernard Lewis, *The Emergence of Modern Turkey*, 1st ed. (Oxford: Oxford University Press, 1961), 356.

129. Ronald Grigor Suny, "Writing Genocide: The Fate of the Ottoman Armenians," in *A Question of Genocide: Armenians and Turks at the End of the Ottoman Empire*, ed. Ronald Grigor Suny, Fatma Müge Göçek, and Norman M. Naimark (Oxford: Oxford University Press, 2011), 31.

130. Suny, *"They Can Live in the Desert but Nowhere Else,"* xiv.

131. Lewis, *The Emergence of Modern Turkey*, 1st ed., 356, emphasis added.

132. Bernard Lewis, *The Emergence of Modern Turkey*, 2nd ed. (Oxford: Oxford University Press, 1968), 356, emphasis added.

133. Bernard Lewis, *The Emergence of Modern Turkey*, 3rd ed. (Oxford: Oxford University Press, 2002), 356, emphasis added.

134. Lewis, *Notes on a Century*, 287.

135. *Le Monde*, an interview with Bernard Lewis, November 16, 1993, quoted in Auron, *The Banality of Denial*, 228.

136. Ibid.

137. Lewis, *Notes on a Century*, 287–288.

138. Nimet Unan, ed. *Atatürk'ün söylev ve demeçleri*, vol. 2 (1906–1938) (Ankara: Türk Tarih Kurumu, 1959), 12, quoted in Erik Jan Zürcher, "Renewal and Silence: Postwar Unionist and Kemalist Rhetoric on the Armenian Genocide," in *A Question of Genocide*, 312.

139. Lewis, *Notes on a Century*, 288.

140. Ibid.

141. Suny, *"They Can Live in the Desert but Nowhere Else,"* xii.

142. Auron, *The Banality of Denial*, 230. He paid a fine of ten thousand francs, with punitive damages of one franc to each organization. Lewis, *Notes on a Century*, 290.

143. Ibid., 291. He mentions later accepting the honor of the Atatürk Peace Prize by the Turkish Academy of Sciences but turning down the $50,000 prize in 1998. Ibid., 292.

144. Ibid., 294.

145. Gilles Veinstein, "Trois questions sur un massacre," *L'Histoire*, no. 187 (April 1995). Veinstein argues that the number of Armenian deaths is exaggerated, relying on McCarthy's figure of six hundred thousand; that many more Muslims than Christians were victims, as there was a civil war; that Armenians joined the Russian army in large numbers and caused a number of rebellions in the eastern provinces (the provocation thesis); and that there is no proof that the regime ordered their total annihilation. Phillipe-Jean Catinchi, "Gilles Veinstein, historien, spécialiste de l'Empire ottoman," *Le Monde*, February 12, 2013.

146. Lewis, *Notes on a Century*, 296. In 1997, a proposal was made to honor Bernard Lewis with an honorary citizenship of Tel-Aviv. This led to an outpouring of support by influential Israeli politicians and scholars, but also condemnation of the honor due to Lewis's denial of the Armenian genocide. In the end, he was not made an honorary citizen of the city. Auron, *The Banality of Denial*, 230–232.

147. Shaw, *The Jews of the Ottoman Empire and the Turkish Republic*, 258.

148. For a withering critique, see Hovannisian, "The Critic's View." Hovannisian concludes that "such uncritical acceptance and reiteration of Turkish denials, rationalizations, and subterfuge turns revisionism into falsification." Ibid., 386.

149. "Crude Bomb Explodes at UCLA Professor's Home," *Los Angeles Times*, October 4, 1977, D1. The group that claimed responsibility called itself the "Iranian Group of 28," the same group that had assassinated the Turkish ambassador to France two years earlier.

Two days before that assassination, the Turkish ambassador to Austria had been assassinated, a murder claimed by a Greek-Cypriot group. But according to the permanent Turkish ambassador to the United Nations in New York, the assassinations were carried out by Armenian groups. The ambassador told the newspaper that Shaw "is considered an objective teacher" and "wrote a good history of the Ottoman Empire." Shaw was quoted by police "as saying that he had been threatened by Armenian and Greek students" and having told a reporter for the newspaper that "he tries to teach 'the truth as I see it.'"

150. Anderson, "'Down in Turkey, Far Away,'" 100n70; Stanford J. Shaw and Ezel Kural Shaw, *History of the Ottoman Empire and Modern Turkey*, vol. 2, Reform, Revolution, and Republic: The Rise of Modern Turkey, 1808–1975 (Cambridge: Cambridge University Press, 1977), 203–204.

151. Shaw and Shaw refer to "an Armenian uprising in Adana that stimulated a severe repression on the part of the local garrison, with massacre and countermassacre following until as many as 30,000 people of all religions were killed." Shaw and Shaw, *History of the Ottoman Empire and Modern Turkey*, 2:281.

152. They refer to how the Armenians "launched a new wave of terrorism in eastern Anatolia and intensified their European propaganda campaign accusing the Ottomans of massacre" just as "the Greek terrorists in Macedonia were equally active" during the period 1910–1912. Ibid., 287. Explaining why the Ottoman Empire sided with Germany during World War I, they mention how Russia "continued to foment Armenian agitation and terrorism." Ibid., 310. Shaw and Shaw include among the Ottoman war aims "the liberation of the Turkish people of the Caucasus and Central Asia from Russian and Armenian tyranny." Ibid., 314. They depict all Ottoman Armenians as traitors siding with Russia. As proof, they place the following statement in quotation marks but provide no footnote: "Several prominent Ottoman Armenians, including a former member of parliament, slipped away to collaborate with Russian military officials." Ibid., 314. See also Gutman, "Review," 172. They also quote inflammatory statements from Russian Armenians, and describe the actions of Russian Armenians, rather than Ottoman Armenians. They float another unattributed quotation that it would "be impossible to determine which of the Armenians would remain loyal and which would follow the appeals of their leaders." Shaw and Shaw, *History of the Ottoman Empire and Modern Turkey*, 2:315.

153. Ibid., 316.

154. Ibid., 316.

155. Ibid., 329, 333.

156. "Prof. Dr. Stanford J. Shaw vefat etti," *Şalom*, December 20, 2006, http://arsiv.salom .com.tr/news/detail/4397-Prof-Dr-Stanford-J-Shaw-vefat-etti.aspx.

157. Bali, *Model Citizens of the State*, 267.

158. Ibid., 269.

159. The House of Representatives Legislation Resource Center, Office of the Clerk, declarations of lobbying agreements nos. 10334017, January 25, 1989 and 16067014, September 3, 2001, cited in Bali, *Model Citizens of the State*, 272.

160. Ibid., 269–270.

5

"FIVE HUNDRED YEARS
OF FRIENDSHIP"

ONE SHABBAT MORNING IN 1986, TERRORISTS STORMED ISTANBUL'S largest Sephardic synagogue, Neve Şalom, built in 1951 on the site of a synagogue established in the fifteenth century by Andalusian refugees. Throwing bombs and firing machine guns, they murdered twenty Turkish Jews and two Iranian Jewish refugees. In the official narrative, the attack is blamed on foreigners, as it is assumed Turkish Muslims are incapable of such outrages against Jews. In it, we are led to believe that in the days before Google Earth and sophisticated mapping technologies, two foreigners dropped from the sky, carried out the attack alone, and committed suicide, all without local assistance.[1] The identities of the terrorists and their accomplices have never been revealed.[2]

At the time of the bombing, the spokesmen for Turkish Jewry repeated the tolerance mantra.[3] Three years later, in 1989, as Turkey faced increased pressure to recognize the massacres of the Armenians as a genocide, and as the Turkish state and its Kurdish allies waged a brutal war against the ruthless guerrillas of the Kurdistan Workers' Party (PKK), the motif was expanded and institutionalized in the *500. yıl vakfı*, the Quincentennial Foundation. The organization was established to celebrate the anniversary of the arrival of Spanish Jews in the Ottoman Empire five hundred years before and, significantly, with the express aim to publicize the "tolerance" that Ottomans and Turks had always displayed toward Jews in Turkey and abroad.[4]

Foundation president Jak Kamhi would later describe the impetus and aims behind the foundation's creation, narrating how at a time when the anti-Turkish efforts of the Armenian and Greek lobbies in the United States and Europe continued unabated, "on the request of President

[General] Kenan Evren [in office 1980–1989] the 'Quincentennial Foundation' was established under my presidency" to "advertise the supreme human values of Turkish society more effectively abroad."[5] The 1980 coup had served to further damage Turkey's already poor international image, and Kamhi, who supported the coup and had close relations with its regime, was again tapped to improve that image.

Kamhi and a delegation of Turkish Jews that included the chief rabbi in his ceremonial dress met with Prime Minister Özal (in office 1983–1989) and President General Evren in early 1988 to explain their plans to celebrate the five hundredth anniversary of the arrival of the Sephardim. The two leaders "expressed their belief that these celebrations would be highly beneficial in presenting Turkey's real face to the world and they proposed that we should also engage in celebrations and promotional efforts abroad."[6] It was decided that "the Turkish Jewish community should establish a foundation to coordinate the celebrations and to promote Turkey more effectively in the world."[7] Rather than having been established by a group of Jews and Muslims, as others claim, Kamhi notes that in 1989 "the Quincentennial Foundation was established along those lines by 114 founding members from the Turkish Jewish community." Yet "the duty of coordinating all efforts was given to Foreign Minister Mesut Yılmaz and every Turkish Embassy was instructed to support the activities of the Quincentennial Foundation."[8] Özal ordered retired ambassador Tevfik Saraçoğlu to be seconded from the Ministry of Foreign Affairs "to act as an advisor to our foundation and we cooperated successfully on these promotional efforts."[9]

The leading Jewish members of the foundation were wealthy industrialists. In considering their motivations, it is worth bearing in mind that from the 1920s to the 1950s, as Turkey established a state-run economy, the Christian and Jewish bourgeoisie had been largely eliminated to create a Turkish Muslim middle class. Being allowed a share in an economy controlled by state officials and the military meant having the right ethnoreligious background, being loyal to the state and its single ruling party, and not appearing to pose a security threat.[10] To make it in business one had to toady up to the regime. Those few Jews allowed to grow their business, secure government contracts, obtain export and import licenses, and become industrialists were acutely aware that each decade they ran their business was marked by episodes of discrimination and violence targeting Christians and Jews. This constant awareness of threat made them wary; at any moment they could lose their wealth, even their lives. Not far from their minds were the 1915 genocide of the Armenians; the "Population Exchange" between Greece and Turkey in 1923 and 1924; the 1934 pogrom in and expulsion from Thrace, which resulted in a mass exodus of Jews from the region; the Twentieth Reserve Corps, the forced conscription in 1941–1942 of Christians and Jews into special army reserve labor units, where some died in poor conditions; the Capital Tax of 1942–1944, a massive wealth transfer to Muslims whereby Christians and Jews were levied extraordinary and excessive taxes, with those unable to pay being stripped of their wealth, property, and businesses and sent to a concentration camp, where some died; the pogrom of September 6–7, 1955, in which thousands of Armenian, Greek, and Jewish homes, houses of worship, schools, and businesses were plundered and individuals attacked; and the mass expulsions of Greeks in 1964, where, similar to what had occurred in Egypt in 1956, the expellees' wealth and property were seized by the government. These traumatic events, which caused fear and anxiety to be added to the Turkish Jewish affective disposition of gratefulness, form the backdrop to the foundation's creation.

The "driving force and principal financial benefactor" of the foundation has been Turkish Jewish industrialist Jak Kamhi, who gave up to $5 million of his own money to the cause.[11] In a chapter of his Turkish-language autobiography entitled "The Armenian Problem," renamed "A Big Problem: The Alleged 'Armenian Genocide'" in the English translation edited by Lowry, Kamhi explicitly states that the aim of the foundation was to prevent Armenian genocide recognition around the world. "Turkey," he argues, "was unable to take effective counter-measures in Europe and the United States, because large numbers of Armenians lived in those countries . . . they had powerful electoral blocs . . . and had also been coordinating their efforts with the Greek lobby on this issue."[12] Turkish Jews stepped up to the plate. "As the Quincentennial Foundation, we engaged in efforts that supported the work being conducted on this issue by our Ministry of Foreign Affairs officials and ambassadors in the concerned countries." As a result, in the United States, "the Jewish lobbies in the House of Representatives and the Senate [were] able to prevent the passage of Resolutions recognizing April 24 as a day of [Armenian] 'genocide' commemoration."[13]

As Kamhi notes, the foundation was backed by powerful entities. "I like to think of the Quincentennial Foundation as the part of the iceberg that is visible above water."[14] Less visible are the Office of the Prime Minister and the Turkish Ministry of Foreign Affairs, which provide half the funding for the foundation. In his autobiography, Kamhi relates how he "always reported directly to the Prime Minister" regarding his lobbying activities, "to brief him and get his instructions."[15] In an internal memo from 1989, Eli Aciman, a foundation board member and head of the public relations firm responsible for publicizing the foundation in the United States, explained the relationship between Turkish Jewry, the foundation, and the Turkish state. "For once, the true owner of all of these activities—or, if you prefer, we may say the true 'customer'—is the state. Naturally, this will not be the official version! By all appearances, the agency responsible will be the Quincentennial Foundation."[16] That the Turkish government understood the effort by Turkish (and American and Israeli) Jews on its behalf to be an indispensable tool that would serve its international propaganda interests is evidenced by President General Evren's words to Kamhi, Chief Rabbi Asseo, and Jak Veissid when they first proposed the idea to him. "Through this you will have broadcast the noble values of the Turk to the world." Plans were thus set in motion for what was to become a closely choreographed propaganda effort.[17]

The participants clearly understood that their efforts on the part of the foundation were at the same time propaganda work for the Turkish state. In correspondence between Kamhi and Aciman, the two men discuss how their efforts would "improve the tattered image of our Turkey."[18] When Foreign Minister Yılmaz pledged government funding for the foundation in 1989 on the condition that the ministry and foundation would work hand in hand in its public relations campaign, Kamhi responded that the activities of the foundation "will reflect the spirit and . . . views of your Ministry."[19] This dual role was also stated explicitly by a leader of the American Sephardic Association in a letter to one of the heads of the American branch of the foundation:

> Unfortunately, Turkey has undeservedly received much bad publicity in the U.S. and Europe, engendered, in part, by highly vocal indigenous minority groups [Armenian Americans and Greek Americans] that have been able to gain the attention of the media. These groups have focused attention upon civil conflict [the Armenian genocide] that they have characterized as atrocities. . . . Under these circumstances, we should not let pass an opportunity to achieve a well-deserved public relations coup by having the Turkish Government replicate an historic act of kindness [the ingathering of the Sephardim] towards perhaps the most oppressed minority group the world has ever known.[20]

As Jewish industrialist and informal ambassador for Turkey Üzeyir Garih (murdered in 2001) explained in 1989, Jewish organizations and the

Turkish government repeated the same mantra because "people from the Promotion Foundation of Turkey, the Foreign Ministry, and the Turkish general staff in Ankara have been assigned to this matter. We maintain contact with them and ask, 'How do you want us to present (Turkey's case)?' . . . We consult with one another in order to make sure this work is in accordance with Turkey's interests." He noted how "until now, this has all been done by amateurs. Now, with the Quincentennial Foundation, a professional mechanism has been put in place."[21] That same year the American Association of Jewish Friends of Turkey was founded to "spread the knowledge that the Jews who live in Turkey and previously in the Ottoman Empire experienced religious freedom."[22] A member of the Turkish Jewish community and promoter of the foundation would later argue that the foundation gained "the support of Sephardic Jews abroad while silencing countervoices," joining with "American Jewish organizations to engage in public relations to reach the goals of the foundation, leading to the American Jewish lobby supporting Turkey in the U.S. Congress, and securing improvement of Turkish-Israeli relations."[23] The foundation can be considered a Turkish lobby.

To achieve their ideology-laden goals abroad, the foundation's public relations campaign turned to the creation of educational materials and opportunities, including model school curricula for Jewish schools in the United States; academic publications and conferences; university lectures; heritage tourism for Jewish Americans; sponsored trips for journalists and politicians, especially US congresspeople; tours by spokespersons; docudramas; and affiliated traveling exhibits to promote the message that Turks have always been tolerant of Jews. A representative publication is a poem published in English, Ladino, and Turkish in 1992 and appearing in *The Quincentennial Papers*. It begins, "Oh, most noble Turk! Compassionate savior of the Sephardim" and continues with lines extolling how "your valiant men instilled terror in Christendom. Blind to their own savagery, they called you cruel . . . Not so, we Sephardim. We remember what Bayezid decreed." But "the benevolence granted by your forefathers did not end in 1492, for five hundred years we have lived side by side, Turk and Jew." So "on this five hundredth anniversary of 1492, we wish to express to you our gratitude."[24] Turkish Jews repeat "the number 'five hundred' like a mantra."[25] This mantra serves as a counterweight to the criticisms and accusations of others in Turkey's attempts to manage its international image.

The image promulgated by the foundation was an explicitly utopian one, an idea of Muslim-Jewish harmony designed to edge out any lachrymose accounts of anti-Semitic events in Turkish history. As the foundation declared, "Jewish history is full of sad events which are marked by commemorations and memorial services. But now there was a major event to celebrate. To celebrate both the 500th anniversary of the welcoming of the Sephardic Jews to the Ottoman Empire and the five centuries of continuous and peaceful life in Turkey."[26] Therefore, "Turkish Jews felt it was both fitting and proper to launch an extensive celebration in Turkey, in the United States and in Europe." Yet events would conspire against this rosy depiction. On March 1, 1992, just three days after a ceremony celebrating the five hundredth anniversary of the arrival of the Sephardim was held in Neve Şalom, with Turkish Jews offering prayers of thanks to the Ottomans for having accepted their ancestors and to the Turks for having tolerated them ever since, terrorists attempted to bomb the synagogue again.[27]

Despite this attack, Turkish Jews pressed forward with their campaign, adding new myths to the fantastic narration of their history. They restored a fifteenth-century synagogue that boasts a *bima*, a raised platform where the Torah is read, in the shape of the prow of a boat, symbolizing the "Ottoman ships which transported the Sephardim from Spain to Turkey."[28] Not even Elijah Capsali had thought to invent the claim that Bayezid II sent ships to the clogged harbors of Spain to bring the Jews to his empire. This legend is so preposterous that even Jewish historians outside Turkey who faithfully transmit all the other Turkish Jewish historiographic myths failed to accept it—with the exception of Bernard Lewis.[29]

One Turkish Jewish researcher has related that "the Quincentennial Foundation's goal is not historical accuracy, but a kind of public relations 'theater.'"[30] To such a theater, Vitali Hakko added the elements of music and fashion, thereby making theater into spectacle. Hakko maintained good contacts at the highest level of the Turkish government throughout the 1980s and 1990s. He recalls having good relations with Süleyman Demirel and Turgut Özal (both prime ministers and presidents during those decades), playing a role in foreign diplomacy, producing a fashion show for visiting president George H. W. Bush, and creating a special tie for the then prime minister Tansu Çiller (in office 1993–1996) to give to President Clinton when she visited the United States.[31]

Hakko's cultural propaganda missions were duly utilized by the foundation in 1992. As he notes in his autobiography, "Just like the celebrations for the one hundredth anniversary of Atatürk's birth," in 1981, in which he arranged fashion shows across Europe celebrating the Turks, "I was very happy for Vakko to participate as much as we could" in the five hundredth anniversary celebrations of the arrival of Spanish Jews "on Turkish soil."³² "As is known," he continues, after Sultan Bayezid II permitted their arrival, "for five hundred years our ancestors lived and worked in peace in Ottoman Turkish lands." The statement flies in the face of what he has narrated one hundred pages earlier, however: his father was fired from his job and not rehired because he was a Jew; the family's resulting difficult economic conditions caused him and his siblings to abruptly end their schooling. As Hakko notes in his preface, he did not start out with nothing; he started out with less than nothing—all on account of anti-Jewish discrimination. And what of the traumatic experience he recounts elsewhere of the reserve labor unit and the Capital Tax in 1942? Fifty-five years later Hakko states that, when compared with what the Jewish people have faced throughout history, "it is easier to understand what this having lived in peace means." Like so many before him, Hakko chose to expunge the memory of his own lived experience of persecution, and that of Turkish Jewry in the early Turkish Republic, from the long history of Jewish persecution.

As for his Vakko company, "we did nothing less than help our good friend Jak Kamhi, who devoted all his time and energy to the activities of the foundation."³³ Vakko was given the task of designing the décor, arrangements, and music and fashion show for the grand reception at Dolmabahçe Palace in summer 1992. Hakko was worried about the evening, to be held outdoors, as the forecast called for rain; miraculously, a divine omen appeared and the clouds cleared as the event began.³⁴ The audience included the Israeli president, the Turkish president, the Turkish prime minister, the Turkish chief rabbi, and all government ministers, diplomats, and leaders of the Turkish Jewish community, as well as President George H. W. Bush, who appeared by video link. Vakko presented its show entitled "Turkey: Land of Hope, Tranquility, and Peace." Hakko explains that the subject of this performance, which was replete with actors dressed as Ottoman sultans, was how "two peoples, differing in religion and language, lived together in peace and tolerance." What of the "third people," the Christians? He does not consider what happened to them. Nor does he remember his own experiences of anti-Semitism in the 1940s. It is also striking that he praises the Turks for being able to live in peace with others in their midst while at that very moment the low-intensity conflict between Kurdish and Turkish forces raged in the country. At the end of the evening, when Hakko rose to dance with his wife, it started to rain. Hakko told her, "'Our prayers have been answered, you see, God is now sanctifying us.' The rain that began to fall may have been . . . a sacred rain."[35] While he may have been speaking on a personal level as the relieved organizer of the open-air evening's events, the reader is led to feel that he is also speaking on behalf of the descendants of the Sephardim granted refuge in the Ottoman Empire.

Quincentennial Foundation Efforts to Influence Historiography

Although the ostensible aim of the foundation was to promote the perception in world public opinion that the Turks had displayed tolerance toward Jews for five centuries, "as a matter of fact, the foundation aimed to counter the anti-Turkish lobbying of the Armenian and Greek lobbies in the U.S."[36] It is for this reason that it concentrated its efforts on US public opinion, politicians, civil society organizations, and academics. Accordingly, rather than endow Jewish studies chairs in Turkey, it supported efforts to endow chairs in Ottoman and Turkish studies in the United States that would promote utopian visions of Muslim-Jewish relations as part of an explicit effort to deny the Armenian genocide.

The foundation found Galanté's utopian approach to relations between Muslims and Jews in the empire and republic to be amenable to its aims. By overlooking or downplaying lachrymose events, it was able to promote the view that anti-Semitism did not exist in Turkey—a statement made repeatedly by the chief rabbi, the chief historian of the rabbinate, and other spokespeople for the foundation.[37] Turkish Jews were depicted as not having suffered at all.[38] In this way, presenting a uniformly positive experience of Turkish Jews became a means of defense to counter criticism of Turkey in the international arena. Whenever and wherever Turkey is criticized for its human rights violations, its treatment of the Kurds, its need to recognize the Armenian genocide, Turkey's supporters point instead to the purported tolerance displayed toward Jews. Remaining silent on the fate of Armenians, Greeks, and Kurds, and simultaneously referring to the myth about the tolerance of Jews has allowed individuals like this senior member of the Ministry of Foreign Affairs to argue that, because of the 1492 experience of giving refuge to Jews, "Turkey might just be the [one] nation in the world that has the least need to take lessons from others about tolerance."[39]

As the Jewish community of Turkey celebrated the anniversary, the myth of "five hundred years of friendship" between the two peoples was repeated by community leaders and prominent Jewish businessmen in the press and media, including in the Jewish newspaper *Şalom*, and books were published to disseminate the thesis to the widest possible international audience.[40]

One of the most important books published in Turkish as part of this effort was written by Naim Güleryüz, who, despite a lack of professional training in history, is the official historian of the chief rabbinate in Istanbul. His study, *Türk Yahudileri tarihi: 20. yüzyılın başına kadar* (A history of Turkish Jewry to the beginning of the twentieth century, 1993) appeared as an online lecture in English, "The History of the Turkish Jews," with the aim of "celebrating 500 years of peaceful living in Turkish lands of the Jews expelled from Spain in 1492."[41] In the pamphlet, he contrasts Byzantine persecution of Jews with Ottoman tolerance. "When the Ottomans captured Bursa in 1324 and made it their capital, they found a Jewish community oppressed under Byzantine rule. The Jews welcomed the Ottomans as saviors." Citing Bernard Lewis, he promotes an image of loyal Jews benefiting their Ottoman masters, arguing that the Ottomans benefited from the Jewish refugees from Iberia because they brought the most advanced medical knowledge, introduced printing, pioneered the Ottoman textile industry, and transferred knowledge of weaponry and war technology from Western Europe.[42] The argument of the English version reflects his position as spokesperson for Turkish Jewry and vice president of the foundation, as well as his source base, which consisted mainly of Graetz, Danon, Galanté, and Lewis. Güleryüz adds a moral component to this conventional wisdom such that the reader is left with the impression that the Ottoman Empire was not merely a haven, but heaven on earth. "This humanitarianism is consistent with the beneficence and goodwill traditionally displayed by the Turkish government and people towards those of different creeds, cultures, and backgrounds. Indeed, Turkey could serve as a model to be emulated by any nation which finds refugees from any of the four corners of the world standing at its doors. In 1992, Turkish Jewry celebrate[s] not only the anniversary of this gracious welcome, but also the remarkable spirit of tolerance and acceptance which has characterized the whole Jewish experience in Turkey."[43] Written at the height of savage state repression of the brutal guerrilla movement of the PKK, these statements are nothing less than astonishing.

The Turkish version of Güleryüz's book also relies on Graetz, Danon, Franco, Rosanes, Galanté, and Lewis. It presents a chronological account of 668 (not 500!) years (1324–1992) of Jews "living harmoniously together with Turks" and offers an account of their contributions to society.[44] He refers to Tzarfati's letter and offers a Turkish translation in an appendix.[45] Here are the early modern myths: Mehmed II invited the Jews of Anatolia to settle in newly conquered Constantinople.[46] Mehmed II established the position of chief rabbi and elevated him to a seat in the imperial council.[47] Relying on Danon and Franco, he claims that Bayezid II offered a warm embrace to the Iberian refugees. Güleryüz even goes so far as to spin a yarn, without any attribution, that "Ottoman galleys under the command of the famous Piri Reis's uncle Kemal Reis began to transport the hopeless migrants waiting in the ports of Cadiz and Sevilla to the Ottoman coasts," and then quotes the apocryphal line of Bayezid II, "You call Ferdinand [of Spain] a wise king; him, who by expelling the Jews has impoverished his country and enriched mine!"[48] The Jews, who were received "with tolerance by the state and Muslim populace," "settled comfortably into their new fatherland." They offered their expertise in diplomacy and finance to the government, introduced the printing press and new weapons technologies to the Ottomans.[49] Significantly, Güleryüz presents Turks and Jews as having both close relations and a common enemy: Christian empires (Byzantine and Catholic) and the Ottoman Greeks and Armenians were prone to foment blood libels from the sixteenth through nineteenth centuries and engaged in palace intrigue to have their Jewish rivals executed in the nineteenth-century era of reform.[50] In contrast with their Christian rivals, he asserts, in the nineteenth century, Jews began serving in the military "to defend the fatherland" and always sided with the Ottomans against European imperialists and rebellious Christians, by which he means the Armenians, thereby deploying a form of genocide denial—that of blaming the victims.[51]

The work of former Turkish Foreign Ministry official Salahi Sonyel (1932–2015) is representative of a group of historical writings produced by non-Jewish Turkish foreign ministry officials who consistently promoted the foundation's views. Sonyel earned a PhD at the University of London, was an honorary member of the Turkish Historical Society, and the recipient of the State Medal for Distinguished Service. The Turkish Historical Society published many of Sonyel's books denying the Armenian genocide.

Sonyel claimed that Muslims and Jews were massacred by Armenians and Greeks and blamed all violence on the intrigues of foreign powers.[52] He published numerous articles in the organ of the Turkish Historical Society, *Belleten*, promoting the foundation's theses.[53] In a typical article, he recycles many of the old historiographic myths: he counters Christian persecution and anti-Semitism with Muslim tolerance; claims that Bayezid II sent his own ships to receive the Jews expelled from Spain; cites the utopian views of Capsali and Tzarfati, as well as the alliance's positive views of Abdülhamid II; and claims that Jews were always loyal to the empire and the republic while Christians fomented blood libels and pogroms and even massacred Jews during Turkey's War of Independence.[54] He cites Haim Nahum and Abraham Galanté as examples of loyal Jews. In one 1990 article, he expresses outrage that some Jews, "the real victims of the Holocaust," recognize the Armenian genocide: "Tenacious and systematic attempts are being made by a number of Armenian 'scholars' to sway, especially Jewish public opinion, that there is a link between the experiences of the Armenians in the Ottoman Empire during World War I, which they label as the 'first genocide of the twentieth century,' and those of the European Jewry during World War II. By their persistent attempts, skillful manipulation of the feelings of some Jewish and other sympathisers, and masterful use of distorted, tendentious, and even forged 'documents,' they have succeeded in winning over some of those who are the real victims of the Holocaust."[55]

To promote its view of Turkish-Jewish harmony among the public, the foundation established a Jewish museum in Karaköy, Istanbul. Inaugurated in 2001, the Quincentennial Foundation Museum of Turkish Jews was billed as a "tolerance museum," where the only tolerance presented is that of Turks for Jews. Located in the Zülfaris (*zülf-ü arus*, Ottoman for "lovelock of the bride") synagogue built by the seventeenth-century chief rabbi Haim Kamhi, it was restored and converted to a museum thanks to the financial support of the rabbi's descendant, foundation president Jak Kamhi.[56] None of the museum curators had any formal training in museum studies. The official opening ceremony was led by then deputy prime minister Mesut Yılmaz at a ceremony attended by Turkish Jewish leaders; the commander of the Turkish First Army; the ambassadors of the United States, Israel, United Kingdom, France, and Spain; and the consul generals of Israel, the United Kingdom, Switzerland, Belgium, Holland, and others.

Kamhi claims in his autobiography that the museum teaches the visitor "about the tolerance and respect for all religions shown by the Ottoman

Empire even in an era when concepts such as human rights and freedom of belief did not even exist." He suggests that its exhibition demonstrates "the lofty values of Turkish people and society that ensured various religious communities could live in safety for centuries in the Ottoman Empire."[57] In fact, the museum focuses on Turkish Muslim tolerance of Jews alone. Accordingly, the panels of the museum are, according to one scholar, "saturated" with "tolerance terms" including "Turkish-Jewish friendship," "peace," "religious freedom," "harmony," "co-existence," "mutual respect," and "humanitarianism," while nowhere are violent episodes against Jews and anti-Semitism in Turkey presented.[58] In contrast to the Museum of Tolerance in Los Angeles, whose exhibits present a lachrymose conception of Jewish history and demand "that we learn from Jewish experience to be tolerant" of the persecuted, the Jewish Museum of Turkey offers instead a utopian or "markedly anti-lachrymose interpretation of the Ottoman Empire's and Republic of Turkey's exemplary tolerance for their Jewish subjects."[59]

According to the bilingual brochure given out at the museum in Istanbul, the foundation aims to "promote, both within the country and abroad, the story of 700 years of amity between Turks and Jews, beginning with the Ottoman conquest of Bursa (1326), continuing with Bayezid II's warm welcome of the Sephardic Jews who preferred expulsion from Spain to giving up the faith and traditions of their ancestors, and carrying on until today. To show through the past 700 years how the two cultures influenced each other. To display the humanitarian spirit of the Turkish nation."[60] The Quincentennial Foundation had inexplicably expanded its historical scope to embrace not half a millennium, but seven hundred years of "togetherness."[61] Quoting verbatim from Güleryüz's 1992 book, the museum brochure goes beyond the theme of "togetherness," however, citing instances from over the course of six hundred years where Ottomans/Turks rescued Jews from oppression by Christian-majority societies. Significantly, Ottoman saviors are contrasted with Christian persecutors:

> At the time of the conquest of Bursa (1326) the Jewish community—oppressed under Byzantine rule—welcomed the Ottomans as saviours. . . . Early in the 14th century, when the Ottomans had established their capital at Edirne, many Jews from Europe, mostly Ashkenazim, migrated there. When Mehmed the Conqueror conquered Byzantium in 1453 he encountered an oppressed Romaniote Jewish community which welcomed him with enthusiasm. He had called upon the Anatolian Jewish communities and invited them 'to ascend the site of the Imperial Throne, to dwell in the best of the land, each beneath his vine and fig tree, with silver and gold, with wealth and cattle.' In

1464/1469, Rabbi Isak Sarfati [Isaac Tzarfati] from Edirne sent a letter to the Jewish communities in Europe, inviting 'his coreligionists to leave the torment they were enduring in Christendom and seek safety and prosperity in Turkey.' In 1492 Sultan Bayezid II, learning about the expulsion of the Sepharads—the Jews from Spain—ordered his governors 'not to refuse the Jews entry or cause them difficulties, but to receive them cordially.' . . . Russian Jews fleeing the pogroms in 1881, 1891, 1897, 1903 and the Bolshevik Revolution in 1917, found refuge in Turkey. In 1933 Atatürk invited famous scientists under threat in Nazi Germany and Austria to find shelter and settle in Turkey and continue their academic careers at Turkish universities. . . . Turkish diplomats serving in countries under Nazi occupation endeavoured greatly and succeeded in saving the lives of Jews from Nazi atrocities and extermination camps. In 1990 Selahattin Ülkümen, consul general at Rhodes (1943–1944) was honored by Yad Vashem as Righteous Among the Nations. During World War II Turkey served as a safe passage for many Jews fleeing the horrors of Nazism.[62]

The museum brochure contrasts the vicious anti-Semites of Christian Europe, as represented by Nazis, Russian pogromists, Spanish Inquisitors, and Byzantine oppressors, with the tolerant Ottomans and Turks, as personified by the perpetual saviors and rescuers Mehmed II, Bayezid II, Atatürk, and Selahattin Ülkümen. The brochure does correct Güleryüz's 1992 book, which had misleadingly claimed that "several Turkish diplomats—Ambassadors Behiç Erkin and Numan Menemencioğlu; Consuls General Fikret Şefik Özdoğancı, Bedii Arbel, Selahattin Ülkümen; Consuls Namık Kemal Yolga and Necdet Kent, just to name only a few of them, spent all their efforts to save from the Holocaust the Turkish Jews in those countries, and succeeded."[63] Yad Vashem has only recognized Ülkümen for his role in saving Jews in Rhodes. Yet in the museum, a "Wall of Honor" continues to list the names of the foreign minister and the entire Turkish diplomatic staff who served in Nazi-occupied Europe during World War II, implying that all these men saved Jews when they did not.

Jewish Historians outside Turkey Promote the Foundation's Aims

As Kamhi relates, the foundation's efforts were "certainly not restricted to gala evenings and cocktail parties," held in Hollywood, Tel Aviv, and New York City, attended by presidents, prime ministers, and prominent journalists, for "we also focused on the academic front."[64] Research into related subjects "was carried out by world-leading Turkologists such as Professors Bernard Lewis, Avigdor Levy, Stanford Shaw, and Heath Lowry," and this research "was presented to the public at various universities and published" in Turkey, America, Israel and Europe.[65]

The most influential book published as part of the effort to promote the utopian thesis outside Turkey was written by Stanford Shaw, the one-time student of Bernard Lewis. Riddled with factual errors and mistranslations, *The Jews of the Ottoman Empire and the Turkish Republic* (1991) violates the standards of the historical profession, for its author fails to document most of the outrageous claims he makes. Much of the book is in fact taken verbatim from the work of Franco and Galanté without attribution. The book was first presented as a series of public lectures at a Sephardic synagogue in Los Angeles, which may explain its tone, point of view, and amateurishness.

Shaw's acknowledgments read as a genealogy of Jewish utopian approaches to Muslims from Ottoman times to the present. He credits a number of influences: Rabbi Haim Nahum, the last chief rabbi of the Ottoman Empire, for inspiring him and providing "the first inklings as to the actual nature of the relationship among the different religious communities in the Ottoman Empire"; Rabbi David Asseo, chief rabbi of Turkey, who allowed him access to the otherwise inaccessible archives of the chief rabbinate; Abraham Galanté, for giving him "the initial direction as to how" he "should approach the subject of Ottoman and Turkish Jewry"; Naim Güleryüz, historian and counselor to the Grand Rabbinate, and foundation vice president, who "opened many doors" for him; Jak Kamhi, the head of the foundation; and Eli Aciman, foundation board member and head of the public relations firm responsible for publicizing the foundation in the United States.[66]

With such acknowledgments, it is no surprise that *The Jews of the Ottoman Empire and the Turkish Republic*, the standard reference book on the topic, is dedicated "to the Muslim and Jewish Turks of the Republic of Turkey, in celebration of five hundred years of brotherhood and friendship, 1492–1992."[67] It is deeply indebted, in both form and content, to the works that precede it: Tzarfati and Capsali, Graetz and Danon, Franco, Galanté, Roth, Baron, and Lewis. He contrasts the Byzantine yoke with Ottoman liberation, depicting Jews as being "overjoyed at the opportunity to throw off their Greek oppressors," asserting, without providing any evidence, that local Jews assisted the Ottomans in conquering Bursa, Edirne, and Constantinople.[68] He ignores evidence to the contrary demonstrating that Byzantine Jewry's "view of the Ottomans was no different from their view of Gentile rulers under whom the Jews in these parts of the world had lived for generations."[69] Here, too, are most of Capsali's and other Sephardic "talking points," as reflected through Graetz and a century of Jewish scholarship: Mehmed II's "inviting" Jews to newly conquered Constantinople; Bayezid II's inviting the Spanish exiles, giving them a "gracious welcome," and quipping, "You call Ferdinand a wise king, he who impoverishes his country and enriches our own."[70]

Shaw's work is peopled by the same stereotypical figures we have come to expect from this genre: magnanimous Muslims and tolerant Turks, loyal and grateful Jews, and anti-Semitic Christians. Shaw argues that the Ottoman Empire was an interfaith utopia that contrasted with the tragic life Jews suffered in Christian Europe. What he finds most significant about Ottoman Jewry is not any of their own achievements, but how they were treated by the Ottoman/Turkish Muslims, as "the Ottoman Turks provided a principal refuge for Jews driven out of western Europe by massacres and persecution between the fourteenth and twentieth centuries, particularly from blood libel massacres in western and central Europe, pogroms in Russia, and from the Holocaust."[71] Reflecting medieval Jewish messianic history writing, he sings the praise of the Ottomans for bringing together the Jewish diaspora for the first time "since the destruction of the Temple and exile of Jews from the Holy Land," which "can truly be taken as an ingathering of the Jewish people, particularly since it took place in the Empire which now ruled the Holy Land, thus providing the first opportunity for their long-awaited return to their homeland."[72] Mirroring the sentiment Jews had publicly employed since 1892, Shaw adds that another significant aspect of Ottoman Jewry is that, in contrast with the Armenians and Greeks, who "were constantly attempting to undermine and destroy this Muslim empire so as to restore the supremacy which they had exercised in late Roman and Byzantine times," Ottoman Jews had been loyal and useful to their rulers.[73] They had contributed "significantly to the Empire's economic development," and they benefited "from toleration and protection in return. They therefore resisted all efforts to get them to join revolts and movements against it [the Empire], particularly during its last century of existence."[74] This is rather a surprising claim when one considers Zionist efforts to establish a Jewish state in Palestine.

Asserting a claim established by Graetz and echoed for a century by Ottoman and then Turkish Jews and Jewish historians outside Turkey, Shaw blames any persecution of Jews in Ottoman domains on Christians, even when Muslims are the perpetrators.[75] For example, repeating an argument made by Franco, he accuses Janissaries "recently converted from Greek Orthodoxy" for one seventeenth-century ritual murder allegation and subsequent pogrom; he blames Janissaries "of Christian origin" for another.[76]

Shaw's illogical claim that Christians—who had the same sociolegal status as Jews—are to blame for oppressing Jews in the empire would be repeated by other Jewish scholars of Ottoman history for the next two decades. This included French historian Gilles Veinstein, who asserted in 2013 that Jews were "liable also to persecution by the Christians of the empire, the inheritors of Byzantine anti-Semitism" and that they "had no other recourse than the sultan himself," who served as "protector of the Jews," demonstrated most clearly in the way he handled blood libel accusations.[77] This is the old saw about the sultan as the protector of last resort of the Jews. Admitting that Muslims were responsible for several sixteenth-century accusations of ritual murder made against Jews, Veinstein nevertheless declares that such allegations "clearly reflect locally entrenched anti-Semitic traditions," by which he means older, Byzantine, Greek, and Armenian anti-Semitism present before the Turks arrived in Anatolia. In other words, even when Muslims deploy anti-Jewish tropes, he argues, Christians are to blame. This serves as a good example of a historian doing his best to avoid the uncomfortable truth of Turkish anti-Semitism, which Turkish Jews and their foreign supporters go out of their way to silence.

The utopian view expressed by the foundation of centuries of Jewish goodwill toward the Ottomans continued to find resonance among Jewish historians outside Turkey. Shaw's doctoral student and US-based Israeli scholar, Avigdor Levy, published three volumes dedicated to five centuries of positive interaction between Muslims and Jews in the Ottoman Empire and Turkey, including *The Jews of the Ottoman Empire* (1994), for which he wrote a 150-page introduction. The book was the outcome of a conference at his home institute of Brandeis University, funded by Turkish Jewish community leader Jak Kamhi and the Institute of Turkish Studies, and published "in cooperation with" the institute.[78] Referring to Baron's claim that Jews experienced a "golden age" in the Ottoman Empire, Levy argues that the Ottomans offered Jews fleeing persecution in Christian Europe "a secure and friendly haven" and that the Jews responded with "loyalty and patriotism."[79] Repeating Galanté's thesis, Levy presents the Jews as useful for the Ottomans. "They were instrumental in developing and expanding the Ottoman economy and administration. . . . Jews made significant contributions to Ottoman society in science, technology, culture, and entertainment. In return, Ottoman Jewry experienced unprecedented individual and religious freedom and long periods of material comfort, security, and prominence."[80] This was because "compared with contemporary Christian Europe, the Ottoman Empire afforded its religious minorities an unequaled degree of tolerance."[81] In fact, Levy asserts, "in its attitude towards its non-Muslim subjects, the Ottoman Empire was one of the most tolerant Muslim states ever to exist," and this tolerance "persisted, on the whole, until the end of the empire."[82] Such a remarkable claim can only be made when one denies the annihilation of the Armenians by the Ottoman government in 1915.

A section concerning "Jewish attraction and allegiance to the Ottoman state," relies on Tzarfati, Usque, and ha-Kohen, although Levy recognizes the role that messianism played in that attraction.[83] Already in the fourteenth (*sic*) and fifteenth centuries, Levy asserts, the Ottomans "came to regard the Jews" as "politically more reliable than the local Christian Greeks and Slavs."[84] Yet Levy, like other historians of Ottoman Jewry, does not offer an explanation, for why, if this was the case, Ottomans would for centuries risk staffing the most important and sensitive positions in their administration, military, and harem with hundreds of thousands of converted Christians, rather than the "trustworthy" Jews. Levy focuses on the "Jewish immigrant contributions to Ottoman expansion and economic development," on the useful "knowledge, experience, and skills" of the Jews in the fields of banking, commerce, international trade, science, medicine, and financial administration, giving rise to an elite class of Ottoman Jewish male "physicians, financial advisors, translators" and "political advisors," and "private bankers" to the sultan and provincial officials, and female "purveyors, agents, and political advisors" to the imperial harem.[85]

Throughout his study, Levy emphasizes the "Turkish-Jewish mutuality of interests."[86] Yet such a mutuality of interests is as true for Ottoman and Turkish Jews as it is for the historians, both premodern and modern, who narrate their history. Levy's promotion of the utopian thesis and denial of the Armenian genocide was recognized by Turkey. Levy received the Promotion Award from the Promotion Foundation of Turkey for "writing a great many works on Turkish history that are based on objective and positive truths, for signing a statement against the Armenian [Genocide] Draft Resolution as a scholar with a realistic world view . . . and for broadly communicating his positive and realistic views of Turkey and Turkish history."[87]

Turkish Anti-Semitism Undercuts the
Harmony Narrative

In 1993, the Quincentennial Foundation published a series of interviews that was ultimately to undermine their carefully crafted myth of Turkish-Jewish harmony. In conjunction with the foundation's activities during the quincentennial celebrations of 1992, Turkish Jewish newspaper *Şalom* editor Lizi Behmoaras conducted twenty-five interviews with non-Jewish Turkish intellectuals so as to probe their views of Jews and of the foundation. Primarily leftist, secularist writers in their sixties, but ranging from forty-year-old Orhan Pamuk to seventy-seven-year-old Aziz Nesin, and including some who self-identify as Muslim or Dönme, the descendants of the followers of Sabbatai Zevi who converted to Islam, they represent the first and second generations raised in the republic. The interviews appeared in book form the following year as *Türkiye'de aydınların gözüyle Yahudiler* (Intellectuals' views of Jews in Turkey), by the same Turkish Jewish press that had published Güleryüz's apologetic works.[88]

What is most striking about the interviews is how often they undermine the foundation's aims of promoting favorable views of Jews in Turkey, of Turks abroad, and of Jewish-Turkish harmony through the ages. The interviewees not only describe in detail the low public opinion of Jews in Turkey; most also depict Jews in a negative way. All confirm the presence of anti-Semitism in Turkey and deploy anti-Semitic stereotypes; several had heard of the malicious anti-Semitic blood libel when growing up. The reader learns from the interviewees about Jews' "special characteristics," including shrewdness, miserliness, and cowardliness, which many intellectuals conclude "run in their genes." The reader is also introduced to conspiracy theories about the "Jewish lobby" as Jewish "dominance" of world finance and media are evoked, as is the view that "Jew" and "capital" cannot be separated. Many hesitate to use the term *Yahudi* (Jew), noting that the word is "shameful," so prefer *Musevi* (Mosaic). Almost all the interviewees discuss various anti-Jewish measures in Turkey. Because the book presents an overall unflattering view of Turkish Jews and of Turkish Muslims' views toward them, the reader is left to wonder why, given the foundation's aims, the interviews were not redacted before publication, or why they were published by the foundation at all. While such views had long been propagated by Turkish Islamists and Rightists, their articulation by leading secularist, leftist intellectuals serves to undercut entirely the myth of Jewish-Turkish harmony in modern-day Turkey.[89]

Two interviews in particular that appear early in the book sit very uncomfortably with the aims of the Turkish Jewish community. The first is with writer Necati Cumalı (1921–2001) who describes "the Jewish proto-type" that appears in his work as a person who has no honor, a person who "changes according to whichever way the wind is blowing, never reveals his true identity, never says no to anyone."[90] In the author's 1979 short story, "Yakub'un koyunları" (Jacob's sheep), an extract of which is included with his interview, he narrates how "as I got to know the Jews' unlikeable aspects, I understood that the creature known as a Jew was a person no longer connected to Judaism who had over time turned into a prototype," who could belong to any religion, speak any language, and possess any nationality. "In the end [the Jew] was a type of human created by usury and lust for money, beyond national or religious belonging."[91] He was "untrustworthy, selfish, cowardly, greedy and covetous, addicted to pleasure, someone for whom nothing was sacred. Money was the Jew's religion and faith. He had no fatherland. Although he bore no burden of responsibility for any bit of land, he enjoyed living in the most beautiful homes in the most beautiful cities, took pleasure in the best food, and chased after the most unbelievable pleasures of the flesh." He was "repulsive; he tried to get ahead of everybody, everywhere. He was like that when driving a car and shopping. When he got on a bus, if he saw a single empty seat at the front, he would push women and children out of the way to try and snatch it for himself." In sum, "he was a pitiful person who would do no good for anyone but himself. He was a creature loathed by the world. A name was found for him: Dirty Jew!" Astonishingly, worse was to come in the interview that follows.

The most embarrassing interview, and unfortunately the most typical in that it brings together in one sitting all the themes present in the others, is that given by satirist Aziz Nesin (1915–1995), the oldest of the interviewees. Nesin refers to Jews as shrewd and miserly; as geniuses; as superpower-ful lobbyists; as cowardly; as a group whose behavior justified the Holo-caust. He describes the prototypical Jews in his works as "quick-witted, cunning businessmen," as Jews in Turkey are "extremely frugal."[92] When he was young, what drew his attention to Jews was his discovery that "in the branches of psychology, philosophy, and sociology, many of the trail-blazers" were Jews; at the time of the interview, at the age of nearly eighty, he still is of the opinion that most of the important people in the sciences and humanities are Jews. So "there must be something different about this race, because it is not only those Jews who have gathered in one particular place, but Jews in America, France, Germany . . . in short, everywhere in the world Jews in different regions are always way ahead in every sphere."[93] After meeting Jews abroad in socialist countries, he realized that "(Jews) must have another important characteristic: most of the people leading the world are Jews." After sharing these anti-Semitic thoughts, Lizi Behmoaras, the interviewer, asks him where he first encountered anti-Semitism. He responds that he first came upon it in the Arab world, when meeting with professors at Cairo University. When asked how he views the Middle Eastern problem, he responds by saying, "I support the Arabs and the Palestinian position. I believe that Jews living outside of Israel usually do not oppose Israel's position, do not think any differently [than Israel]. If we talk about percentages, it would be more than 50%! I don't approve of this. What a pity—it will sound very heavy—but on this topic they behave as if they want to show that what Hitler did to the Jews was right." Behmoaras interjects, "'Showing what Hitler did was right!'" "Yes," he continues, "this is what I think."[94]

When Behmoaras asks Nesin why Turkish Jews do not enter politics, he responds, "Because they are very prudent of course . . . the Jew does not take risks." When asked if he is calling Jews cowards, he responds, "That cowardice is a very interesting thing. In Turkey, Jews are known as cowards. But the ones in the United States are bullies. . . . Jews are cowards because their environment made them cowards." When asked whether they should have raised their heads, he responds, "If they raised their heads they would not have been successful. They preserved their existence by accommodating behind the scenes." Unlike America where they are truly free, he asserts, the conditions in Turkey have "forced them to submit and humiliate themselves." In this way, they have managed to exist.[95] They may not hold government positions, but they "are in the place where they can direct the government behind the scenes [to achieve their interests]."

These two interviews are not outliers. Many of the interviewees first deny that anti-Semitism exists in Turkey and then either refer to its presence, or worse, deploy it. Writer and journalist Oktay Akbal (1923–2015) declares that "whether in the Ottoman period or during the Turkish Republic, the Jewish community was never excluded, repressed, never faced difficulties. Of course, other than the Capital Tax!"[96] But then he confirms that he prefers the term *Musevi* to *Yahudi* because "the term *Yahudi* is always used in ugly expressions such as 'Jewish coward,' 'dirty Jew,' and so on. When I was a child they would always frighten me by saying, 'I will give you away to the Jewish junk peddler.' It was said that Jews put children in needle-filled barrels."[97] When Behmoaras asks how such expressions could have found their way into Turkish, "since there generally is no anti-Semitism in Turkey," Akbal responds, "Christian propaganda. . . . The antagonism Christians have toward Jews is worse than everyone else's."

When journalist and writer Atillâ İlhan (1925–2005) is asked by Behmoaras why he depicts Jews in his works in a negative way, he responds in part by saying that his Jewish friends are disturbed by his characterization of the role Jews played in the empire's decline. Yet he defends himself by ensuring her that he is no anti-Semite.[98] She asks him whether it is possible for any human to be completely free of racist thoughts, and he responds, blatantly unaware of the form his own racism takes, by saying, "Among us Turks it is possible." Furthermore, "Turks are a strange group, for they definitely do not have any prejudice toward any other group." He agrees with her that "Christianity is considered the cradle of anti-Semitism," claiming that "because they [the Jews] knew this, they defended the Ottomans until the end!" At the same time, he contends, Jews controlled trade in the Ottoman Empire such that when the West decided to exploit Turkey, Jews made up the comprador class enabling it to happen.[99] When she asks him directly whether there is anti-Semitism in Turkey, he responds by saying that it does exist. "Had there been no Israel, there definitely never would have been anti-Semitism in Turkey."[100] But then he blames the "Jewish lobby" for organizing and financing the United States' imposition of its imperial order on the whole world. "I am opposed to the Jewish lobby not because it is Jewish, or because it supports Israel, but because it supports those [the United States] who impose an imperialist order in the world."

Other interviewees also mention the "needle-filled barrel," a malicious anti-Semitic myth promoted during the Nazi era with the publishing of Cevat Rifat Atılhan's 1937 book, *İğneli fıçı: Tarih boyunca Yahudi mezalimi* (The needle-filled barrel: Jewish atrocities throughout history). Psychologist and writer Suna Tanaltay (b. 1933) remembers the effect the myth had on her as a child: "Something that made my hair stand on end was that Jews threw children in needle-filled barrels. But . . . at the same time . . . my mother had very dear [Jewish] friends. . . . I did not think about who they were. Or, more correctly, [I thought that] they were *other* Jews. They were not those ones [who threw children in barrels]!"[101] Poet Özdemir İnce (b. 1936) also mentions that during World War II everyone was talking about the "needle-filled barrel."[102]

When asked when he first met or heard of Jews, political scientist Mete Tunçay (b. 1936) responds, "When I was a child, I remember, my father would often mention his anger toward the Jews.... It was the literature of the 1940s: 'These Jews exploit everybody, they also live very well, etc.' ... These 1940s claims were probably fanned by the Nazis and were also reflected in the Turkish press. In my opinion, anti-Jewish sentiment increased in intensity with German money" and that "when Turkism became the dominant ideology in Turkey, and then adding Nazi influence to it, the situation" for Jews worsened.[103] He also mentions how leftists do not hesitate to use "the Jewish type for bankers, money changers, and usurers." He mentions the Capital Tax, the Thrace Pogrom, concurring with Behmoaras that the World War II era "is the most anti-Semitic in Turkish history."[104] There were rumors "that the Jews were going to be sent from work camps to concentration camps. There is also the famous story about the gas ovens in Balat [a fearful rumor about giant incinerators being built in a predominantly Jewish neighborhood in Istanbul].... I definitely believe that these are legends. But I do not know what would have happened had Turkey been occupied by Germany."

Ashkenazi Geniuses and Sephardic Bourgeoisie, Stingy Cowards and Powerful String-Pullers

The anti-Semitic stereotypes that appear in the interviews with Cumalı and Nesin are repeated by the others: Ashkenazi Jews are geniuses but Sephardic Jews are not; Jews are stingy cowards; Jews are a secret power pulling the strings behind closed doors; Jews constitute a powerful lobby.

The trope of Ashkenazi (European) genius and Sephardic (Turkish) lack peppers the interviews. Writer Tomris Uyar (1941–2003) asserts like many others that "there is no doubt that a large percentage of the most important people in the world—Freud, Marx, Einstein, etc.—are Jewish."[105] To writer İlhan Selçuk (1925–2010), "All music virtuosos on the face of the earth are Jews.... All of them!"[106] Political scientist Cengiz Çandar (b. 1948) regrets that, in his view, Turkish Jews have not produced any important figures because all the important Jewish figures are Ashkenazi."[107] Like the others, Nobel Prize–winning novelist Orhan Pamuk (b. 1952) always wondered "why Jews in other countries are the most creative group (whether in the sciences or in literature), while in Turkey they are not ... why did they not produce an Einstein?"[108] And again, what strikes İnce about Turkey's Jews is how they pale in comparison with Jews in other countries, while "it is even said that there is an international Jewish writers' lobby," while in Turkey there is only novelist Mario Levi (b. 1957).[109] Writer, poet, and artist Ferit Edgü (b. 1936) complains that Turkey's Jews, unlike Jews everywhere else, are not artists, writers, or scientists, but that they concentrate instead in business and the professions.[110] He waxes nostalgic for the few exceptions, such as Abraham Galanté, "who were not only interested in their own community but in Turkish society as well."[111]

The trope of stinginess appeared in an unusual manner during the interviews with Tarık Dursun K. (1931–2015). The writer is praised by Behmoaras for depicting Jews in positive ways in his writing, but when he reflects in the interview on his time growing up in Izmir and the Jewish families he knew, he says that "thriftiness is in their genes" giving several examples of Jews being stingy.[112] Behmoaras, a Turkish Jew, notes that she had left her sunglasses behind in the place where they held the interview and was unable to meet him again for six months. When they finally meet again, he says jokingly to her, "Being this uninterested in your possessions is not proper behavior for your race."[113]

A number of the interviewees discussed the cowardly stereotypes they had grown up with, some repeating them, other suggesting that cowardliness may be a heritable trait. İlhan Selçuk noted that "when I was a child, whenever someone said Jew you would twist your lips . . . as in 'Jewish coward.'"[114] Journalist Ali Sirmen's (b. 1939) definition of being Jewish includes "a type of behavior . . . a reaction . . . a psychosis of fear," and he refers to Jews as cowards.[115] Çandar mentions how "My mother's side is Salonican, probably Dönme . . . When I was a child I would visit [my mother's relatives], and all of them, my cousins, my aunt, even my mother, were like the prototypical [stereotypical] Rachels and Salomons [of anti-Jewish jokes]."[116] Tunçay remembers hearing his Jewish neighbor in Ankara beating his children while screaming, "What did you say? Say it again!" They had called him a phrase they had learned at school: Jewish coward.[117] When asked why the term cowardly Jew is used, he responds, "This phrase has become so much a part of the language that people use it without thinking. . . . Sometimes my wife calls to our cat, 'come out of there cowardly Jew.'"[118] Psychiatrist Özcan Köknel (b. 1928) notes, "When I was a child, my first conceptions of Jews came from the caricature magazines . . . [that Jews are] stingy and cowardly."[119] Köknel, a psychiatrist with a medical degree, declares that cowardice may be passed on in their genes.[120]

Politician, journalist, and poet Çetin Altan (1926–2015) notes that Jews were always involved in politics in the Ottoman Empire and Turkey, asking rhetorically, "Is it possible that they were not? . . . Could they have survived any other way?" Furthermore, "The reason the Jews survived is because they followed an obvious political approach."[121] The clear implication is that Jews survived by operating behind the scenes. He alleges that the Jews' "most special trait" is that "they possess a culture that is able to determine how to live, whether in East or West"; in other words, they were able to follow the same political approach and survive. The Jew displays solidarity with Jews internationally, he claims, which he refers to in English as, "the Jewish connection."[122] "They even taught us this in sociology," he declares, and perhaps "they do carry it in their genes!" Jews are like "moths whose wings are the color of stars."

The cavalcade of anti-Semitic stereotypes marches on for nearly three hundred pages: Jews "do not care about anything other than making a profit;"[123] are incredibly shrewd, "possessing a quickness of mind that can immediately understand and adapt to the situation;"[124] possess phenomenal organizational skills; they are ostentatious; they form a powerful lobby that achieves its aims because they "are dominant in world financial spheres and the media."[125]

Jewish Friends, Christian Enemies . . . Or Have They Really Exaggerated It?

The dozens of interviews of non-Jewish Turkish intellectuals published first in the Turkish Jewish newspaper *Şalom* and later redacted in book form present an often unflattering view of relations between Muslims and Jews and of the opinions Muslims hold of Jews. They also have much to say about the foundation's public awareness activities. Consistent with the foundation's aims, many interviewees articulate the conventional view contrasting Jewish friend and Christian enemy. These dichotomous categories of friend/enemy are then linked to the claim that Turks are not anti-Semitic, even when some speakers contradict themselves a few moments later by displaying their anti-Semitic views in the very same interview. Turks have always treated Jews well, and Jews have responded to this magnanimity with loyalty.

Many repeat the trope of the Jew as the friend of the Muslim Turk against the common Christian internal and external enemy—Armenians, Greeks, the Russian Empire. According to Oktay Akbal, "Among all the minority communities in Turkey, the Jewish community is the one that got along best with the Turks."[126] Atillâ İlhan argues that when "the West decided to break the Ottoman Empire into pieces" in the nineteenth century, the Jews "defended the Ottomans," remaining loyal. Although seemingly unaware of the Zionist independence movement in Ottoman Palestine during the first part of the twentieth century, İlhan posits that Jews did not form independence movements "because they knew that the tolerance that they would have in the Ottoman Empire would never be given" to them by the Greeks. Jews "had a five-hundred-year relationship with the Ottomans, and this relationship had never caused them to suffer! They knew what the Greeks had done to them, and what they were capable of doing to them."[127] Nazlı Ilıcak (b. 1944), a right-wing journalist interviewed for the volume, considers Jews "as a community that was never in conflict with Turkey."[128] She contrasts Jews with Greeks and Armenians, minorities that turned to nationalism and fought for independence. With Jews "there was never any disagreement or conflict." But when Turks speak of Armenians, "it can be very uncomfortable now," since "in the past they collaborated with Russia and stabbed Turks in the back. Even though we do not love Armenians for these reasons, there may be Armenians with whom we get along very well. But these realities are undeniable. Because of the past . . . we can feel uncomfortable. But as for the Jews . . ."[129]

The theme of Jews "repaying" Ottoman tolerance with their loyalty is also often expressed. Cengiz Çandar narrates how "[the Jews] arrived here to an open-armed embrace. . . . Bayezid II . . . embraced the Jews and behaved tolerantly toward them. He even called King Ferdinand of Aragon a fool, for he had expelled a great treasure from his kingdom, the Jews, giving them as a gift to the Ottoman Empire." The Jews in the Ottoman Empire and Turkey "were accepted without any problem, they always lived that way. And later, when the empire was dissolving, when the Greeks and Armenians were influenced by nationalism and turned rebellious, the Jews never took part in this, remaining completely united with the majority society and state." Accordingly, "the Jews' situation is very different than that of the Armenian or Greek minority in Turkey."[130] Mete Tunçay opines that "the Armenians may have been labeled the 'loyal community,' but actually the Jews were the loyal community." As the Ottoman Empire was collapsing "only the Jews did not have a serious separatist movement."[131] He, too, seems to have forgotten about Zionism. Moreover, "During World War I the Jews were neutral, which was different than the Armenians and Greeks."[132] French teacher and poet İsmet Özel (b. 1944) argues that "when the Ottoman Empire was breaking into pieces, the Christians demanded territory. But because the Jews did not [follow suit], they acted in solidarity with the empire's Turkish and Muslim elements," and this was also true in the republic.[133] Özcan Köknel claims that all the Turkish Jews that he knows "have identified with the majority's [Turkish Muslims'] aims, rules, principles and sentiments as much as, if not more than, the majority." He also has Armenian and Greek friends, "but with them you feel like it is better not to discuss known subjects beyond a certain limit; once you begin talking about them, hurtful things may come out." The reason is that "no matter how hard people try to be civilized, at a certain point they become more emotional. It is very difficult to get beyond this!" But he thinks the Jews have "gotten beyond it."[134] Moreover, "when talking with a Greek friend . . . I have to stop [the conversation] at a certain point. If I feel that the political discussion is beginning to cause hurt feelings, I end it. . . . But let me say very frankly that when such a thing happens with a Jew, I do not feel any need to stop the conversation."[135] Politician and diplomat Coşkun Kırca (1927–2005)—who, while serving as Turkish ambassador to Canada, broke many bones jumping out of a window when Armenian terrorists occupied the embassy in Ottawa in 1985[136]—argues that "when the Ottoman Empire went into decline, powerful nations like Russia and France began protecting certain minority groups living in the Ottoman Empire. But not the Jews."[137] He claims, "If anyone would protect them it would be the Turks. . . . When the Greeks and Armenians were given the idea that outside forces would be able to protect them, they began to rebel, and to betray the state. . . . But the Jews did not betray the state."[138] Regarding the counterexample of Zionist plans to establish a Jewish state in Ottoman Palestine, he claims that Ottoman Muslims did not perceive Ottoman Jews as supporters of the Zionists, and thus did not see them as treacherous. More important for him is how in 1918 at the time of the armistice, when "the religious leaders of the Greeks and Armenians collaborated with the occupying forces [the Allies]," Chief Rabbi Haim Nahum "declared 'I do not intervene in politics.' It was a demonstration of loyalty, displaying the degree to which this minority was ready to live in Turkish society."[139] He credits Nahum's pledge of loyalty for hindering the outburst of anti-Semitism in Turkey, relating Jews' "good behavior" to Turkish Muslim tolerance.[140]

Seeing the Jew as the friend united against the common enemy, some of the interviewees confirm how useful the foundation is for Turkey abroad, especially in countering Armenian genocide claims. İlhan states that "Jews seek to balance" the view of Turkey abroad concerning its human rights record, "as Turkey is sometimes unjustly accused in international fora."[141] To improve this view, "they give the message to the whole world that 'Look, we are fine, they did not slaughter us, even if sometimes we faced insignificant hindrances, we are still here.'" Altan finds the foundation to be useful as a means of "hindering Armenian propaganda, and finding a spokesperson on the world stage."[142] Ilıcak, while contrasting the Jewish friend with the Christian enemy, declares that with the foundation, the Jewish community "acts on behalf of Turkey in the outside world."[143] Çandar claims that Jews "have played a more important role for Turkey, for Turkish society, for Turkey's interests, than seventy-five percent of Turks. . . . I view this very positively." For example, the five hundredth anniversary celebrations occurring in 1992 "constituted a very important trump card for Turkey's image in the West." He attended the gala evening in New York City and the ball at Dolmabahçe Palace [in Istanbul, organized by Hakko]. The latter event "was perfect in every way, the best event that I have ever seen, offering the imperial image and sentiment that we feel necessary. . . . That day was one of the rare situations where I felt proud to be a member of this society, and this is in part thanks to the Jews."[144] When asked whether he believes the foundation's celebrations have played a role in improving Turkey's image in the West, he responds, "I believe so. The Turks have a very undeserved image in the West. . . . For this reason, it is very important that the Jews were welcomed five hundred years ago, and from that age until now never were subjected to any serious difficulties." Behmoaras adds that "the West still acts in a prejudiced way regarding the Armenian and Kurdish assertions. The Armenians claim there was a 'genocide' and have succeeded in making people believe it, especially in France and the United States." Çandar praises the Jews: "This is partly because of the Jews. . . . They do not appear to support allowing the Armenians to share such terms as 'Holocaust' and 'genocide.' If they had given the Armenians the support they desired, the Western image of Turkey and Turks would be many times worse than it is today."[145] To Kırca, "the activities of the foundation abroad, especially in countries where Greek and Armenian groups are relatively powerful, give the message that the Turks are not at all barbarians. This manages to elicit question marks in the minds of people whose heads have already been filled [with Greek and Armenian propaganda]."[146]

While a good number of the interviews repeat the foundation's view on the Jewish friend and Christian enemy, a surprising number offer critiques of the way the foundation has represented the past. Numerous intellectuals expressed dislike for what they viewed as the foundation's exaggerated presentation of Ottoman and Turkish tolerance and the utopian view of Muslim-Jewish relations, and of the deferential and uncritical attitude of Jews toward Turkish Muslims and their coziness with the government. Some even deploy anti-Semitic stereotypes when describing it, such as the suggestion that the foundation's success is a good example of Jews' supposed organizational skills and cleverness.

When asked what she thinks of the efforts of the foundation and the message it communicates, physician and writer Selçuk Erez (b. 1936) responds, "I find the use of the term 'gratitude' to be very wrong. . . . One cannot have gratitude for something that is necessary or required. Because the Turkish community perceives this [presentation of history] wrongly, as 'Look, do you see? Look how magnanimous I am.' No, you [the Turks] have done the right thing, you did what was required. You truly behaved gentlemanly. During the tension with the Armenians, from time to time you acted wrongly, and for this they censure you. But do not use it [treatment of the Jews] to say 'Look, I am not a cruel nation. I treated the Jews well.'"[147] Aziz Nesin declares, "Of course because of the five hundredth anniversary you say wonderful things. But as an impartial and just person I am opposed to skipping over some [negative] historical events."[148] Furthermore, "I do not forget the shameful acts that we Turks have committed."[149] In his view, this approach "is a good example of Jewish intelligence, for no [Turks] will object to the [praise propagated by the] foundation!"[150] "But," he continues, "on the topic of this empty word, 'gratitude,' as always, I think the opposite of the majority. I think it is an insult to Turkey. People either are unaware, or we agree with it, it pleases us. The foundation saying 'You did not slaughter us, you did not mow us down, you did not hang us, you are more or less human, not bad,' to me is as heavy as saying 'You slaughtered us, you mowed us down, you hanged us.'" Behmoaras interjects that this is said in comparison with other countries. "Fine, if we say we never did anything to the Jews . . . in fact, we always treated them as inferior."[151]

Tomris Uyar also criticizes the efforts of the foundation, this time in terms of their work with the ruling party. "They have cozied up too much to the government's propaganda. It would have been much better had they celebrated only among themselves [without the involvement of government officials]. While it is true that anti-Semitism was never the policy of the Ottoman Empire or Turkey, I just cannot understand their saying, 'We never experienced any difficulties.' They feel pressured [to say so]. If the pressure does not come from the state, then it is felt in daily life—a taxi driver making fun of a Jewish accent."[152] She warns Turkish Jews that "if you act too long, in the end you will identify with the role," and then relates her critique to a stereotype: "When you ask a Jew even the most simple question, they always respond with a variant of 'What answer should I give?' or 'Which is the most appropriate answer?'"[153] In a feat of conspiratorial thinking about the power of Turkish Jews, İlhan Selçuk notes that Turkish Jews have declared that the foundation would "be Turkey's lobby in the United States, because Turkish Jews [are the ones who] establish relations between Turkey and the United States."[154] He also notes that "representing the state is one thing; establishing a foundation to be the tool of state politics is another."[155] He also declares the term "tolerance" to be archaic; tolerance came before freedom. If the sultan tolerated the Jews, fine, but the concept of "tolerance" is not relevant in today's world. The foundation is speaking of the past—while there was no tolerance in Spain and Portugal, the Ottomans were tolerant. But what matters today, Selçuk argues, is freedom.

Ali Sirmen acknowledges that "the Ottoman Empire was multinational and was endowed with a manifest tolerance." But, he cautions, "it is important not to exaggerate this tolerance. Recently our Jewish citizens have really exaggerated it . . . as we [Turks] immediately jumped on the band wagon. The 'great tolerant Ottoman' image pleased us of course. But no nation is more or less tolerant than the others."[156] Journalist Mehmet Ali Birand (1941–2013) declares that he supports the foundation's aims, argument, and international efforts, and is ready to work with the foundation to spread its message, but with one caveat: "For goodness sake . . . do not make it too exaggerated."[157] He mentions that if he were a Jew, "honestly, I would not be able to live here very comfortably."[158] It is difficult, he says, for a Jew to become a high state official, work in the foreign ministry, be a diplomat, or in a high position in the military "due to discrimination" against "everyone who is not a Turk."[159] Pamuk notes how "a Jew in Turkey knows that it is his fate from birth that he will never be the prime minister, never be the leader of a political party. And because he knows this, it is as though it kills certain ambitions in his mind. For this reason, Turkish Jews will not "present radical views, offer radical criticism of the government."[160] Concerning treatment of minorities, Pamuk declares that Turks are "extraordinarily silent" on the matter and turns to criticize the passivity of Turkish Jews in the face of anti-Semitism.[161] The difference with other countries, he argues, is how the affected minorities respond. "In other countries, Jews seem to lead the way. In other countries, if a writer claims that İnönü's era was a paradise, the Jews would put pressure on this writer, reminding him that there was something called the Capital Tax, as a result of which people from certain races were sent to concentration camps."

Conclusion

In 1989, in preparation for celebrating the quincentennial of the arrival of the Iberian exiles in the Ottoman Empire, Turkish Jews established the *500. yıl vakfı,* the Quincentennial Foundation, in association with the Turkish government, primarily the Office of the Prime Minister and the Ministry of Foreign Affairs. Reviving the trope of benevolent Turkish rescuers acting in the face of external and internal Christian enemies, the foundation promoted a history of Ottoman tolerance toward Jews, who responded with gratitude. According to its president, long-time Turkish Jewish lobbyist Jak Kamhi, the aim of the foundation was "to promote the true values of our Turkey, a country whose reputation had been sullied by various groups and lobbies [Armenians and Greeks]."[162] The efforts of the foundation "were the most effective and important of all the promotion efforts we had conducted up to that time," as "we were able to promote our important values to the world, thus generating a sense of affection and respect for our country." Through its efforts in promoting the work of sympathetic non-Turkish Jewish historians abroad, the foundation also succeeded in "changing negative perceptions and attitudes towards Turkey, especially in America and Europe."[163] As one historian has remarked, "The image of the Ottoman authorities in Jewish historiography has been a very positive one."[164] This is borne out by the influential works of such Turkish Jewish historians as Naim Güleryüz and like-minded Jewish historians abroad, including Stanford Shaw and Avigdor Levy, who worked closely with the foundation.

None of the foundation's organizers, leaders, or spokespeople were professional historians, educators, or museum curators. A collection of influential industrialists, businessmen, and lay community leaders working hand in hand with the Turkish state, these Turkish Jews sought to influence public opinion in Turkey and abroad by referring to a single legitimating historical event, the medieval Ottoman "welcome" given their Iberian ancestors. Understandings of this significant medieval event were manipulated by Turkish Jews without any historical training in order to sell an image of themselves as grateful and Turks as tolerant. When the official historian of such a community is an amateur, one cannot expect the resulting narrative to withstand critical historiographic analysis. One might reasonably ask what a medieval event occurring in a defunct empire has to do with the way minorities are treated in a modern nation-state? How can premodern tolerance be equated with modern equality? How can a government's good treatment of the smallest ethnoreligious minority rebut the same government's annihilation of the largest? In the foundation's narrative, we see all the elements of suppression of historical memory at play: distortion of the broad spectrum of historical experience; silencing of negative events, including persecution of and discrimination against Jews; and redirection of attention from the genocide of Armenians. Rather than tell a tale that is believable and true, their purpose was to express and manipulate collective emotions toward Turks in such a way as would serve their interests as Turkish Jews and those of their ally, the Turkish state. A leading member of the community told me openly that they promote the image of Turkey as savior of the Jews in part because they seek to promote their own international business relations, which are best afforded when Turkey has strong diplomatic relations with the United States and Israel.[165]

Just as historians are dependent upon access to sources in order to carry out their research, businessmen are reliant on access to materials and markets. If a foreign scholar writes openly of the Armenian genocide, she will not be given a research visa in Turkey. Likewise, a Jewish businessman who criticizes the Turkish state or Turkish society will not obtain government permission to engage in large-scale projects. Just as Turkish synagogues and churches voluntarily fly the Turkish flag at their entrance—unlike mosques, which no one would mistake as being foreign—so, too, are Turkish Jewish industrialists required by an unspoken rule to prove themselves more patriotic and loyal than Turkish Muslims. The aims and activities of the foundation are expressions of these everyday facts of being a minority in Turkey.

If Turkish Jews faithfully promote an idealistic image of Turks, the same cannot be said of Turkish Muslim views of Jews; even the opinion of leftist, secularist Turkish intellectuals on Jews are not always so flattering. The foundation was seen as little more than "a great hubbub, a 'show,' whose function was "to try and prove to the outside world from the point of view of Turkey 'how good we were.'"[166] Lizi Behmoaras, editor of the Turkish Jewish journal *Şalom*, may have objected that such an approach was not factually wrong, as the Ottomans really *had* been good to and for the Jews, but one of her interlocutors disagreed: "It was wrong. The important thing is not to say 'We were not that bad' or 'We were good.' . . . For Jews to be able to live in this land as equal citizens alongside me and my children there are clearly things that need to be done. What need is there to sit around and invent a past?"[167] Rather than inventing the Ottoman and Turkish Jewish past, historians have leveraged it in such a way as to deny the genocide of Armenians. When Behmoaras asked another interlocutor to clarify whether the image the foundation projects of Turkey to the outside world correlated with reality, he disagreed, undermining the long-standing effort to present the genocide as an if/then proposition, that if the Turks are tolerant toward Jews, then they could not have committed genocide against the Armenians: "It is exaggerated. And because it is exaggerated it is not believable. If I am this tolerant, what happened with the Armenians?"[168] Only rejecting the myth that Turks and Jews have lived in peace and brotherhood for five hundred years allows one to accept that Turks could have perpetrated a genocide against the Armenians.

Notes

1. "Neve Şalom'a hain terör saldırısı!," *Cumhuriyet*, September 6, 1986. The first bombing of the synagogue occurred in 1969. Bali, *Model Citizens of the State*, 149. Bali discusses the 1986 attack in ibid., 302–303, quoting a Turkish security official who could not believe only two foreigners could have carried out such an attack without local assistance.

2. Bali, *Model Citizens of the State*, 304.

3. Ibid., 302.

4. For the establishment and aims of the foundation, see Marc Baer, "Turkish Jews Rethink '500 Years of Brotherhood and Friendship," *Turkish Studies Association Bulletin*, 24, no. 2 (2000): 63–73; Brink-Danan, *Jewish Life in 21st-Century Turkey*, 35–62.

5. Kamhi, *Gördüklerim yaşadıklarım*, 249.

6. Ibid., 393–394.

7. Ibid., 394.

8. Ibid., 394–395.

9. Ibid., 249.

10. Göçek, *Denial of Violence*, 279.

11. Sachar, *Farewell España*, 111.

12. Kamhi, *Gördüklerim yaşadıklarım*, 343.

13. Ibid., 343.

14. Letter from Jak Kamhi to Rıfat Bali, November 13, 2001, cited in Bali, *Model Citizens of the State*, 310.

15. Kamhi, *Gördüklerim yaşadıklarım*, 263.

16. Archives of Manajans Thompson A.Ş., internal communiqué, October 30, 1989, cited in Bali, *Model Citizens of the State*, 310.

17. Ibid., 311.

18. Cited in ibid., 312.

19. Cited in ibid., 317.

20. Letter from Bernard Ouziel, vice president of the ASA, to Paul Berger, vice president, Quincentennial Foundation, United States, May 24, 1991, Archives of the American Sephardi Federation, Records of the Quincentennial Foundation, Series 1, General Agenda 1989–June 1991, cited in Bali, *Model Citizens of the State*, 314.

21. Cited in Bali, *Model Citizens of the State*, 321–322. On his murder, see "Üzeyir Garih öldürüldü," *Hürriyet*, August 25, 2001.

22. Ibid., 319.

23. Ojalvo, "Le Lobbysme juif en Turquie."

24. Quoted in Brink-Danan, *Jewish Life in 21st-Century Turkey*, 39.

25. Ibid., 35.

26. Statement currently available on its website, "Turkish Jews: Turkish-Jewish Friendship over 500 Years," http://www.turkyahudileri.com/index.php/en/12-turkish-jewish-community and in its original printed form, Güleryüz, *The History of the Turkish Jews*, 25.

27. "Neve Şalom'a ilk saldırı değil," *Hürriyet*, November 11, 2013. The article was written on the occasion of the third bombing of the synagogue.

28. Güleryüz, *The History of the Turkish Jews*, 21–2. Jak Kamhi would repeat the myth: Kamhi, *Gördüklerim yaşadıklarım*, 26.

29. Compare with Shaw, *The Jews of the Ottoman Empire and the Turkish Republic*, 32–34.

30. Quoted in Brink-Danan, *Jewish Life in 21st-Century Turkey*, 51.

31. Hakko, *Hayatım. Vakko*, 238–240.

32. Ibid., 240.

33. Ibid., 241.

34. Ibid., 243.

35. Ibid., 244.

36. Bali, *Cumhuriyet yıllarında Türkiye Yahudileri*, 15.

37. "Heureux comme un juif en Turquie," *Le nouvel observateur* 2092, December 9, 2004. The next year historian Naim Güleryüz informed the European Union's "Seminar on Racism and Antisemitism" held in Istanbul that Turkey is an exemplary nation for its lack of anti-Semitism. Cited in Mallet, *La Turquie, les Turcs et les Juifs*, 469.

38. Bali, *Cumhuriyet yıllarında Türkiye Yahudileri*, 19–20.

39. Onur Öymen quoted in ibid., 22.

40. Baer, "Turkish Jews Rethink '500 Years of Brotherhood and Friendship.'" For an example of work that follows the same directive emphasizing Ottoman tolerance, welcome, and humanitarianism and Ottoman-Jewish peaceful coexistence, see Gülnihal Bozkurt, "An Overview on the Ottoman Empire-Jewish Relations," *Der Islam* 71, no. 2 (1994): 255–279. For a further paragon of this genre that uncritically repeats all of the standard myths, see Yusuf Besalel, *Osmanlı ve Türk Yahudileri* (Istanbul: Gözlem, 1999). Despite being based mainly on the work of Galanté and Güleryüz and to a lesser extent on various encyclopedias and Shaw, it was awarded a prize in the "research monograph" category by the newspaper *Şalom*.

41. Naim Güleryüz, *Türk Yahudileri tarihi I: 20. yüzyılın başına kadar* (Istanbul: Gözlem, 1993); Güleryüz, *The History of the Turkish Jews*. The lecture is also available online: http://turkishjews.com/history/.

42. Lewis, *The Jews of Islam*, 129–135.

43. Güleryüz, *The History of the Turkish Jews*, 3–4.

44. Güleryüz, *Türk Yahudileri tarihi I*, 13.

45. Ibid., 44, 80. The translation is based on the document presented in Galanté and Lewis.

46. Ibid., 50, citing Galanté.

47. Ibid., 51–52.

48. Ibid., 61.

49. Ibid., 62–63, 67.

50. Ibid., 52–53, 73–74, 170, 183–186. He notes that Franco blames the 1530 Amasya blood libel on Greeks while Galanté blames it on Armenians.

51. Ibid., 180, 182.

52. *Minorities and the Destruction of the Ottoman Empire* (Ankara: Türk Tarihi Kurumu, 1993); *The Assyrians of Turkey: Victims of Major Power Policy* (Ankara: Türk Tarihi Kurumu, 2001); *The Great War and the Tragedy of Anatolia* (Ankara: Türk Tarihi Kurumu, 2001); *Osmanlı Ermenileri büyük güçler diplomasisinin kurbanları* (Ottoman Armenians: victims of Great Powers' diplomacy, Istanbul: Remzi, 2009); *İngiliz gizli belgelerine göre Adana'da vuku bulan Türk-Ermeni olayları* (Temmuz 1908–Aralık 1909) (The Turkish-Armenian events in Adana according to secret English documents, Ankara: Türk Tarihi Kurumu, 2014).

53. See for example, "The Fifth Centenary of the First Jewish Migrations to the Ottoman Empire," *Belleten* 56, no. 215 (April 1992): 207–212.

54. Salahi Sonyel, "Turco-Jewish Relations during the First World War and Turkey's War of Liberation," in *Turkish-Jewish Encounters: Studies on Turkish-Jewish Relations Through the Ages*, ed. Mehmet Tütüncü (Haarlem, the Netherlands: SOTA, Research Centre for Turkestan, Azerbaijan, Crimea, Caucasus and Siberia, 2001), 225–238.

55. Salahi Sonyel, "Turco-Armenian Relations in the Context of the Jewish Holocaust," *Belleten* 54, no. 210 (August 1990): 757–772, here 757. Sonyel is sure to mention Armenian support for the Nazis during World War II.

56. Kamhi, *Gördüklerim yaşadıklarım*, 403.

57. Ibid., 404.

58. Brink-Danan, *Jewish Life in 21st-Century Turkey*, 45.

59. Ibid., 44.

60. "700 yıllık bir beraberliği keşfedin," 500. yıl vakfı Türk Musevileri Müzesi, n.d.

61. Naim Güleryüz, *The Turkish Jews: 700 Years of Togetherness* (Istanbul: Gözlem, 2009).

62. "700 yıllık bir beraberliği keşfedin."

63. Güleryüz, *The History of the Turkish Jews*, 14.

64. Kamhi, *Gördüklerim yaşadıklarım*, 400.

65. Ibid.

66. Shaw, *The Jews of the Ottoman Empire and the Turkish Republic*, ix.

67. Ibid.

68. Ibid., 26. One source of Shaw's view may have been a mid-sixteenth-century *fetva* (legal opinion) of Shaykh al-Islām Ebussuud Efendi. In response to the question of whether Sultan Mehmed II conquered Constantinople by force, which would have allowed the Ottomans to confiscate its churches and synagogues, the mufti answered, "As is well known he conquered it by force. . . . In 1538–1539 an investigation was made in this matter. A 117 year-old-man and a 130 year-old-man were found who testified saying that 'Jews and Christians secretly allied with Sultan Mehmed, and did not help the Christian ruler in battle, Sultan Mehmed did not take them captive.'" Accordingly, ancient churches and synagogues could not be confiscated by the Ottomans. M. Ertuğrul Düzdağ, *Şeyhülislâm Ebussu'ûd*

Efendi'nin fetvalarına göre kanunî devrinde Osmanlı hayatı: Fetâvâ-yi Ebussu'ûd Efendi (Istanbul: Şule, 1998), 165. Ebussuud Efendi's *fetva* is a legal fiction that allowed the pragmatic Ottomans recourse to permit the rebuilding of synagogues. As Minna Rozen demonstrates, there is no evidence that Jews assisted the Ottomans in taking Constantinople, and in fact, Greek Jews were taken captive and treated no differently than other Byzantines. Rozen, *A History of the Jewish Community in the Istanbul*, 15. A seventeenth-century imperial decree based on the same logic as the sixteenth-century *fetva* "should not be taken as historical fact, but most probably as a useful, late invention concocted jointly by the Jewish community and the Ottoman authorities." Ibid., 11.

69. Rozen, *A History of the Jewish Community in the Istanbul*, 38.

70. Shaw, *The Jews of the Ottoman Empire and the Turkish Republic*, 29–30, 33, 41.

71. Ibid., 1.

72. Ibid.

73. Ibid., 2.

74. Ibid. This paragraph is repeated verbatim, without quotation marks, in Sonyel, "Turco-Jewish Relations During the First World War and Turkey's War of Liberation," 230.

75. See also his article published by the Turkish Historical Foundation, "Christian Anti-Semitism in the Ottoman Empire," *Belleten* 54 (1990): 1073–1149.

76. Shaw, *The Jews of the Ottoman Empire and the Turkish Republic*, 85, 198.

77. Gilles Veinstein, "Jews and Muslims in the Ottoman Empire," in *A History of Jewish-Muslim Relations*, 187.

78. Levy is the author of *The Sephardim in the Ottoman Empire* (Princeton, NJ: Darwin, 1992), and editor, *The Jews of the Ottoman Empire* (Princeton, NJ: Darwin, 1994). On the ITS role in genocide denial, see Roger Smith, Eric Markusen, and Robert Jay Lifton, "Professional Ethics and the Denial of Armenian Genocide," *Holocaust and Genocide Studies* 9, no. 1 (Spring 1995): 1–22.

79. Avigdor Levy, introduction to *Jews, Turks, Ottomans: A Shared History, Fifteenth Through the Twentieth Century*, ed. Avigdor Levy (Syracuse, NY: Syracuse University Press, 2002), xix. Levy's work was used by other studies, such as Mark Mazower's *Salonica: City of Ghosts*, a beautiful, moving account that aims to revive memories of a city that serves for its author as a model of "religious co-existence" and also offers a nostalgic perspective on relations between Ottomans and Jews. Mark Mazower, *Salonica, City of Ghosts: Christians, Muslims, and Jews, 1430–1950* (New York: Vintage, 2006), 11.

80. Avigdor Levy, preface to *The Jews of the Ottoman Empire*, xiii.

81. Avigdor Levy, introduction to *The Jews of the Ottoman Empire*, 15.

82. Ibid., 16–17.

83. Ibid., 19–21.

84. Ibid., 21.

85. Ibid., 28–29.

86. Ibid., 105.

87. "Türkiye'yi dunyaya tanıttılar," *Hürriyet*, November 29, 1988; "TüTAV ödülleri sahiplerini buldu," *Güneş*, November 29, 1988"; Communication no. 322: TüTAV to Professor Avigdor Levy, December 2, 1988, cited in Bali, *Model Citizens of the State*, 319.

88. Lizi Behmoaras, ed., *Türkiye'de aydınların gözüyle Yahudiler* (Istanbul: Gözlem, 1993).

89. Marc David Baer, "An Enemy Old and New: The Dönme, Anti-Semitism, and Conspiracy Theories in the Ottoman Empire and Turkish Republic," *Jewish Quarterly Review* 103, no. 4 (Fall 2013).

90. Behmoaras, *Türkiye'de aydınların gözüyle Yahudiler*, 45.
91. Quoted in ibid., 46.
92. Ibid., 71.
93. Ibid., 71–72.
94. Ibid., 73.
95. Ibid., 78.
96. Ibid., 15.
97. Ibid., 17.
98. Ibid., 23–24.
99. Ibid., 26.
100. Ibid., 29.
101. Ibid., 192.
102. Ibid., 212.
103. Ibid., 243–244.
104. Ibid., 245.
105. Ibid., 92.
106. Ibid., 111.
107. Ibid., 227.
108. Ibid., 182.
109. Ibid., 213–214.
110. Ibid., 136.
111. Ibid., 138.
112. Ibid., 34.
113. Ibid., 38.
114. Ibid., 111.
115. Ibid., 155.
116. Ibid., 225.
117. Ibid. 247–248.
118. Ibid., 248.
119. Ibid., 265.
120. Ibid., 266.
121. Ibid., 125–126.
122. Ibid., 127.
123. Ibid., 130.
124. Ibid., 202.
125. Ibid., 232.
126. Ibid., 14.
127. Ibid., 25.
128. Ibid., 145.
129. Ibid., 146.
130. Ibid., 226–227.
131. Ibid., 240.
132. Ibid., 243.
133. Ibid., 256.
134. Ibid., 264.
135. Ibid., 267.
136. See Göçek, *Denial of Violence*, 453–454.

137. Behmoaras, *Türkiye'de aydınların gözüyle Yahudiler*, 272.

138. Ibid.

139. Ibid., 273.

140. Ibid.

141. Ibid., 30.

142. Ibid., 129.

143. Ibid., 145.

144. Ibid., 231.

145. Ibid., 232.

146. Ibid., 278.

147. Ibid., 66.

148. Ibid., 74.

149. Ibid., 75.

150. Ibid., 76.

151. Ibid., 77.

152. Ibid., 94.

153. Ibid., 97.

154. Ibid., 116.

155. Ibid., 117.

156. Ibid., 158.

157. Ibid., 172.

158. Ibid., 168.

159. Ibid., 170.

160. Ibid., 182.

161. Ibid., 183.

162. Kamhi, *Gördüklerim yaşadıklarım*, 393.

163. Ibid., 268, 400.

164. Hacker, "Ottoman Policy toward the Jews and Jewish Attitudes toward the Ottomans during the Fifteenth Century," 117.

165. Interview with author, Istanbul, October 2015.

166. Mete Tunçay, quoted in Behmoaras, *Türkiye'de aydınların gözüyle Yahudiler*, 248.

167. Ibid.

168. Ali Sirmen, quoted in Behmoaras, *Türkiye'de aydınların gözüyle Yahudiler*, 158.

6

WHITEWASHING THE ARMENIAN
GENOCIDE WITH HOLOCAUST HEROISM

IN 1993, STANFORD SHAW COLLABORATED WITH TURKISH CAREER foreign
service personnel and Turkish Jewish leaders committed to denying the
Armenian genocide in the promotion of a polished image of Turkey for an
international audience. Two years after publishing *The Jews of the Ottoman
Empire and the Turkish Republic*, Shaw published *Turkey and the Holocaust:
Turkey's Role in Rescuing Turkish and European Jewry from Nazi Persecution, 1933–1945*, a book that brought together Armenian genocide denial and
an updated version of the centuries-old theme of utopian relations between
Muslims and Jews in the face of the Christian enemy.[1] In *The Jews of the Ottoman Empire and the Turkish Republic,* Shaw had repeated the old saw that
"Muslim Turks themselves never at any point showed any anti-Semitism"
whereas Christians, especially Armenians, "persisted in their anti-Semitic
attitudes and activities" in Turkey during World War II.[2] It was a short step
to take—hand in hand with the document cullers in the Ministry of Foreign Affairs—to add to this the myth that Turkey rescued its Jews from the
Nazis. All Shaw needed was evidence. And so he was handed the unverified
testimonies of Turkish ambassadors who claimed to have saved Jews.

With the staking of this new claim, a new layer was added to the old
myth: Turkish Jewish loyalty across more than five hundred years of friendship was in the long run repaid by Turkish benevolence during the Nazi
regime; Turkish universities opened their gates to German Jews seeking
refuge; Turkish ambassadors in Europe saved Turkish Jews from their Nazi
oppressors.[3]

Turkey and the Holocaust introduced the myth of the Turks as the rescuers of Turkish Jews during the Holocaust.[4] Such a claim—introduced in
the early 1990s as Turkey sought to join the newly established European

Union—corresponds well to postwar US and European worldviews, which judge the tolerance level of a state and a people in reference to their moral standing during the Holocaust.[5] Notably, Shaw had not mentioned Turkey's alleged role saving Turkish Jews living in Europe from Nazi persecution in his previous study.[6] There, he had argued instead that, according to Zionist agents based in Istanbul during the war, it was *"their [Zionist] activities alone*, done with the full knowledge and silent support of the Turkish government, that provided European Jews" deliverance from the Nazis.[7] He did not mention Turkish Jews living in Nazi-occupied Europe. In his earlier account, he claimed that the Turkish government played a secondary role, offering the Zionists "passive approval" for their efforts to rescue European Jews from "Poland, Yugoslavia, Bulgaria, Greece, Hungary, Rumania, and Czechoslovakia . . . Estonia, the Ukraine and Russia."[8] Shaw's list did not include France. While he credited Turkish diplomats in Europe with "at times helping and even arranging for Jews to flee to Turkey," these actions were depicted as part of "Zionist rescue activities," not Turkish government policy. In other words, prior to the publication of his 1993 book, Shaw did not treat these events as examples of Turkish humanitarianism or good relations with Jews, nor as the heroic deeds of individual Turkish ambassadors and diplomats.

Two years later, however, Shaw argued that Turkish diplomats—in particular, those in France where most European Turkish Jews lived—acting on orders from Ankara, whose policy he claimed was to rescue Jews, regularly intervened to save the lives of European and Turkish Jews, those with Turkish citizenship and those without, at risk to their own lives.[9] What had changed in the intervening two years? Why did Shaw suddenly present Turkey as the main agent of Jewish rescue from the Nazis and why had he not mentioned Turkish Jews in Europe before? How is it that over the course of "thirty-five years of research" in "the libraries and archives of Turkey, Great Britain, the United States and France," he had failed to uncover such material?[10] If such evidence had long existed, why had Abraham Galanté not exploited it in place of judging Turkey as a beneficiary of German Jewish immigration? If Turkey's heroism was an established fact, why had Joseph Néhama not documented it in his comprehensive account, published shortly after the war, of the annihilation of Sephardic Jewry by the Nazis?[11] What sense can we derive from this puzzling state of historiographic affairs?

The picture comes sharply into focus the moment that Shaw relates in the preface to *Turkey and the Holocaust* that the thesis and documentation supporting "Turkey's role in rescuing thousands of Jews from the Holocaust" were both introduced to him by Turkish diplomats in a meeting facilitated by Turkish Jewish community leaders, all of whom were on the directorial board of the Quincentennial Foundation. During "a visit to the offices of Jak V. Kamhi, head of the Quincentennial Foundation, retired ambassadors [and foundation vice president] Tevfik Saraçoğlu and [foundation general secretary] Behçet Türeman, historian [and foundation vice president] Naim Güleryüz, and the foundation's administrative director Nedim Yahya showed me copies of a number of letters exchanged between Jewish Turks resident in wartime France, the Turkish consulate in Paris, and German diplomats, Gestapo officers, and concentration camp commanders as well as French officials involved in persecution of Jews at that time."[12] Despite being a historian who prides himself on archival research based on the reading of original historical documents, he was pleased to see these "copies." He then thanks the Turkish foreign minister, the director of its research department, and other ambassadors and retired ambassadors. These include two long involved in Armenian genocide denial—Kâmuran Gürün and, notably, Bilâl Şimşir, "also an active member of the Turkish Historical Society, who as a young Turkish Foreign Service officer catalogued the embassy archives in Paris, London, and elsewhere in Europe."[13] The documents that appear in Şimşir's published work have not been made available to independent researchers.

The Incredible Tale of Turkish Consul Necdet Kent

The most preposterous counterevidence of the Turkish rescue effort is the manufactured story of Necdet Kent (1911–2002), consul at Marseilles, who allegedly jumped into a cattle car full of Jews destined for a concentration camp, forcing the Germans to release the Turkish Jews with the consul. Kent's claims appeared for the first time in the form of a statement, included as an appendix in Shaw's 1993 book on the Holocaust, published courtesy of the foundation, after having been narrated to Jak Kamhi, head of the foundation, six years earlier.

Kent, a Turkish Muslim, narrates how "one evening, a Turkish Jew from Izmir named Sidi Iscan, who worked at the Consulate as a clerk and translator," came to his house and told him "that the Germans had gathered up about eighty Jews and had taken them to the railroad station with the intention of loading them onto cattle wagons for shipment to Germany." Iscan "could hardly hold back his tears. Without stopping to express my grief, I immediately tried to calm him and then took the fastest vehicle available to the Saint Charles railroad station in Marseilles."[14] Reference to the Turkish Jewish rescuer would later be dropped in cinematic and novelistic retellings of the narratives, for his inclusion confuses the ethnoreligious boundary between rescuer and rescued so necessary to the tale of Turkish Holocaust heroism.

Claims at the beginning of Kent's statement have given historians pause. The train in question left at ten o'clock in the morning, not in the evening.[15] Moreover, "it is impossible to confuse the magnificent building of St. Charles station with the pitiful environment" of the Arenc freight train station from which the train actually departed.[16]

Kent's description of the arrested Jews is credible, but then his narrative falters on another detail. He relates how "the scene there was unbelievable. I came to cattle wagons which were filled with sobbing and groaning people. Sorrow and anger drove everything else from my mind. The most striking memory I have of that night is the sign I saw on one of the wagons, a phrase which I cannot erase from my mind: This wagon can be loaded with twenty head of large cattle and five hundred kilograms of hay."[17] Reviewing photographic evidence, one scholar realized that the sign on the cattle car would have actually read either "*Hommes* (People) 60—*Chevaux* (Horses) 8" or "*Hommes* (People) 40—*Chevaux* (Horses) 8."[18] The small inconsistencies in the story begin to add up. But no matter, the consul reaches the point in the narrative where he can boast of his heroism. When the Gestapo officer asked him why he was there, "I told him that these people were Turkish citizens, that their arrest had been a mistake, and that it should be remedied at once by their release."[19] When the Gestapo officer replied that these were not Turks but Jews, Kent narrates his response: "Seeing that I would get nowhere by making threats which could not be carried out if they were fulfilled, I returned to Sidi Iscan and said, 'Come on, let's board the train ourselves' and pushing aside the German soldier who tried to block my way, I boarded one of the wagons with Sidi Iscan beside me." The Gestapo officer begged them to alight, but the train began to move. The dramatic scene would be replayed in several Turkish novels and films.

But here the author admits that his memory falters. He cannot remember all of the details. "Since it was a long time ago, I cannot remember too well, but I remember that the train came to a stop when we came to either Arles or Nimes. A number of German officers climbed onto the car and immediately came to my side." The officers "told me that there had been a mistake, the train had left after I had boarded, the persons responsible would be punished, as soon as I left the train I could return to Marseilles on a car that would be assigned to me." He told them "it was not a mistake, that more than eighty Turkish citizens had been loaded onto this cattle wagon because they were Jews, that as a citizen of a nation as well as the representative of a government which felt that religious beliefs should not be the reason for such treatment, there could be no question of my leaving them alone, and that was why I was there." The officers asked him to ascertain whether "all those in the wagon were Turkish citizens."[20]

The consul depicts himself as having the ability to make life or death decisions. He will depict himself as having saved them all. The Jews unabashedly show their gratitude, as Turks expect them to do. "All of the people around me, women, men, and children, stood petrified while they watched this game played for their lives. Most likely because of my refusal to compromise, as well as an order received by the Nazi officers, we all descended from the train together."[21] He "will never forget what followed. The people who had been saved threw their arms around our necks and shook our hands, with expressions of gratitude in their eyes. I have rarely experienced in my life the internal peace which I felt as I entered my bed towards morning of that day."[22]

The statement's mawkish closing scenario poses the most questions about its veracity, for in it, Kent claims to have been sent letters of gratitude by many of those he saved. "I have received letters from time to time over the years from many of my fellow travelers on the short train ride of that day. Today who knows how many of them are still in good health and how many have left us. I remember them all affectionately, even those who may no longer remember me."[23] As it turns out, none have remembered him. This is because, as Holocaust scholars have pointed out, this tale, as moving as it is, is "hardly credible."[24] It is fiction. During the actual January 24, 1943, raid in Marseille, seventy Turkish Jews were arrested; nine were released.[25] One scholar asks why Turkish diplomats would later "demand the release of people who apparently had already been rescued by Kent?"[26] Kent's own communications to the Turkish embassy the following day, January 25, about events he claims to have taken place that day, reveal that the train in question *had already departed* for the camps the morning before.[27] One Turkish Jewish woman narrates escaping from the deportation train *that Kent allegedly boarded*.[28] Why would she remember having to escape and not remember embracing Kent who saved her life?

Most significant is the lack of eyewitness and documentation to support Kent's claims. For this reason, no international Holocaust organization, not even the Israeli Holocaust Memorial and Museum Yad Vashem, has acknowledged Kent's self-declared rescue of Turkish Jews. Kent was never able to name a single survivor or produce any of the letters he claimed to have received over the years. In point of fact, no Turkish Jew has remembered him. Just as Kent could not name a single Jew on that train, not a single Jew could be found to provide testimony of Kent having saved her life.

From the Historical Frying Pan into Fiction

Despite being little more than baseless fiction, Kent's claims do make for a great story, and on the surface his seemingly heroic actions have proven irresistible to those wishing to present Turkey in a positive light. The story has been repeated ad nauseum. It was dramatized first nearly verbatim in the film *Desperate Hours* (2000), which was produced with the support of the Quincentennial Foundation and the Turkish Ministry of Foreign Affairs and promoted by Jewish American congressmen well known for their work defeating resolutions recognizing the Armenian genocide.[29] The filmmaker Victoria Barrett admitted that the idea to make the film came to her after Turkey's ambassador in Washington, DC, had explained to her how Turkish diplomats had rescued Jews.[30] The story then appeared in Ayşe Kulin's best-selling novel, *Nefes nefese* (Out of breath, 2002), which became an international bestseller as *The Last Train to Istanbul*.[31] In both Barrett's film and Kulin's novel, we see a good example of how genocide denial and Holocaust heroism go hand in hand; both present Turkish (or Ottoman) Muslims in the best possible light. On the one hand, referring to the fate of the Armenians, Kulin can state during a television interview, "I love the Armenians very much, but that was a deportation [as opposed to being a genocide]. It happened in the midst of war. It is difficult to label something that happens in the midst of war as a genocide. We did not begin to slaughter them for no good reason, like what happened to the Jews."[32] Kulin's argument is not too different from what Shaw's mentor Bernard Lewis had claimed some twelve years earlier: "To make this a parallel to the Holocaust in Germany, you would have to assume that the Jews of Germany had been engaged in an armed rebellion against the German state, collaborating with the Allies against Germany."[33] Or, as Justin McCarthy put this "blame the victim" perspective rather bluntly in his congressional testimony six years before Lewis, "Our remembrance of the evils of Nazi Germany has unfortunately caused us to see other events of history through the glass of the Holocaust. In the Holocaust, an innocent people was persecuted and annihilated. There was no Jewish threat to the German State. Yet the full force of a modern state was mobilized to slaughter the innocent."[34] In contrast, McCarthy averred, in Anatolia in 1915, "both sides were armed, both sides fought, and both sides were victims." In other words, finding the Armenians guilty of having threatened the empire, McCarthy, Lewis, Shaw, and Kulin hesitate neither to label the fate of Armenians undeserving of the term genocide, nor to label the fate of the Jews a genocide, despite it having happened "in the midst of war."

Like Shaw, Kulin thanks Naim Güleryüz, official historian of the chief rabbinate in Istanbul, and the foundation for providing documentation— the "various booklets, documents, and newspaper clippings provided by the 500 Year Trust"—which are nowhere referenced.[35] The contents of official documents are presented throughout the novel in italics, without attribution, and the reader is led to believe that they refer to the documents allegedly provided Kulin by the foundation. The novel repeats the old historiographic myths that Ottoman and Turkish Jews have long told and which the foundation promotes: that Sultan Bayezid II "invited" the "250,000" (!) Jews expelled from Spain to his realm; that "the Turks were the only nation that came to their aid"; and that Bayezid stated, "You call Ferdinand [of Spain] a wise king; he, who, by expelling the Jews, has impoverished his country and enriched mine."[36] Moreover, she has a character claim that the Jews were the Ottomans' "most loyal and hardworking subjects, who unlike the other minorities, did not stab the state in the back as the empire was crumbling."[37] Kulin adds that, by taking advantage of the freedom they had been granted, "the Jews became wealthy" in their new land. She includes among her reference material the works of longtime Armenian genocide denier Kâmuran Gürün and credits the foundation's "Turkish Jewish Museum" for having provided the list of the nineteen "Turkish diplomats who saved the lives of Jews" during World War II. In return, the foundation honored Kulin for her novel, which by 2017 had been translated into twenty-five languages.[38]

Kulin's acknowledgments show just how blurred the line between fact and fiction is when it comes to narrating Muslim-Jewish relations in Turkey. As with historians like Shaw, one suspects that for the novel's author, the difference between the two does not really matter. As Kulin states in her acknowledgments, "*Last Train to Istanbul* is not the biography of an actual person. The novel is based on the experiences of a number of Turkish diplomats who were posted to Europe during the Second World War who succeeded in saving many Turkish and non-Turkish Jews from Hitler's grasp."[39] She thanks two diplomats "who devoted so much of their precious time to narrating their memories of that era, which enabled me to write this novel": Kent and Namık Kemal Yolga, vice-consul at the Paris consulate general during World War II. Subsequent research has proven that, rather than "protecting" Jews as he had claimed in an account published as an appendix in Shaw's study of the Holocaust, Yolga was actually instrumental in *stripping* Jews of protection, in particular, the France-born *children* of Turkish citizens.[40] The novelist inadvertently disturbs the boundary demarcating where fact and fantasy diverge.

Kulin's claim that "the book is not based on the lives of real characters" becomes disconcerting when the reader finds Necdet Kent thinly disguised as "Nâzım Kender" in the novel. When Kent/Kender jumps on the train in the novel, the episode adheres almost verbatim to Kent's testimony published in Shaw's book, following the same sequence of events with virtually all the same details.[41] The text that appears as an independently unverified primary document in a historical study (*Turkey and the Holocaust*) becomes a fictional account in a novel (*Last Train to Istanbul*). The author darkens the atmosphere and heightens the drama by making the train journey longer, adding a man suffering from an apparent heart attack and the smell of urine. Otherwise there is little difference between the "fictional" account in the novel and the alleged "nonfictional" account in the history book.

The author ends the scene with Kent's depiction of how he must have wanted to have been treated had he actually carried out the actions he claims to have—the way Jews are expected to treat Muslims in Turkey: with gratitude. "Eighty people wanted to kiss Nâzım Kender one by one; all tried to hug him. Those who could not reach him stretched out their arms and hands, like people trying to touch a sacred object. 'Don't lift me up on your shoulders' the Consul pleaded. But there was no way he could control the torrent of love rising around him. There were no words to describe the gratitude felt by these people."[42]

The flood of love continued in Turkey. A postage stamp was issued in Kent's honor in 2008 as part of the Turkish Postal Service's "Precedent for Humanity" series. The stamp features a dour-looking Kent with a flock of doves flying above a speeding train. The other stamp in the series, dedicated to Selahattin Ülkümen, the only Turkish diplomat mentioned by Galanté, recognized by Yad Vashem for saving forty-two Jews, appears to show the same flock of birds flying out of a concentration camp.

Politicians and journalists often repeat the claim that Turkey saved Jews during the Holocaust, and they invariably cite Kent. A typical example appeared in the English-language *Turkish Daily News* the same year the postage stamp was issued. In "Turks Saved Jews from Nazi Holocaust," which cites Shaw's book as a reference, Eyüp Erdoğan begins by discussing Kent's heroics: "Some took the risk of forcibly getting on Nazi 'death trains' as they were to set off for death camps, prying Jews on them from the hands of the SS officers."[43] Although the International Raoul Wallenberg Foundation (IRWF) posts this article on its website, it appends a note stating that although it has conducted "a thorough and worldwide research into the role played by Turkish diplomats in France and in other countries" during World War II, it has uncovered "no evidence as to the role played by the said diplomats vis-à-vis Turkish Jews" and "to date, it was not possible to receive any independent, objective third party corroboration to the self-testimony of Mr. Necdet Kent, regarding his having boarded a Nazi deportation train and released a number of Turkish Jews from deportation or death. No single survivor or survivor's descendent, has ever come forward verifying this account. All the IRWF attempts to get access to the official Turkish Archives, utilized by Shaw, have been ignored."[44]

Turkish Passport, "The Only Holocaust Film with a Happy Ending"

Kent's tale was most recently dramatized in *Türk Pasaportu* (*Turkish Passport*, 2011), a film largely produced by Turkish Jews.[45] *Turkish Passport's* project director was Yael Habif; its producer, Bahadır Arlıel; its director, Burak Arlıel; its historical advisor, Naim Güleryüz; it was also supported by the chief rabbinate, the foundation, and community leader Bensiyon Pinto; additional financial support came from the Turkish Foreign Ministry and Turkish Ministry of Tourism and Culture.[46] One of the most dramatic scenes in the film, shown at the Cannes Film Festival, depicts Kent and his aide jumping into the train destined for a concentration camp in order to force the Germans to release the Turkish Jews. The aide's Jewishness, part of Kent's original statement, has been edited out of the film, for it would confuse the boundary between Turkish savior and grateful Jew indebted to the Turk for his beyond-the-call-of-duty tolerance.

The film begins with a harrowing scene. A dark-haired boy with a yellow Jewish star pinned to his jacket is running through darkened streets from a Nazi soldier. Clutching at the star as he tries to remove it, he runs in and out of doorways, in and out of shadows, until finally coming face to face with the soldier. Crumpling to the ground and putting his hands over his head, he awaits his death, as the audience holds its collective breath. But then the scene shifts, and the same boy, without a Jewish star, awakens from what the audience understands to have been just a nightmare; he is warm and safe sitting in a Turkish train car with his family, traveling away from the danger of Nazi Europe toward safety in the Turkish Republic. It was all just a dream. It was a fiction.

Or was it? The ninety-minute film, which the director calls a documentary, mainly features Turkish Jews speaking in French narrating their rescue by Turkish diplomats in wartime France as actors pantomime the actions the interviewees describe. An early scene in the film shows a girl wearing a yellow Jewish star being denied entry to a café, where the owner has put up a "No Jews Allowed" sign. But as the audience is watching this scene, the narrator, a Turkish Jewish woman who survived Nazi-occupied France, tells the audience that Turkish Jews did not have to wear the yellow star because they were citizens of a neutral country. If Turkish Jews did not have to wear the star in Nazi-occupied France because of their status as Turkish citizens, why did the filmmaker add this detail? And if the Turkish Republic did not discriminate between citizens on the basis of race or religion, then how could the repatriation of Jewish citizens of Turkey be considered an act of rescue above and beyond the call, rather than a mere discharge of diplomatic duty?[47] Here, yet again, the "rescued" Turkish Jew is expected to express her gratefulness to her "saviors" in perpetuity. Less an equal citizen than a guest offered safe harbor, such an outsider's repaid gratitude is a given. For while a citizen has the right to expect its government to act impartially on her behalf, an outsider is expected to repay such a feat with gratitude; she would find it natural for a foreign government to congratulate itself on having bestowed the heroics of rescue upon her. The viewer wonders what happened to these Jews after the war and why they speak French today. Did they not remain in Turkey, the welcoming heroic land where Muslim-Jewish relations are so amicable?

As an annotation to the film's main claim that Turkish diplomats risked their lives to save many Jews, the final image is a listing of the names and posts of nineteen Turkish diplomats in Europe beneath the Turkish foreign minister at the time, Hüseyin Numan Menemencioğlu. At an autumn 2014 cocktail reception and film screening I attended in London hosted by the Turkish ambassador to the United Kingdom, the crowd of mostly Turkish Muslims gave the film—or more specifically, Turkish diplomats—a standing ovation. When Turkish Muslims congratulate themselves for being a part of a great Turkish nation devoted since time immemorial to humanitarianism, Turkish Jews step up to play their part in lending credence to the claim. One representative of the Turkish Jewish community spoke before the screening of the film, expressing his gratitude to the Turks for having received the Spanish refugees in 1492 and for having allowed them to flourish thereafter in their midst. He mentioned Turkey's Ülkümen, conspicuously absent in the film, as having been recognized as a "Righteous Among the Nations," noting that the Turkish Jewish community had recently founded a primary school in his name in Van following a recent earthquake. Bringing the story more vibrantly into the room, he projected a photo of the chief rabbi in ceremonial dress surrounded by school-uniform-wearing (Kurdish) children in front of the modest Ülkümen school. Why Van, a southeastern Anatolian city closely associated with the Armenian genocide? Why not a Jewish neighborhood in Istanbul?

According to its website, *Turkish Passport* is a true story, a documentary "based on the testimonies of witnesses who travelled to Istanbul to find safety."[48] It also presents written historical documents and archival footage "to tell this story of rescue and bring to light the events of the time." As professor of international relations Umut Uzer—a Turkish scholar who condemns Turkish anti-Semitism and promotes Holocaust education but denies the Armenian genocide—stated to the audience before the screening of the film in London, "We know this story is true; we have Stanford Shaw's study proving the case."[49]

Just before the final image naming the twenty Turkish diplomats featured in the film, one after another, a succession of Turkish Jews express their thanks to Turkey. These are passengers on what the film calls the "Rescue Train"—not the train Kent is supposed to have boarded, but a train that carried them from Nazi-occupied France all the way through war-torn Europe to Turkey. "The Turkish government saved our lives . . ." "The debt I owe Turkey . . ." "It is a miracle I am still alive . . ." "Thank you . . ." "The Turks saved our lives . . ." "I am grateful . . ." "We owe our being here today to the Turkish government . . ." "Thank you very much . . ." A reviewer of the film expresses bewilderment as to why "in the documentary, some of the most categorically pro-Turkish arguments are made by Turkish Jews. Having ethnic or religious minorities advocate Turkish nationalist arguments is a time-tested strategy of the Kemalist establishment."[50] But rather than having anything to do with Kemalism, such Jewish myth-making takes us back to 1892 and the Jewish commemoration of the four hundredth anniversary of the ingathering of Spanish Jewry.

As the myth of Turkey as rescuer of Turkish Jews was being created throughout the 1980s, 1990s, and 2000s, scholars in genocide studies realized that what is unique to Turkey is "the determination to deny the Armenian genocide by acknowledging the Holocaust."[51] Yet in point of fact, the problem is more deep seated: *Turkish Passport* and efforts like it are actually a form of Holocaust denial. By promoting the film as "the only Holocaust film with a happy ending," the story silences the many measures Turkey took to prevent Turkish Jewish return. Because Turkish Jews were not considered "members of the Turkish race,"[52] Turkey denaturalized approximately 3,000 to 5,000 Turkish Jews during the war. The film also silences the Nazis deportation of between 2,200 and 2,500 Turkish Jews to death camps (Auschwitz and Sobibór) and another three to four hundred to concentration camps (Ravensbrück, Buchenwald, Mauthausen, Dachau, Bergen-Belsen), where many succumbed.[53] Others died in detention in the Drancy and Westerbork camps or were murdered by the Gestapo. Contrary to the film's claim that "Turkey was the only country to take a stand against" Nazi persecution of Jews, Turkey was in reality the only neutral country to implement restrictions on its own Jews, which is to say that even fascist Spain made more efforts to save its Jews.[54]

Shaw had argued that Turkey had been a lifesaver for one hundred thousand persecuted Jews transiting through Turkey en route to Palestine. In fact, "the legal escape route to Palestine was enormously limited."[55] Because of this, Jewish organizations chose to brave the much more dangerous illegal sea route. Turkey generally did not allow the ships to put in at its ports; at the time, Turkish satirical journals and the press mocked the refugees with anti-Semitic depictions. Most tragic was the sinking of the refugee ship *Struma* with 769 aboard in the winter of 1942. Referring to the dead, the then Turkish prime minister, Refik Saydam (in office 1939–1942)—who had already stated in 1939 after the war had broken out that Turkey "would not accept masses of Jews, nor individual Jews who were oppressed in other countries"—asserted that Turkey bore no responsibility for the disaster; it had only adhered to its principle that "Turkey will not become the home of people who are not wanted by anyone else."[56]

When Nazi Germany offered Turkey the opportunity to repatriate its Jews, Turkey explicitly instructed its diplomats "not to send Jews back 'in large numbers."[57] In September 1943, the secretary of the Turkish embassy in Berlin informed the Nazi authorities that "*a mass immigration of Jews into Turkey was to be prevented, especially by Jews who had correct Turkish papers but had not had any contact with Turkey for decades.*"[58] Germany did not send those Turkish Jews arrested in Germany to the death camps, preferring to send them to concentration camps in case Turkey demanded their repatriation later. Turkey never did so. When compared with the frequent interventions by other countries in response to attacks against their citizens, "scarcely any records of Turkish interventions on behalf of Turkish Jewish citizens can be found."[59]

Again, historical facts contradict the assertions made by Shaw; consular officials did not extend protection to Turkish Jews living in France whose Turkish citizenship had expired or was "unascertained." In the one case where an honorary Turkish consular official either gave or sold identity papers to Jews, the Turkish ambassador in Vichy, Behiç Erkin (1876–1961), reported the "improper behavior" to Ankara, launching an investigation into the official's actions. Realizing that the honorary consul "*had acted for purely humanitarian reasons,*" Erkin warned him to cease violating policy.[60] In February 1943, the Turkish consul general in Paris went so far as to strip a majority of these Jews of their citizenship rights; in keeping with its policy to hinder the mass return of Turkish Jews to Turkey, Turkey recognized the citizenship of only 631 of the 3,000 to 5,000 Jews in the French northern zone that Nazi authorities asked them to verify. The consul general told German authorities that no steps would be taken for the rest, even though he referred to these Jews as people "who had up to now been Turkish citizens."[61]

Between February and May 1944, Turkey repatriated less than 10 percent, a total of 314, of the 3,900 Turkish Jews living in the northern zone of France. While films have been made about the trains carrying these 314 Jews, with the addition of 100 from the southern zone of France, to safety in Turkey, during the same months 700 Turkish Jews were deported to death camps.

Neutral Turkey had "tremendous opportunities" to save its Jews.[62] Some Turkish consular officials, contrary to orders from Ankara and working under their own initiative, did save small numbers of Jews by either recognizing them as Turkish citizens, or by obtaining their release from detention and thus deportation. While some may have been driven by humanitarian zeal, compassion was not always the motivating factor; some officials demanded bribes and other favors from their fellow Jewish citizens in exchange for documentation that was their right.[63] Issuing laws and secret decrees, Ankara went out of its way to prevent the repatriation of a large number of Turkish Jews. When Nazi authorities demanded in 1942 that Turkey repatriate its Jews living in Europe, Ankara stripped them of their citizenship and instructed its consulates not to pursue mass repatriation. The cost of the repatriations were paid for not by the Turkish state, but by Jewish organizations. Many of the repatriated did not want to return to Turkey, which, as they learned from relatives, had subjected Jews to forced labor and taxes, reducing many to poverty. Having nowhere else to go, most sojourned in Turkey temporarily and then left once the war was over. The majority of Jews who survived did not do so thanks to Turkish officials; only once did Turkey intervene at the ambassadorial level to save Jews who had been deported. Contrary to Shaw's history and the history presented in *Turkish Passport*, Turkey "made relatively little effort" to save Turkish Jewry from the Holocaust.[64]

Turkish Passport—which does not acknowledge any of these historical facts, focusing instead on the 414 Jews repatriated to Turkey between February and May 1944—is not without references to the Armenian genocide. For no apparent reason, the only historian to appear in the film is a man long associated with Armenian genocide denial, Heath Lowry, the then holder of the Atatürk Chair in Turkish History at Princeton University.[65] He is the author of *The Story Behind Henry Morgenthau's Story*, which presents genocide testimony of the Jewish American ambassador to the Ottoman Empire as "lies motivated by anti-Turkish sentiments."[66] An exposé subsequently revealed that at the time Lowry was writing that study, he was in frequent contact with the Ankara government regarding global denialist efforts and was paid to ghostwrite denialist letters on behalf of the Turkish ambassador to the United States.[67] Calling out these kinds of subversions of scholarship, the authors argue after Terrence Des Pres that in these narratives "'knowledge' is what serves the interest of the powerful (particularly the state), the goal of knowledge is seen as control rather than freedom, and 'truth' is whatever officials (and their adjuncts) say it is."[68] Or, as another scholar has put it quite succinctly, "denial aims to reshape history in order to rehabilitate the perpetrators."[69]

With just such a rehabilitation in mind, the film presents Behiç Erkin, Turkey's ambassador to Paris and Vichy from 1939 to 1943, as a rescuer of Jews. Erkin had been involved in "the dismissal, persecution, removal, and deportation of Armenian railway staff" in 1915. *Turkish Passport* "attempts to whitewash a perpetrator of the Armenian genocide by painting him as a rescuer in the Holocaust."[70] The same year that *Turkish Passport* appeared, the English translation of another hagiography of Erkin was published, this one by his grandson, Emir Kıvırcık.[71] The original Turkish version was first published in 2007 by a publishing house founded by Turkish Jews.[72] Entitled *The Ambassador*, the book's first Turkish printing was published with a long and unsubtle subtitle: *The story of a Turkish hero of the War of Independence who saved 20,000 people from the Nazi genocide and changed the fate of his honorable nation.* The author's acknowledgments mention Shaw, Paris ambassador Osman Korutürk, and the Turkish Ministry of Foreign Affairs, which opened their archive to him. The polemics of the book are explicit: "This work provides a lesson to humanity, authored by the Turkish nation during Hitler's genocide, the only genocide recognized by the United Nations [i.e., the Armenian genocide is not a genocide]. In an atmosphere where our nation and people are subjected to slander, this work provides a lesson to humanity that anyone who lives abroad, is in contact with foreigners, and is proud of being a Turk must read and know."[73] In other words, this book will be useful for Turks in countering Armenian genocide recognition. Kıvırcık claims that during World War II, while employed at the Turkish embassy in Paris, his grandfather, Behiç Erkin, "showed courage in opposing Hitler as he implemented his terrible genocide; as millions of people were being murdered, he showed the courage to save the lives of close to 20,000 Jews by offering them certificates stating that they were Turkish citizens."[74] In blatant disregard of the actual historical record, Kıvırcık claims that by the time he left France in August 1943, Erkin had provided ten thousand Jews who had not managed to maintain their Turkish citizenship and ten thousand more who had—in other words, twenty thousand in total, every single Turkish Jew in France—with certificates of citizenship, thereby ensuring that they were able to return to Turkey.[75] "Perhaps he was given this duty by God."[76] In his own autobiography, however, Erkin "only briefly mentions the subject twice," once referring to a repatriation of 121 Jews having been organized on the personal initiative of the Paris consul general, not Erkin himself, and again noting that he had received orders from Ankara not to repatriate "Jews by the trainload."[77] Additional historical evidence suggests that Erkin, dutifully carrying out orders from Ankara, played his part in preventing the vast majority of Turkish Jews in Nazi Europe to find safety, by explicitly rejecting suggestions to send convoys to Turkey.[78]

Contrary historical evidence has not stopped some scholars of Ottoman Jewish history—particularly those who have published works since Shaw and who have insisted on contrasting Jewish loyalty to the Ottoman regime during World War I with the disloyalty of the Armenians and Greeks during that time—from repeating the myth of Turkey being a safe haven for many Jews fleeing the Nazis as Turkish diplomats across Europe allegedly stood up to the racial laws.[79] Their scholarly efforts echo those of the Turkish Jewish community leaders who use Turkey's alleged savior role in the Holocaust to deny the Armenian genocide.

The If/Then Proposition of Tolerance and Genocide

In 2007, Kamhi wrote a letter to a major American Jewish organization that had recently recognized the genocide, countering that rather than "acceptance of the much-disputed claim that the historical events in question constituted a 'genocide,'" Turks "deserve your praise for their centuries-long tradition of compassion and their culture of humanity and cohabitation that remains an example to the world."[80] According to this view, genocide is an if/then proposition: if one accepts the fantasy that Turks and Jews have lived in harmony for five hundred years, then Turks could not possibly have perpetrated a genocide against the Armenians.

This trope was repeated in 2011 when the Turkish Jewish community was given permission to commemorate the Holocaust for the first time, an event that was to become a yearly tradition.[81] At that commemoration, the president of the Turkish Chief Rabbinate Holocaust Commission, Süzet Sidi, repeated the standard narrative of Turkish Jewry's leadership, using the provocation thesis that Armenians had been disloyal and rebellious to negate comparisons between the Holocaust and the Armenian genocide. She argued that the Holocaust is unique in that Jews were annihilated despite not being at war with Germans. Unlike the Armenians, loyal Jews had not rebelled or tried to establish a state within a state.[82]

Sidi's logic is similar to how Jak Kamhi had argued against the "so-called Armenian genocide" by claiming that "it was the Jewish community that remained most loyal to the Ottoman state." Only by ignoring and repudiating the Zionist movement in Ottoman Palestine could they make the argument that Turkish Jews "had never rebelled, demanding sovereignty or territory," nor "had they ever received any weapons or support from anyone, even for self-defense."[83] Kamhi's summary of the horrors that occurred in the Ottoman Empire in 1915 was that "the Armenians' uprising paved the way for the deaths of so many innocent people."[84] In support of blaming the victim, Kamhi notes that "objective academicians and historians," such as Bernard Lewis, "have examined what occurred in 1915 and determined that it is best to term them uprisings."[85] Rebellion, uprising, provocation; these are the behaviors that transform victims into perpetrators.

In 2012, at a Holocaust commemoration at Bergen-Belsen concentration camp, Turkish officials commemorated the Turkish dead without accepting the role the Turkish government in Ankara had played in their deaths. The Turkish Jewish spokesperson attending the commemoration praised the Turks for having always offered Jews a safe refuge, be it for Iberian Jews in the fifteenth century or Turkish Jews during World War II. He remained apparently oblivious to the irony of praising a country whose diplomats had been unable to save the very ones they were commemorating and who lay at their feet.[86] Beginning in 2014, Turkish Jewish community leaders have been joined in their annual Holocaust commemoration by high-ranking Turkish officials who have used the occasion each year to promote the image of Turks as rescuers of Jews, from 1492 through to World War II. Playing the part of Jewish savior against the tide of genocide, the Turkish government can vaunt its pride and claim never to have engaged in such historical crimes, thereby denying, sometimes obliquely, sometimes explicitly, the annihilation of the Ottoman Armenians. Turkish Jews stand at their side, contributing to the historical whitewash.

Representatives of the Turkish Jewish community have told me they feel obliged to participate in state-sponsored Holocaust commemorations abroad.[87] They want to honor their dead but acknowledge these ceremonies are hijacked by the state for its own ends, where officials deny and falsify history. But they fear what would happen if the state invited Jewish representatives, and they refused to come. The state needs Jews for the ceremonies, just as Jews, who have no allies in Turkey but the state, feel they need the state. They cannot, or will not, say no to the state. They agree to collaborate, so as to remember their dead, but internally disagree with the official approach.

A young advisor to the chief rabbi of Turkey told me about their conflicted feelings regarding Turkish state memorialization of the Holocaust. Participating as a member of an official Turkish state delegation to a concentration camp in Europe, they noted the irony of flag-waving Turkish officials remembering the murder of "Turkish citizens." Had these Jews been recognized as citizens they probably would not have been killed. No matter how uncomfortable they are misrepresenting the actions of Turkey during wartime, however, they continue to take part, believing it is better to have any public commemoration than none at all.

Conclusion

Armenian genocide denialists operate like tobacco industry lobbyists and global warming skeptics. They "labor to construct denialism as a legitimate intellectual position within a historical debate"; fund biased research while supposedly striving for objectivity; and work with public relations firms to sow doubt, create a new reality, and erect a "permanent smokescreen of controversy."[88] They engage in tactics of denial, distraction, and distortion: denial that the genocide occurred; distraction from the perpetration of one genocide through boasts about heroics in another; and distortion of historical events surrounding both events. Turks as saviors of Jews is their new reality. These denialist methods are utilized in the scholarship on Ottoman Jewish and Turkish Jewish history promoted by the foundation, most notably in Stanford Shaw's *Turkey and the Holocaust: Turkey's Role in Rescuing Turkish and European Jewry from Nazi Persecution, 1933–1945*. Promoting the foundation's myth of the Turk as the eternal redeemer of Jews persecuted by Christians both at home and abroad, the book introduced the antihistorical claim that Turkey's wartime policy was to rescue Jews persecuted by the Nazis. This historical distortion has been repeated ad infinitum in history books, novels, and films, including the widely distributed propaganda film *Turkish Passport*. The film's logo, a Turkish star and crescent rising above a locomotive, was designed to evoke the image of the Turk as steadfast rescuer of Jews. In defiance of the well-established Holocaust image of the cattle car, icon of Jews as passive victims traveling on death trains to the gas chambers, these Jews, the image proclaims, have been diverted to safety in Turkey where they can breathe free in a land without anti-Semitism.

Notes

1. Stanford J. Shaw, *Turkey and the Holocaust: Turkey's Role in Rescuing Turkish and European Jewry from Nazi Persecution, 1933–1945* (New York: New York University Press, 1993).
2. Shaw, *The Jews of the Ottoman Empire and the Turkish Republic*, 254–256.
3. Mallet, *La Turquie, les Turcs et les Juifs*, 249–252.

4. İ. İzzet Bahar, *Turkey and the Rescue of European Jews* (London: Routledge, 2015), 260.

5. Ibid., 11.

6. Shaw, *The Jews of the Ottoman Empire and the Turkish Republic*, 244–271.

7. Emphasis added. Ibid., 257–258.

8. Ibid., 257.

9. Shaw, *Turkey and the Holocaust*, 60.

10. Shaw, *The Jews of the Ottoman Empire and the Turkish Republic*, ix.

11. Néhama argues that during the war there were sixty thousand Sephardim in France (of Salonican, Turkish, and Balkan origin) of whom fifteen thousand became victims of the Nazis in the camps in Poland and Germany, or in France itself. He makes no mention of Turkey making any effort to save or protect any of these Jews, or even of Ülkümen having saved several dozen Jews in Rhodes. *In memoriam: Hommage aux victimes Juives des Nazis en Grèce*, Tome II, ed. Joseph Néhama (Salonique: Communauté Israélite de Thessalonique, 1949), 235–236.

12. Shaw, *Turkey and the Holocaust*, ix. On foundation office holders, see Kamhi, *Gördüklerim yaşadıklarım*, 395.

13. Shaw, *Turkey and the Holocaust*, ix-x.

14. "Testimony of Retired Ambassador Necdet Kent Regarding His Rescue of Jewish Turks at Marseilles during World War II," Appendix 4, translated by Stanford Shaw, in Shaw, *Turkey and the Holocaust*, 342.

15. Bahar, *Turkey and the Rescue of European Jews*, 190.

16. Corry Guttstadt, *Die Türkei, die Juden und der Holocaust* (Hamburg: Assoziation A, 2009) was translated into Turkish as Corry Guttstadt, *Türkiye, Yahudiler ve Holokost* (Istanbul: İletişim, 2012), and into English as Corry Guttstadt, *Turkey, the Jews, and the Holocaust*, translated from German by Kathleen M. Dell'Orto, Sabine Bartel, and Michelle Miles (Cambridge: Cambridge University Press, 2013). Guttstadt, *Turkey, the Jews, and the Holocaust*, 220.

17. "Testimony of Retired Ambassador Necdet Kent," 343.

18. Bahar, *Turkey and the Rescue of European Jews*, 190.

19. "Testimony of Retired Ambassador Necdet Kent," 343.

20. Ibid.

21. Ibid.

22. Ibid., 343–344.

23. Ibid., 344.

24. Guttstadt, *Turkey, the Jews, and the Holocaust*, 220.

25. Ibid., 218, 220–221.

26. Ibid., 220–221.

27. Bahar, *Turkey and the Rescue of European Jews*, 190.

28. Guttstadt, *Turkey, the Jews, and the Holocaust*, 221.

29. Bali, *Model Citizens of the State*, 398.

30. Rıfat Bali, *Türkiye'de Holokost tüketimi, 1989–2017* (Istanbul: Libra, 2017), 209–210.

31. Amazon lists it as the number-four best seller in Middle Eastern literature on its website (accessed June 2016).

32. "Biz, Ermenileri Yahudiler gibi durup dururken kesmeye başlamadık." CNNTürk, "Aykırı Sorular," February 3, 2014.

33. Bernard Lewis, speech at the National Press Club, Washington, DC, broadcast on C-Span, March 25, 2002.

34. "Armenian Allegations: Myth and Reality," testimony delivered by Professor Justin McCarthy before the House Committee on International Relations, May 15, 1996.

35. Ayşe Kulin, *The Last Train to Istanbul*, translated by John Baker (Istanbul: Everest, 2006).

36. Ayşe Kulin, *Nefes nefese* (Istanbul: Remzi, 2002), 110–111.

37. Ibid., 171.

38. Bali, *Türkiye'de Holokost tüketimi*, 213–214. Ayşe Kulin's latest best-selling novel, *Kanadı kırık kuşlar* (Birds with broken wings, Istanbul: Everest, 2016), which has already sold over 150,000 copies, concerns German Jewish academics who took refuge in Turkey during World War II.

39. Kulin, *Nefes nefese*, vii.

40. Bahar, *Turkey and the Rescue of European Jews*, 184–185.

41. Kulin, *Nefes nefese*, 185–196; Kulin, *The Last Train to Istanbul*, 190.

42. Kulin, *Nefes nefese*, 197; Kulin, *The Last Train to Istanbul*, 200.

43. Eyüp Erdoğan, "Turks Saved Jews from Nazi Holocaust," *Turkish Daily News*, October 25, 2008.

44. http://www.raoulwallenberg.net/highlights/turks-saved-jews-nazi/. For further examples of the propagation of the myth of Turkish rescue by such consuls as Kent in Turkey and abroad, see Mallet, *La Turquie, les Turcs et les Juifs*, 478–484.

45. Burak Arlıel, director, *The Turkish Passport* (Imaj, Interfilm Istanbul, Turkey, 2011).

46. Bali, *Türkiye'de Holokost tüketimi*, 225, 231–233.

47. Uğur Ümit Üngör, review of Burak Arlıel, *The Turkish Passport*. H-Genocide, H-Net Reviews, March, 2012, http://www.h-net.org/reviews/showrev.php?id=35380.

48. The website is no longer online, but one can still find it on the Internet Archive: https://web.archive.org/web/20120425034845/http://www.theturkishpassport.com/holocaust_story.asp.

49. For examples of Uzer's explicit denial of the Armenian genocide, see Umut Uzer, "The Fallacies of the Armenian Nationalist Narrative," *Jerusalem Post*, April 27, 2015; Umut Uzer, "Ermeni meselesine farklı bir bakış," *Şalom*, May 27, 2015; and Umut Uzer, "Hayal ve gerçek arasında Balakian'ın kara köpeği," *Şalom*, April 27, 2016, cited in Bali, *Türkiye'de Holokost tüketimi*, 205. Also see M. Hakan Yavuz ve Umut Uzer, "Ermeni meselesi, devlet ve aydınlar," *Zaman*, Yorum, February 23, 2013.

50. Üngör, review of Burak Arlıel.

51. Smith, Markusen, and Lifton, "Professional Ethics and the Denial of Armenian Genocide," 11.

52. Rıfat Bali, *Bir Türkleştirme serüveni (1923–1945): Cumhuriyet yıllarında Türkiye Yahudileri* (Istanbul: İletişim, 1999), 340–341.

53. Guttstadt, *Turkey, the Jews, and the Holocaust*, 309.

54. For a comparison of how the neutral nations Argentina, Portugal, Spain, Sweden, Switzerland, and Turkey responded to Jewish refugees and the needs of their own Jewish citizens in Nazi Europe during the Holocaust, see the collection of essays *Bystanders, Rescuers or Perpetrators? The Neutral Countries and the Shoah*, ed. Corry Guttstadt, Thomas Lutz, Bernd Rother, and Yessica San Román, International Holocaust Remembrance Alliance series, volume 2 (Berlin: Metropol, 2016).

55. Guttstadt, *Turkey, the Jews, and the Holocaust*, 112.

56. Bali, *Bir Türkleştirme Serüveni (1923–1945)*, 341, 361; Guttstadt, *Turkey, the Jews, and the Holocaust*, 116.

57. Guttstadt, *Turkey, the Jews, and the Holocaust*, 157.

58. Ibid., emphasis added.
59. Ibid., 162.
60. Ibid., 199, emphasis added.
61. Ibid., 212.
62. Ibid., 309.
63. Ibid.
64. Ibid., 313.
65. Üngör, review of Burak Arliel.
66. Heath Lowry, *The Story Behind Henry Morgenthau's Story* (Istanbul: Isis, 1990).
67. Smith, Markusen, and Lifton, "Professional Ethics and the Denial of Armenian Genocide."
68. Ibid., 2.
69. Deborah Lipstadt, *Denying the Holocaust: The Growing Assault on Truth and Memory* (New York: Free Press, 1993), 217, cited in Smith, Markusen, and Lifton, "Professional Ethics and the Denial of Armenian Genocide," 13.
70. Üngör cites Ziya Gürel, "Kurtuluş savaşında demiryolculuk," *Belleten* 44, no. 175 (July 1980): 539–73; Behiç Erkin, *Hâtırat 1876–1958* (Ankara: Türk Tarih Kurumu, 2011); and Arnold Reisman, *An Ambassador and a Mensch: The Story of a Turkish Diplomat in Vichy France* (CreateSpace Independent Publishing Platform, 2010).
71. Emir Kıvırcık, *The Turkish Ambassador* (CreateSpace Independent Publishing Platform, 2011).
72. Emir Kıvırcık, *Büyükelçi: Yirmi bin insanı Nazi soykırımından kurtaran, Kurtuluş Savaşı kahramanı bir Türk'ün ve şerefli ulusunun tarihi değiştiren öyküsü!* (Istanbul: GOA, 2007). By its third printing in 2010 with a larger press, it had sold a hundred thousand copies. Bali, *Türkiye'de Holokost tüketimi,* 217.
73. Kıvırcık, *Büyükelçi,* 9.
74. Ibid., 10.
75. Ibid., 191.
76. Ibid., 193.
77. Guttstadt, *Turkey, the Jews, and the Holocaust,* 150, 211–212; Erkin, *Hatirât.*
78. Guttstadt, *Turkey, the Jews, and the Holocaust,* 212.
79. Levy, introduction to *Jews, Turks, Ottomans.*
80. Jak Kamhi, "Letter to Abraham H. Foxman," August 22, 2007, available on the website of the Turkish Coalition of America, http://www.tc-america.org/issues-information /armenian-issue/letter-to-abraham-386.htm. See also "Turkish Jews Disavow 'Genocide' Move," *Today's Zaman,* August 23, 2007.
81. In 2008, Turkey became an observer member of the International Holocaust Remembrance Alliance, founded in 1998 "to promote education, remembrance and research about the Holocaust." https://www.holocaustremembrance.com/international-holocaust -remembrance-alliance.
82. Cited in Bali, *Türkiye'de Holokost tüketimi,* 121.
83. Kamhi, *Gördüklerim yaşadıklarım,* 340.
84. Ibid., 352.
85. Ibid., 358.
86. Cited in Bali, *Türkiye'de Holokost tüketimi,* 102–103.
87. Conversations with the author, June 2018, Graz, Austria.
88. Mamigonian, "Academic Denial of the Armenian Genocide in American Scholarship," 62, 63.

7

THE EMERGENCE OF CRITICAL
TURKISH JEWISH VOICES

THE 1990S IN TURKEY WITNESSED COMPETING TRENDS IN history writing concerning the nation-state's first decades (1923–1945). In the years
leading up to and following 1998, the 75th anniversary of the Turkish
Republic, many memoirs by or biographies of "the children of the republic"
were published, teachers in particular, sometimes by the Turkish Ministry
of Culture.[1] Repeating the official textbook version of the country's origins
and makeup, they deploy the main tropes of republican historiography,
promoting its principles and remaining mute on its many silences. Inherent to this nostalgic republican memoir writing was a biting critique of the
competing narratives then present in Turkey in the 1990s—Islamist, Kurdish, nationalist, and liberal—which were wont to paint Kemalism as oppres-
sive and authoritarian.[2] These years witnessed the rise to prominence of
Islamists, as Necmettin Erbakan became prime minister (1996–1997) until
deposed by a warning from the military. Erbakan's protégé, Recep Tayyip
Erdoğan, served as the influential mayor of Istanbul (1994–1998) until he
was jailed and his party outlawed, reemerging later as the leader of the new
Islamist *Adalet ve Kalkınma Partisi* (AKP, Justice and Development Party,
2001–present). Conflict between the Turkish state and the guerrillas of the
Kurdistan Workers' Party (PKK) raged during these years, claiming tens
of thousands of lives until the capture of their leader Abdullah Öcalan in
1999. The liberal *ikinci cumhuriyetçiler* (second republicans) intellectuals
criticized the role of the army in the state and the state in the economy,
promoting civil society and more democracy and transparency.

In addition to the specific partisan criticisms of the republic during
these years by Islamists, Kurds, and liberals, a small group of journalists,
novelists, and scholars began to reappraise and critique the official state

narrative, particularly the silence regarding the nation-state's often violent Turkification policies directed against Christians, Jews, and Kurds. Through their texts, public attention was drawn to past traumatic events, including the Armenian genocide of 1915, the 1934 anti-Jewish pogrom in Thrace, the Capital Tax of 1942–1944, the sinking of the Jewish refugee ship the *Struma* in 1942, and the pogrom of September 6–7, 1955.[3] While the most prominent spokespeople of the Jewish community appeared to side with the children of the republic in promoting the official nationalist myth of the Turkish state—to wit, the Quincentennial Foundation's claim that Turks have ever been model humanitarians—a minority within the Jewish community was moved by the revisionist critiques.

The Quincentennial Foundation in Retrospective

As we have seen in previous chapters, the main promoter of the myth of Turkish rescue has been the foundation. Deploying baseless historical claims and suppression of facts about the actual role of Turkey, the foundation also stifled knowledge of the increasingly precarious position of Jews in the Turkey of the 1990s. In 1996, the foundation offered a retrospective account of its efforts on its website.[4] The account remained notably silent on a number of disturbing developments: the attempted assassinations of its head, Jak Kamhi, by Turkish Islamists in 1993 and the head of the Jewish community in Ankara in 1995; the increase in anti-Semitic publications, including many separate printings of *The Protocols of the Elders of Zion*, which the Jewish community was helpless to stop; and public Islamists' lament that the foundation aimed "to erase or at the very least minimize the image of Turkey as anti-Zionist and anti-Jewish."[5] Over the course of a generation, the size of the Turkish Jewish community had halved again, to less than twenty thousand members.[6]

Disregarding these significant developments in Turkish-Jewish relations, Kamhi reiterated the foundation's two main aims on the retrospective published on their website at the time: "The first one is to remind the whole world of the high human qualities of the Turkish people, to those who approached with goodwill, by showing what they did not know and confronting the malicious with historical facts."[7] For Kamhi, the "malicious" are those who accept what befell the Armenians as genocide, the "facts" are those of Ottoman tolerance of Jews. Kamhi implicitly assumes that were these malicious genocide promoters confronted with "facts," they would no longer accept that a people with "high human qualities" could commit genocide. The second goal of the foundation, Kamhi relates, "was to assist the Jewish citizens of Turkey, who are an inseparable part of the Turkish nation, in expressing their gratitude for the humanly embrace that their ancestors encountered in the Turkish lands five centuries ago." Featuring a photo of then president and long-serving Turkish leader Süleyman Demirel, the foundation reiterated its goals in even more exaggerated fashion: "To reiterate the superior humanist character of the Turkish nation. The savior hand that the Turkish people extended throughout the centuries to those who suffered from cruelty and bigotry became a monument of honor for all nations. The humanly attitude of the Turkish nation towards Jews, Poles, Tsarist Russians, the people of Bangladesh, Afghans, North Iraqis was an example dedicated to mankind. It is a distinguished honor for the Quincentennial Foundation to continue to relate to the whole world this highly human quality of the Turkish nation."[8] Conspicuous by their absence are Armenians, Greeks, and Kurds.

"Ottoman Tolerance" Redux

The foundation was not alone in promoting these views. In 1999, the Turkish government and numerous NGOs in Turkey celebrated the seven hundredth anniversary of the founding of the Ottoman dynasty. Museums commissioned special exhibits for the occasion, ranging in content from royal robes to calligraphic styles, showing them in Istanbul and abroad. Universities hosted conferences with presentations by Turkish and foreign scholars glorifying the Ottomans. Popular television programs, aired during prime time and going on until dawn, assembled historians, journalists, and politicians to discuss the achievements of the Ottomans. Many of the major daily newspapers offered beautiful, leather-bound reprints of multivolume histories of the empire in exchange for coupons clipped out by their eager readers. The mass circulation Istanbul dailies *Hürriyet* and *Sabah*, for example, offered İsmail Hakkı Uzunçarşılı's 1970s *Osmanlı tarihi* series and a Turkish translation of Joseph von Hammer-Purgstall's early nineteenth-century *Büyük Osmanlı tarihi*, respectively. Ottoman-style restaurants serving "palace favorites" popped up in big Turkish cities. While not matching the fervor of the 1998 75th anniversary of the establishment of the Turkish Republic, what with its torch-carrying marchers accompanied by refitted trucks blasting a disco-remix of the 1938 *Onuncu yıl marşı*

(*Tenth Anniversary March*), the 1999 celebration of the Ottoman Empire was a full-on display of national pride.[9]

While living and conducting dissertation research in Istanbul from 1996 to 1999, I was able to take part in both celebrations. The best example of the tenor of the Ottoman anniversary was a conference I attended hosted by the right-wing NGO *Marmara Grubu Stratejik ve Sosyal Araştırmalar Vakfı* (Marmara Group Strategic and Social Research Foundation), whose motto is an adaptation of John F. Kennedy's famous quote: "Ask not what my country Turkey can give me, but what I can give my country Turkey." Founded in 1985 and affiliated with the far right party *Milliyetçi Hareket Partisi* (MHP, Nationalist Action Movement), the Marmara Group promotes Eurasian economic summits, close ties with Central Asian Turkic republics, Turkey joining the European Union, and relations with Turkey's "sister republic" Azerbaijan. Their activities in connection with Azerbaijan focus on opposing Armenians' claims in the disputed territory of Nagorno Karabagh and denying the Armenian genocide. Most recently, its chairman was Dr. Akkan Suver, who served as MHP spokesman from 1987 to 1995. Its honorary chairman in 2016–2017 was none other than Jak Kamhi, who offers very favorable views of the MHP in his autobiography.

One activity the Marmara Group supports in this regard is what it calls *interreligious dialogue*. For this reason, in 1999 it organized the "Ottoman Tolerance" conference, which I attended at Yıldız Palace in Istanbul. To an Ottoman historian, the choice of location was peculiar, for the builder and resident of that palace, Sultan Abdülhamid II, is not known for his tolerant approach to his Christian subjects. Dressed in their ceremonial robes and headdresses, the leaders and representatives of the Jewish, Syriac, and Greek Orthodox communities appeared as living ghosts of the Ottoman past, in attendance in order to speak of peace, brotherhood, and respect in Ottoman society, without any mention of the Armenian genocide. The Armenian patriarch was conspicuously absent.

The conference schedule was full. The Syriac Christian spoke on the topic of "Ottoman-Syriac Friendship." A representative of the Vatican was to hold forth on "Ottoman-Catholic Closeness." A professor from a Greek university addressed "Ottoman-Greek Relations." An aged, secular Turk was permitted the longest presentation, "Humanism in the Ottoman Empire." Professor Heath Lowry, Atatürk Chair in Turkish History at Princeton University, gave a speech entitled "Toleration in the Ottoman Empire." A Turkish professor from Ankara University gave nearly the same talk, "Tolerance in the Ottoman Empire." An Israeli professor lectured on "Ottoman-Jewish Brotherhood." An Armenian professor from a private Istanbul University, in attendance despite the absence of the Armenian patriarch, spoke on the theme of "Ottoman-Armenian Relations." All speakers received a ceramic plate inscribed with the seal of Sultan Abdülhamid II, during whose reign hundreds of thousands of Armenians were massacred.

With the exception of the Turkish humanist, all speakers, including high-level religious representatives, were only permitted five minutes to speak. In fact, the professors from Greece and Israel and the representatives of the Turkish Jewish and Syriac communities were cut off in midsentence by the chairman for having exceeded their allotted time. The brevity of the minitalks confirms that the aim of the conference was not to relate the historical details of "tolerance in the Ottoman Empire," but rather to show to the world in a pageant-like spectacle of grateful advertisements and little to no scholarly substance how tolerant Turks have been since medieval times. Despite the Ottoman Empire having collapsed, these ghosts of empire yet remain, demonstrating for the conference organizers (at least) that Turks have ever been humanist, tolerant, magnanimous to their religious Others, the guests in the lands over which Turks rule. At the end of the choreographed three-hour performance of gratitude, after yet another speaker had been silenced by the chairman—rushed off stage, given his or her Sultan Abdülhamid II plate and a handshake, smiling for the press photographers—some elderly members of the audience rose to their feet in protest. The secular representative of the Syriac Christians had begun to explain how his community had lived in Anatolia for thousands of years—in other words, before the Turks had arrived—when he, too, was silenced. Suddenly, an older woman rose to her feet and shouted, "Enough already; let the man speak! You cut off all the speakers. It is too short. He was about to teach us about his community. This conference is a disaster!" The Syriac Christian left the stage, and the chairman decided to not let the Vatican representative speak, announcing instead that it was time for the buffet lunch in the garden followed by a tour of the palace. But then the representative of Catholics in Turkey was inexplicably given permission to speak. The salon had half emptied by then. He concluded his brief remarks claiming, "It has been repeatedly mentioned today how the Jews of Spain were expelled. This is a reality. But the reason why they were kicked out has not been mentioned. The reason is that King Ferdinand owed the

Jews a great deal of money, so in order not to pay it he expelled them from his kingdom." The comment was met with appreciative laughter and nods of agreement from the chairman and audience, who were still chuckling as they filed out to enjoy *hünkâr beğendi* ("the sultan approved of it," a dish of puréed eggplant and meat) and other imperial delicacies. Cracks in the myth had begun to appear.

Abraham Galanté's Angry Descendants

In the face of sustained, centuries-long efforts at promoting a utopian vision of history and silencing countervoices, it is perhaps not surprising that until the 1990s, no Turkish Jewish author had been interested in examining the darker side of Muslim-Jewish relations. In part as a response to broader trends in society, in part as a reaction to the public dissemination of the thesis of five hundred years of brotherhood on their behalf by the representatives of Turkish Jewry, a thesis that did not match their own experience, a handful of Turkish Jewish historians, memoirists, and writers, including some who had migrated to Israel, were compelled to publish critical, revisionist works of history or novels focusing on life in the Turkish Republic.[10] The first to do so were Avner Levi, Vitali Hakko, Eli Şaul, Rıfat Bali, and Mario Levi.

Avner Levi, born and raised in Izmir in 1942, emigrated in 1968 to Israel, where he served as professor in the Institute of Asian and African Studies at Hebrew University in Jerusalem. He published *Jews in the Turkish Republic: Legal and Political Statuses* in Hebrew in 1992; translated in 1996 into Turkish and redacted by Rıfat Bali, it has not yet been translated into English.[11] Levi broke a taboo by being the first to discuss the negative episodes Turkish Jews have experienced in Turkey in the modern period. Reflecting a Zionist approach, his brief book covers the period from the birth of the Turkish Republic in 1923 to the establishment of the Jewish state of Israel in 1948. The book is valuable for summarizing the facts of the Thrace pogrom and the Capital Tax, and for exploring the writings of Turkish anti-Semites. The book is also significant for its discussion of the debilitating blows that the transformation from pluralist empire to nationalist republic dealt to Turkish Jews, four-fifths of whom fled the country in response.

Levi refutes Shaw's contention that the bad press Turkey has received about the Capital Tax is a result merely of "anti-Turkish political groups" who "subsequently used the fact that many of those who suffered from the Capital Levy were Christians and Jews to claim that the measure was directed primarily against the minorities."[12] It also serves to counter Shaw's humiliating contention—based on purported interviews that he cites nowhere of events that have been contradicted by scholars in Turkey and abroad and by the published accounts of Turkish Jews who experienced that era—that Jews happily payed the tax, which "helped the Jews of Turkey by showing Turks that the Jews were suffering so much that they should not give in to Nazi demands to deport their Jews to the death camps."[13] How could Shaw claim that Jews happily paid an unfair tax that ruined them financially and psychologically? Many Jews unable to pay the tax who served at the labor camps in Aşkale returned broken men. Some died there. Not only is Shaw's statement unattributed to any source, but it is also factually inaccurate; the Nazis never demanded that Turkey deport its Jews to death camps. Moreover, adding that "the deprivation of their wealth by the government drained what resentment there might otherwise have been among Turks against Jewish wealth while the mass of the population was suffering because of the war," Shaw repeats the anti-Semitic campaign at the time depicting Jews as war profiteers. This statement even serves to undermine his own contention, again refuted by subsequent scholarship, that "Muslim Turks themselves never at any point showed any anti-Semitism either before, during, or after the program was in force." In this case, as with the Armenian genocide, Shaw holds a more extreme view than his mentor, Bernard Lewis, who offers several critical pages on the "sad affair" of the tax, albeit concluding that "its effects should not, however, be exaggerated." For compared with Nazi Europe, "Turkey's one essay in persecution was a mild and gentle affair."[14] Yet here he contradicts his own advice elsewhere, downplaying anti-Semitism in Turkey. "If, as the term of comparison for Christendom, we take the Spanish Inquisition or the German death camps, then it is easy to prove almost any society tolerant."[15] If the Holocaust is the standard by which we measure anti-Semitism, all other manifestations will be belittled.

Levi's study is genre bending in that it was the first to break the taboo of writing about the dark side of Jewish-Turkish relations. The sources he uses for his history—the Turkish Jewish press and interviews conducted with elderly Turkish Jews—document the fear and loss suffered by Turkish Jews during that period. The emotional content of Jewish newspapers of the time illustrates the response of Turkish Jews to the whirlwind that turned their world upside down. The book also helps us to understand Galanté's work and public campaigns in the context of the time.

Levi's theses were supported by the publication the following year of the autobiography of Turkish Jewish fashion designer and Quincentennial Foundation collaborator Vitali Hakko, who recounts episodes of anti-Jewish discrimination faced by his family.[16] Hakko was born in Yedikule, Istanbul, just before the beginning of World War I. As he relates in his 1997 autobiography, his neighborhood at the end of the Ottoman era was a cosmopolitan, interfaith utopia, where Armenians, Greeks, Jews, and Muslim Turks lived in the same apartment buildings, spoke each other's languages, overlooked their religious differences, and got along well.[17] He quickly skips ahead to the establishment of the Turkish Republic when he was ten, telling the reader nothing about World War I, the Allied occupation, and what is known in Turkey as the Turkish War of Independence. Hakko's account is silent regarding what happened to his neighborhood during these years and the diverse peoples who lived there, especially the Greek majority.

Yet his description of the establishment of the republic begins with a dark omen. At the local neighborhood celebrations, a woman was killed by a stray celebratory bullet.[18] Offering his own life story as a way of symbolizing the experience of Turkish Jewry, he notes how lucky he was; he had intended to sit in the fateful chair just before the bullet found its unlucky target.

His account of the early republic offers examples of anti-Jewish discrimination and the fear pervading Turkish Jewry, which had life-changing effects for him. In 1925, his father was fired from his job at the railway company when it was nationalized, and non-Muslims were not permitted to work for it thereafter. This also meant the end of twelve-year-old Vitali's formal education.[19] The family could no longer afford school fees, and he and his siblings were compelled to begin to work.[20] Several years later, his family moved to a Jewish-majority neighborhood in Istanbul, Kuledibi, Beyoğlu, adjacent to the future Neve Şalom synagogue.[21] Thereafter, most of Hakko's autobiography becomes a compelling rags-to-riches story detailing his hat business before World War II and the creation of the Vakko brand after, as well as aphorisms illustrating his optimistic life philosophy. As he states in the preface, "Had it not been for the hat revolution and clothing revolution [in Turkey], there is no doubt Vakko would not exist today."[22] For this reason, Vakko "owes its existence to the Kemalist revolutions and Turkey's westernization effort." Yet as a Jew, Hakko and his business faced constant difficulties during World War II.

Like other Turkish businessmen, Hakko was adjusting to the difficult economic conditions of the war era when he was suddenly called up in 1942 to military duty for the third time, after having only recently been discharged from his second stint. The third time was odd and unsettling. He received no orders from the military. Instead, the police showed up at his store and took him to the Selimiye Barracks.[23] He quickly noticed that "there was not a single Turkish Muslim among us." This fact made he and the others wonder why, only one week after their discharge from military service, they had all been called up for the third time. Why were there only Christians and Jews? Why had they been so suddenly assembled, without being given the chance to contact their families? Why did the authorities not tell them why and where they were being taken?[24] The fact that there were no Muslim Turks among them only served to increase their fear and anxiety. There were sixty-year-old, white-bearded Greeks, Armenians, and Jews among them, crying over their fate. Hakko shared a tent with a sixty-five-year-old Jewish man. What kind of military call-up was this? For obvious reasons, many feared something terrible would be done to them should Germany occupy Turkey. The people around him were "pessimistic, hopeless, hungry, and depressed."[25] They feared they would not survive the war, that they would be subject to Nazi persecution. In short, it was as though everyone was prepared to meet their maker.[26] Ever the optimist, Hakko kept up his spirits and after eighteen months was released.[27]

But then, immediately following his release, "such a black cloud darkened the skies of the nation that there was no chance of escape. The name of the black cloud was the Capital Tax."[28] The convinced Kemalist believed that the tax was a "terrible policy that violated Republican principles," discriminating between theoretically equal citizens.[29] As he explains, while foreigners and Muslim Turks were to pay one-eighth of their wealth and Dönme one-fourth, non-Muslims were to pay half.[30] Deeply worried, he had no idea how he would be able to pay the tax. His company had neither enough cash nor assets to sell. He had no friends to turn to for help, as they were all in a worse state than he. He witnessed people crying, banging their heads against the wall, and pounding their fists on their empty store cash registers.[31] He notes that "Hitler's armies occupied all of Europe. There was nowhere to go," but then corrects himself: "There was in fact only one place to go: Aşkale." A footnote explains how 90 percent of the 1,400 men who could not pay their tax assessment and were sent to the concentration camp in eastern Anatolia were Christians and Jews from Istanbul. Seeing the silver lining in every situation, however, Hakko explains how in those "dark war years, even during the drama of the Capital Tax," he was an eye-witness to the fact that "humanity did not die."[32] He describes how, while writing these lines fifty years later, his hands still shook and his eyes still filled with tears explaining how he was saved.

He traveled to Ankara unannounced to the hat store of an acquaintance, the religious Muslim he called Hacıbaba. The pious Muslim welcomed him, offered him tea, told him "God is great, do not be sad," and slipped an envelope into his pocket, containing cash in the amount of one-fifth of his Capital Tax assessment, repeating "You will see, God is great."[33] When Hakko returned to Istanbul he went straight to the office of the Istanbul Finance Director Faik Ökte, handed him the cash, and asked for permission to pay the rest of the amount by installment. Ökte was reportedly so delighted he kissed him on the forehead and told Hakko he would do everything he could to help such a "well-intentioned citizen," agreeing to accept the rest of the tax on installment without any specified date for payment. Hakko concludes the narrative of the episode, "May you rest in peace, Hacıbaba."[34]

More critical still is another autobiography published two years later. Eli Şaul (b. 1916) was a dentist originally from Istanbul, and one of the ten Turkish Jews who founded a local branch of the *Hovevei Zion* (True Lovers of Zion) movement following the pogrom in Thrace in 1934. The author was born in Hasköy and grew up in Balat, two Istanbul neighborhoods with centuries-old and sizable Jewish populations. In 1941, he graduated from Istanbul University's dental school and attended the Military Medical Practice School in Ankara. He was sent to posts in eastern Turkey, such as Doğubayezit, to serve as a military dentist. Because of what he experienced in the 1930s and 1940s, Şaul concluded that Jews had no future in Turkey. He wrote editorials in the Turkish press between 1947 and 1950 defending Jews before deciding to emigrate with his family to Israel.

Şaul's very personal account of the 1930s and 1940s complements Levi's more historiographic approach. His book, *Balat'tan Bat-Yam'a* (From Balat [Istanbul] to Bat-Yam [Tel Aviv]), redacted and translated like Avner Levi's work by Bali, consists of recollections of growing up in Balat; diary entries and letters from his time in high school, university, and military service in the 1930s and 1940s; editorials from the late 1940s defending Jews who emigrated to Israel after having been attacked; and letters published in Turkey while the author resided in Israel.[35] Almost half the book consists of Şaul's

1943 diary entries and letters concerning the Capital Tax and the discrimination Jews and Christians faced in the republic.

Şaul's book allows the reader to understand how Turkification policies and the public's attitude toward non-Muslims affected individual Jews. In a letter home, written from his post in Doğubayezit in 1943, Şaul complains that, despite serving his country as an officer, he is addressed by titles reserved for non-Muslims and foreigners. He argues that if Turks could not treat them as equals, non-Muslims would stand no chance of assimilating into Turkish society. He complains about how in the theater, the cinema, and the press of the time, non-Muslims were mocked for speaking Turkish with accents. Announcements in newspapers for government jobs stated that the applicant "had to be a Turk," thereby excluding Christian and Jewish citizens. While he was in Ankara at the Military Medical Practice School, over fifty Christians and Jews who were students at the reserve officer school sat for exams, but none passed. Many told him that there was not a question on the exam they did not know. They believed that non-Muslims were let into the school, educated, and permitted to take exams but not allowed to pass. He writes of being constantly reminded of his difference, whether by other students, by the police, or even by his closest Turkish Muslim friends.

Şaul devotes an entire section of the book to the Capital Tax and how it affected those near him. When he returned home to Kuledibi in Istanbul in 1943, he found that his father had been devastated by the Capital Tax. He had been sent to Aşkale and had returned a crushed man. Despite being poor, his wife's father had had to pay a hefty tax. Because he could not pay, he was arrested, beaten, and sent to Aşkale. When she went to the police to find out about her father, the chief of police mocked her, saying, "Why are you crying, girl? Your father went to Aşkale for a change of scenery."[36]

The Istanbul chief of police from November 1942 to September 1943 was Nihat Halûk Pepeyi, and the police official in charge of the office of foreigners and minorities was Salahattin Korkud. The two traveled to Germany in January and February of 1943, ostensibly to bring back to Turkey the remains of Talat Pasha, the Ottoman interior minister who was the architect of the Armenian genocide. The minister had issued written orders to provincial governors in western, central, and eastern Anatolia to deport Armenian women, children, and the elderly to Deir ez-Zor in the Syrian Desert and was assassinated in retaliation by an Armenian in Berlin in 1921.[37] As guests of the Gestapo and the SS, Pepeyi and Korkud traveled from Nazi-occupied Holland and France in the West to Poland and the Crimea in the East. They visited Krupp and I. G. Farben factories run on slave labor. In Berlin, they stayed at the SS guesthouse in Wannsee, where only one year before, fifteen high-ranking representatives of the SS, Nazi Party, and various ministries, including Reinhard Heydrich and Adolf Eichmann, met to discuss their cooperation in the ongoing annihilation of European Jewry.[38] On February 1, 1943, "due to their special request," the two Turkish police officials visited the Sachsenhausen concentration camp in Oranienburg outside Berlin, where two hundred thousand people were held in brutal conditions over the course of the war, and at least thirty thousand were murdered by gassing, hanging, shooting, and torture.[39] Sachsenhausen was set up by Heinrich Himmler as a model for other camps, was used by the SS to train and prepare people such as Rudolf Höss, the camp commandant of Sachsenhausen and then Auschwitz, and was the home of the Inspectorate of Concentration Camps, the administrative center for all concentration camps in Nazi-occupied Europe.[40] At the SS club at Sachsenhausen, separated from "the screaming, the stench, the cramped conditions, and the violence" by merely a road and a wall, the Turkish police dined on a six-course lunch, including goose liver, and drank wine with SS officers.[41] They made a careful tour of the camp, which would serve as a model for what they planned to construct in Turkey.[42]

Rıfat Bali Takes a Sledgehammer to the Sugary Puff of History

Above all others, it is Rıfat Bali (b. 1948) of Istanbul who has written the most significant and exhaustively researched work about the history of republican-era Turkish Jews, the six-hundred-page study, *Cumhuriyet yıllarında Türkiye Yahudileri: Bir Türkleştirme serüveni, 1923–1945* (Turkish Jews in the early republic: An adventure in Turkification, 1923–1945). Unlike the works of Levi and Şaul, it does not offer a Jewish nationalist resolution to the problems facing Turkish Jewry. It also has yet to be translated into another language. Like the leaders of the foundation, the official historian of the Turkish chief rabbinate, and the Turkish diplomats who spearheaded Turkish state denial of the Armenian genocide, Bali is an amateur historian. He first began writing history while still a small business owner and had no training whatsoever in historical methods. He had not even earned a bachelor's degree. Not being a member of the Jewish elite, Bali is free of the worries of those Turkish Jewish industrialists who rely on the support of the state. Driven by an affective disposition that makes him Abraham Galanté's angry twin, he writes not to promote an imagined harmony of interests between Muslims and Jews, but to catalogue the sad state of Jews in the Turkish Republic. His method is to offer lengthy quotation from Turkish sources illustrating how the Muslim public imagined Jews in negative terms.

In *Cumhuriyet yıllarında Türkiye Yahudileri*, Bali argues that in their memoirs and with few exceptions, Turkish Jews have sterilized their pasts and have chosen to forget harsh anti-Jewish measures.[43] Bali was first motivated to take up the pen by a realization that the public statements and writings of the leaders of the Jewish community contrasted starkly with what he and other Jews had experienced. He uses his typewriter like a sledgehammer smashing a century of sugary puff. His aim is to counter the widespread view that the Jews had never suffered any troubles from the Turks, and that Jews and Muslims had had good relations throughout the same years.[44] Bali's method is thus to counter this utopian image with six hundred pages of hate-filled quotes from Turkish sources, showing just how Muslims really viewed Jews, and how they treated them accordingly. Bali depicts the early republican era in decidedly lachrymose terms, to show that the Jews suffered prejudice.

Bali first aims his sledgehammer at Jewish writers who have "used history as a means of defense" against the accusation that Jews have been disloyal, writers who have gone out of their way to display only the positive interactions between Jews and the Turkish state and society. This focus on the positive has led, ironically, to Turks having used these Jewish writers' positive valuations as a shield against those who would criticize the treatment of Jews in Turkey.[45] Bali asserts that the best example of such an approach is the work of Galanté. He reminds the reader that Galanté saw it as his personal duty to defend the Jews in the minds of the public and of regime officials into the 1950s, citing Galanté's *Türkler ve Yahudiler* as the best example of this effort. He notes that in that book, Galanté only reflected the positive aspects of Muslim-Jewish relations and Jewish interaction with the regime and either ignored or minimized negative episodes. In Bali's view, this utopian treatment gives the reader the feeling that Muslims are angels, perfect in their treatment of others.

Bali's main aim in the book was to examine the relations Jews had with the ruling CHP, how the Turkish public perceived Jews, and how the application of the politics of Turkifying the nation's culture and economy during the first decades of the republic affected Jews. The result is an account that provides evidence of official and popular anti-Semitism in the early republic; demonstrates that far more Jews suffered from Turkish policies in World War II than were saved by them; argues convincingly that the Capital Tax specifically targeted Christians and especially Jews; and shows how Jews were systematically excluded from the public sphere. Despite the convincing historical evidence that Bali provided to substantiate these claims, scholars in Turkey continue to argue that while the republic may have engaged in policies that have negatively affected non-Muslims, it has not enacted any that are anti-Semitic or anti-Jewish.[46]

The most significant part of Bali's book is his narrative of the World War II era. In it, Bali counters one of the main pillars of the thesis of Turkish tolerance of Jews: that Turks rescued many Jews during the war as part of a timeless Turkish penchant for helping Jews in need. In fact, Bali's research demonstrates that Turkey did not give permission to German Jews to immigrate in 1933 when approached by Turkish Jews, individual foreign Jews, or international Jewish relief organizations. The only Jews allowed were those who could fill empty positions at the new Istanbul and Ankara universities. A total of fifty-eight scholars were accepted in 1933. The limited migration of small numbers of German Jews is celebrated by the Turkish government as an example of Turkey's humanitarian treatment of Jews facing persecution. As scholars have subsequently demonstrated, however, Turkish officials of the 1930s and 1940s did not view these Germans as Jews. They preferred to see them as representatives of Europe who were instrumentalized to modernize and Westernize the secularizing republic's newly established universities.[47] Turkey's actions regarding these German Jewish academics were motivated by state interest in improving its educational system rather than by humanitarianism or an intention to help Jews.[48] The same officials viewed Turkish Jews neither as Europeans (and thus useful for Turkey), nor as Turks (and thus worth saving).

Crucially, Bali was the first to present evidence that far more Jews suffered from Turkish policies in World War II than were saved by them.[49] Because the study has not been translated out of Turkish, it has had no impact on Holocaust studies. Bali found that in contrast to the small numbers of Jews saved by the efforts of Turkish diplomats in Nazi-occupied Europe, many more Turkish Jews had their citizenship revoked by the Turkish government and as a consequence were sent to the camps where they died.[50] In 1938, as the position of Jews in Europe had significantly worsened,

Turkey outlawed foreigners from entering for purposes of transit if they did not possess visas to their destinations (read: Palestine). Another law enacted that year disallowed people who were not "members of the Turkish race" (read: Jews) from receiving residence permits.[51] Officials made it clear in 1938 and 1939 that they would not accept Jewish refugees: Turkish consulates received an order not to give visas to Jews with German, Hungarian, Italian, or Romanian passports unless they could "help" Turkey. Some Turkish consulate officials did manage to save Turkish Jews. But many more Turkish Jews in Nazi-occupied France who had their citizenship cancelled by the Turkish government or whose passports were not renewed were sent to death camps. The irony is that many of these Jews had fled the Turkish Republic in the 1920s and 1930s in order to escape Turkish anti-Semitism, widespread discrimination, and violence against them. Despite these facts, the collaboration of Turkish consular officials in the persecution of Turkish Jewry has to this day been neither acknowledged nor commemorated in Turkey, Germany, France, or the rest of Europe.

Levi and Şaul claimed that the Capital Tax targeted Christians and especially Jews, since only members of these groups were sent to labor camps for nonpayment. Using more convincing evidence, including political cartoons and the speeches of leading Turkish government and CHP officials, Bali makes the same point. A cartoon in the satirical magazine *Akbaba* from 1941, for example, is entitled "Basement of Profiteering Stores" and depicts a Jewish man given the stereotypical Jewish name Salamon with a phone to his ear on the first floor standing before empty shelves and a Turkish customer. Speaking with a Jewish accent, he says to the customer, "I just got word over the phone, our goods are at customs and will not clear for as long as a month." The bottom half of the cartoon depicts the basement of the store, where a Jewish man sits among piles of goods and talks to Salamon upstairs on the phone.[52] Many claimed that the Capital Tax was a "Blood Tax" because Christians and Jews had not "spilled blood" (read: fought) as had Turks or Muslims, but had instead become wealthy at the Turks' expense.[53] Others argued that in order to prevent this, the government had to put an end to Jews' profiteering and hoarding.[54] Prime Minister Şükrü Saraçoğlu (in office 1942–1946) stated that the tax would be implemented "with all due severity" on those who "benefited from the hospitality of this nation and became rich" yet avoided fulfilling their duty during the war years.[55] He also argued that the Capital Tax was "an opportunity to win our economic independence. Removing the foreigners [non-Muslims] who control our market, we will turn the Turkish market over to Turks [Muslims]."[56] A CHP official declared that the tax would force non-Muslim merchants to leave the country.[57] Many Jews believed that the second half of the Sephardic proverb, "Neither take a Romanian bride, nor own possessions in Turkey" (*Ni mujer de la Romanya, ni mülk en la Turkiya*) was thus verified.[58]

In view of the Twentieth Reserve Corps—the recruitment of Christians and Jews to serve in forced labor units disguised as a reserve military corps, to which Hakko had been called—and the Capital Tax the following year, Jews expected an even bigger disaster to follow in the event that Germany should occupy Turkey. Rumor spread that the huge ovens being constructed in Balat and Sütlüce in Istanbul and in Bahri Baba in Izmir were going to be used to annihilate them. Although the rumor proved to be false, the fact that many Jews believed it illustrates their fear and distrust of Turkish authorities.

In the final section of the book, Bali analyzes the republican social plan to create Turkish citizens, and the hindrances that stood in the way. Bali argues that because the government distinguished citizens by religion, and many believed that the term "Turk" denoted a Muslim, efforts at making Armenians, Greeks, and Jews into Turkish citizens were not successful. The aim of winning a "second War of Independence" by "liberating" the economy from Christians and Jews and creating a Turkish (read: Muslim) bourgeoisie also hindered the full realization of the project to create equal citizens. Sakıp Sabancı (1933–2004), head of the second-wealthiest family in Turkey (the wealthiest was Vehbi Koç, 1901–1996), accurately and succinctly explained how "formerly, İshaks and Salamons (read: Jews) conducted Turkey's business. Now this has changed."[59] Unlike Levi and Şaul, Bali also places responsibility for the lack of integration upon the attitudes and behavior of Jews, especially their insistence on continuing to speak French and Ladino. Many Turks did not understand why Jews would not adopt Turkish instead of these languages. Bali argues that Jews were not anxious to integrate despite the attempts of their leaders and the mass swearing of oaths in synagogues every Jewish New Year to speak Turkish. But anti-Jewish public opinion, incited by newspapers such as the regime mouthpiece, *Cumhuriyet*, and humor magazines that depicted Jews in the most grotesque fashion, along with constant humiliation of Jews in public and print for speaking heavily accented Turkish, worked to hinder their efforts and discourage them. Bali contends that another stumbling block was that the leaders of Turkish Jewry emphasized that the Ottomans had welcomed their ancestors in 1492, so Jews owed Ottomans and Turks an everlasting debt of gratitude. Ironically, emphasizing their having come from a foreign land and having guest status encouraged the public to view Jews as foreigners and therefore as being ungrateful by not speaking Turkish.[60]

Bali discusses how, in order to prove their loyalty, Jews raised funds for public institutions, a public effort that had also been undertaken by Ottoman Jews. Bali demonstrates that Jews were accused in the press of making these donations for their own material gain, not because of loyalty to the nation. Jews were considered incapable of true patriotic feeling toward Turkey and were accused of celebrating national holidays only because there were opportunities to make money, for example, by stitching and selling Turkish flags. According to Bali, the ruling CHP's view of Armenians, Greeks, and Jews crippled the success of the government's social blueprint. He quotes from a CHP party report written in 1944 that argued that Christians and Jews did not integrate, spoke their own languages, played no role in the foundation of the republic, served the interests of foreign powers, and never demonstrated their loyalty to Turkey.[61] The report stated that Jews never mixed with others because they remained separate, their only goal being to earn money. The report also proposed that Turkey should not permit the Jewish population to grow and should instead ease restrictions on Jewish emigration, decrease their population, and remove them from important spheres of the Turkish economy.

According to Bali's study, based largely on an examination of the Turkish press, the image Muslims had of Jews during the period from 1923 to 1945 was that Jews were disloyal, untrustworthy, and unpatriotic; eternal foreigners incapable of learning Turkish or assimilating; greedy, caring more about money than people; and wealthy. They were often depicted holding money bags marked with the dollar or pound sign. They were believed to possess considerable control over the economy and to have enriched themselves during wartime by hoarding goods and selling them on the black market while the nation's sons spilled their blood on the battlefield. One finds in the press of the era political cartoons such as one from summer 1939 where, as a ship full of European Jewish refugees approaches the Turkish shore, one large-nosed Jew calls out, "We are hungry, we are penniless. For God's sake, permit us to disembark for five minutes so we can get rich!"[62] Or another from 1944 depicting the deck of another overcrowded refugee ship attempting to land in Turkey where one large-nosed Jew in bowtie, bowler hat, and topcoat says to another, "We will have Palestine to ourselves, as our fatherland alone," with the other responding, "How can that be? What are we going to do, swindle ourselves there?"[63]

"He Had Believed That He Could Be Rescued"

The year Bali's monograph was published, Turkish Jewish novelist Mario Levi wrote a sprawling, multivocal, multiplot, disunified, stream-of-consciousness, eight-hundred-page family saga, *İstanbul bir masaldı* (Istanbul was a fairy tale).[64] In his novel, Levi offers the reader a different take on the theme of rescue, loyalty, and betrayal, casting doubt on the myth of Turks as saviors of Jews. Rather than depicting Armenians betraying Turks, to which the Turkish reader is accustomed, Levi transforms Turks into disloyal characters, who betray loyal Jews. Declaring that Jews are Turks, he attempts to inscribe Jews in a multicultural Istanbul landscape. His Turkey is a kaleidoscope of intimately connected ethnic characters: Jewish, Christian, Muslim, Arab, Armenian, Greek, Jewish, and Turkish. Levi's Jews are either true *Istanbullular* (Istanbulites), having lived in Istanbul for five centuries since arriving from al-Andalus, and thus originally Spanish Jews; or are contemporary Spanish Jews. Despite this fact, these Jews appear "stateless" and "foreign" in the eyes of others.[65] Levi's real-life Turkish English translator, Ender Gürol, proves this point, for he is unable to linguistically accept Jews as Turks. Gürol consistently changes passages in the original Turkish referring to Jews as *Türkler* (Turks) with a rightful claim to *Türklük* (Turkishness), choosing instead to refer to them in the English translation as "Turkish citizens" who possess "Turkish nationality." At times, he simply does not translate passages that refer to Jews as Turks. In this way, the translator betrays the author by denying a Jew the ability to call himself a Turk, an ideology that had deadly consequences during World War II as depicted in the novel.[66]

Two of the novel's many main protagonists are Consul Fahri (Turkish: honorary) Bey and Nesim. Fahri "*spoke of having* rescued many Turkish Jews from the concentration camps," a disbelieving gloss that modifies the conventional history that Turkish consuls "rescued many Turkish Jews."[67] His innocent foil is Istanbulite Sephardic Turkish Jew, Nesim, whose "admiration for the German language had not prevented him from being sent to the concentration camps." Nesim the Jew was "a real Ottoman who had never forsworn his attachment to Istanbul. In that small city on the shore of the Atlantic Ocean, *he had believed that he could be rescued from that road to death by taking refuge in his Turkishness*" [English version: "taking refuge in his Turkish nationality"].[68] Already at the novel's outset the reader confronts four fantasies: Istanbul is a fairy tale built on untruths because its inhabitants are afraid to tell the truth, fearing annihilation if they say or do the wrong thing; Fahri's fantasy of having rescued many Jews in Nazi-occupied Europe; and Nesim's naïve double fantasy, first that his Germanness [his ability to speak German and admiration for German culture] would save him from the Nazis, and then, when it did not, that his Turkishness would rescue him.

Five hundred pages into the novel, the reader comes to the fateful scenes involving Nesim and Fahri. Nesim and his wife Rahel have emigrated from Istanbul to Biarritz, France near the Spanish border; the author thus places Turkish Jews in Europe. The couple's best friend is Spanish Jewish communist Enrico Weizmann who had fled Spain to Biarritz when the republicans were defeated. Enrico serves as Nesim's confidant, allowing the reader to follow the fate of Nesim's family. Enrico's function as a survivor is to convey the words of the victims of the Holocaust.

We learn of the fate of Rahel and Nesim and their daughters Annette and Paulette through "the letter from those [concentration] camps" written by Enrico in 1945.[69] That a novel dedicated to the memory of Nesim's long-established Istanbul Sephardic Jewish family should have such a chapter demonstrates how unique and subversive of the conventional historical narrative this novel is. The family had been expecting arrest by the Nazis but believed all the while that they would find a way to escape. After all, "Spain was nearby, if worst came to worst. Spain was nearby."[70] Spain as the escape route symbolizes the Spain of Jewish memory, al-Andalus, where Sephardic Jewry experienced their "golden age" under Muslim rule. They did not try to escape while there was still time because "*Nesim trusted that the 'privilege' of his 'Turkishness' would make him safe,* [English version: "being a Turkish citizen"] and at every opportunity would say 'They won't be able to touch me.'"[71] For the second time, the reader is told that the Turkish consul does not save him, despite his tale of having saved many Jews.

Nesim grows wistful about Istanbul. As Enrico relates in the letter, "during one of those nights when we could practically feel the Gestapo breathing down our necks," Nesim "longs for his home overlooking the Golden Horn. . . . But rather than conceive this as a reality, he defines his longing more correctly as the ability to continue living with the Istanbul of his imagination."[72] Istanbul is envisioned as a place of refuge, a home. It is dreamed by a man yearning for safety. But Istanbul is only a fantasy realm of safety for Jews, for we know that he will never reach it again.

The Turkish Jewish men, women, and children were sent on cattle cars to Drancy, the concentration camp whose commandant was Adolf Eichmann's deputy, Alois Brunner, and from where Jews were sent to Auschwitz.[73] For the third time, the reader is confronted with the fantasy of the consul who rescued many Jews. After they were taken to the French concentration camp, Enrico relates how he *"still entertained a tiny bit of hope for Nesim and his family. After all they were Turks* [English version: "after all they were Turkish nationals"], *citizens of a nation with which Germany had close relations at that time.* We knew that it was too late. But hope is hope."[74] The close relations between the Ottoman Empire and Germany during World War I, their *Waffenbruderschaft* (brotherhood in arms), in which German generals commanded Ottoman armies, is alluded to here. In this novel, it is an allusion to the Armenian genocide. Alluding to the genocide serves as an omen for the grim outcome awaiting the Turkish Jews. For the fourth time, we read: *"We waited in vain for the Turkish consulate to attempt to save Nesim and his family."*[75] They are murdered at Auschwitz.[76]

At the end of *İstanbul bir masaldı*, we read "the 'confessions' of Consul Fahri Bey."[77] It is significant that Levi chose the term *confessions*, which has a very different meaning than *testimony*. *Testimony* is the word used in the apologetic work of Stanford Shaw, *Turkey and the Holocaust*, in an appendix entitled, "Testimony of Retired Ambassador Necdet Kent Regarding His Rescue of Jewish Turks at Marseilles during World War II."[78] As we have seen previously, subsequent research has cast considerable doubt on the veracity of Kent's claim to have rescued a cattle car full of Turkish Jews.[79] Such laudatory titles will not work here. Levi uses the word *confessions* because there is something amiss with his tale; it cannot be considered an objectively factual account. By this point the reader of the novel has long been aware that Nesim, Rahel, and their daughters are representative of all the Turkish Jews that had been murdered because their government did not save them. The surviving Jewish men shove gassed bodies into ovens, fearful of coming across the body of their wife or daughter.[80] The reader has been told four times that Nesim expected Turkey to save him, but it did not. The author informs his reader that Enrico's account is credible.

When Consul Fahri Bey finally speaks, the retired consul declares, "In those days I saved many people, I tried to save [many people]."[81] Is he correcting himself? Which is it? Did he *save* many people, or did he *try* to save many people? The reader is prepared to meet the claim with skepticism. According to Fahri, "We were in a position to be able to save him up until the last day of 1943. They had until that date to do whatever they could do, they had to return to Turkey, or to get to a more secure region. . . . I told him this." The consul claims that "at that time none of us completely understood what was happening in those 'death regions.' It is not as if bad news did not reach us. But I cannot lie, we never thought that the calamity would reach such proportions. Who knows, perhaps we preferred not to believe it."[82] The consul knew that they were taken away ten days later.[83] Was it Nesim's decision to make, to return to Turkey or not, or was it the consul's? Is Nesim responsible for his own death? This part of Fahri's narrative seems credible to the reader as specific dates are given. In fact, they match the historical record; Turkey was given several ultimatums by Germany during that period to repatriate its nationals in Nazi-occupied Europe lest they be subjected to the measures taken against other Jews.[84] Then the consul states, "Many years have passed since then; like all my peers I have begun to confuse some events and details. Perhaps my memory deceives me."[85] The fuzzy status of his memory casts doubt on his narrative, especially on what will come later. Unlike the letter written by Enrico, the interview with the consul contains no testaments to credibility. The consul asks, "Am I trying to ease my conscience? Am I trying to cover up my guilt for not having been able to do more for him? Who knows?"[86] Levi implies that Turkish narratives of rescue are meant to assuage guilt for *not* having done enough to save Jews.

The consul explains how he had acted immediately upon hearing that a new group had been brought to Drancy, because he believed he "would be able to save a few more people," Nesim included. He narrates handing over a list of "the last Turks" he had been able to reach [The translator of the English version excises reference to these Jews as Turks, omitting "the last Turks"].[87] "Every name meant a life," he narrates, "One had to see and experience that scene . . . Later they called out Nesim . . . I was going to succeed, at that moment I very much believed that I was going to succeed. But at that precise moment something unexpected happened."[88] A man he does not know claims to be Nesim. Because they had collected the identity papers he would not be able to prove the man was lying. In addition, "Before me was a person struggling desperately to be saved, ready to assume another's identity in order to save his life. A person, do you understand? How could I send him to his death when he was on the verge of being saved?" What was important to him "at that moment was to be able to save several lives."[89] He takes credit for managing to have all on the list returned safely to Turkey.

A Turkish Muslim is in a position to decide whether a Turkish Jew lives or dies. Rather than take the blame for allowing Turkish Jews to be sent to their deaths, however, the consul narrates finding himself in a position to spare one life, which he knew meant condemning another. Levi has the consul admit that Turkish Jews were sent to their deaths. "A few days later we learned that they had all been transferred together . . . to Auschwitz, they said. . . . But frankly speaking, we were not able to learn the truth about this matter."[90] Levi has the consul say in his confessions a word that has never appeared in the celebratory narratives of Turkish rescue—*Auschwitz*. If all Turkish Jews were saved, what need would there be to mention the place from which none returned?

Levi does not try to prove to the reader that Turks have been tolerant to Jews. Liberated from a pedantic approach by the genre of fiction, he creates Muslim and Jewish characters that are far more believable than those depicted in the historiography. In fact, considering the way he treats the consul's account, Levi's novel is quite remarkable. It is one of the only texts in Turkish, fictional or nonfictional, published up to that time to cast doubt on Turkey's self-serving myths about World War II.[91] Using Sephardic rather than Ashkenazi Jews who can reach neither Spain nor its replacement, Turkey, and a Turkish Muslim perhaps modeled on the so-called Turkish Schindler—the Turkish consul at Marseille, Necdet Kent—Levi questions the honorary story that Turkey tells about itself. In so doing, his novel most effectively undermines the utopian view of Turkish-Jewish relations.

After having narrated the Holocaust, Levi introduces the Armenian genocide, weaving the experiences together. The reader learns that the letter from the concentration camps written in 1945 by Enrico was addressed to a Monsieur Jacques, Nesim's younger brother, whose best friend is an Armenian. Thus is a connection made between the Holocaust and the Armenian genocide. The narrator reminds us that 1942 was the year when the decision was made to "gather together" (Turkish: *toplama*, same as Turkish: *toplama kampı*, concentration camp) twenty thousand non-Muslim men in one place for a special military conscription, the Twentieth Reserve Corps.[92] Those were also the years, the narrator explains, when it was rumored that Turkey had made a secret agreement with Germany and had begun to construct a giant oven [for murdering Jews] in Sütlüce, the site of Istanbul's largest slaughterhouse.[93] Some feared that the conscription (*toplama*) was the first step in the plan to murder them. Fears that their own government was constructing a giant crematorium in their main neighborhood to annihilate them expresses the state of mind of Turkish Jewry in that era, the narrator tells us. Not only Jews were worried: "When one remembered what had happened in the past," it was understandable why the Armenians were also afraid.[94] Most were to be sent from Istanbul to Yozgat, an explicit genocide reference Levi uses to good effect, for it is where Ottoman lieutenant governor Mehmed Kemal was found guilty of mass murder of Armenians and plunder of Armenian property during the genocide and was hanged by the postwar Ottoman government in 1919.[95] The author makes further references to the Armenian genocide, describing how, during the morning muster roll at the Twentieth Reserve Corps, a sergeant used to say, "Where, oh where are your corpses? Are you *still* alive?'"[96] One morning when the mass of recruits is commanded to separate themselves according to ethnoreligious identity, the Armenians become the most afraid and some try to sneak into the Greek and Jewish groups. "Once more [the Armenians] felt the cold breeze of fear on their necks. . . . They were in Yozgat. . . . In Yozgat." When the conscripts arrive in Yozgat, local Muslim Turks shout at them. "To hell with the infidels! Kill off these infidels!"[97]

In the final chapters of Levi's book, Armenians fear a repetition of their past in Anatolia, while Jews, panicked by the construction of what they believe to be crematoria in Istanbul, fear the measures being taken in the present and planned for the future. Revisiting places such as Yozgat at different historical times, Levi brings together the Ottoman genocide of Armenians, the Nazi Holocaust of Turkish Jews, and discrimination against Christians and Jews in the Turkish Republic, all in the same frame. In Levi's telling, Anatolia and Europe are lands where all Ottoman/Turkish minorities suffer at the hands of their own government.

The "letter from those [concentration] camps" written by Levi's fictional character Enrico appears to the narrator as if "it had come from a completely different world and time, despite its authenticity and bare simplicity."[98] He explores how those who were able to return from the camps "had to wait for years, had to battle with their own ghosts, with the hope of being able to find a place for themselves in others' tales" after the war. Their tales must overcome both the reticence of the tellers and the disinterest or incomprehension of others given that they do not fit into the dominant Turkish, German, and Israeli tales about that era.[99] How could a Turk possibly be a Jew? How could there be Turks in Nazi-occupied Europe? Conventional wisdom holds that since Turks did not arrive in Germany until the 1960s, Turks have nothing to do with what happened in the war. The realities recounted in the camp survivor's letter is counterposed with the doubtful credibility of the consul's account, he who had facilitated their transfer to Auschwitz, wielding power over life and death. The narrator hopes that relating this awful tale will embolden himself and other Turkish Jews to tell more tales about their collective experience.

Levi's narrator is uncertain of the tale the consul has told for years about having saved Turkish Jews. He asks whether Consul Fahri has told "a 'concocted tale' about himself, consisting here and there of parts he had made up, hiding behind some images [of how he wished to be portrayed], avoiding some facts that he no longer wished to remember," or whether he had told a sincere tale about what he had actually experienced.[100] The consul's "confession" could be fiction or nonfiction, but the reader is compelled to not believe it.

The reader of *İstanbul bir masaldı* never discovers the answer to the question of whether Fahri Bey's account is fiction or nonfiction. Levi begins the novel with a tongue-in-cheek disclaimer: "Should the names, places, and dates 'used' in the tales in this novel resemble 'actual' names, places, or dates, it is purely coincidental." Nevertheless, "the author will not object" should what is related in the novel "cause the reader to recall 'past' experience or records of that experience." Ayşe Kulin claims that her novel *Last Train to Istanbul*, a one-dimensional rehash of the same old tired historiographic tropes that have circulated since 1892, is based on historical documents provided by the foundation and interviews with retired ambassadors, including Necdet Kent, "who recalled their experiences" for her. Her book, then, is a novelization of the dominant historiography. Levi's tale does not pretend to offer historical truths, yet his account presents the more believable characters. In place of the cardboard cutouts of Turkish rescuers and grateful Jews we are used to encountering in Turkish and Ottoman historiography, Levi's novel tells a more complicated and therefore believable tale of troubled souls negotiating upsetting events. It is ironic that only a novelist can portray Turkish and Jewish protagonists that are far more convincing than those presented by centuries of historians.

Using repetition and ellipses to heighten the reader's focus, underlining points for emphasis, Levi ends his novel with a cry for a new, true story to be told. He imagines himself asking the characters "Tell me. . . . Tell me again. . . . For the sake of that place, time, and person. . . . Tell me for the sake of that nation, our nation. . . . Tell me again a new tale that I can believe in. . . . Tell me a tale that is more honest, more genuine, that is 'unguarded.' Tell me . . . Tell me . . . Tell me . . . "[101] Levi's fictional account implores Turks to write histories that are believable, to talk about their past in a way that acknowledges the gray areas. But accustomed to tales of Turkish heroism, would the reader believe them?

Conclusion

Faced with the pervasive myth of peaceful relations between Turks and Jews that continues to be expressed by community leaders, Rıfat Bali offered a needed corrective in 1999, publishing a groundbreaking work in Turkish without which this book could not have been written. A one-man wrecking ball, Bali redacted and brought to publication accounts of other embittered Turkish Jews, including Avner Levi and Eli Şaul. As a necessary rejoinder to a century of mythmaking, Bali's writing shades over into the lachry-mose spectrum of Jewish historiography. As Zionists who left Turkey, Levi and Şaul reflect a counternarrative to the official and popular discourse on Muslim-Jewish relations. While a vast improvement on the history writing that Mark Cohen describes as depicting a "'golden age' of Jewish-Muslim harmony, an interfaith utopia of tolerance and *convivencia*," a noncritical reader could see the work of Bali, Levi, and Şaul as part of another type of history writing on Jewish-Muslim relations, that of the "counter-myth of Islamic persecution."[102]

The weakness of this group's contribution, however, lies in their unwill-ingness to examine how the same Turkification policies that had such det-rimental effects on the lives of Jews also affected Armenians, Greeks, and Kurds. None of these terms appear in Bali's index. Rather, these groups are primarily mentioned in the preface and conclusion, particularly in the context of the Quincentennial Foundation being used to counter Armenian and Greek lobbying efforts in the United States.

Despite these flaws, Bali, Levi, and Şaul have achieved their aim. They have uncovered and exposed a wealth of documentation and testimony concerning the negative side of the lives of Jews in early republican Tur-key, illustrating their arguments with grotesque political cartoons from the period, gripping personal anecdotes, and blood-curdling quotations from Turkish officials and newspapers. It is hard for the reader to complete these books without acquiring a negative perspective on the fate of Turkish Jews and skepticism toward those who argue anything different. But because Levi and Bali's works remain untranslated from Turkish, their impact is limited.

So long as a much more powerful and well-funded Muslim-Jewish alliance of interests, manned by politicians, journalists, novelists, and filmmakers promotes the myth of rescue within a utopian frame, such countervoices will remain a whisper that is lost in the cacophony of Turkey promoters. Who will gasp at the racist images so typical of the 1940s Turkish press, such as a 1943 political cartoon depicting a large-nosed Jewish man in bowler hat hugging a large safe, happy to be "reunited" with his money upon release from a labor camp? Rather than these horrors, the image that remains is that of Turkish consul Necdet Kent boarding that train.[103]

Novelist Mario Levi went further than Avner Levi, Vitali Hakko, Eli Şaul, or Rıfat Bali, all of whom offered critical accounts of Turkish-Jewish relations in the early republic, for he touched upon the last Ottoman era as well. Levi is the only Turkish Jewish author to recognize the Armenian genocide instead of ignoring or denying it. Yet even Mario Levi's imagination has its limits. As with all other authors who wax nostalgic for the Ottomans, whether critical of the Turkish Republic or not, he still clings to the Ottoman ingathering of the Sephardim as an idealized past. And like Hakko, he uses that idealized Sephardic past as a foil to the violence suffered by Jews in modern Turkey. In Levi's novel, al-Andalus is a place of memory that informs utopian visions in the present. *Sefarad* (Spain) serves as a vision of peace in a time of war. Its extension, the Ottoman Empire, is seen by Turkish Jews as an unchanging cultural and historical reference point for Muslim-Jewish intimacy, Muslim tolerance of Jews, and Jewish refuge.

Notes

1. Esra Özyürek, *Nostalgia for the Modern: State Secularism and Everyday Politics in Turkey* (Durham, NC: Duke University Press, 2006), especially "The Elderly Children of the Republic: The Public History in the Private Story," 29–64.

2. Özyürek, *Nostalgia for the Modern*, 30–31.

3. *Unuttukları ve hatırladıklarıyla Türkiye'nin toplumsal hafızası*, ed. Esra Özyürek (Istanbul: İletişim, 2002); and *Politics of Public Memory in Turkey*, ed. Esra Özyürek (Syracuse, NY: Syracuse University Press, 2007). The most significant works are Taner Akçam, *Türk ulusal kimliği ve Ermeni sorunu* (İstanbul: İletişim, 1992); Taner Akçam, *İnsan hakları ve Ermeni sorunu—İttihat ve Terakki'den kurtuluş savaşına* (Ankara: İmge, 1999);

Rıdvan Akar, *Varlık vergisi—Tek parti rejiminde azınlık karşıtı politika örneği* (Istanbul: Nadir, 1992; revised 2nd edition); Rıdvan Akar, *Aşkale yolcuları: Varlık vergisi ve çalışma kampları* (Istanbul: Belge, 1999); Hülya Demir and Rıdvan Akar, *İstanbul'un son sürgünleri* (Istanbul: İletişim, 1994); Yelda, *İstanbul'da, Diyarbakır'da azalırken* (Istanbul: Belge, 1996); Yelda, *Çoğunluk aydınların'da ırkçılık* (Istanbul: Belge, 1998); Leyla Neyzi, *İstanbul'da hatırlamak ve unutmak: Birey, bellek ve aidiyet* (Istanbul: Tarih Vakfı, 1999); and Ayhan Aktar, *Varlık vergisi ve Türkleştirme politikaları* (Istanbul: İletişim, 2000), which includes revised versions of articles published between 1996 and 1999. Additional authors who could be cited include Elçin Macar, Herkül Milas, and Baskın Oran.

4. The retrospective webpages were then found on the website of Sephardic House: Institute for Researching and Promoting Sephardic History and Culture at the Center for Jewish History in New York, but today only exist on the internet archive: https://web.archive.org/web/20010220164801/http:/www.sephardichouse.org:80/quincentennial-foundation.html.

5. M. Ahmet Varol, "Türkiye Yahudileri'nin 500. yılı," *Millî*, August 9, 1992, cited in Bali, *Model Citizens of the State*, 324. On the attempted assassination of Kamhi, see Kamhi, *Gördüklerim yaşadıklarım*, 415–420.

6. According to the World Jewish Congress, there are approximately 18,500 Jews in Turkey today; 61,000 have migrated to Israel since 1948. In 1965 the last Turkish census to record religion found 38,000 Jews in the country. http://www.worldjewishcongress.org/en/about/communities/TR; Shaw, *The Jews of the Ottoman Empire and the Turkish Republic*, Appendix 3, 285.

7. https://web.archive.org/web/20010220164801/http:/www.sephardichouse.org:80/quincentennial-foundation.html.

8. https://web.archive.org/web/20010304204734/http:/www.sephardichouse.org:80/500b.html.

9. For an analysis of the 1998 celebrations, see Özyürek, *Nostalgia for the Modern*.

10. For a review of the works of three of these authors, where I first raised these issues, see Baer, "Turkish Jews Rethink '500 Years of Brotherhood and Friendship.'"

11. Avner Levi, *Türkiye Cumhuriyetinde Yahudiler: Hukukî ve siyasi durumları*, ed. Rıfat N. Bali (Istanbul: İletişim, 1996).

12. Shaw, *The Jews of the Ottoman Empire and the Turkish Republic*, 256.

13. Ibid.

14. Lewis, *The Emergence of Modern Turkey*, 2nd ed., 301.

15. Lewis, *The Jews of Islam*, 7.

16. Hakko, *Hayatım*. The book was finally translated into English by Rıfat Bali's publishing house: Vitali Hakko, *My Life: Vakko* (Istanbul: Libra, 2011).

17. Hakko, *Hayatım*, 15.

18. Ibid., 28.

19. Ibid., 28–29.

20. Ibid., 30.

21. Ibid., 39.

22. Ibid., 12.

23. Ibid., 88.

24. Ibid., 89.

25. Ibid., 91.

26. Ibid., 92.

27. Ibid., 93.

28. Ibid., 95.

29. Ibid., 95–96.

30. Ibid., 96.

31. Ibid., 97.

32. Ibid., 98.

33. Ibid., 99.

34. Ibid., 100.

35. Eli Şaul, *Balat'tan Bat-Yam'a*, ed. Rıfat N. Bali and Birsen Talay (Istanbul: İletişim, 1999). The book was also finally translated into English by Rıfat Bali's publishing house: Eli Şaul, *From Balat to Bat Yam: Memoirs of a Turkish Jew* (Istanbul: Libra, 2012).

36. Şaul, *Balat'tan Bat-Yam'a*, 89.

37. The complete official travel itinerary recorded by the Nazis is translated into Turkish in Rıfat Bali, "Sachsenhausen temerküz kampı'nın Türk ziyaretçileri," *Toplumsal Tarih* 151 (July 2006): 43. The top army generals traveled to Europe that summer, meeting with Hitler in Berlin and touring the western and eastern fronts. See Rıfat Bali, "Hitler ile görüşme: Ordu komutanı Orgeneral Cemil Cahit Toydemir'in Almanya gezisi," *Toplumsal Tarih* 165 (September 2007): 38–42. On the purpose of the police chiefs' visit, see Rıfat Bali, "Talat Paşa'nın kemiklerini mi? Nazi fırınları mı?" *Toplumsal Tarih* 150 (June 2006): 42–47; and Bali, "Sachsenhausen temerküz kampı'nın Türk ziyaretçileri."

38. On the Wannsee Conference, protocols of the meeting, and other documentation on the genocide of European Jewry, see https://www.ghwk.de/en/.

39. On Sachsenhausen, see https://www.sachsenhausen-sbg.de/en/.

40. *Sachsenhausen Concentration Camp, 1936–1945: Events and Developments*, Günter Morsch and Astrid Ley, eds., Schriftenreihe der Stiftung Brandenburgische Gedenkstätten Band 24 (Berlin: Metropol, 2011), 79, 182.

41. These are the words of the Dutch camp survivor Ab Nikolaas. Quoted in *Sachsenhausen Concentration Camp, 1936–1945*, 12.

42. The Nazis had drawn up plans for murdering the Jews of Arab lands—along the lines of the Mobile Killing Units (*Einsatzgruppen*) deployed in the USSR—in the wake of the defeat of the British and French in the Middle East and North Africa. Nazi occupation forces murdered Jews in Tunisia but were largely unable to carry out massacres elsewhere. See Peter Wien, "Coming to Terms with the Past: German Academia and Historical Relations between the Arab Lands and Nazi Germany," *International Journal of Middle East Studies* 42, no. 2 (May 2010): 312–313.

43. Bali, *Cumhuriyet yıllarında Türkiye Yahudileri*, 27.

44. Ibid., 19–20.

45. Ibid., 14.

46. See Şule Toktaş, "Perceptions of Anti-Semitism among Turkish Jews," *Turkish Studies* 7, no. 2 (2006): 203–223. Toktaş criticizes her Turkish Jewish interviewees by asserting that their perception of discrimination is baseless. "A Turkish Jew may believe that there are special laws in Turkey that restrict the recruitment of Jews to the Turkish Armed Forces or prevent a Jew from being nominated for Presidency, whereas, in fact, there are no laws of any kind specifically making such restrictions." Ibid., 205.

47. Kader Konuk, *East West Mimesis: Auerbach in Turkey* (Stanford, CA: Stanford University Press, 2010), 81–101.

48. İzzet Bahar, "German or Jewish, Humanity or Raison d'Etat: The German Scholars in Turkey, 1933–1952," *Shofar* 29, no. 1 (2010): 48–72.

49. Bali, *Cumhuriyet yıllarında Türkiye Yahudileri*, 331–368.

50. Ibid., 362–368.

51. Ibid., 332–333.

52. Reproduced in ibid., 429.

53. Ibid., 464.

54. Ibid., 426.

55. Ibid., 445.

56. Ibid., 478.

57. Ibid., 447–448. See also Rıfat Bali, *The "Varlik Vergisi" Affair: A Study on its Legacy—Selected Documents* (Istanbul: Isis, 2005); Rıfat Bali, *L'affaire impôt sur la fortune* (Istanbul: Libra Kitap, 2010); Rıfat Bali, ed. *Varlık vergisi: Hatıralar—tanıklıklar* (Istanbul: Libra Kitap, 2012); and Rıfat Bali, ed., *The Wealth Tax (Varlık Vergisi) Affair—Documents from the British National Archives* (Istanbul: Libra Kitap, 2012).

58. Quoted in Bali, *Cumhuriyet yıllarında Türkiye Yahudileri*, 482.

59. Quoted in Ibid., 551.

60. Recently, in response to a Turkish Jewish reporter expressing his community's "sense of gratitude" to Turkey, the Turkish consul-general in Marseilles replied, "In order to feel gratitude, you cannot be one of us. If you actually feel that you are Turks, there is no need to feel gratitude." Cohen, *Becoming Ottomans*, 142.

61. Bali, *Cumhuriyet yıllarında Türkiye Yahudileri*, 538–541.

62. *Akbaba*, August 24, 1939, reproduced in Bali, *Cumhuriyet yıllarında Türkiye Yahudileri*, 344.

63. *Akbaba*, December 14, 1944, reproduced in Bali, *Cumhuriyet yıllarında Türkiye Yahudileri*, 368.

64. Mario Levi, *İstanbul bir masaldı* (Istanbul: Remzi, 1999), 19th printing, November 2014. The novel has sold roughly thirty-eight thousand copies in Turkish. The English version, *Istanbul Was a Fairy Tale*, translated by Ender Gürol (Champaign, IL: Dalkey Archive Press, 2014), is riddled with errors and unreliable.

65. Levi, *İstanbul bir masaldı*, 17.

66. I witnessed this being confirmed at a presentation by Levi at a Turkish cultural center in London in 2015 when two Turkish audience members asked the Yunus Nadi Novel Prize–winning Istanbul author whether he spoke Turkish or wrote in Turkish.

67. Ibid., 34, emphasis added.

68. Ibid., 40, emphasis added. Levi, *Istanbul Was a Fairy Tale*, 33.

69. Levi, *İstanbul bir masaldı*, 587–607.

70. Levi, *İstanbul bir masaldı*, 590.

71. Ibid., 590–591, emphasis added. Levi, *Istanbul Was a Fairy Tale*, 489.

72. Levi, *İstanbul bir masaldı*, 591.

73. Ibid., 494.

74. Ibid., 596, emphasis added. Levi, *Istanbul Was a Fairy Tale*, 494.

75. Levi, *İstanbul bir masaldı*, 597, emphasis added.

76. Ibid.

77. Levi, *İstanbul bir masaldı*, 728–732.

78. "Testimony of Retired Ambassador Necdet Kent."

79. Guttstadt, *Turkey, the Jews, and the Holocaust*, 219–221.

80. Levi, *İstanbul bir masaldı*, 602–603.

81. Ibid., 729.

82. Ibid.

83. Ibid., 730.

84. Guttstadt, *Turkey, the Jews, and the Holocaust*, 209–240.

85. Levi, *İstanbul bir masaldı*, 730.

86. Ibid.

87. Levi, *Istanbul Was a Fairy Tale*, 599.

88. Levi, *İstanbul bir masaldı*, 730–731.

89. Ibid., 731.

90. Ibid., 731.

91. Incidentally it was published the same year as Turkish Jewish writer Bali's still untranslated *Cumhuriyet yıllarında Türkiye Yahudileri*, the most critical historical account of the experience of Turkish Jews written in any language.

92. Levi, *İstanbul bir masaldı*, 741.

93. Ibid. Not "bakery" as in the English translation! Levi, *Istanbul Was a Fairy Tale*, 608.

94. Levi, *İstanbul bir masaldı*, 741.

95. Suny, *"They Can Live in the Desert but Nowhere Else,"* 337–338.

96. Levi, *İstanbul bir masaldı*, 742.

97. The translator of the English version censors this passage to read "Down with the infidels!" alone. Levi, *Istanbul Was a Fairy Tale*, 609.

98. Levi, *İstanbul bir masaldı*, 587.

99. See Baer, "Turk and Jew in Berlin"; and Marc David Baer, "Mistaken for Jews: Turkish PhD Students in Nazi Germany," *German Studies Review* 41, no. 1 (February 2018): 19–39.

100. Levi, *İstanbul bir masaldı*, 606–607.

101. Ibid., 803, ellipses in original.

102. Cohen, "The 'Golden Age' of Jewish-Muslim Relations: Myth and Reality," 28.

103. *Akbaba*, Kanun II 7, 1943, reproduced in Bali, *Cumhuriyet yıllarında Türkiye Yahudileri*, 474.

8

LIVING IN PEACE AND HARMONY,
OR IN FEAR?

THROUGHOUT THE 2000S, A NUMBER OF TURKISH JEWS, primarily those who had left Turkey, were compelled to tell their life stories, thus countering the narrative promoted by the foundation and its supporters abroad. Shaw continued to perpetuate the same well-worn myths of the humane Turk as the rescuer of Jews. His 2001 article concerning Turkey during World War II begins with a scene not from that era, but with a harkening back to the 1492 arrival of Iberian Jewry in the Ottoman Empire, whose sultans he credits with having protected Jews from "Christian bigotry and persecution."[1] He makes this anachronistic commendation in connection with his argument that "as had been the case for more than five centuries, Turks and Jews continued to help each other in times of great crises."[2] But did they?

The Sephardic Past Becomes a Fairy Tale in Thrace

Erol Haker (formerly Elio Adato, b. 1930), an Istanbulite Jewish economist who left Turkey for Israel in 1956, was having none of this. He published a Turkish translation of his unpublished English memoir as *Bir zamanlar Kırklareli'de Yahudiler yaşardı . . . Kırklarelili Adato ailesin'in öyküsü* (Once upon a time Jews lived in Kırklareli . . . The story of the Adato family of Kırklareli).[3] Once again, the work was redacted by Bali. Bittersweet memoir, oral history, archival study, and folkloric description of a lost culture, Haker's account traces his Sephardic Adato family of Kırklareli in eastern Thrace from 1800 to 1934. While in 1912 the entire extended Adato family lived exclusively in the town, by 1977 none of the family was left: they had all emigrated, first to Palestine, and later Israel, France, Mexico, Cuba, or the

United States. They shared the fate of other Jews of the town: whereas in 1912, 1,300 Jews resided in Kırklareli, when Haker visited in 1997 he found only seven elderly members of the community.[4] What had happened? If Turks and Jews had lived together in peace and brotherhood, why were there no longer any Jews in the Thracian town of Kırklareli? Haker explains that the narrative ends in 1934 "due to the anti-Semitic events that took place in Thrace that July," the nail in the coffin to the Jewish community's continuing existence in Kırklareli.[5] The reader also soon discovers that Haker had lost nine members of his extended family in the Holocaust. One wonders why that is the case when we have been constantly told that Turkey not only remained neutral during the war, but that all of its ambassadors and diplomats were busy saving Jews in Europe.

Born in the Ottoman Empire, Haker's ill-fated family members had settled in France during the second decade of the twentieth century, "hoping for a better future."[6] We discover later in the book how Hayim Adato and his family were "arrested by the French police and sent to their death in Auschwitz."[7] Marko Adato, another relative, hid with his family in the home of a non-Jewish French friend in Paris. At the end of July 1944, thinking that the tide of war had turned and that the Germans were about to be defeated, Marko left his hiding place to buy a packet of cigarettes. He paid with his life. The French police arrested him because he had no identity papers and sent him to Drancy from where he was immediately sent to Auschwitz and gassed at Birkenau. Drancy was liberated by the US Army less than three weeks later.[8] Why had the Turkish consuls in France not saved him?

Haker contrasts the sad fate of Jews in the early Turkish Republic with positive relations between Turks and Jews in the Ottoman Empire until 1912, deploying the theme of friend versus enemy as he narrates the Balkan Wars that erupted that year. In his account, the Jews of Kırklareli sided with the Ottomans, whereas the Greeks (and Bulgarians) were clearly the Jews' enemy. Haker describes how his grandfather Lia took his uncle and his father, Menahem (b. 1904), to cheer on the Ottoman soldiers gathering near the family home. The civilians who gathered to view their "heroic army" were "either Turks or Jews. The town's Bulgarians and Greeks were nowhere to be found."[9] Menahem never forgot the "Ottoman Army March" he learned at the time, whose lyrics include "Let us sacrifice our blood for the fatherland."[10] The Ottomans were routed, and the Bulgarians would take the town. "There was not a moment to lose. The Turks and Jews, who had never forgotten the Bulgarian occupation after the Russians took Kırklareli in 1878, fled the town en masse, deciding to become refugees [rather than face that fate again]."[11] His father drew a vivid comparison between the columns of wounded, shocked, defeated Ottoman soldiers "moving like ghosts, saying nothing, with frozen expressions on their faces" and the Jews expelled from Rome two thousand years earlier.[12]

Predictably, the Bulgarians took Kırklareli a couple of hours after the family had fled by horse cart and train to Istanbul. For Haker, the Turks' defeat was also the Jews' defeat. The family was able to return six months later, only to find their home being used as a Bulgarian headquarters, a situation that continued for another three months. When the Ottoman army retook Kırklareli in July 1913, the Jews had reason to hope that good days had returned. But the Bulgarian army would again destroy Turkish villages and towns only a few months thereafter in the Second Balkan War. As an outcome of the wars and the attendant shrinkage of the borders of the empire, Kırklareli became a border town with poor economic prospects, compelling the migration of young men in his extended family. Those who went to France would be murdered by the Nazis.

During World War I, which followed on the heels of the Balkan Wars, most Jewish men of Kırklareli were exempted from military service, but due to his excellent Turkish, his grandfather Lia served during the war in the main post and telegraph office as a military censor.[13] His grandfather's brother Menahem also became a reserve officer and was assigned to the intelligence bureau of the general staff, serving until the end of the war, responsible for censoring articles in the press.[14] Haker does not reveal what they learned about the deportation of Armenians.

Haker's narrative again emphasizes Turkish-Jewish solidarity during the Greek occupation (1920–1922), when the Adatos "openly sided with the Turks," providing drinking water from the spring that ran behind their home to the Turkish guerillas, despite the presence of a Greek military police station across the street.[15] In November 1922, when the armistice agreement stipulated that eastern Thrace would be given to the Turks and the Greeks would withdraw, "the Greeks of Kırklareli decided to burn the town down [as they withdrew]. When the Jewish community learned of the plan, they joined forces with the Turks to save the town. Members of the community, including [grandfather] Lia, participated in the night patrols," thereby preventing the Greeks from setting fire to any building save the municipality.[16]

The tone in the second half of Haker's account changes as the author explores the new Turkish Republic's abandonment of the tolerant principles of the Ottoman Empire, detailing the onset of anti-Jewish events in Thrace soon after the founding of the republic in 1923.[17] But "miraculously" the small Jewish community of Kırklareli "was able to maintain friendly relations" with the Turks, and his family prospered until the depression of 1929. But in fact, one of the main reasons the family prospered was that the Greeks had been deported in the "population exchange" of 1923–1924. Greek merchants had been the Jews' main economic competitors. In their absence, his grandfather Lia was able to greatly expand the family business. But without Greeks, Jews suddenly became much more visible. There were ill omens on the horizon.

In 1925, the new republic nationalized the importation, production, and sale of alcohol, putting one of his grandfather's brothers out of business. More ominously, in August 1927, while the family was visiting Istanbul, the young Jewish woman Elza Niyego was murdered by an older Turkish Muslim man, an event "that shocked Turkish Jewry."[18] Being an eyewitness to the events following her murder "played a determining role" in the lives of grandfather Lia, father Menahem, and aunt Sultana, who would all migrate to Israel after its foundation in 1948. Thousands of Jews, possibly these three included, joined her funeral, "which turned into a protest against worsening Turkish-Jewish relations relative to the Ottoman period."[19] The government responded to the mass protest by prohibiting Jewish travel within the country. The family had to remain in Istanbul for a year. Haker's father, Menahem, had found a good job working for an Italian firm in Istanbul, but in 1931, the republic nationalized all foreign firms. Moreover, since its establishment, the new nation-state had fired all Jews working in the public sector and government offices. Menahem's only choice was to return to Kırklareli and rejoin the family cloth business.[20] In 1935, Lia's brother Simanto and his family emigrated to the Zionist settlement in British Palestine. Haker explains that while Simanto was already a committed Zionist, the immediate reason to migrate had been a humiliating episode. His wife, Sultana, was arrested for violating a law passed in 1926 that made "insulting Turkishness" a crime. Her crime had been to harshly scold some Turkish youth who had accidentally hit her in the head with their ball while she was sitting on her balcony.[21] The family managed to get her released from jail before her trial and promptly fled the country.[22] But the reader suspects that the underlying reason for the family's decision to emigrate was the July 1934 pogrom the year before, to which Haker devotes a long section of the book. The twenty pages devoted to the pogrom are the most difficult to read, and yet they are the most gripping, vivid, and memorable part of the memoir, for they provide the answer to the question of why there are virtually no Jews left in Kırklareli—and why the Sephardic past is a fairy tale, to use Levi's formulation. Based on oral histories he conducted with members of his extended family, Haker narrates the experiences of individuals one by one. At the beginning of July, his family had heard that anti-Jewish attacks had taken place in other Thrace towns the previous week, but they and other Kırklareli Jews thought that since they had good relations with their Turkish neighbors, they had nothing to fear. Even in the worst-case scenario, they thought, should their neighbors turn on them, they could trust the Turkish police to protect them.[23] They were mistaken. The narrative of what happened next reads as a horror story.

The three-story Adato family home was located next to the town's central police station. Their proximity to the police station notwithstanding, their house was stoned after dark on July 3, and all its windows were broken. During the attack, the extended family retreated to the second floor and shouted out to the nearby police station for help, to no avail. Instead, as they heard the unmistakable sound of an axe destroying their wooden front door, Lia's and Simanto's families rushed downstairs and ran out the back door, fleeing across the inner courtyard to the home of another family member to hide in the coal cellar.[24] That relative's home was then plundered. Lia's Arab friend, an army colonel, led them out and promised that his men would patrol the family block so nothing would happen. The family thought it wise for the young women to remain hiding in the coal cellar. The Adato home had been plundered, especially Simanto's floor, and whatever could not be taken was being destroyed. The family assumed the attack was because he was an open Zionist. But then just before dawn, another mob came to the family compound, chasing away the Arab friend's appointed guards and looting what had not been taken before. The young men asked where the young women were hiding, naming them.[25] Told that they were away visiting relatives in Istanbul, the mob left with more of the family's possessions. After returning to their hiding place on the other side of the inner courtyard for the remainder of the night, they ventured back to their own home at dawn, coming face to face with a third mob of looters. A large wrestler was carrying their heavy Singer sewing machine on his back.[26] Haker's grandmother Esther upbraided the man, "How can you do this to a friend of the Turks like Lia Adato? You should be ashamed of yourself!" The wrestler froze in his tracks, dropped the machine with a great crash, and ran away. Little else remained in the house apart from some old carpets and clothes.

Later that morning, most of the Jews of Kırklareli, including most members of the extended Adato clan, fled by train to Istanbul. While heading to the station, they were surrounded by large, jeering crowds of Turks. They came across one of the would-be rapists from the night before. Upon seeing the young woman whom he had asked for by name, he shouted, "We will settle our account next time!"

The reader learns that other members of Haker's extended family had been warned by Turkish friends that bad things would happen that night and that they should stay indoors. As the pogrom began, they were told that "the aim was not to kill Jews, but to plunder them. So long as Jews did not resist, blood would not be spilled."[27] But blood was shed in his family. Some relatives were beaten, others knifed. Mosse Levi suffered the pain and indignity of having his gold crowns pulled from his mouth by the mob.[28] Rabbi Moşe Fintz and his wife, Mazalto, suffered worse humiliation. When the looters entered the rabbi's home, they split into three groups. While one plundered their belongings, one attacked the rabbi. They told him he did not need his beard. Taking out a razor, they started to cut it off. He resisted, and they cut his face. As Haker narrates, "It was obvious they bore a grudge against him and wanted to humiliate him."[29] He gave up resisting, and they finished cutting off his beard. The third group set out to rape his wife. The would-be rapists had started to rip off her clothes and beat her but were suddenly distracted when they discovered she had hidden a pocketbook in her underwear. Instead of raping her, they fought over the money in the pocketbook, leaving her disrobed and in a state of shock on the floor. They finished stripping the house clean and left.[30] Within a year the rabbi and his wife migrated to Bulgaria, and then Cuba, finally settling in Israel in 1950.

Accompanying these violent images, other vignettes haunt the reader, such as that of Moşon Mitrani's family the morning after, sitting on the bare floor in the ruins of their home, silently making Turkish coffee over a coal brazier. Even the chairs had been stolen.[31]

The Jews were told that they had been ordered to leave the town, for they were no longer wanted.[32] The police had not raised a finger to prevent the looting and violence. Neither their good relations with Turkish neighbors nor with the state had protected them. In some cases Turkish friends and business partners had warned them beforehand to hide their valuables and stay out of sight. Some homes had been guarded by Turkish army officers and neighbors. But the damage was done. Jews felt betrayed. Haker's grandfather Lia never recovered from the shock of that night.[33] He had thought the only difference between Turks and Jews to be a minor one—their religion. He had done everything in his power to be considered a Turk. But the pogrom "demonstrated to him that the difference was greater than he had thought or wished. During the events, no Turkish friends stood by his side."[34]

Oral histories conducted with three dozen members of his extended family exposed no memories of Turkish anti-Semitism during the Ottoman era.[35] But the Balkan Wars changed everything for the worse, he argues. Where once the Jews of Kırklareli had been on good relations with the authorities and their Turkish neighbors, after 1912 the relations frayed with the rise of Turkish nationalism and the abandonment of Ottomanism.[36] During the chaotic years that followed World War I, when it was unclear whether the Greek, Bulgarian, or Turkish side would rule in Thrace, some Adato family members turned to Zionism.[37] The situation worsened in the new republic after the Greeks had been expelled and the Jews remained as the only Thracian minority.[38] As Haker concludes, "Relations between the small Jewish community and Turks in Kırklareli gave the false impression that everything would be fine despite the rising nationalism, that relations [in their town] were better than elsewhere." The anti-Semitic events in 1934 "destroyed this belief. The Jews were struck in their most vulnerable psychological and economic spot."[39] And they realized they could never recover it in Turkey.

"Making the Jewish Monkey on the Back Disappear"

In 2003, the same year his account of the Jews of Thrace appeared in English,[40] Haker published a memoir of his own life in English, *From Istanbul to Jerusalem: The Itinerary of a Young Turkish Jew*. The account covers his life in Istanbul from his birth in 1930 to his migration to Israel in 1956, which he views, like Avner Levi and Eli Şaul before him, as the resolution to his own and Turkish Jewry's existential problems. He describes Turkey in the 1930s as a country where "anti-Jewish attitudes were gathering strength, at times to the point of active discrimination against them, agitation, and even organized physical violence."[41]

The memoir expresses the anxiety and fear of Turkish Jews during the 1930s and World War II. Haker's list of anti-Semitic and discriminatory incidents is long. In 1939, while visiting his grandmother in Kırklareli, local children threw stones at them and called them *pis Yahudiler* (dirty Jews).[42] Anti-Semitism punctured his school life as well.[43] His third-grade teacher, Ms. Selma, would upbraid the children when they were being too noisy by shouting, "This is not a synagogue!" When children asked what "stingy" meant, the same teacher explained the term with the example of how "*Kırk Yahudi bir toriğin başını yer*" ("Forty Jews share one fish head"). His fourth-grade teacher, Ms. Saime, asked him who his prophet was; when he responded that it was Moses, she turned to another student who answered the question correctly, saying "Muhammad." As Haker narrates, "a triumphant smile appeared in Ms. Saime's face. Well there it was. She had exposed the 'Nigger in the pile.'"[44] (Haker uses this old-fashioned, offensive phrase to draw parallels between African American slaves and Turkish Jews.) Haker's bench mate, Necati, turned to him to ask if he was "really a Muslim," as the family had officially converted to Islam to avoid stigmatization and discrimination. When Haker answered in the affirmative and showed his identity card to prove it, Necati "broke into a big smile and exclaimed, 'In this case when we throw the Jews out of the country, you will not be among them?'" When Haker confirmed the fact, he said, "I am so glad, then we can remain friends."[45] Haker unfairly labels these teachers Nazis and his classmates "young Nazis to be."[46] Yet the very next year, there were no anti-Semitic incidents, and he was given the coveted role of "the Turk" in a class play.[47]

In the winter of 1941, German troops arrived at the Turkish border. Haker describes how the national climate had already become "more anti-Jewish."[48] He mentions the call-up of non-Muslim men to serve "as a form of forced labor" in the guise of a reserve military corps, the Twentieth Reserve Corps. All of his Jewish acquaintances served, except his father, who had converted to Islam, compelling the rest of his family to do the same. Jews wondered why the men were sent to central Anatolia rather than the border region of Thrace if the purpose was to build fortifications to prepare for a German invasion. By early 1942, "the unspecified period of time attached to the general call up for non-Muslims assumed an ominous ring to it."[49] What was its purpose? Rumors began to circulate among Jews that Turkey was preparing to annihilate them. The rumors were "a telltale sign of how Jews felt at the time" based on the call-up, anti-Jewish sentiment in the press, and personal experience. In 1942, his father's Turkish business client told him that should Germany invade Turkey, he had made arrangements for the family to stay with him in distant Kars in eastern Turkey.[50]

Haker judges his overall primary school experience from 1936 to 1942 to have been positive, for he believes that he had "made considerable progress with getting assimilated," passing as a Muslim and speaking Turkish. His middle school experience from 1942 to 1946, not coincidentally the war years, would see his "progress in integration" be "severely jolted." Attacked for being a Jew, filled with fear and anxiety, Haker began to lose his self-esteem in the face of public humiliation.[51]

In his recounting of how the Capital Tax initiated in 1942 affected his family, Haker argues that two uncles received light assessments because they had Turkish (rather than Jewish) names. Another uncle, who was hospitalized, committed suicide rather than become a burden to a family already saddled with a heavy tax.[52] His father had been taxed two-thirds of his net worth. After paying off two-thirds of the amount due, he told the tax collector he was a Muslim. The official changed his demeanor and arranged that the rest of the tax would not have to be paid. Instead, the state would sell off the family's household goods at public auction, use the revenue to close his file, and look the other way when his father bought back all his goods. Haker's father arranged for a Dönme friend to just so happen to always be the highest bidder for every item, and afterward his father paid the man back and recovered all his household goods.[53] Although the family was relatively lucky, Haker's story prompts the reader to reflect upon the weighty financial and emotional burden of the tax and the public humiliation of selling off businesses and household goods. The tax caused families to lose their wealth and personal possessions. People's businesses were liquidated, resulting in the loss of stores and homes. In the worst cases, people were sent to a remote concentration camp, returning psychologically and financially ruined. Narrating the death of his grandmother, he notes how "she made herself her morning coffee, but did not finish drinking it, and its contents spilled onto the now barren floor, all the lovely carpets that once covered it sold . . . in a state auction to pay the Capital Tax."[54]

His classmates at the elite Robert College in Istanbul were gleeful about the tax and mocked him, asking him if he had already lost his furniture, one offering to pay his weekly allowance if his father no longer could.[55] While Haker felt that the Turkish state was out "to screw the Jews and other non-Muslims," as far as his Muslim classmates were concerned, "this was well deserved and therefore they were enjoying the show." Of his closest friends, he notes that all but one "were antisemitic to varying degrees."⁵⁶ At the end of 1944, when his Jewish background was revealed, he was treated by his friends "as if I had been discovered in a delinquency I had committed."⁵⁷ He denied "the accusation" and they laughed at him even more, promising to "overlook" the fact. In 1945, some members of his group of friends advocated the annihilation of Jews because they were all "dishonest."⁵⁸ As he recalls, "most of us knew about the extermination of the Jews . . . The argument was not about whether it was taking place or not, but rather about whether or not Jews should be exterminated." These arguments were "one of the most traumatic experiences" of his entire life, "namely, that one of my best friends was in favour of exterminating all of my kind!"⁵⁹ He recalls how the pro-German Turkish dailies, with their racist caricatures of Jews, also caused him "great grief" during the war years. One cartoon he has never forgotten concerned the *Struma* refugee ship. In it, a port pilot tells the captain of a service boat that if he wanted to find the stricken vessel in Istanbul's harbor, he need only follow his nose toward the stinking Jews.⁶⁰ Haker notes that during these years all Jews were considered black-market profiteers. He counters with the argument that "the majority of Jews . . . were bone-poor because of the limited economic opportunities that they faced as a result of being discriminated against" and it is for this reason that "such Jews were first to leave Turkey, 'en masse' for Israel" when the Jewish state was established.⁶¹

Haker faced constant harassment. Classmates told him they hated Jews.⁶² They referred to Jews as "Salamon" (Solomon), the stereotypical name given to Jewish men in Turkey. Older boys bullied him, calling him *ulan Yahudi* (Jew boy, similar to calling an adult African American "boy"), or *pis Yahudi* (dirty Jew). One boy attacked him, both verbally and physically, with such words. An older girl told him she did not like "gym shoes, I don't like carrots, and I don't like Jews."⁶³ The mention of gym shoes calls to his mind Haker having witnessed an uncle's humiliation as he was forced to wear white gym shoes rather than military boots during his army training, visible from the Haker family home.⁶⁴

The reader learns of the young man's constant social ostracism. At the age of nineteen, his first girlfriend, a Muslim, put an end to their relationship, stating, "I heard that you were Jewish."⁶⁵ He felt that "something deep inside me had been permanently damaged and was beyond repair," sparking his first plans to migrate to Israel.⁶⁶ Haker describes his feelings of "insecurity," being "a Jew in the eyes of a Turk," but a Turk in the eyes of Jews. This dichotomy, a result of his school choice, social circle, and language spoken, led to him experiencing "the worst of both worlds."[67] Trying to pass as a Turk, Haker was constantly exposed to anti-Jewish remarks and sentiment that, although not usually directed at him personally, nevertheless "undermined" his belief that he could ever feel or be accepted as a true Turk.[68] It is ironic that in trying to integrate into the majority society, Haker was "more exposed" to anti-Semitism than were his Jewish classmates who kept their distance and thereby protected themselves "from being hurt."[69] Despite Haker's theory about the protection that remaining openly Jewish offered, his own Jewish relatives ended up emigrating to Israel or whatever land would take them, embittered by the Turkish treatment they had endured over the past two decades, what with its humiliating and terrorizing military reserve call-up and its ruinous Capital Tax. One relative accepted a visa from Belgium on condition that he agreed to serve in a remote province of the Belgian Congo as an engineer for a specified number of years.[70] Contrary to his young assessment of their protected status, most of Haker's Jewish classmates migrated to Israel.

Despite his "determination to become a Turk," after eight years at Robert College, Haker emerges an anglophone European lacking in self-esteem, due in part to his "false conversion" to Islam at a young age, in part to anti-Semitism during his adolescence.[71] Conceiving a Zionist resolution to his social and personal problems, Haker's life narrative comes to symbolize the plight of Jewry outside the Jewish state. Graduating in 1950, he realizes that there is no future for him in Turkey, neither as a Turk, nor as a Jew. What was growing within him was "a nascent identification with Israel."[72]

The reconversion of his family to Judaism in 1951 facilitated his migration to the new Jewish state. By that point, Haker recalls having "ceased wanting to be a Turk."[73] He conceives his migration to Israel as a way to end his exposure to anti-Semitism and falls in with Israeli and British Zionists while a student at the London School of Economics and Political Science in the early 1950s.[74] He first visits Israel in 1953 thanks to a Jewish Agency program designed to entice Jewish university students to migrate.[75] He describes feeling at home in Israel, for it was only there that for the first time "the Jewish monkey" on his back "disappeared."[76] After six weeks in Israel, he was determined to migrate following his immanent graduation from university.[77] Returning first to Turkey in 1954 to complete his required military service, reexposure to anti-Jewish discrimination confirmed his belief in Turkish Jewry's lack of a future in the country. After being commissioned as an officer—their ranks opened to Jews only a few years earlier—he was appointed to military intelligence in the general staff in 1955. On his first day at his post, his commander tried to adduce his views on Jews. When Haker confessed that he himself was Jewish, the officer excused himself and told him to report for duty the next day. When he did, he was barred from entering the building, told that a mistake had been made, and given another, less prestigious assignment.[78] His career with military intelligence lasted only as long as it had taken them to ascertain that he was Jewish—one day. Haker, realizing the state of affairs, expresses relief that his dismissal occurred so quickly and not later when he would have had knowledge of military secrets. He fantasizes darkly that "when found out as a Jew, I probably would have been fed straight into the nearest meat grinder."[79] After completing his military service, he returned to Istanbul without job prospects, alienated from his parents, and suffering from very low self-esteem.[80] He migrated to Israel in 1956. When his parents tried to convince him to return to Istanbul, he refused; once he had migrated to Israel, the "Jewish monkey" on his back had "disappeared completely, and forever."[81] He felt justified, for there was no reason to remain in Turkey where his experience taught him that Jews were viewed through the lens of contempt: as devilishly clever, dirty, noisy, rich but stingy, cowardly, secretive, untrustworthy, treacherous, and exploitative—as profiteers and crooks. For him, Turkey was a land where "Jew" itself is a pejorative term, "an expletive," shorthand for this concatenation of contemptuous attributes.[82]

Everyday Instances of Anti-Jewish Sentiment and Violence

Haker's memoirs focus heavily on the violence suffered by Jews in the early Turkish Republic. The first volume covering the experience of his family in Thrace, *Once Upon a Time Jews Lived in Kırklareli*, ends with its longest and most unforgettable section documenting the 1934 pogrom. His point is to leave the reader with the impression that Jews have no future in Turkey. The second volume covering his own life until his migration to Israel, *From Istanbul to Jerusalem*, is meant to confirm his Zionist thesis that only in Israel can Jews escape the stigma, discrimination, violence, and loss of self-esteem that burdens Jews in the diaspora. His work is in this way similar to that of Avner Levi and Eli Şaul. Having narrated the suffering of Turkish Jewry since the republic's establishment in 1923, Levi ends his account with the 1948 birth of Israel, that destined homeland of a persecuted Jewry. Şaul's writing is also colored by a Zionist interpretation of Jewish life in the diaspora, evident in his section on growing up in Balat, where he tars nearly all Turks with the brush of racism and anti-Semitism. Together, their works narrate the discrimination, anti-Semitism, and violence Jews have faced in modern Turkey. Emphasizing the impossibility of Jewish life in Turkey, they offer migration to Israel as a resolution.

These Zionist biases are overcome in the work of Jewish poet and playwright Beki Bahar (1927–2011). In 1992, the mayor of Beşiktaş municipality in Istanbul honored Bahar by reading her poem "Boğaz'da Ortaköy'de" (In Ortaköy on the Bosphorus) at a ceremony and inscribing it on a sign in the central square of the showcase multireligious neighborhood of Ortaköy, where church, mosque, and synagogue stand almost side by side. It is not difficult to understand why the poet was celebrated: her poem depicts Sephardic Jews expelled from Spain dropping to their knees and kissing the ground when they first arrive in Ortaköy, grateful to Bayezid II for granting them freedom and peace.[83] A year later Bahar published a prizewinning play about the sixteenth-century Portuguese Conversa turned Ottoman Jewish patroness, Doña Gracia Mendes Nasi, about whom Abraham Galanté and Cecil Roth had written as evidence of the imagined harmonious Turkish-Jewish symbiosis.[84] It seemed as if she, too, would follow the same pattern of depicting utopian relations between Turks and Jews. Yet a decade later, she published a bittersweet account of the history of the Jews of Ankara, *Efsaneden tarihe Ankara Yahudileri* (Ankara Jews from legend to history), focusing on its vanished Jewish neighborhood. As a Turkish Jew who had not emigrated, Bahar argues that the establishment of Israel in 1948 sounded the death knell for the community. Migration was exacerbated by the 1955 pogrom in Istanbul. By 2000, there were only ten or fifteen Jews—mainly old widows—remaining in the old Jewish quarter of Ankara.[85] The quarter became an island. She likens the barbed-wire-topped synagogue enclosure to "a prison wall."[86]

Bahar clings to a utopian vision of Ottoman-Jewish harmony, arguing that the Jews are indebted to the Ottomans, whose "tolerant attitude" allowed them to flourish in the wake of Spanish persecution. She admonishes her reader that this fact "must not be forgotten, must be emphasized, and must be commemorated with gratitude."[87] She expresses the old Turkish Jewish affective disposition of gratefulness while casting Armenians and Greeks as the anti-Semitic enemies. She claims that during the

Ottoman period, the peaceful existence of Ankara Jewry was only violated by Armenian and Greek blood libels.[88] Bahar emphasizes how the Jews of Ankara always had good relations with Ottoman administrators and Muslim neighbors. Nevertheless, her book is important in that she narrates instances of lachrymose events in the Ottoman period, including the lynching of the Jewish lady-in-waiting to the harem in 1600, although she hastens to add that the kira's brutal death did not have a negative effect on the lives of Ottoman Jews in general.[89]

Despite the varnish she paints on the Ottoman centuries, her account is less like the foundation's narrative and more like that of the other memoir writers for two reasons. First, she undercuts the foundation's aims by emphasizing that Turkish Jews are not exclusively the descendants of the immigrants from Iberia. Importantly, she argues that the Jewish presence in Turkey predates not only the arrival in Anatolia of the Sephardic migrants, but that of the Turks themselves. She correctly traces the history of the Jews of Anatolia to ancient times and claims that the Ottomans encountered Turkish-speaking Jews when they conquered Ankara in the fourteenth century.[90] But she falsifies history when she makes the ancient Hittites, based in central Anatolia, into Turks, and implies that the good relations between the ancient Israelites and the Hittite kingdom served as precedent for the friendship between Jews and Turks.[91]

Second, like the other memoir writers, she offers devastating details of discrimination against Jews during the early republic, expressing how fear was the prevailing emotion of Turkish Jewry during the 1940s. Bahar focuses on everyday instances of anti-Jewish sentiment, recalling how Muslim customers dubbed one Jewish-owned shop, the "Refined Jew's"; they called another, the "Dirty Jew's."[92] One Ankara Jewish family was compelled by officials to accept the surname *Paracanlı* (Money-Lover) when surnames became mandatory in 1934.[93] Beki became Bedia in 1937 when her family moved from Istanbul to Ankara. Yet she remembers "feeling upset when during middle school finishing exams, the principal . . . insisted on my using the [Jewish] name [Beki] on my identity card rather than [the Turkish Muslim name] Bedia."[94]

Turkish Jewish fear is expressed in several episodes in the memoir. The most haunting section concerns the emotional state of Ankara Jewry during the "anxious" World War II era.[95] To avoid drawing attention to themselves, Jews spoke Turkish in public, and quietly; Jewish youth including Bahar admonished older members of the community when they spoke

Judeo-Spanish.[96] Moreover, as she recalls decades later, the belittling caricatures of Jews in the press and Nazi-influenced writings "did more than just trouble us, they frightened us." They frightened them because the Nazis were at Turkey's doorstep; Jews were "anxious" wondering whether the Nazis would fulfill the German-Turkish Friendship Treaty and nonaggression pact they had signed with Turkey. Every night they listened to the Free French Radio broadcast from London, and Bahar's father was "rather anxious." They worried about a coup by pro-Nazi groups. All the possible German machinations in Turkey "frightened us." The 1934 Thrace Pogrom "troubled all of us." She notes how Turkish Jewry became unsettled by the fact that some sectors of society and some of the important press organs sided with the Nazis.[97]

Turkish Jews were especially worried when the government created the Twentieth Reserve Corps, the special military reserve units of eighteen- to forty-five-year-old minority men, who were given uniforms but no weapons and no military training and were not allowed to leave their camps. The men believed they had been interned. The author remembers bringing food to Jews her father's age at one such camp established at Gençlik Park. Armenians and Greeks were also taken into these reserve units, but in a move that discounts the Armenian massacres and genocide and expulsions of Greeks, she muses, "It was natural that the Jews were even more troubled by this. Could there have been a secret article regarding Jews in the pact signed with Germany? Terrifying rumors circulated."[98] The Jews were relieved when the reserve units were disbanded in 1942, but "this happiness did not last long" for soon after the "nightmare" Capital Tax was implemented.[99] Bahar surmises that the Jews of Ankara did not find themselves in the "unbelievable situations" facing Istanbul and Bursa Jews who could not pay the tax—that of being sent to the labor camp at remote Aşkale—because Ankara was the location of foreign embassies.[100] Nevertheless, several Ankara Jewish families lost their wealth. Bahar remembers how "very upsetting and frightening" it was seeing those sentenced to Aşkale, as they passed through Ankara's train station.[101] In her mind she can still see the image of her "old, broken down uncle [from Bursa], Avram Alkaş, in that train car pass before my eyes like in a film reel."

Nevertheless, just as her father was spared from serving in the reserve units for minorities, so too was his initial Capital Tax levy reduced. Their main worry was about what would happen should Germany invade Turkey, and how Jews should respond. Her father thought that the family should turn on the gas in the apartment and commit group suicide the moment the

Germans crossed the border. But in the end, life continued, the family maintained good relations with Muslim Turks—even with their Nazi-supporting landlord—and they enjoyed themselves as best they could while Europe was being destroyed and Jews were being annihilated. As she concludes, "We always laughed, we did not cry." No matter how bad Turkish Jewry had it during those years, she reiterates, European Jews had it worse.

In 2003, the same year Haker and Bahar's autobiographical accounts were published, twin truck bombings targeted two Istanbul synagogues, Neve Şalom in Beyoğlu, and Beth Israel in Şişli, killing twenty-three people and injuring three hundred. A far-right Turkish Muslim group claimed to have carried out the attacks.[102] Two days after the double synagogue bombings, a professor of political science and philosophy at Yale University, Seyla Benhabib, responded in the way one has come to expect from Turkish Jews. Just as the chief rabbinate spokesman told the press in response to the bombings that "there is no antisemitism in Turkey, but international terrorism is very strong,"[103] so Benhabib proclaimed in a *New York Times* opinion piece the non sequitur that Turks were tolerant of Jews. In the piece, she mentions how her ancestors had arrived in Istanbul "when they fled the Spanish Inquisition after 1492 and were given refuge by the Ottoman Empire."[104] The presence of Jews in Turkey, not the recent terrorist attacks against them, is "testament to the peaceful coexistence of Jews and Muslims not only in medieval Spain but throughout the old Levant." Adopting Shaw's nonsensical argument, she claims that while Nazis murdered the Jews of neighboring Greece, Turkey "closed its border" to the Nazis and would not murder its Jews, even though Nazi Germany had not demanded these things from Turkey. She mentions that her father and uncles may have been sent to camps in the interior of the country to appease the Nazis, but "they were only labor camps," repeating a cringeworthy argument made by Shaw. Benhabib claims that the decision to send Jewish citizens to concentration camps—where, it must be remembered, some died in the harsh conditions—"underscores the peaceful coexistence of Jews and Muslims since the 15th century in a Muslim country that respects the democratic equality of citizens of different faiths." Where else but Turkey do Jews argue that being sent to concentration camps by their government is a sign of democracy, respect, and good intercommunal relations? These arguments are no different from those of the foundation that the Turks have been the rescuers of Jews—as in 1492, so in 1942. Ignoring the Zionist movement and Jewish colonization of Ottoman Palestine, Benhabib concedes that "some of Turkey's other minorities," including Greeks and Armenians, "who unlike the Jews, have had territorial claims on Turkish lands—have fared less well." She thus implies that Otto-man Christians were traitors, blaming them for their own comparably worse fate. "What matters now, though," she concludes, is not the fate of the Armenians, Greeks, or Kurds, but "which historical model Turkey will be encouraged to embrace"—tolerance or terrorism. Two days after her arti-cle appeared, two more truck bombs attacked British interests in the city, killing 35 people, wounding 450. Seven people—six of whom were Turkish citizens—were convicted for the four bombings.[105]

After the twin synagogue bombings, in marked contrast to the response of other Turkish Jews, Bali published an unusually frank op-ed in a major leftist daily proffering a harsh critique of Turkish Muslim and Jewish toler-ance of anti-Semitism.[106] The terror attack "gave Turkish society an oppor-tunity to confront the anti-Semitism internalized within political Islam. But everyone—led first by the ruling party, the media, intellectual elites, Israel, his eminence the chief rabbi, the representative of the Turkish Jew-ish community, and the secular leaders under him—was determined not to take advantage of the 'opportunity' created by this event." Arguing that Muslims and Jews in Turkey promote the false view that "in Turkey there never has been anti-Semitism," he then catalogues the many manifesta-tions of it appearing in Turkey from 1950 to the recent bombings. Blam-ing society and the government for failing to confront anti-Semitism, he ends with a cri de coeur: "Everyone should confront reality and call their conscience to account. Turkish Jews are not dhimmis in need of the Mus-lim majority's tolerance and protection. They are citizens of the Turkish Republic. The only expectation is the end of the traditionalized tolerance for anti-Semitism. The time for saying 'enough' has come and gone. Now, unfortunately, we realize that it is too late."[107]

"Centuries in This Land, Living in Peace and Happiness"

In 2008, long-serving Turkish Jewish community leader Bensiyon Pinto published his autobiography. By that point, the cat had been let out of the bag. The public knew about the anti-Semitic incidents that marred Jewish life in Turkey. How would this community spokesman narrate them?

Pinto's aims in writing the autobiography are twofold. The first is to have Turkish society "embrace its Jewish community, rather than exclude it," to trust it and not discriminate against it. The second is for Turkish Muslim

readers to understand that because Turkish Jews love Turkey as their homeland, they are as Turkish as other Turks and do not deserve to be treated as
the Other.[108] He wants the younger generation to "be able to live in peace
and harmony, [with Muslims] as brothers, as was the case for centuries [in
the Ottoman Empire]. He complains that Turkish Jews are still viewed as
not being "full citizens who share the nation with the rest of the population,
but rather as mere subjects of the sultan." This mentality is one that never
allows Jews "to be seen as an intrinsic part of mainstream society," which
continues to view them "with an indulgent superiority."[109] Interestingly,
Pinto objects to the terms "tolerance" and "mosaic" that are often used to
describe Muslim-Jewish relations in Turkey.[110] They are not a community
in need of tolerance, he argues. "We are Turks who have been living here
for centuries . . . We are not slaves of the [Ottoman] sultan. We are citizens
of the Turkish Republic." Mosaics, moreover, are "fragile" and made up of
"tiny separate pieces." He prefers the term *ebru* (paper marbling), where
"all colors mix harmoniously and merge with each other." Nevertheless,
despite his plaintive appeals for acceptance, when he is abroad, he always
explains how "we live very comfortably and happily in our country."[111]

Pinto was born in Kuledibi, Istanbul, the same neighborhood where
Vitali Hakko and Eli Şaul grew up, on Büyük Hendek Street in a building
adjacent to the future Neve Şalom synagogue. In his autobiography, which
has been translated into English and German, Pinto narrates how in 1941,
already at age five, he experienced "some of the darkest days of my life."[112]
He can never forget the day the men of the family gathered at his home and
his grandfather told his father, "Don't feel sad. . . . You must leave, but God
will secure your return." The little boy wondered "what kind of journey
required God to guide the way back?" And why was his mother crying? His
fortysomething father had been called up like other non-Muslims in the
Twentieth Reserve Corps, even though he had already completed his military service. Pinto argues that the call-up turned their lives upside down
and frightened them. Indeed, the day his father left "was the most frightening day of my life. I did not know where he was going, when he would come
back, how long he would stay away and what I would do if I missed him."[113]
Not only was his mother crying, "That day was the first and last time I
saw my father cry." Pinto learned later that the men "were badly treated."
He notes that "the wounds had not yet healed" after the pogrom in Thrace
in 1934, "and this conscription policy caused great fear." Because of these
violent events, Jews fled from Thrace to Istanbul, and many then migrated

to Israel, including his grandfather and both aunts in 1949, and his brother decades later. Jews feared it would happen to them in Turkey again, and "unfortunately, it did happen."[114]

He recounts the 1942–1944 Capital Tax, "which completely changed the destiny of religious minorities living in Turkey." The aim was to weaken Jews' "ties with their own nation, to turn friends into enemies." He uses the terms "calamity," "major injustice," and "plunder" to describe the tax, asking "what could be more painful for people than to suddenly find themselves second-class citizens in their own country?" Over sixty years later, Pinto "still cannot get my head around this situation," a state discriminating "against its own citizens."[115] He remembers being "scared."

He offers a vivid memory of having breakfast at a neighbor's home when two men from the revenue office came in and asked, "Jew, why didn't you pay the money you owe?" Pinto had never heard anyone addressed as "Jew" before. The six-year-old wondered, "Was being Jewish a bad thing? . . . Was it a crime?" The men literally "grabbed the rug and pulled it right out from under our feet," knocking little Bensiyon to the ground and causing him to bang his head on the bare floor. Pinto still remembers the fear and uncertainty he experienced in that era.

The terrible events continued. As a young man, he dreamed of becoming a professional soccer player. He was talented and played for the Galatasaray Club youth team in the early 1950s. But one day a team trainer referred to him as "Jew," and he was "old enough to understand what calling me a Jew with this tone of voice meant. It was discrimination itself. It was racism. . . . He was shouting at me with hatred, as if being Jewish was a crime."[116] Not only did the incident end his fantasy of a professional soccer career, but he realized that "they no longer liked us in this country," and that his friends who argued that the only choice was to leave were right.[117] Jews were not seen as full citizens. "Whatever we did, no matter how close we came to our goal, they pushed us away." The anti-Semites compelled him to make up his mind that day to migrate to Israel. He bought a one-way ticket and left Turkey in 1954 at the age of seventeen.[118]

Overwhelmed by homesickness, however, he decided to visit his mother in Turkey during the Jewish New Year in 1955. As fate would have it, the very next day was September 6, the day of the pogrom targeting Greeks, Armenians, and Jews. He saw the large mob looting shops in Beyoğlu, and ran home past broken shop windows, through mounds of merchandise strewn across the streets.[119] The whole neighborhood "looked like hell."[120] When he reached his apartment building, the mob had turned toward his street, shouting "Burn everything down!" Because a plywood shop was located in the ground floor of the family's apartment building, his family feared being burned alive. But the building's Muslim resident door keeper, Hüseyin, had run to the mosque to alert the imam, who arrived and shouted to the mob, "Stop! This place does not belong to *gavurlar* (infidels). All the people who live here are Muslims." Convinced by the imam's white lie, they left the building alone. The imam turned to Pinto and said, "Do not be scared, my son. It's over!" He was as stung by the use of the term "*gavur,*" as by the fact that had the imam not arrived at that moment, his parents and brother would have been burned alive, with him "a spectator" and without any guarantee "that the crowd would have let me live." He returned to Israel the next day. His mother's illness the next year served as a pretext to return to Turkey, where he would often face violence and treatment as a foreigner.

Referring to the earlier bomb attack on Neve Şalom synagogue in 1986 without assigning blame, Pinto describes how he has "been scared at times . . . for myself," but that "love and friendship can conquer fear."[121] When he heard the news, he could not grasp it. Despite the experiences of his youth and the anti-Semitism that had compelled him to migrate to Israel, Pinto declares that "nothing like this had happened in the history of the Turkish republic. In fact, the Jewish community has been living in this land for centuries without ever before facing such an event."[122] He even doubted it was true, for "no such thing could happen to us," a conviction grounded in his "complete trust in his state and nation."[123] The reader finds this statement to be incredible. What of the 1955 riots when his family narrowly escaped being burned alive? Pinto avers that "even if the past had included some painful days," like Hakko, he was an optimist and preferred to always look on the bright side. The attack came as a "dreadful shock" the truth of which he "had refused" to believe could be true. Pinto rushed to the synagogue, finding it "a scene from hell. Body parts . . . were strewn all over the place. . . . Those who had been reading the Torah inside the synagogue had been blown to bits. Tears of grief were pouring from my eyes." He struggled to accept what had come to pass: "Such things did not happen here."[124]

Yet it happened again. Pinto narrates his experience of the truck-bomb attack on the Beth Israel synagogue in Şişli, Istanbul, in 2003, noting that there is nothing more painful "than living in fear in your own homeland," waiting for the next inevitable terrorist attack to occur,[125] despite Turkish

Jewry's patriotism, despite the fact that Islam and Judaism are so close to one another, Pinto averred. The attack made him feel "the cold breath of death on the back of my neck." A deafening blast was followed by his deputy telling him, "They have hit us again."[126] Covered in the blood of the people killed around him, he thought that "the world had ended, and we were all dead!" All he saw "was carnage and destruction! Beyond the open door was a scene from hell!" It was a nightmare come to life. He saw the son of the chief rabbi, "with blood squirting from his neck! His face was unrecognizable."[127]

Pinto describes another episode—the 1993 Istanbul Water and Sewage Administration corruption scandal—where he was groundlessly targeted by a media that referred to him as a bribe-giving Jew and mistreated by a police force that treated him "like a criminal and second-class citizen."[128] Although he was exonerated by a judge and the case for bribery against him was dropped, he was so humiliated that he considered suicide.[129]

Despite the horrible events he experienced firsthand, Pinto does not find it ironic that he tells foreigners, including visiting Spanish ministers, "When you expelled us, the gates of the Ottoman Empire opened for us. Now we are Turks and we are very happy. We love our country." Jews, he assures them, have lived in Turkey "for centuries in this land, in peace and happiness."[130]

Pinto articulates the Turkish Jewish community's politics of memory when, speaking of the Capital Tax, he says that the community has chosen "to push this painful episode aside" and relegate it to "a corner of its past, acting as though it had never happened." Jews had decided not to live "in constant remembrance" of such horrors, the implication being that the Armenians did do so.[131] This is an important admission from the head of the Turkish Jewish community. In his opinion, such a view is superior to focusing on lachrymose episodes, as, "no good comes from dwelling on wrongdoings." He admonishes the reader that "planning your life accordingly or building your world outlook based on [mournful episodes] is not useful to anyone." He agrees with the Turkish proverb, "Private things should remain private," especially what goes on in Turkey. "When we go abroad, we need to keep our mouths shut."[132] But has publicly denying their own past and that of others been helpful to Turkish Jewry?

Without any sense of irony, Pinto repeats the old tropes. "In Ottoman times as well as during the Republican era, Jews have lived a very happy life. . . . Turkish Jews are among the few Jewish communities in the world that are able to live comfortably in their homeland."[133] Preferring to see the glass half full when it comes to the problems the Jewish community faces, he argues that "those who want to create problems can turn life itself into a problem."[134] In contrast, the Turkish Jewish community "has chosen to live free of problems as a principle; it has devoted itself to the Turkish nation," trusting that over time the problems that do arise will be solved.

Paradoxically, Pinto's autobiography demonstrates how "keeping private things private" has not worked to resolve the problems for Turkish Jews that have arisen over the course of nearly a century. They are still viewed as strangers in their own land. Pinto marvels at the irony that "no Jew lives here thinking he is the Other," yet "he comes to a point where he has to ask the state for help to protect him from his fellow countrymen in his own country."[135] Pinto feels compelled to declare, "We are not the Others. We are not Israelis," Turkish Jews are not the "enemy of this country."[136] What wearies him the most is Turks who implore him, "Tell your people to stop this war." He responds that he is a Turkish Jew, not an Israeli, that the Turks are his people, not the Israelis, that if he is an Israeli, "then why is he living in Turkey? Why does he keep talking about his country, Turkey, wherever he goes? Why does he work with all his might to change the opinion of people prejudiced against his country?"

Pinto finds himself repeatedly having to declare, "We [Turkish Jews] are citizens of this country. Israel's . . . policies are its own concerns. As a Turkish Jew, I only follow the . . . policy of the Turkish Republic because I was born in this country and grew up here. Furthermore, whether as chairman or honorary chairman of the Jewish community, I have worked for Turkey by conducting trips to Israel and other countries. My country always comes first for me."[137] He claims that he goes to bed "planning what I can do for the Turkish Republic the next day," such as accepting a lobbying assignment from the foreign minister. Yet even high-level Turkish officials fail to make the distinction between Turkish Jews and Israelis. He notes how distressing it was when, during a dinner held for the Israeli prime minister visiting Turkey, Turkish officials referred to the Israeli Prime Minister as Pinto's leader.[138] He has repeatedly found himself having to say, "Hey, what country do you think I am a citizen of? . . . I am a Turk, my prime minister is the Turkish prime minister." Moreover, he finds himself having to repeat, "I am a Turkish patriot. . . . I cry in the presence of my flag." To illustrate the importance of his homeland, he offers as proof the fact that he uses the term "homeland" on "every second page" of his autobiography.

His account of what he experienced over the course of sixty years reads as a desperate plea to Turkish Muslims to accept Turkish Jews as their equals. In Pinto's account, Jewish lives in Turkey are marred by fear, exclusion, discrimination, treatment as foreigners or second-class citizens, and repeated episodes of deadly violence. Regardless, neither this litany, nor his own personal experience of anti-Semitism, which once drove him to migrate to Israel, and even to consider suicide, prevent him from presenting utopian visions of Turkish-Jewish relations to a foreign audience while at the same time expending considerable energy preventing Armenian genocide recognition.

The Foundation Strikes Back

In contrast to the bold publications of Turkish Jewish countervoices and the admissions of one of the Quincentennial Foundation's most prominent leaders, Jak Kamhi's 2013 autobiography is a picture in reverse perspective. The prominent lobbyist and community leader uses the occasion of his autobiography as an opportunity to describe Jews as friends of Turks and Armenians and Greeks as their common enemy. He denies the existence of anti-Semitism in Turkey altogether and praises Turks' exceptional character. Writing of the loyalty of Turkish Jews in relation to Greeks' disloyalty, he claims that "the first people to rebel against the English occupation [of the Ottoman Empire] in the First World War were Jews. Again, it was Jews who lowered the Greek flag and hoisted the Turkish flag when Atatürk entered Izmir on September 9, 1922."[139] He asserts that "the Jews did not get along with the Greeks," whose "imagination was so rich they would claim that we sacrificed a Christian child during our Passover holiday!"[140] He also claims that during the Ottoman period, "whenever we wanted to build a synagogue anywhere, the Greeks would be the first to oppose it. But because the sultan permitted it, they could do little more than grumble."

Describing the World War II era, he declares that, contrary to claims that Turkish Jewry experienced anti-Semitism, in fact a spirit of philo-Semitism reigned, as many refugees were welcomed into society. One of his professors at Yıldız Technical University was "a German Jew who had taken refuge in our country."[141] His father spent all his time thinking about what would happen should Germany invade Turkey and march on Istanbul. He purchased a farm in Adapazarı so that the family could hide in the countryside if needed.[142] But Kamhi repeats that Jews had nothing to fear: "The most important thing causing anxiety among Jews living in Istanbul was the possibility that society would change its [positive] attitude toward them, for anti-Semitism was wreaking havoc in Europe like a virulent plague. And yet in Istanbul such a wind was definitely not blowing."[143] The only anti-Semite he encountered at the time was a French teacher at Saint Michel High School in Istanbul. Since they did not have to concern themselves with anti-Semitism within Turkey, Turkish Jewry was mainly concerned during the war with whether or not Germany would attack Turkey, he argues, and in that event, "no one could know what would become of us." They need not worry, he claims in a remarkable passage, for the nation's leaders sought to protect them. Just before the end of the war, German forces massed on the Bulgarian border, apparently to launch an attack on Turkey. Yet "in order to save Turkish Jewry from the fate of the Jews of Europe, Marshall Fevzi Çakmak was authorized by President İnönü to establish the famous Çakmak Line, which may have deterred the planned German invasion." Incredibly, Kamhi claims that the defensive measure was undertaken not merely to defend the nation, but to protect the nation's Jews, as though that were a concern of Turkish government policy at the time. The same Turkish government had already issued policies that allowed thousands of Turkish Jews in Europe to be murdered in the camps rather than recognize them as citizens and save them.

Following a detailed denial of the existence of anti-Semitism in Turkey during the war years and his claim that Turkey was motivated to protect its Jews from the Nazis, Kamhi devotes a section to "The War Heroism of Turkish Diplomats."[144] Accurately, he maintains that "years later, the actions of Turkish diplomats, especially in France and on the island of Rhodes, would be narrated like legends (*efsaneler*)."[145] Legend is the right word, and it is the only historically accurate aspect of his account. He notes "the extraordinary efforts of Namık Kemal Yolga" in Paris, who "even succeeded in securing the release of people who had already been put on the trains to the camps." Heath Lowry, a historian involved since the 1980s in Armenian genocide denial, and the editor of the English version, makes the passage read, "the release and salvation of people," deploying the myth of Turks as saviors of the Jews.[146] Necdet Kent is "another legendary name."[147] Legendary, indeed. Kamhi narrates Kent's having boarded the train—"this was simply inconceivable"—and claims that he was accompanied by another consul, Bedii Arbel, rather than the Turkish Jew Kent relates was with him. Kamhi never stops to consider why they would have to rescue their own citizens, given that Turkey was a neutral country and its citizens were not subject to anti-Jewish measures at the time. He refers to the alleged rescue as "a true miracle."[148] He concedes without any explanation that "unfortunately, the heroic efforts of these Turkish diplomats did not succeed in rescuing the husbands" of two of his Turkish Jewish aunts in France. Did they not receive Turkish passports from the consuls? Finally, he states that "those who were able to reach Turkey crossed the border without any difficulty," which like most of what he writes in this section, does not accord with Turkish actions during that period actively hindering the arrival of Jewish refugees.

More significant is his depiction of Turkish exceptionalism. The Turks, he argues, are a people that cannot be anti-Semitic. Turkish diplomats risked their lives to save Jews as part of a timeless, Turkish humanitarianism. "They undertook this risk in order to do justice to the lofty human values that they had inherited from their ancestors. . . . Just as they had embraced the Jews fleeing Spain centuries before, so now did they embrace those Jews fleeing Nazi persecution."[149] He compares Turkey favorably to Christian European nations, which are riven by anti-Semitism, a hatred he insists does not exist in Turkey. Turkey is "an exceedingly important exception [among the nations]. The country's origins in a multi-confessional, multi-cultural empire constituted a major ingredient in fostering a spirit of cohabitation."[150] Yet how did that empire end? Only by denying the Armenian genocide could he make such a claim.

Kamhi explains away the Capital Tax and other discriminatory policies during the World War II era by blaming Nazi Germany. Deploying yet another legend, he claims that Turkey's government was actually protecting Jews through its policies. "The Germans wanted the Jews of Turkey to be sent to the camps, but the government resisted this."[151] The Germans never demanded such a thing. He claims that the Capital Tax was meant to endear Turkey to Germany. He suggests that although there had been a pogrom in Thrace in 1934, it had been instigated by "many German agents," not the Turkish governor who actually was behind it.[152] He argues that it is important to point out that the Capital Tax was not simply an anti-Jewish measure, as it targeted all non-Muslims. Its effects on his own family were nevertheless disastrous. His uncle Bensiyon's assessment was exorbitant. Despite the family's attempts to pay it off, the uncle was sent to Aşkale, identified by the contemporary Turkish newspaper clipping that accompanies Kamhi's text as "a concentration camp." Within a week, he died of

typhus; his wife died shortly after of heartbreak.[153] "Officials came periodi-
cally to our house to cart off our possessions," Kamhi notes, and "on one
of those distressing and sinister days" his mother fell and broke her hip,
which never healed, and then she suffered a stroke, spending the rest of her
life in that condition. "In reality," he concludes, "we did not only sacrifice
my uncle to the Capital Tax, but my mother as well."[154] Despite the sad state
of his own mother, Kamhi continues to extol the virtues of Turks and their
treatment of Jews, even when they hurl abuse at him and try to assassinate
him, such as occurred in 1993.

Kamhi had paid for the refurbishment of the Zülfaris synagogue and its
conversion into the Quincentennial Foundation Museum of Turkish Jews
in 2001. Striking for a city that has no museum let alone a monument to the
Armenian genocide—there *is*, however, a monument to the so-called genocide of the Turks murdered by Armenians in eastern Anatolia—Istanbul
boasts this "Tolerance Museum" established by the Quincentennial Foundation. In the winter of 2016, the museum reopened at Istanbul's thrice-bombed
Neve Şalom synagogue. Rather than focus on the repeated bombings of its
new home, the museum repeats the same themes as in its previous incarna-
tion: the welcome the Ottomans gave the Sephardim; five hundred years of
peace and harmony; and Turkish Jewry's loyalty and patriotism. At a press
conference celebrating the reopening, Moris Levi, the museum's president,
boasted that the grateful Jews responded in a way that contributed to Ottoman renown. "The Quincentennial Foundation accepts 1492 as its beginning. It is the date when the Sephardic Jews were expelled from Spain. Sultan
Bayezid II, who sent their vessels and brought our ancestors to this land,
showed a human duty ahead of his time. On the other hand, he thought that
Jews would be very useful here." To emphasize their usefulness, he added a
historical myth. "It is rumored that Sultan Bayezid II, referring to the Spanish king, said: 'How can you define this emperor as smart and wise? He
makes his country poor while making mine rich.' Our ancestors worked
hard to become useful for the country in which they lived."[155]

A sculpture depicting the "Jewish soldiers who fell while defending
their homeland" greeted visitors at the entrance to the original museum.
All the pre-modern Sephardic myths are on display inside the museum:
that Mehmed II appealed to Jews to settle in Constantinople; that he named
Moses Capsali to be the first chief rabbi; and that sultans always saved Jews.
Museum panels declare the Ottoman Empire was "a haven of tranquility"
and quote the apocryphal line of Bayezid II, welcoming Spanish Jewry, by

mocking "Wise Ferdinand." The museum organizers chose to quote Cecil Roth to confirm their affective disposition of gratefulness: "The Jewish people must always recall the Turkish Empire with gratitude [because] it flung open its doors widely and generously for the reception of the fugitives, and kept them open."

A panel labelled "Turkish Jews in Public Life" declares "Through their words and actions, Turkish Jews have always proven their loyalty to their country." As evidence, an 1893 petition from the chief rabbi and rabbinical council requests that Jews be allowed to serve in the army in order to defend the fatherland; a panel displays a picture of Dr. Nesim Karidi, who fought during the war with Greece in 1896. Another panel declares that during the Turkish War of Independence (1918–1923), "during the violent and painful days of the invasion of Anatolia, Turkish Jews in Istanbul, Bursa, the Aegean coast, Southeastern Anatolia and in all cities and towns under occupation always remained loyal to the motherland and never collaborated with the invaders." To further illustrate the point, and to make clear which groups were disloyal, a panel shows a photo of Nesim Navaro "who lowered and then ripped the Greek flag during a banquet given in honor of [Allied] General Dixon at the Grand Hotel Kraemer Palace in Izmir." To prove Turkish Jewry's unflinching loyalty and to ensure the visitor does not associate the community with any treasonable act, a museum exhibit devoted to Sabbatai Zevi and the Dönme declares that after the conversion of Sabbatai Zevi and his followers, "there has been no religious or social connection with Turkish Jews and no relationship exists with them and the Rabbinate or directors of Jewish civic organizations."

Before leaving the museum, the visitor is invited to sign a guest book beneath two suggestive panels emblazoned with utopian quotes from Atatürk and more recent Turkish presidents and prime ministers extolling Turkish-Jewish loyalty, bragging that Jews in Turkey have always lived "in comfort and happiness," and praising the "deep and lasting friendship between Turks and Jews." The visitor cannot help but note the irony of having to pass through very strict security measures to learn about how much Turkish Jews are appreciated and how safe and secure they feel.

Conclusion

In the early 2000s, Rıfat Bali continued to redact critical accounts of Turkish Jews, such as those of Erol Haker. Haker's countervoice sours the image of Turkish-Jewish relations by providing the reader horrible images such as an angry mob in Thrace in 1934 ripping Mosse Levi's gold crowns from his mouth, cutting off Rabbi Moşe Fintz's beard, and tearing the clothes off his wife as they beat her. Beki Bahar and Bensiyon Pinto also offered dark depictions of the affective disposition of Jews, marked by fear and anxiety, set against a remembered past of idyllic Ottoman rule. As Haker argues, anti-Semitism "of a visceral kind" may have "ruled the day" in the early Turkish republic, but it "had no equal under five hundred years of benevolent Ottoman rule,"[156] while Pinto wishes a return to "the peaceful, happy, and carefree days of our [Ottoman Jewish] ancestors."[157] Despite his and his family's lived experience that has been anything but happy—pogrom, exorbitant taxation and incarceration in a concentration camp, mob violence, repeated synagogue bombings, discrimination, being treated like a foreigner—community leader Pinto, who even migrated to Israel as a young man to escape Turkish anti-Semitism, persists in propagating utopian visions of Turkish-Jewish relations to a foreign audience while devoting all his efforts to oppose the recognition of the Armenian genocide. In his 2013 autobiography, community leader Jak Kamhi presents the same well-worn myths about Turkish-Jewish brotherhood and friendship in the face of anti-Semitic Armenian and Greek enemies, denies there is anti-Semitism in Turkey, depicts the Turk as the perennial savior of Jews, and boasts about his success in hindering Armenian genocide recognition.

His approach to the genocide mirrors his response to Turkish anti-Semitism. During the occupation of one of his Profilo factories in 1976, a striking worker shouted at Kamhi, "You are not even a Turk, what are we going to talk to you about?" He responded, "Hey you, I am more of a Turk than you are."[158] Reflecting on this incident he admits that, "unfortunately I would also experience the discriminatory and exclusionary attitude betrayed by that worker's outburst . . . that so infuriated me at other times in my life." One of these moments occurred in 1993 when an Islamist member of parliament told a television audience that if Kamhi was Turkish, "let him change his name. If he does not, he is a fraud."[159] Kamhi's response to such provocation is placid. "Whenever I come across this isolated attitude, which by no means reflects the feelings of the Turkish nation, rather than being upset for myself, I am sad that such people do not share the lofty human values of their own [Turkish] nation."[160] When a Turkish Muslim insults him for being a Jew, and not a real Turk, or when a team of Turkish Muslim assassins tries to murder him, Kamhi declares that their sentiment is not authentic. Turks cannot be anti-Semitic, he insists. Turks can only be tolerant. When they are intolerant, they are not real Turks. This same exclusionary logic has been deployed by Turkish and non-Turkish Jewish scholars to blame anti-Jewish sentiment and violence in the Ottoman Empire and Turkey on Christians, even when voiced or committed by Muslims. It has also been used to deny the genocide: because the Ottoman Empire was *only* capable of tolerating difference, when it did not, it was not the empire and thus cannot have committed atrocities.

Notes

1. Stanford Shaw, "Turkey and the Jews of Europe during World War II," in *Turkish-Jewish Encounters: Studies on Turkish-Jewish Relations through the Ages*, ed. Mehmet Tütüncü (Haarlem, the Netherlands: SOTA Research Centre for Turkestan, Azerbaijan, Crimea, Caucasus and Siberia, 2001), 309.

2. Ibid., 325. Shaw then repeats exaggerated or inaccurate assertions, including the claim that due to the diligence of all Turkish diplomats in Europe—especially the half dozen in France, including Necdet Kent, who were "most involved" in this work—Turkey "rescued" fifteen thousand Turkish Jews from France. Ibid., 312, 325.

3. Erol Haker, *Bir zamanlar Kırklareli'de Yahudiler yaşardı . . . Kırklarelili Adato ailesin'in öyküsü*, translated by Natali Medina (Istanbul: İletişim, 2002).

4. Ibid., 15.

5. Ibid., 19.

6. Ibid., 28.

7. Ibid., 145.

8. Ibid., 145–146.

9. Ibid., 137.

10. Ibid., 138.

11. Ibid., 139.

12. Ibid.

13. Ibid., 154–155.

14. Ibid., 156–157.

15. Ibid., 180–181.

16. Ibid., 182.

17. Ibid., 183.

18. Ibid., 185.

19. Ibid.

20. Ibid., 210.

21. Ibid., 191.

22. Ibid., 192.

23. Ibid., 250.

24. Ibid., 251–252.

25. Ibid., 253.

26. Ibid., 254.
27. Ibid., 255.
28. Ibid., 260.
29. Ibid., 265.
30. Ibid., 266.
31. Ibid., 257.
32. Ibid., 262.
33. Ibid., 269.
34. Ibid.
35. Ibid., 315.
36. Ibid., 317.
37. Ibid., 319.
38. Ibid., 322.
39. Ibid., 323.
40. Erol Haker, *Once Upon a Time Jews Lived in Kırklareli: The Story of the Adato Family* (Istanbul: Isis, 2003).
41. Erol Haker, *From Istanbul to Jerusalem: The Itinerary of a Young Turkish Jew* (Istanbul: Isis, 2003).
42. Ibid., 36.
43. The following examples are also cited in Göçek, *Denial of Violence*, 289.
44. Haker, *From Istanbul to Jerusalem*, 40.
45. Ibid., 41.
46. Ibid.
47. Ibid., 43.
48. Ibid., 47.
49. Ibid., 48.
50. Ibid., 50–51.
51. Ibid., 58.
52. Ibid., 61–63.
53. Ibid., 63–65.
54. Ibid., 68.
55. Ibid., 63.
56. Ibid., 87.
57. Ibid., 86.
58. Ibid., 87.
59. Ibid., 89.
60. Ibid., 91.
61. Ibid., 90.
62. Ibid., 93.
63. Ibid., 94.
64. Ibid., 95.
65. Ibid., 143.
66. Ibid., 145.
67. Ibid., 149.
68. Ibid., 153.
69. Ibid., 155.
70. Ibid., 152.

71. Ibid., 165–166.
72. Ibid., 166.
73. Ibid., 179.
74. Ibid., 189–190.
75. Ibid., 201.
76. Ibid., 202.
77. Ibid., 209.
78. Ibid., 239.
79. Ibid., 241.
80. Ibid., 253.
81. Ibid., 256.
82. Ibid., 267–268.
83. For a photograph of the author with the sign and the full text of the poem, see Beki Bahar, *Efsaneden tarihe Ankara Yahudileri* (Istanbul: Pan, 2003), 198–199.
84. Beki Bahar, *Donna Grasya Nasi* (Istanbul: Isis, 1993).
85. Bahar, *Efsaneden tarihe Ankara Yahudileri*, 119.
86. Ibid., 127–128.
87. Ibid., 185–186.
88. Ibid., 43–44.
89. Ibid., 47.
90. Ibid., 36.
91. Ibid., 14–19, 27–28.
92. Ibid., 127.
93. Ibid., 126.
94. Ibid., 165. Also cited in Göçek, *Denial of Violence*, 321.
95. Bahar, *Efsaneden tarihe Ankara Yahudileri*, 164.
96. Ibid., 165.
97. Ibid., 109.
98. Ibid., 166.
99. Ibid., 167.
100. Ibid., 168.
101. Ibid., 169.
102. Sebnem Arsu and Dexter Filkins, "20 in Istanbul Die in Bombings at Synagogues," *New York Times*, November 16, 2003. According to the article, "A militant Turkish Islamic group, the Great Eastern Islamic Raiders' Front, claimed responsibility for the attacks in a telephone call to the Anatolia News agency. But NTV, the Turkish television network, quoted the police as saying the attack appeared to have been too sophisticated to have been carried out by that group." Four months later, Islamists intent on killing Jews attacked a Mason lodge in Istanbul. Bali, *Model Citizens of the State*, 436–437. Earlier in the year, Turkey also witnessed the murder of dentist Yasef Yahya, whose killers claimed their only motivation in killing him was that he was Jewish. Gürkan Akgüneş, "Diş hekimine infaz," *Milliyet*, August 22, 2003, 5.
103. Quoted in Bali, *Model Citizens of the State*, 434.
104. Seyla Benhabib, "In Turkey, A History Lesson in Peace," opinion, *New York Times*, November 18, 2003.
105. "Seven Jailed for Turkey Bombings," *BBC News*, February 17, 2007; Karl Vick, "Al Qaeda's Hand in Istanbul Plot: Turks Met with Bin Laden," *Washington Post*, February 13, 2007.

106. Rifat Bali, "Antisemitizmi hoşgör(me)mek," *Radikal 2*, November 23, 2003. The editorial is cited and a different passage quoted in Brink-Danan, *Jewish Life in 21st-Century Turkey*, 58.

107. This is the paragraph quoted in Brink-Danan, *Jewish Life in 21ˢᵗ-Century Turkey*, 58.

108. Pinto, *Anlatmasam olmazdı*, 169.

109. Ibid., 210.

110. Ibid., 215.

111. Ibid., 211.

112. Ibid., 32.

113. Ibid., 33.

114. Ibid., 34.

115. Ibid., 35.

116. Ibid., 51.

117. Ibid., 52.

118. Ibid., 53.

119. Ibid., 65–66.

120. Ibid., 66.

121. Ibid., 135.

122. Ibid., 137–138.

123. Ibid., 138.

124. Ibid., 139.

125. Ibid., 141.

126. Ibid., 143.

127. The son would survive the attack.

128. Ibid., 156.

129. Ibid., 157.

130. Ibid., 157.

131. Ibid., 35.

132. Ibid., 232.

133. Ibid., 250.

134. Ibid., 284.

135. Ibid., 162.

136. Ibid., 163.

137. Ibid., 230.

138. Ibid., 164.

139. Kamhi, *Gördüklerim yaşadıklarım*, 56–57.

140. Ibid., 57.

141. Ibid., 69.

142. Ibid., 71.

143. Ibid., 73.

144. Ibid., 74–76.

145. Ibid., 75.

146. Jak V. Kamhi, *What I've Seen What I've Experienced*, ed. Heath Lowry (Istanbul: Bahçeşehir University Press, 2013), 45.

147. Kamhi, *Gördüklerim yaşadıklarım*, 75.

148. Ibid., 76.

149. Ibid., 76.

150. Ibid., 78.
151. Ibid., 79.
152. Ibid., 80.
153. Ibid., 82.
154. Ibid., 82–83.
155. "Turkish Jewish Museum Reopens after Update," *Hürriyet Daily News*, February 27, 2016.
156. Haker, *From Istanbul to Jerusalem*, 11.
157. Pinto, *Anlatmasam olmazdı*, 140.
158. Kamhi, *Gördüklerim yaşadıklarım*, 222.
159. Ibid., 224.
160. Ibid., 223–224.

CONCLUSION:
NEW FRIENDS AND ENEMIES

IN THE MODERN PERIOD, JEWS AND MUSLIMS TOGETHER forged an idealized vision of Muslim-Jewish harmony that was rooted in early modern Jewish accounts. This ideal became the established portrayal of Ottoman relations with Jewry both in Turkey and abroad. For political reasons, this history writing has since the nineteenth century postulated a state of harmony, conviviality, and common purpose, forged by two very different peoples involved in a mutually dependent, symbiotic relationship. It is based on a selection of the rosiest premodern and modern Jewish accounts, a dismissal of contradictory details (such as the uprooting of Byzantine Jews by Mehmed II's conquest of Constantinople), and a silencing of counternarratives (such as Jewish nationalism, Zionism). It has also largely ignored Muslim imaginings about Jews.

This dominant utopian narrative was fashioned in the context of Ottoman Jews' political awareness beginning in the late nineteenth century and has been maintained by most Turkish Jews and their historians outside Turkey to the present day. Jews were not the only non-Muslim ethnoreligious group in the Ottoman Empire. Because they were the smallest of the three recognized non-Muslim communities, the fate of the Armenians and the Greeks served as a cautionary tale for Jews, compelling them to promote a distorted view of their circumstances and of the state that ruled them. Far from being a vision that reflects confidence and happiness, this utopian historical narrative reflects fear and anxiety at what had befallen others with similar legal, cultural, linguistic, and religious status. The context of war, ethnic cleansing, genocide, population exchange, pogroms, discrimination, and forced assimilation moved Jews to take sides. Jews were compelled to place their bets on who would be victorious—Muslims or Christians. History writing became the means for articulating an acceptable past so that Jews might be accepted by Muslims in the present and future.

These idealized narratives were forged in the fifteenth century in collusion with Ottoman authorities, and their influence was heightened in the sixteenth century by messianic expectations and then replaced by messianic were embodied in Sabbatai Zevi. But in the seventeenth century, s were dashed. By the nineteenth century, the history was secularized and reconfigured with an eye to the treatment of Greek and Armenian Christians. This latter version is perpetuated to this day, conflating, as all versions since the fifteenth century have, echoes of religious sentiment and ecstatic feelings of gratefulness with political awareness. It persists as the dominant narrative through a twofold repression: by silencing critical internal voices and ignoring contrary memories.

The Quincentennial Foundation, established by Turkish Jews in 1989 with the close involvement of the Turkish foreign and prime ministries, explicitly promotes a vision of Ottoman tolerance toward Jews in order to deny the annihilation of the Armenians. In the words of its president, Jak Kamhi, while Jews were always loyal, "some other minorities [Armenians and Greeks] who lived at peace in our country for nearly four centuries took advantage of the breakup of the Ottoman Empire to stage rebellions . . . [and] these uprisings, which were openly encouraged and armed by Russian and other European powers, led to numerous bloody events that have always been explained to the world in a one-sided manner." But "through their Quincentennial celebrations, Turkish Jewry has told the world the 500-year story of their attachment to the Ottoman Empire and the Republic of Turkey where they have always lived in peace; in so doing, they have clarified the truth about these events."[1]

Kamhi credits the foundation with having brought about the defeat of resolutions to recognize the Armenian genocide in the US Congress over the past four decades and with having changed the views of many a country's leaders. "Countries influenced by the negative effects of certain groups [Armenians and Greeks] and lobbies were finally able to see the realities of the Ottoman Empire and the Republic of Turkey. Instead of criticizing the alleged ill-treatment of minorities, they were now unanimous in praising the respect, love and tolerance shown by the Ottoman Empire and the Republic of Turkey towards different religions."[2]

The foundation's efforts are evidence that, even when confronted with Muslim sentiment and treatment they knew to contradict the utopian portrayal of history they promoted, leaders of the Turkish Jewish community strove ever harder to accentuate Jewish contributions to the Turkish state in a desperate attempt to convince Muslim Turks that Jews should belong. To their international audience, Muslims and Jews presented a common front of the Turk as rescuer of the Jews: Muslims in order to improve an international image stained by genocide, Jews in order to ensure their own survival.

As anti-Semitism traveled from the crude fringes to the well-heeled mainstream and Muslims adopted racialized conceptions that prevented Jews from being regarded as Turks, fewer and fewer Jews chose to remain in Turkey, and conspiracy theories about them flourished.[3] The Turkish Jewish population, once a sizable and dynamic minority within Ottoman society, dwindled to the point of serving as little more than a symbolic relic. Brought out for display at public celebrations dressed in his archaic robes, the chief rabbi expressed the Jews' gratitude, and, by his very otherness, Jews' eternal foreignness in their own country.

It is ironic that although Turkish anti-Semitic conspiracy theories imagine Jews serving foreign interests, Turkey's foreign interests may have been best served by Jewish historiography on Ottomans and Turks. Beginning with the 1993 publication of Stanford Shaw's *Turkey and the Holocaust: Turkey's Role in Rescuing Turkish and European Jewry from the Holocaust*, new myths were added to the already incredible account of Muslim-Jewish relations narrated since 1892. Shaw's study introduced the myth of Turkey as the rescuer of Turkish Jews during the Holocaust, portraying its ambassadors as having risked their lives to save Jews. The most thrilling example put forth at that time was the tale of the Marseille consul, Necdet Kent, whose self-proclaimed exploit—in fact, contradicted by Jews and controverted by the irreconcilability of his own account with the historical record—is to have leapt into a cattle car of Jews destined for the death camps and to have ensured their release, thereby obliging Jews' perpetual gratitude to him as a "Turkish Schindler." This fairy tale, which first appeared in Shaw's book as a "testimony," has been uncritically repeated in other histories, novels, and films. The internationally popular film *Turkish Passport* was labeled by its Muslim and Jewish creators as "the only Holocaust story with a happy ending" because the ideology of Turkish exceptionalism maintains that unlike all other nations, Turkey always saves Jews. Facilitated by the Quincentennial Foundation, Shaw based his argument for that book on documents prepared for him by Turkish diplomats long active in Armenian genocide denial, documents that have not been viewed by any other scholar. The myth of Turkey rescuing Turkish Jews was concocted as a stew of denial of the Armenian genocide, promotion of a sanitized and saintly image of Turkey presented to an international audience, and appeal to older Jewish affective dispositions of gratefulness and historiographical tropes of utopian relations between Muslims and Jews in the face of the Christian enemy. Because its message has been repeated for decades, amplified by best-selling novels translated into English and popular films screened at the Cannes Film Festival, the rescue myth has not been dislodged as the conventional narrative—despite contrary historical evidence and lachrymose countervoices, the most compelling of which has been neglected because it has not been translated from Turkish (discussed in the next section).

Another unique aspect of Muslim-Jewish relations in the Turkish context is that Turkish Muslim ambassadors found themselves in a position to save or condemn Turkish Jews in Nazi-occupied Europe. One Turkish ambassador, Selahattin Ülkümen, is recognized for having saved *several dozen* Turkish Jews from certain murder at the hands of the Nazis on Rhodes, despite the fact that nearly *two thousand* other Jews—including family members of Turkish Jewry's unofficial spokesman, Abraham Galanté— were deported from the same island to their deaths at Auschwitz. Ülkümen's life-saving actions are nevertheless leveraged as an if/then proposition to counter claims that the Ottomans committed genocide against Armenians. How can the only people noble enough to have stood up to Nazism, the only people to have saved and given refuge to Jews persecuted in Europe, be perpetrators of a genocide?

Turkish heroism in rescuing Jews and their oft-touted constitutional immunity to anti-Semitism is invariably contrasted not only with European barbarism—thereby turning the tables on centuries-old European labeling of the Turk as the barbarian—but also with a depiction of Armenians and Greeks as anti-Semites. "While the Nazis largely exterminated the remaining Jewish populations of the former Ottoman possessions of Greece during World War II, thus culminating the persecutions begun in these countries following their achievement of full independence during the nineteenth century," Stanford Shaw argues, "neutral Turkey defended its Jews and rejected Nazi demands for them to be deported for extermination in the death camps."[4] Eager to contrast Christian anti-Semitism with Turkish tolerance, Shaw falsifies history. For just as the Nazis never demanded that Turkey deport Jews from Turkey to death camps in Europe, neither did Turkey defend all of its Jews in Europe. Such arguments have been used as a way of showing that Turks are superior to Europeans, as an argument for admittance into the Christian club of the European Union, or, in more recent years, as reason for not bothering to join the EU given its anti-Semitism and Islamophobia.

In Turkish Jewish and Turkish Muslim history writing and fiction, the myth of Turkish rescue is itself a form of Holocaust denial, for it covers up the extent to which Turkish ambassadors facilitated the Holocaust by not recognizing Turkish Jews living in Europe as their fellow citizens. This Holocaust denial goes hand in hand with denial of the Armenian genocide (Shaw was literally handed documents by genocide deniers), with "blame the victim" rhetoric that tars Christians in Turkey with the brush of anti-Semitism, and with that other form of denial—silence.

Toppling the House of Cards

Beginning in 1999 with Rıfat Bali's seminal *Cumhuriyet yıllarında Türkiye Yahudileri: Bir Türkleştirme serüveni, 1923–1945* (Turkish Jews in the early republic: An adventure in Turkification, 1923–1945), Turkish Jewry finally found a critical voice. Bali's public outspokenness is unlike that of any other Turkish Jew living in Turkey. Since his first work, Bali has written over three dozen books, edited twenty-six, and published hundreds of articles in multiple languages, all of them countering the utopian narrative and conventional view that Jews have not been the targets of discriminatory government policies.[5] His historical monograph, *Model Citizens of the State: The Jews of Turkey during the Multi-Party Period* (2012), catalogues Turkish Jewry's woes from 1950 to 2003. Unlike his first monograph, which barely mentioned Armenians and Greeks or what had befallen them, *Model Citizens of the State* also describes discrimination and persecution of Armenians and Greeks in the republic. The book details events during the September 6–7, 1955, riots that mainly targeted Greeks but also Armenians and Jews,[6] and has lengthy sections exposing the Turkish Jewish role in international genocide-denial efforts. Adopting language absent in the original Turkish work, he argues that "the most important tool in Turkey's strategy for countering the forces pushing for recognition of the Armenian genocide was its claim of past and present tolerance of the Jews."[7] For Bali, "the official version of this history, according to which the Ottoman Empire and its successor, the Republic of Turkey, always treated their minorities, particularly the Jews, with great compassion and tolerance" has "been one of the linchpins of Turkey's ongoing campaign against Armenian claims of genocide. An admission of Turkish intolerance in one area is liable to bring down the whole theoretical house of cards."[8]

Bali's lead was followed by other Turkish Jews, especially memoir writers, whose works he edited. These were surpassed by novelist Mario Levi, who criticized the early republic's discriminatory and violent treatment of

Jews, linking it to the Armenian genocide. The autobiographies of leading Turkish Jews echo Levi's *İstanbul bir masaldı* in that they narrate their lived experience of discrimination, harassment, occasional violence, and being treated like second-class citizens or foreigners in their own country. Such a lived experience of precarious minority "guest" status results in an affective disposition of fear and anxiety. This emotional world compelled Levi to use his fictional characters to cry out against such injustices. It also motivated memorialists Eli Şaul and Erol Haker to leave the country, settling in Israel instead so that they could get the "Jewish monkey" off their back for good. The same affective disposition of fear and anxiety drove community leaders and spokespeople Vitali Hakko, Bensiyon Pinto, and Jak Kamhi to invoke the ecstatic gratefulness of their Sephardic ancestors as it was experienced in the early modern period and later projected onto Muslims in the modern period. Their reanimation of that earlier emotional world under changed present conditions resulted in the Quincentennial Foundation's dual ideological survival strategy for allowing Jews to flourish and prosper in Turkey: present a utopian vision of Muslim-Jewish relations to foreigners while playing a leading role in denying the Armenian genocide. Revisionism among historians aimed at reassessing the foundation's ideological twins—harmony and denial—would occur only as Turks and Kurds began to come to terms with the Armenian genocide.

At the turn of the new millennium, Turkish Jewish historians outside of Turkey began to engage more critically with the Ottoman Jewish past and for the first time began to consider the Armenian genocide. The best example is the work of Aron Rodrigue (b. 1958?), one of the leading scholars of Sephardic Jewry in North America, who has trained a generation of historians holding Sephardic studies positions in the United States. Rodrigue's 2000 publication, *Sephardi Jewry: A History of the Judeo-Spanish Community, 14th–20th Centuries*—a revised version of the 1993 French original coauthored with Esther Benbassa (b. 1950)—offers a more critical approach to early modern Ottoman Jewish historiography, its "idyllic vision" of the empire and its rulers, and the politicization of this vision during the quincentennial celebrations.[9] Yet it still deploys the standard functionalist approach depicting Jews as useful, reliable, and loyal, and the Ottoman sultans as their tolerant protectors.[10] Most of the study focuses on the Jewish role in the Ottoman economy, internal communal and cultural developments, and the politicization of Jews in the nineteenth and twentieth centuries. It barely mentions Armenians and Greeks during the Ottoman

era, other than to associate Greeks with economic rivalry and child murder accusations.[11] In the modern era, Greeks are discussed in relation to
anti-Semitism in Greece.[12] The "decimation" of the Armenians is mentioned
in passing in relation to Turkey,[13] where anti-Semitism is downplayed and
discriminations and pogroms in the republic, and worse treatment during
World War II, are explained through the concept of a general "antiminority
xenophobia."[14]

Rodrigue would finally engage the genocide in a cautious article published in 2002.[15] In it, he asserts he is not interested in debates concerning
designations such as "genocide" as he wishes to avoid "ahistorical sterile
semantic quibbles," a remark that could be misinterpreted, considering the
context of long-standing Turkish Jewish denial of the genocide.[16] Rodrigue's
caution and discomfort with the term "genocide" is reflected in the work of
his student, Julia Phillips-Cohen, who, her own convictions to the contrary,
chooses the qualified phrase "ongoing debates over the Armenian genocide"
rather than simply "the Armenian genocide."[17] This slippage, however unin-
tended, serves to highlight the minefield that surrounds discussion on the
Armenian genocide within Ottoman and Turkish studies; in this context,
the term "debates" is leveraged by genocide deniers as a pseudoscientific
qualifier of the term "Armenian genocide." Suggesting that the genocide is
up for "ongoing debate" places a question mark around it ever having happened at all. Rodrigue also repeats the conventional historiography depicting a near-utopian Jewish experience under Ottoman rule. Comparing
Jews and Armenians, he narrates how Jews "had, on the whole, a relatively
harmonious experience."[18] He argues that the ruling elite correctly perceived Ottoman Jews as "developing no significant nationalist politics" and
comprising one of the "last remaining *staatserhaltende* [state-supporting]
groups that were committed to the survival of the empire." Moreover, they
were "the model 'tolerated' community with a 'happy' history, the exemplar
of 'toleration' in recent discourses on the Ottoman and Turkish past."[19] But
the article is explicit. Rodrigue argues that "the Empire under the rule of
the Committee of Union and Progress was not a nation-state, nor was there
a meaningful attempt to turn it into one."[20] The aim of the CUP "was to
'save the Empire.' This was still, first and foremost, an imperial polity."[21] The
Ottoman Empire perpetrated the crime.

In 2003 Beki Bahar had dedicated her *Efsaneden tarihe Ankara Yahudileri* (Ankara Jews from legend to history) to her son İzzet Bahar (b. 1953),
including a photograph of his bar mitzvah in the book. Electrical engineer

İzzet would leave Turkey and pursue a doctoral degree in history in the United States, where he was briefly a student of mine, authoring two works in the new millennium. The first, his MA thesis, published in 2008, looked critically at the tolerance myth promoted by Ottoman and Turkish Jewry and its reflection in modern non-Turkish historical accounts.[22] The second, his doctoral dissertation, published in 2015, criticized the myth of Turkey as a rescuer of Jews during World War II.[23] This book has benefited from his research. Despite his important and timely critical readings of Ottoman and Turkish Jewish history, when it comes to the Ottoman Armenians, İzzet Bahar promotes the "provocation thesis," blaming their "deportations and emigration" (not genocide) on their own actions.[24] Old affective dispositions linger. Shaped by the lived experience of being a Jew in Turkey, or of a desire to defend Jews living in Turkey, they continue to hinder critical analyses wherein the scholar may approach the historical record from a noncompetitive point of view of the Armenian Other. For a Jew living in Turkey, and their allies, empathy is what is needed as the new affective disposition toward Armenians. Missing is the ability to accept that Jews and Armenians have both been victims of genocide. The caring imagination necessary to bridge the denial gap would allow Jews to place themselves in the position of Armenians in the Ottoman Empire in 1915, just as German Jewish author Franz Werfel did with his 1933 novel, *The Forty Days of Musa Dagh*. İzzet Bahar has begun to go down that path, as demonstrated by his tracing the long-lasting myths created by early modern Jews and criticism of Turkey for failing to rescue Turkish Jews in Europe during World War II, but acknowledgement of the genocide remains the sticking point because of the hurtful contest between Jews and Armenians to be recognized as victims of genocide.

From Dialogue to Trialogue and Other Efforts at Reconciliation

Non-Jewish Turkish scholars and journalists in Turkey, Germany, and the United States were more radical in their breaking of taboos. Shattering the official silence by criticizing nationalist historiography and denial, they utilized Ottoman archival and literary sources to demonstrate conclusively that an Armenian genocide was planned and committed by the last Ottoman regime. Individual Turkish human rights activists had long been outspoken on the topic. Ragıb and Ayşenur Zarakolu founded Belge publishing house in 1977 and began publishing or translating works into Turkish on the Armenian genocide, among other taboo subjects. What was new about this group of scholars was how many more Turkish intellectuals joined the cause of breaking the silence. The taboo breakers in Turkey include a long roster of leftists and foreign-educated scholars: Halil Berktay, a former Maoist educated at Birmingham University in the United Kingdom who was a professor at Boğaziçi University and then Sabancı University in Istanbul; Selim Deringil, also at Boğaziçi University, who earned his PhD in the United Kingdom at the University of East Anglia; Edhem Eldem, another Boğaziçi University history professor who earned his PhD at the University of Provence in France; Murat Belge at Istanbul Bilgi University, another Marxist who was forced to resign his university positions following the 1971 and 1980 coups; Fikret Adanır, who earned his PhD in history at the University of Frankfurt am Main and taught at Ruhr University, Bochum; Taner Akçam, a leftist revolutionary adopted by Amnesty International as a Prisoner of Conscience in the mid-1970s, who fled Turkey following the 1980 coup, gained political asylum in Germany, earned a PhD in sociology at Hanover University, and since 2008 has served as the Robert Aram, Marianne Kaloosdian and Stephen and Marian Mugar Chair in Armenian Genocide Studies at Clark University in the United States; and Fatma Müge Göçek, who earned a PhD at Princeton as the student of Bernard Lewis and teaches sociology at the University of Michigan, also in the United States.

Working together with Armenian American historian Ronald Grigor Suny and Armenian political scientist Gerard Libaridian, beginning in 2000, Göçek organized a nearly two-decade-long series of workshops in the United States, Europe, and Turkey in which I participated, as would Rıfat Bali and Aron Rodrigue.[25] Entitled the "Workshop for Armenian-Turkish Studies," it brought together Armenian and Turkish scholars and journalists, and other historians of the Ottoman Empire and Turkish Republic to debate the history of Armenians in the late empire behind closed doors. The workshops constituted the first time that "normal scholarly exchange" was able to replace "unyielding confrontation" on the matter.[26] The collaboration was opposed viciously in Turkey and by many Armenian Americans. Turkish participants were vilified in the Turkish press; many were charged with Article 301 of the penal code for "insulting Turkishness." Despite these attacks, the collaboration has resulted in the edited volume, *A Question of Genocide: Armenians and Turks at the End of the Ottoman Empire*; Göçek has most recently published the 680-page tome *Denial of Violence: Ottoman*

Past, Turkish Present, and Collective Violence against the Armenians, 1789–2009, a direct counter to Bilâl Şimşir's, *Ermeni meselesi, 1774–2005.*[27]

In 2005, Berktay, Deringil, Eldem, and Belge organized the first academic conference in Turkey to acknowledge the Armenian genocide, "The Ottoman Armenians during the Era of Ottoman Decline."[28] Cancelled by two public universities, it was finally held at a private university, where outside the conference hall hundreds of nationalist protesters pelted the academics with trash. Justice Minister Cemil Çiçek publicly insulted the organizers as traitors who had stabbed Turkey in the back. Other Turkish public figures, including popular novelist Elif Shafak and Nobel Prize–winning novelist Orhan Pamuk joined the growing list of Turkish academics and writers acknowledging the fate of the Armenians. Shafak's novel, *The Bastard of Istanbul*, published in English in 2006, counters denial of the Armenian genocide with a tale of a family made up of Turks and Armenians, perpetrators and victims, bound by the violent past.[29] Pamuk declared that same year in an interview in a Swiss journal that "thirty thousand Kurds and a million Armenians were killed in these lands."[30] Because of remarks such as these, each of these individuals were brought to trial or threatened with prison sentences for having allegedly violated Article 301. While most of the cases were dismissed, Turkish Armenian journalist Hrant Dink was convicted and given a suspended sentence. A decade earlier, Dink had founded the left-leaning, genocide-mentioning, Turkish-language, Istanbul-based Armenian newspaper, *Agos*, which was everything the Jewish community's *Şalom* was not—namely, confident and critical.[31] Dink had also been a participant in the second Workshop for Armenian-Turkish Studies organized by Suny and Göçek in Ann Arbor in 2002.

The year 2006 also witnessed a sea change in the field of Turkish studies outside of Turkey. One of the most respected Ottoman historians, Donald Quataert, himself a signatory to the 1985 letter of petition opposing the recognition of the Armenian genocide by the US Congress, wrote an article documenting the long-standing practice of self-censorship by foreign scholars of Ottoman history regarding annihilation of the Armenians.[32] In that article, Quataert argues that from when he began graduate studies in the 1960s through to the turn of the millennium, "there was an elephant in the room of Ottoman studies—the slaughter of the Ottoman Armenians in 1915." Ottoman historians, he wrote, "fall into a camp of either silence or denial—both of which are forms of complicity," but "it now appears that the Ottomanist wall of silence is crumbling."[33] Such an admission would have been unthinkable a decade earlier. But much had changed in the course of the 1990s. US universities had begun to reject Turkish offers to establish chairs, such as happened at UCLA in 1997. They had seen how other Turkish-funded chairs, including that at Princeton, had been misused as springboards for genocide denial. Unlike at the other universities in the past, faculty at UCLA objected to the conditions attached to the chair that its holder "must have used Turkish archives and must maintain 'close and cordial relations with academic circles in Turkey.' Anyone, of course, who acknowledges the Armenian Holocaust is not going to have any kind of cordial relations with Turkish academics, let alone access to Ottoman archives."[34] For his "indiscretion," Quataert was pressured to resign his position as president of the Institute of Turkish Studies, and many of the board members resigned along with him. A decade later, one of the leading scholars of late Ottoman and early republican history, Erik Zürcher, based in the Netherlands, could write openly of genocide without any repercussions.[35] One understands the transformation best by comparing his 1984 book, *The Unionist Factor: Role of the Committee of Union and Progress in the Turkish National Movement, 1905–1926*, in which the Armenian genocide "is hardly discussed and largely limited to footnotes," with his 2010 book, *The Young Turk Legacy and Nation Building: From the Ottoman Empire to Atatürk's Turkey*, and 2011 article, "Renewal and Silence: Postwar Unionist and Kemalist Rhetoric on the Armenian Genocide," where Zürcher reveals "the fundamental importance of the deportations and massacres in the story of the final years of the empire."[36] His Turkish student Uğur Ümit Üngör has recently published a series of critical studies on the topic.[37]

In Turkey, there were limits to such free expression. In 2007, Dink was assassinated in broad daylight outside the office of *Agos*.[38] The ultranationalist assassin claimed to have avenged the 1921 Berlin assassination of Talat Pasha. While ultranationalists and members of the police, who had failed to protect Dink despite his having received explicit death threats for years, celebrated the murder, posing for photos with the murderer, over one hundred thousand Turkish citizens of all ethnic and religious backgrounds filled the streets of Istanbul following Dink's funeral in protest. Many held signs that read, "We are all Armenian."

The assassination was a watershed for Turkish-Armenian reconciliation. In the aftermath, two of Dink's close friends wrote books that broke new ground. Taner Akçam's *The Young Turks' Crime against Humanity: The Armenian Genocide and Ethnic Cleansing in the Ottoman Empire*, became the first book on the Armenian genocide to be awarded the prestigious Albert Hourani Award for the Best Book in Middle East Studies given by the Middle East Studies Association of North America in 2012.[39] Akçam notes how his book "may also be read as a critical reflection on the silences in Ottoman historiography as practiced both in Europe and in the United States until recently," as the genocide "has been nonexistent" in the work of most Ottoman historians who investigate the period, as if "ignoring mass deportations and annihilation were an academic virtue and noble act."[40] Even more spectacular, that same year Turkish journalist Hasan Cemal, the grandson of Cemal Pasha, one of the men responsible for the genocide, published a Turkish best seller entitled *1915: The Armenian Genocide*.[41] As minister of the navy, commander of the Fourth Army, military governor of Syria, and a key figure in the last Ottoman regime, Cemal Pasha had overseen the deportation of Armenians to their deaths. The author not only acknowledges the Armenian genocide, but apologizes on behalf of his grandfather for having committed it. As Cemal states in the preface, "We cannot remain silent before the bitter truths of the past. We cannot let the past hold the present captive. Also, the pain of 1915 does not belong to the past, it is an issue of today. We can only make peace with history, but not an 'invented' or 'distorted' history like ours and reach liberty." In this way, Cemal promotes rapprochement between Turks (Muslims) and Armenians (Christians) today by means of a reconciliation with their shared past. The genocide's centennial in 2015 saw many more Turkey-based intellectuals, journalists, and novelists criticize the official policy of silence and denial, to wit, the "Letter to the Armenians," authored by eight important Turkish figures, including Cengiz Çandar.[42] As one of them observes, "Today a growing number of Turks understand that 1915 was a genocide and want to confront our shared history." Accordingly, the *Tarih Vakfı* (History Foundation) in Istanbul dedicated an entire year-long weekly speaker series confronting the history of the genocide and its aftereffects in Turkish society, just as Can publishing house released *İçimizdeki Ermeni, 1915–2015* (The Armenian within us), with contributions from three dozen authors.[43]

Alongside these stunning new developments among Turks, another grassroots movement emerged in the very part of Turkey most affected by the Armenian genocide: southeastern Anatolia—Kurdistan. Kurdish "intellectuals, activists, and organizations addressed the Armenian Genocide in various ways long before the shift in the Turkish public debate occurred."[44] This is because the Kurds went from being "perpetrators to victims," from "loyal subjects of the late Ottoman Empire who actively participated in the killings and dispossession of the Armenians," to being the victims of Turkification policies in the republic.[45] Already at the beginning of the new millennium, Kurds began to publicly recognize the genocide and apologize to the Armenians for their role in it. On April 24, 2004, a headline in the pro-Kurdish Turkish daily newspaper *Özgür Gündem* read, "We Apologize."[46] On the same anniversary five years later, another Kurdish-focused daily issued an apology. Upon being voted into office across the southeast in 2012, Kurdish political parties began to hold interreligious memorial services. They rebuilt, reopened, and returned the deeds of Armenian churches, including the largest Armenian church in the Middle East, Surp Giragos in Diyarbakir.[47]

Since 2005, a new generation of Kurdish writers, politicized in the 1990s during the Turkish state's suppression of the Kurdish movement, have published a number of novels which "establish an association of victimhood" between the Armenians, who suffered in 1915 at the hands of the Ottoman Empire, and the Kurds, who were subject to state violence by the Turkish Republic in the 1990s.[48] Setting "aside questions of guilt, intention, responsibility" in favor of "focusing on agentless victimhood and redemptive continuity" between Armenian suffering in the early twentieth century and Kurdish suffering at its end, these writers have sought to mobilize "the former for the sake of bolstering the latter."[49]

On the anniversary of Hrant Dink's assassination, imprisoned PKK leader Abdullah Öcalan published an open letter to the Armenian people in *Agos* in which he recognized the genocide, expressing how both the Kurdish and Armenian peoples have suffered at the mercy of a common enemy, the "forces of international capital and their lobbies."[50] The latter sentiment and finger-pointing offers clues as to how Jews fit into this new constellation, which distinguishes new friends from a new enemy. Two aspects in particular of Turkish and Kurdish efforts to recognize and come to terms with the Armenian genocide committed by the Ottoman Empire bear significance for Jews: the dominant historiography of Muslim-Jewish relations and the Muslim-Jewish-Christian trialogue that is often triangulated in unhealthy ways.

In relation to the first issue of the dominant Muslim-Jewish historiography, the Turkish Jewish community and their allies must acknowledge the role played by its leaders and the Quincentennial Foundation in assisting the Turkish government in its international campaign to deny recognition of the Armenian genocide. The question is whether Turkish Jewish organizations, historians of Jews in the Ottoman Empire based outside of Turkey, and other Turks who promote the myth that Turks have always rescued Jews in need and thus can never be accused of anti-Semitism will be able to confront the historical record and their own past as some Turkish intellectuals and the Kurdish movement have done. Individual Turkish Jews may have finally spoken out, such as industrialist İshak Alaton (1927–2016), who had an epiphany near the end of his life that "denial causes more pain than murder; first you kill them, and then by denying your crime you kill them for a second time." In 2012 he published an open letter in *Agos*, in which he lamented how "we piled the skeletons up in the closet and locked the doors. For ninety years we buried our heads in the sand. . . . We are afraid of facing the facts. They taught us to be afraid. The skeletons have rotted in the cupboard, and the stench has become insufferable. I can no longer breathe. How about you?"[51]

The official Turkish Jewish community does not appear to be moving in this direction. Kamhi and the current chief rabbi, İshak Haleva, adamantly cling to a view of Turkish and Turkish Jewish history that has been discarded over the past decade by experts across the political spectrum; they continue instead to rail against international recognition of "so-called genocides."[52] The editor in chief of *Şalom* continues to the present day to refer to the Armenian genocide prefaced by the same derisive qualifier.[53] Were the official Turkish Jewish community to adopt a critical approach to Ottoman/Turkish history and their own role in genocide denial in place of the old utopian one about Muslim-Jewish harmony, the dysfunctional three-footed stool of the Muslim-Jewish-Christian trialogue would begin to wobble. Adoption of a critical approach would necessarily destroy the carefully constructed image of the Jew as friend to the Muslim and of the Christian as enemy to both. If Muslim reconciliation with the Armenians proceeds without Jewish participation and buy-in, this could lead Muslims to no longer see Christians as the internal enemy, in which case they will have no more need of Jews as their allies when speaking to Christians abroad, and the Jewish friend may be discarded. Jews would then face two enemies where there once was one, both blaming Jews for their past problems. This would then force the Turkish Jewish community, its spokespeople, and its defenders abroad to join in the heretofore bilateral reconciliation process, attempt to repair their relationship with Christians, and rewrite their history in the trilateral interest of Jews, Muslims, and

Christians alike. This in turn may prompt Armenians and other Christians to do the same. This brings us to the second issue of the triangulated relations between communities in the reconciliation process.

Muslims and Christians must for their part come to terms with and find remedies for the anti-Semitism that has at times been articulated in the course of reconciliation by some of the most influential Turkish, Kurdish, and Armenian political figures and journalists, including Hrant Dink and Abdullah Öcalan. In yet another twist on the Muslim-Jewish-Christian trialogue, these figures have reanimated old anti-Semitic themes, pointing to Jews as the all-powerful architects of the genocide. In their imagination, the annihilation of the Armenians was planned and carried out by an alliance between German Jewish capitalists who aimed to rid themselves of their main economic competitors, the Armenians, and secret Jews within the Ottoman Empire, the Dönme, who held positions of power in the ruling CUP regime.[54] If "a Jewish hand" in the form of world Jewry and its local Dönme agents is behind the genocide, and if Turks and Kurds can be imagined as mere pawns in their evil plot, then Muslims can absolve themselves of blame and thereby be forgiven by Armenians for their deeds. Such a view combines hackneyed anti-Semitic themes long prevalent among Muslims in Turkey and Armenians elsewhere with an element of "moral payback" to the Armenians for decades of Turkish Jewish lobbying to silence acknowledgment of their genocide.[55] What projecting blame onto the Dönme, "the perfect scapegoat,"[56] will do for the depiction of Jews held by Turks, Kurds, and Armenians in Turkey is another matter. Such a new dysfunctional triangulation of Muslim-Christian harmony and Jewish enmity will surely not lead to peace and reconciliation.

A new bilateral Muslim-Christian reconciliation based on having Jews and Christians swap places as friend and enemy of the Muslim demonstrates the salience of the Muslim-Jewish-Christian trialogue and the constructions of "friend" and "enemy." Perhaps only by admitting to their entanglement will these three communities break out of this triangle of friends and enemies where the relation between two is constructed against relations with the third, as Muslims and a non-Muslim friend unite against another non-Muslim enemy. Trilateral reconciliation, not bilateral, is the only choice.

As far back as 2008, Turkish Jewish community leader Bensiyon Pinto warned Turkish Jews of the risks involved in trying to repress the past. Referring to the violence Jews have been subjected to in the Turkish

Republic, he declared, "If a person does not know his history, he is condemned to be crushed under the weight of it."[57] To ensure "that history does not repeat itself, it is necessary to know what happened. No one can just wash their hands [in denial] and say 'nothing of the sort happened.'" His argument is apropos, for in making it, Pinto suggests that once the descendants of the perpetrators of violence stop denying the facts of what happened, the descendants of the victims may be able to forgive them. For the ability to "start again from the beginning, to forgive, and to understand" are "among the greatest virtues that make us human." If the official Turkish Jewish community spokespeople and their supporters abroad—along with the leaders of the Turkish Republic—would adopt this approach toward the Armenian genocide, then Jews and Armenians might finally be able to see one another as friends joined together as equals in a harmonious trialogue with Turkish Muslims.

Notes

1. Kamhi, *Gördüklerim yaşadıklarım*, 404–405.
2. Ibid., 409.
3. See Baer, "An Enemy Old and New."
4. Shaw, *The Jews of the Ottoman Empire and the Turkish Republic*, 255.
5. See his home page, http://www.rifatbali.com.
6. Bali, *Model Citizens of the State*, 56–60.
7. Ibid., 310.
8. Ibid., 452.
9. Benbassa and Rodrigue, *Sephardi Jewry*, 8, 194.
10. Ibid., 2, 6, 7.
11. Ibid., 96, 159–160.
12. Ibid., 96–101, 161.
13. Ibid., 101.
14. Ibid., 161–163, 179–184.
15. Aron Rodrigue, "The Mass Destruction of Armenians and Jews in the 20th Century."
16. Ibid., 303.
17. Cohen, *Becoming Ottomans*, 133.
18. Rodrigue, "The Mass Destruction of Armenians and Jews in the 20th Century," 303.
19. Ibid., 304.
20. Ibid., 306.
21. Ibid., 307.
22. Bahar, *Jewish Historiography on the Ottoman Empire*.
23. Bahar, *Turkey and the Rescue of European Jews*.
24. He argues that "in the last decades of the Empire, because of the rebellious activities of Armenian nationalists, friction between the Ottoman Administration and its Armenian subjects was very common. Most notably, an Armenian separatist organization staged

a bloody occupation of the Ottoman Bank in August 1896 to force concessions from the government, and Armenians were behind an assassination attempt against Sultan Abdülhamit II in July 1905." It is noteworthy that Bahar skips over the massacres of hundreds of thousands of Armenians in these years. He continues, "In the critical first years of WWI, the Administration's fears about the loyalty of the Armenians were further exacerbated by the close relationship of militant Armenian organizations with the Empire's archenemy, Russia. The fact that most of the Armenian population was living in territories close to the Russian border was creating a security concern for the government." Bahar, *Turkey and the Rescue of European Jews*, 27.

25. Other participants in WATS workshops over the years who are discussed in this book include Fikret Adanır, Taner Akçam, Margaret Lavinia Anderson, Murat Belge, Halil Berktay, Hasan Cemal, Cengiz Çandar, Selim Deringil, Howard Eissenstat, Ayda Erbal, Dikran Kaligian, Hans Lukas-Kieser, Marc Mamigonian, Mark Mazower, Robert Melson, Elif Shafak, Mete Tunçay, Uğur Ümit Üngör, and Erik Zürcher.

26. Ronald Grigor Suny and Fatma Müge Göçek, "Introduction: Leaving it to the Historians," *A Question of Genocide*, 4. See also Ronald Grigor Suny, "Truth in Telling: Reconciling Realities in the Genocide of the Ottoman Armenians," *American Historical Review* 114, no. 4 (October 2009): 930–946.

27. Göçek, *Denial of Violence*. See also Suny, "*They Can Live in the Desert but Nowhere Else.*"

28. İmparatorluğun çöküş döneminde Osmanlı Ermenileri: Bilimsel sorumluluk ve demokrasi sorunları, Conference at Bilgi University, September 23–25, 2005.

29. Elif Shafak, *The Bastard of Istanbul* (New York: Viking, 2006).

30. Karl Vick, "Turkey Charges Acclaimed Author," *Washington Post*, September 1, 2005.

31. One example comparing the Armenian and Jewish communities in that era will suffice. Because they sought to avoid the appearance of not being grateful for "500 Years of Peace and Brotherhood," the leaders of the Turkish Jewish community did not cooperate in transferring Yılmaz Karakoyunlu's 1990 novel *Salkım Hanım'ın taneleri*, which concerns a Jewish family victimized by the World War II–era Capital Tax, to the big screen, so the main characters were transformed into Armenians. Bali, *Model Citizens of the State*, 425.

32. Donald Quataert, "The Massacres of Ottoman Armenians and the Writing of Ottoman History," *Journal of Interdisciplinary History* 37, no. 2 (2006).

33. Ibid., 249–250, 258, quoted in Eissenstat, "Children of Özal," 25, and in Gutman, "Review: Ottoman Historiography and the End of the Genocide Taboo," 167.

34. Robert Fisk, "Turkish Money Fails to Blot Out the Stain of Genocide," *The Independent*, January 17, 1998.

35. Erik Jan Zürcher, "The Role of Historians of Turkey in the Study of the Armenian Genocide," *Centre for Policy and Research on Turkey (ResearchTurkey)* 4 (2015): 12–17.

36. Suny, "*They Can Live in the Desert but Nowhere Else*," 454n43.

37. Üngör, *The Making of Modern Turkey*; *Confiscation and Destruction: The Young Turk Seizure of Armenian Property*, ed. Uğur Ümit Üngör and Mehmet Polatel (London: Bloomsbury Academic, 2013); and *Genocide: New Perspectives on its Causes, Courses, and Consequences*, ed. Uğur Ümit Üngör (Amsterdam: Amsterdam University Press, 2016). For a review of the first two of these works, see Gutman, "Review: Ottoman Historiography and the End of the Genocide Taboo," 178. For an overview of the development of historiography on the genocide, see Ronald Grigor Suny, "Historians Look at the Armenian Genocide: A Bibliographical Discussion," in Suny, "*They Can Live in the Desert but Nowhere Else.*"

38. "Turkish-Armenian Writer Shot Dead," *BBC News*, January 19, 2007.

39. Akçam, *The Young Turks' Crime Against Humanity*.

40. Ibid., xxv, quoted in Eissenstat, "Children of Özal," 27.

41. Hasan Cemal, *1915: Ermeni soykırımı* (Istanbul: Everest, 2012); Hasan Cemal, *1915: The Armenian Genocide* (London: Gomidas Institute, 2015).

42. Adalet Ağaoğlu, Ahmet Altan, Oya Baydar, Murat Belge, Hasan Cemal, Cengiz Çandar, Perihan Mağden and Bejan Matur, P24, Platform for Independent Journalism (website), http://platform24.org/en/articles/270/a-letter-to-the-armenians.

43. Tarih Vakfı, 100. yılda 1915'e ve bugüne bakışlar, "Tehcir-taktil-soykırım: 1915–2015," Karin Karakaşlı, Rober Koptaş, Zakarya Mildanoğlu. http://tarihvakfi.org.tr/Etkinlik /persembekonusmalari/1; *İçimizdeki Ermeni (1915–2015)*, ed. Yiğit Bener (Istanbul: Can, 2015).

44. Bilgin Ayata, "The Kurds in the Turkish-Armenian Reconciliation Process: Double-Bind or Double-Blind?" Roundtable, One Hundred Years of Denial: The Armenian Genocide, *International Journal of Middle East Studies* 47, no. 4 (2015): 807. Ayata is based in Switzerland.

45. Ibid., 809.

46. Göçek, *Denial of Violence*, 413.

47. Ayata, "The Kurds in the Turkish-Armenian Reconciliation Process," 810; Raffi Khatchadourian, "A Century of Silence: A Family Survives the Armenian Genocide and its Long Aftermath," *New Yorker*, January 5, 2015.

48. Adnan Çelik and Ergin Öpengin, "The Armenian Genocide in the Kurdish Novel: Restructuring Identity through Collective Memory," *European Journal of Turkish Studies* (Online), Complete List, 2016, 7.

49. Ibid., 11. See also Adnan Çelik and Namık Kemal Dinç, *Yüzyıllık ah! Toplumsal hafızanın izinde 1915 Diyarbekir* (Istanbul: İsmail Beşikci Vakfı, 2015); and Özlem Galip, *Imagining Kurdistan: Identity, Culture and Society* (London: I.B. Tauris, 2015).

50. "Öcalan'dan Ermenilere mektup: Bize yardımcı olun," *Radikal*, January 30, 2014.

51. Rober Koptaş, "Cinayetin değil, inkârın özrünü savunuyorum," *Agos*, February 2, 2012.

52. Bali, *Model Citizens of the State*, 392–393, 395.

53. See İvo Molinas, "Hangi 'soykırım'?" *Şalom*, June 10, 1998; and İvo Molinas, "Soykırım endüstrisi," *Şalom*, January 9, 2008, which are cited in Bali, *Türkiye'de Holokost tüketimi*, 50, 202–203, and 204; as well as İvo Molinas, "Holokost ve soykırım," *Şalom*, June 8, 2016.

54. For extensive quotations from Turkish Armenians and Turkish Muslims articulating this view, see Rıfat Bali, *A Scapegoat for All Seasons: The Dönmes or Crypto-Jews of Turkey*, translated from Turkish by Paul Bessemer (Istanbul: Isis, 2008), chapter 9, "A Recent Antisemitic Theme: The Sabbatean Role in the Armenian Genocide," 277–316; Hrant Dink, "Gerçek maskaralık," *Agos*, October 20, 2000.

55. Bali, "A Recent Antisemitic Theme," 315.

56. Ibid., 316.

57. Pinto, *Anlatmasam olmazdı*, 34.

EPILOGUE

ONE OF THE FACTORS PERMITTING THE NEW OPENNESS in Turkey was Recep Tayyip Erdoğan having led his AKP party to its first victory in the general election of 2002. Erdoğan served first as prime minister from 2007 to 2014 and then as Turkey's president. For a decade beginning in 2003, Erdoğan and his party promoted the open expression of religious and ethnic identities long suppressed in secular Turkey. In order to disempower the secular establishment in control of the military and judiciary, an apparatus that had long oppressed Islamists and Kurds, the AKP forged alliances with the Gülenist Islamist movement and the Kurdish political movement. As a consequence of the latter relationship, between 2003 and 2015 Turkish society came as close as it had ever come to acknowledging the Armenian genocide in the Ottoman Empire and the persecution of Kurds in the Turkish Republic.

Regarding Jews, however, Erdoğan took a more schizophrenic approach: on the one hand, he denied the existence of Turkish Muslim anti-Semitism by leveraging Ottoman and Turkish Jewish claims that the Turks had saved Jews persecuted by Christian anti-Semites, while on the other hand, he regularly deployed anti-Semitic topes borrowed from Christian Europe. Erdoğan has denied that the Ottomans annihilated the Armenians by stating that "a Muslim cannot commit genocide."[1] Claiming that same year that "anti-Semitism has no place in Turkey. It is alien to our culture," he accepted the Anti-Defamation League's Courage to Care Award recognizing the efforts of Turkish diplomats to save Jews in Nazi Europe. He told Turkish Jews, "We are the grandchildren of the Ottomans who welcomed your ancestors and treated them as a guest in this land when they were expelled [from Spain]."[2] To prove that Turks still tolerated Jews, the Turkish government paid for the restoration of one of the largest synagogues in Europe, the Great Synagogue in Edirne, at whose opening ceremony the deputy prime minister declared, "There is no anti-Semitism in Turkey."[3] His claim that "European and other countries lag behind Turkey in that sense" is belied by the fact that it was the 1934 pogrom in Thrace that caused the Jews of Edirne to abandon the city and leave their synagogue to fall into disrepair.

The opening in Turkey was not to last. By 2013, Erdoğan had turned increasingly to authoritarianism and suppression of free speech, beginning with a crackdown of the widespread Gezi protests beginning in May that year. In December, Turkish police arrested key members of the business and political elite closely affiliated with Erdoğan. The charges of bribery and corruption reached the president's family. It seemed like his decade-long reign was ending. But then the cases were dismissed. Members of the judiciary and police involved in the investigations were arrested and put on trial for conspiring to overthrow the government. The Istanbul public prosecutor issued an arrest warrant for former Erdoğan ally Fethullah Gülen, in exile in the United States. He allegedly heads a criminal and armed terror group, the "Fethullah Terror Organization/Parallel State."[4] The corruption charges, it is claimed, were fabricated by members of the "terror organization" whose "parallel state" is attempting to take over Turkey from within.[5] This foreign-based movement allegedly embeds personnel within the government, whose members spring into action when "the button is pushed."[6]

Erdoğan saw a Jewish hand behind the various protests against his rule. Despite his contention that Turkey "has never been anti-Semitic in any time in its history at all," he freely deployed anti-Semitic stereotypes.[7] According to Erdoğan, Jews control world media, claiming that the *New York Times* has been campaigning against Turkey's rulers since Sultan Abdülhamid II: "Now, they are spitting out the same hatred on me. . . . It is clear who their patrons are. There is Jewish capital behind it, unfortunately."[8] Erdoğan claims Jews are so clever at managing money and are such geniuses that Turks should take them as a model, for they "print money from where they are sitting" and "still earn dividends from having invented the telephone and the light bulb." He blames unrest in Turkey on the so-called "interest rate lobby."[9] In 2014 the American Jewish Congress demanded that he return the Courage to Care Award due to his having "incit[ed] the Turkish population to violence against the Jewish people," and because his "attacks on Jews call into question" everything he was honored for. In response, Erdoğan referred to the award as a bribe to keep him silent.[10]

Erdoğan's dictatorial tendencies intensified in response to the success of the Kurdish political movement in the summer 2015 general elections. Rather than allowing a coalition government to form, he forced a new election, which returned the AKP to single-party rule. His new government stripped politicians focused on the Kurdish issue of their elected positions, including members of parliament, and jailed them, and shut down pro-Kurdish television stations and newspapers. Turkey resumed the military campaign against the PKK, resulting in devastating effects on civilians living in Turkey's southeast.

By 2015, Erdoğan openly blamed Turkey's problems on the *üst akıl* (Mastermind), whom Erdoğan and his followers allege "rules the world, burns, destroys, starves, wages wars, organizes revolutions and coups, and establishes states within states," an evil cabal that has its sights set on annihilating Islam, Muslims, Turkey, and Turks.[11] According to Erdoğan, "Today very insidious, very vile, and very bloody tricks are being played both on our region and on our country. The thing I call the Mastermind appears before us every day with new deviltry, trying to sow new seeds of enmity and discord in our region. He is trying to blacken the future of our region with bloody tears, civil war, and sectarian wars. We are aware of this reality, that this is a power struggle."[12] According to the two-hour "Mastermind" documentary that was shown on pro-Erdoğan Turkish television channel A Haber in 2015, and which features extensive clips of the president's speeches, the Mastermind, which allegedly secretly controls the world, employing puppets to carry out its nefarious plans, is the "international Jew."

The film begins with Erdoğan speaking in parliament claiming that attacks on his regime are actually part of operations directed against Turkey's very existence. And behind it all is the Mastermind. What is happening in the world today, the narrator claims, can be explained by going back 3,500 years, for that is when Judaism was born. "Experts" filmed by a shaky camera in dim lighting against a background of threatening music assert that Jews are taught to believe that they are "the master" and to treat all other people as their slaves. For this reason they have been oppressing believers for thousands of years, dividing and ruling the world for their own interests.

Crediting the Mastermind with having deposed Ottoman and Turkish rulers from the time of Abdülhamid II onward, Erdoğan also blamed the Mastermind for ordering the followers of Gülen to carry out the unsuccessful coup attempt against his government on July 15 and 16, 2016.[13] The very next day, the front-page political cartoon in the Islamist daily *Yeni Akit*, which is part of the Turkish presidential press pool, depicted a Hasidic Jew marked with a Star of David holding the chain of a barking dog, who is actually a man on all fours, and none other than Gülen, wearing a skull cap topped with a Star of David. Marked with the phrase "parallel things," referring to the so-called "parallel state," the dog and his master move toward a sign pointing toward Turkey.[14] But how could they make a convincing case for Gülen as the cat's paw of a Jewish coup against an Islamist leader? Gülen, former ally to Erdoğan, a Turkish-educated Sunni Muslim religious leader who had fled Turkey in the 1990s prior to the rise of the AKP; Gülen, who had faced indictment for fomenting Islamic revolution; this Gülen would have to somehow be remade to fit the Mastermind. Erdoğan and his advisors relied on the oldest conspiracy theory in their book—they labeled Gülen a Dönme, descendant of the followers of Jewish messiah turned Muslim Sabbatai Zevi, and a Jew, the son of a Jewish mother and an Armenian father.[15] They alleged Gülen, while a mosque preacher in Sabbatai Zevi's birthplace of Izmir, visited the former home of the seventeenth-century Kabbalist, where Dönme proclaimed him their messiah.[16] They called him the "Sabbatai Zevi of our age."[17] One cabinet minister declared that when Gülen dies he will be buried in a Jewish cemetery.[18] They deployed anti-Semitic stereotypes. In the words of a columnist for the Erdoğan mouthpiece, the daily *Sabah*, run by Erdoğan's son-in-law, Gülen "immediately catches the whiff of money and power because he is a Jew....Fethullah Gülen loves money so much there isn't a thing he wouldn't do for money."[19] Thus according to this logic, Gülen is a Jew carrying out "the Jews'" plans against Turkey. Erdoğan declared, "Have you seen him criticize Israel? No, he cannot do it as he cannot criticize his Master, who holds his leash."[20]

In 2016, for the first time, a CEO of the Anti-Defamation League announced that "what happened to the Armenian people was unequivocally genocide," and that his organization "would support U.S. recognition of the Armenian Genocide. Silence is not an option."[21] The recognition of the genocide was partly a response to Erdoğan's anti-Semitism. A number of major US Jewish organizations, including the American Jewish Committee and the Jewish Council for Public Affairs, began to promote Armenian genocide recognition.[22]

Indeed, on October 29, 2019—incited by Turkey's invasion of northern Syria to expel US-allied Kurds and replace them with Arabs—the United States House of Representatives voted in favor of a resolution, sponsored by a Jewish-American congressman, to recognize the Armenian genocide. Finally, despite Turkish state threats and Turkish Jewish lobbying, it seems that in the United States Congress, at least, the spell is broken. Erdoğan's anti-Semitism and open criticism of Israel, and the AKP's close relations with Hamas have also contributed to strained relations with the Jewish state. This has, in turn, produced new efforts in Israel to recognize the Armenian genocide.

The US congressional resolution may yet inspire the Knesset to act. Time will tell whether the leaders of the Turkish Jewish community do the same. The community's affective disposition of gratefulness and fear examined throughout this book and the ongoing government seizure of tens of billions of dollars' worth of assets from AKP opponents, the purging of tens of thousands of civil servants, the jailing of hundreds of academics and journalists, and the takeover of hundreds of opposition media outlets makes it unlikely that they will dare to raise their heads or voices for the foreseeable future.[23] How could they in a country where people are sentenced to aggravated life in prison for "sending subliminal messages" against the regime?[24] The only hope lies with a new generation of Turkish Jews that rejects the myths of the older generation and their ancestors. Such recent interventions as "Avlaremoz" (Judeo-Spanish for "let's speak publically"), a new, Turkish-language online "platform against anti-Semitism" produced by young Turkish-Jewish activists, may yet instigate a broader turning away from previous generations' "Kayedez," or silence and keeping a low profile.[25]

Notes

1. "Prime Minister Erdoğan Reiterates 'No Genocide' in Darfur," *Today's Zaman*, November 9, 2009.
2. "Prime Minister Erdogan Tells ADL That 'Anti-Semitism Has No Place in Turkey,'" ADL Press Release, June 10, 2005; "Osmanlı torunuyuz mazlum yanındayız," *Hürriyet*, January 7, 2009.
3. Yusuf Ziya Durmuş, "Edirne Synagogue Reopens Its Doors After Restoration," *Daily Sabah*, March 27, 2015.
4. "Turkey Issues Arrest Warrant for Erdogan Rival Fethullah Gülen," *Guardian*, December 19, 2014.
5. "'Fethullahçı Terör Örgütü' suçlaması," *Milliyet*, April 4, 2015.
6. "Second Arrest Warrant Issued for Gülen," *Hürriyet Daily News*, February 24, 2015.
7. "Turkey, in no part of its history, has ever been racist. It has never been anti-Semitic in any time in its history at all. I am one of the first prime ministers in the world to have declared anti-Semitism to be a crime against humanity. Turkey, its people and its state, have always stood by the oppressed. When the Jews were under pressure or oppressed, Turkey extended a helping hand to them. When the Jews were expelled from Spain in the 15th century, they sought refuge in the Ottoman territory and they lived peacefully in this land for centuries. Similarly, our country embraced the Jews fleeing Hitler's persecution." Recep Tayyip Erdoğan, Address to the Council of Foreign Relations, New York, September 23, 2014, Presidency of the Republic of Turkey (website), https://www.tccb.gov.tr/en/news/542/3249/president-erdogan-addresses-cfr.html.

8. "Erdoğan Lashes Out at Foreign Media Ahead of Turkey Polls," AFP (Agence France-Presse), June 6, 2015.

9. "Erdoğan'dan Yahudi açılımı," *Hürriyet*, October 7, 2009; Joe Parkinson, "Dismay Over Turkish Rates," *Wall Street Journal*, January 12, 2012.

10. Tolga Tanış, "US Jewish Group Demands PM Erdoğan Return Award," *Hürriyet Daily News*, July 24, 2014.

11. Mustafa Akyol, "Unraveling the AKP's 'Mastermind' Conspiracy Theory," *Al-Monitor*, March 19, 2015, http://www.al-monitor.com/pulse/originals/2015/03/turkey-zion-protocols -akp-version.html. The two-hour "Mastermind" documentary, which was shown on Turkish television channel A Haber on March 15, 2015, can be viewed on YouTube: https://www .youtube.com/watch?v=Zqw2eZ1K6Uw.

12. "Cumhurbaşkanı Erdoğan: Milli seferberlik ilan ediyorum," CNNTurk, December 14, 2016.

13. "Cumhurbaşkanı Erdoğan: FETÖ tam bir maşa, onun üstünde üst akıl var," *Haber 10*, July 31, 2016; "Erdoğan: Üst akıl Fethullah Gülen değil," *Timeturk*, July 31, 2016.

14. Manşetüstü, *Yeni Akit*, July 17, 2016. The same cartoonist had long featured Gülen wearing a skull cap crowned with a Star of David, or depicted him as a spider with fangs, yet the same Jewish headgear: Manşetüstü, *Yeni Akit*, October 28, 2015, November 11, 2015, and November 12, 2015. A cartoon published February 11, 2017, showed Gülen, again wearing a Star-of-David-topped skullcap, sweeping crimes labeled treachery, embezzlement, lying, murder, adultery, dirty tricks, coup, and mafia activity under the rug, an American flag.

15. For example, see "AK Partili vekil açıkladı: Gülen'in babası Ermeni," haber7.com, November 2, 2016, http://www.haber7.com/guncel/haber/2201612-ak-partili-vekil-acikladi -gulenin-babasi-ermeni; "Fethullah Gülen Sabetayist mi?" *Odatv*, August 23, 2016; Tamer Korkmaz, "Sakladım, gizli tuttum, söylemedim, uyuttum!" *Yeni Şafak*, August 23, 2016; "'Gülen babadan Ermeni anadan Yahudi'dir!'" *Yeni Akit*, August 16, 2016; Tamer Korkmaz, "Rabin'in oğlu Fetullah bunalımda!" *Yeni Şafak*, August 12, 2016; Pinar Tremblay, "Is Gulen an Armenian?" *Al-Monitor*, August 12, 2016.

16. "Fethullah Gülen'le ilgili şok bir belge daha," *A Haber*, April 8, 2015.

17. Ferhat Ünlü, "Çağımızın Sabetay Sevi'si: Fethullah Gülen," *Sabah*, October 4, 2015.

18. "Bakan Eroğlu: Gülen, Yahudi mezarlığına gömülecek," siyasihaber3.org, December 9, 2016, http://siyasihaber4.org/bakan-eroglu-gulen-yahudi-mezarligina-gomulecek; "Pis bir Yahudi mahallesi idi," *Şalom*, December 9, 2016.

19. Ersin Ramoğlu (Güney), "Karay Yahudisi Fethullah Gülen," *Sabah*, December 28, 2016.

20. President Erdoğan, Speech in Ordu, Turkey, July 19, 2014, quoted in "Erdoğan's Campaign of Hate Speech: Case of Targeting the Gülen Movement, 2013–2017," Stockholm Center for Freedom, 2017, https://stockholmcf.org/wp-content/uploads/2017/06/Erdogans -Vile-Campaign-Of-Hate-Speech-Case-Study-Targeting-Of-The-Gulen-Movement_2017.pdf.

21. Jonathan Greenblatt, "ADL on the Armenian Genocide," ADL Blog, Anti-Defamation League, May 13, 2016, https://www.adl.org/blog/adl-on-the-armenian-genocide.

22. Lidar Gravé-Lazi and Herb Keinon, "Knesset Committee Recognizes Armenian Genocide," *Jerusalem Post*, August 3, 2016.

23. Kareem Shaheen, "Revealed: The Terror and Torment of Turkey's Jailed Journalists," *Guardian*, March 23, 2017.

24. Kareem Shaheen, "Turkey Sentences Journalists to Life in Jail Over Coup Attempt," *Guardian*, February 16, 2018.

25. www.avlaremoz.com

BIBLIOGRAPHY

Premodern Sources

Aboab, Immanuel. *Nomologia o discursos legales.* Amsterdam, 1629.

Anonymous, "Jewish Account of the Expulsion" (Italy, 1495). Translated from the Hebrew by Jacob Marcus. In Jacob Marcus, *The Jew in the Medieval World: A Source Book, 315–1791*, 51–55. New York: Atheneum, 1979.

Âşıkpaşaoğlu tarihi. Edited by H. Nihal Atsız. Istanbul: Milli Eğitim, 1970.

Âşıkpaşazade, Osmanoğulları'nın tarihi. Edited by Kemal Yavuz and M. A. Yekta Saraç. Istanbul: K, 2003.

Âşıkpaşazâde tarihi (Osmanlı tarihi 1285–1502). Edited by Necdet Öztürk. Istanbul: Bilge, 2013.

Capsali, Eliyahu. *Seder Eliyahu zuta.* 3 vols. (1975–1983). Edited by Aryeh Shmuelevitz, Shlomo Simonsohn, and Meier Benayahu. Jerusalem: Mekhon Ben-Tsvi, 1975.

Defterdâr Sarı Mehmed Paşa. *Zübde-i vekayiât.* Ankara: Türk Tarih Kurumu, 1995.

Düzdağ, M. Ertuğrul. *Şeyhülislâm Ebussu'ûd Efendi'nin fetvalarına göre kanunî devrinde Osmanlı hayatı: Fetâvâ-yi Ebussu'ûd Efendi.* Istanbul: Şule, 1998.

Evliya Çelebi seyahatnâmesi. Edited by Orhan Şaik Gökyay. Topkapı Sarayı Bağdat 304 Yazmasının Transkripsiyonu-Dizini, 1. Kitap: İstanbul. Istanbul: Yapı Kredi, 1996.

Hacohen, Joseph and The Anonymous Corrector. *The Vale of Tears (Emek Habacha).* Translated plus critical commentary by Harry S. May. The Hague: Martinus Nijhoff, 1971.

Ha-Kohen, Joseph. *The Chronicles of Rabbi Joseph ben Joshua ben Meir the Sephardi.* Translated by C. H. F. Bialloblotzky. London, 1835.

———. *Sefer divrei ha-yamim le-malkhei Tzarefat u-malkhei beit Otman ha-Togar.* Sabionetta, 1554.

JPS Tanakh: The Jewish Bible. Philadelphia: Jewish Publication Society of America, 1991.

Katip Çelebi. *Fezleke.* 2 vols. Istanbul: Ceride-i Havadis, 1286/1869.

Kürd Hatib Mustafa. *Risâle-i Kürd Hatib.* Eski Hazine 1400. Istanbul: Topkapı Palace Museum Library.

Marlowe, Christopher. *The Jew of Malta.* In *The Complete Plays.* London: Penguin, 2003, 458–536.

Mehmed Hemdemî Çelebi. *Solakzâde tarihi.* Edited by Dr. Vahid Çabuk. 2 vols. Ankara: Türk Kültür Bakanlığı, 1989.

Mustafa Naima. *Tarîh-i Naîmâ.* 6 vols. Istanbul, 1281–1283/1864–1867.

Naîmâ Mustafa Efendi. *Târih-i Na'imâ (Ravzatü'l-Hüseyn fî hulâsati ahbâri'l-hâfikayn).* Edited by Mehmed İpşirli. 4 vols. Ankara: Türk Tarih Kurumu, 2007.

"Nathan of Gaza, A Letter to Raphael Joseph." Translated by David Halperin. In *Sabbatian Heresy: Writings on Mysticism, Messianism, & the Origins of Jewish Modernity*, edited by Paweł Maciejko, 5–7. Waltham, MA: Brandeis University Press, 2017.

Samuel Usque's Consolation for the Tribulations of Israel (Consolaçam às tribulaçoes de Israel). Translated from the Portuguese by Martin A. Cohen. Philadelphia: Jewish Publication Society of America, 1964.

Selâmikî Mustafa Efendi. *Tarih-i Selâmikî.* Edited by Mehmed İpşirli. 2 vols. Istanbul: Istanbul Üniversitesi Edebiyat Fakültesi, 1989.

Sphrantzes, Georgios. *Memorii: 1401–1477.* Edited by Vasile Grecu. Bucharest: Editio Academiae Rei Publicae Socialistae Romaniae, 1966.

Shaykh al-Islām Karaçelebizade Abdül Aziz Efendi. *Ravzat ül-ebrar el-mübeyyin bi-hakaik il-ahbar.* Cairo: Bulak, 1248/1832.

Modern Sources and Studies

"Aboab, Immanuel." In vol. 2 of *Encyclopaedia Judaica Jerusalem,* 90. Keter: Jerusalem, 1971.

Aciman, André. *Out of Egypt: A Memoir.* Reprint edition. New York: Picador, 2007.

Adak, Hülya. "National Myths and Self-Na(rra)tions: Mustafa Kemal's Nutuk and Halide Edib's Memoirs and the Turkish Ordeal." *South Atlantic Quarterly* 102, no. 2/3 (2003): 509–527.

Ahmad, Feroz. *The Making of Modern Turkey.* London: Routledge, 1993.

———. "Unionist Relations with the Greek, Armenian, and Jewish Communities of the Ottoman Empire." In vol. 1 of *Christians and Jews in the Ottoman Empire: The Functioning of a Plural Society,* ed. Benjamin Braude and Bernard Lewis, 401–434. New York: Holmes & Meier, 1982.

Akar, Rıdvan. *Aşkale yolcuları: Varlık vergisi ve çalışma kampları.* Revised 2nd ed. Istanbul: Belge, 1999.

———. *Varlık vergisi – Tek parti rejiminde azınlık karşıtı politika örneği.* Istanbul: Nadir, 1992.

Akçam, Taner. *The Young Turks' Crime against Humanity: The Armenian Genocide and Ethnic Cleansing in the Ottoman Empire.* Princeton, NJ: Princeton University Press, 2012.

———. *İnsan hakları ve Ermeni sorunu –İttihat ve Terakki'den kurtuluş savaşına.* Ankara: İmge, 1999.

———. *Türk ulusal kimliği ve Ermeni sorunu.* İstanbul: İletişim, 1992.

Aktar, Ayhan. *Varlık vergisi ve Türkleştirme politikaları.* Istanbul: İletişim, 2000.

Alaranta, Toni. "Mustafa Kemal Atatürk's Six-Day Speech of 1927: Defining the Official Historical View of the Foundation of the Turkish Republic." *Turkish Studies* 9, no. 1 (2008): 115–129.

Allagui, Abdelkrim. "The Jews of the Maghreb: Between Memory and History." In *A History of Jewish-Muslim Relations: From the Origins to the Present Day,* edited by Abdelwahab Meddeb and Benjamin Stora, translated by Jane Marie Todd and Michael B. Smith, 985–989. Princeton, NJ: Princeton University Press, 2013.

Anderson, Margaret Lavinia. ""Down in Turkey, Far Away': Human Rights, the Armenian Massacres, and Orientalism in Wilhelmine Germany." *Journal of Modern History* 79, no. 1 (March 2007): 80–111.

Anidjar, Gil. *The Jew, the Arab: A History of the Enemy.* Stanford, CA: Stanford University Press, 2003.

Arşiv belgelerine göre Kafkaslaräda ve Anadolu'da Ermeni mezâlimi I: 1906–1918/Armenian Violence and Massacre in the Caucasus and Anatolia Based on Archives. Ankara: T. C. Başbakanlık Devlet Arşivleri Genel Müdürlüğü, 1995.

Atatürk'ün söylev ve demeçleri. Edited by Nimet Unan. Vol. 2 (1906–1938). Ankara: Türk Tarih Kurumu, 1959.

Atatürk, "Speech," Turkish Ministry for Culture and Tourism, http://ekitap.kulturturizm.gov
.tr/TR,81464/nutuk.html.
Auron, Yair. *The Banality of Denial: Israel and the Armenian Genocide.* London: Transaction,
2003.
———. *Zionism and the Armenian Genocide: The Banality of Indifference.* London:
Transaction, 2000.
Ayata, Bilgin. "The Kurds in the Turkish-Armenian Reconciliation Process: Double-Bind or
Double-Blind?" Roundtable, One Hundred Years of Denial: The Armenian Genocide.
International Journal of Middle East Studies 47, no. 4 (2015): 807–812.
Baer, Marc David. "Death in the Hippodrome: Sexual Politics and Legal Culture in the Reign
of Mehmet IV." *Past & Present* 210, no. 1 (February 2011): 61–91.
———. *The Dönme: Jewish Converts, Muslim Revolutionaries, and Secular Turks.* Stanford,
CA: Stanford University Press, 2010.
———. "The Double Bind of Race and Religion: The Conversion of the Dönme to Turkish
Secular Nationalism." *Comparative Studies in Society & History* 46, no. 4 (October
2004): 678–712.
———. "An Enemy Old and New: The Dönme, Anti-Semitism, and Conspiracy Theories in
the Ottoman Empire and Turkish Republic." *Jewish Quarterly Review* 103, no. 4 (Fall
2013): 523–555.
———. *Honored by the Glory of Islam: Conversion and Conquest in Ottoman Europe.* Oxford:
Oxford University Press, 2008.
———. "Islamic Conversion Narratives of Women: Social Change and Gendered Religious
Hierarchy in Early Modern Ottoman Istanbul." *Gender & History* 16, no. 2 (August
2004): 425–458.
———. "Mistaken for Jews: Turkish PhD Students in Nazi Germany." *German Studies Review*
41, no. 1 (February 2018): 19–39.
———. "Muslim Encounters with Nazism and the Holocaust: The Ahmadi of Berlin and
German-Jewish Convert to Islam Hugo Marcus." *American Historical Review* 120, no. 1
(February 2015): 140–171.
———. "Turk and Jew in Berlin: The First Turkish Migration to Germany and the Shoah."
Comparative Studies in Society and History 55, no. 2 (2013): 330–355.
———. "Turkish Jews Rethink '500 Years of Brotherhood and Friendship.'" *Turkish Studies
Association Bulletin,* 24, no. 2 (2000): 63–73.
Baer, Marc and Ussama Makdisi. "Tolerance and Conversion in the Ottoman Empire: A
Conversation with Marc Baer and Ussama Makdisi." *Comparative Studies in Society &
History* 51, no. 4 (October 2009): 927–940.
Bahar, Beki. *Donna Grasya Nasi.* Istanbul: Isis, 1993.
———. *Efsaneden tarihe Ankara Yahudileri.* Istanbul: Pan, 2003.
Bahar, İ. İzzet. "German or Jewish, Humanity or Raison d'Etat: The German Scholars in
Turkey, 1933–1952." *Shofar* 29, no. 1 (2010): 48–72.
———. *Jewish Historiography on the Ottoman Empire and Its Jewry from the Late Fifteenth
Century to the Early Decades of the Twentieth Century.* Istanbul: Gorgias Press and Isis
Press, 2008.
———. *Turkey and the Rescue of European Jews.* London: Routledge, 2015.
Bali, Rıfat. "Antisemitizmi hoşgör(me)mek." *Radikal* 2, November 23, 2003.
———. *Cumhuriyet yıllarında Türkiye Yahudileri: Bir Türkleştirme serüveni, 1923–1945.*
Istanbul: İletişim, 1999.

———. "Hitler ile görüşme: Ordu komutanı Orgeneral Cemil Cahit Toydemir'in Almanya gezisi." *Toplumsal Tarih* 165 (September 2007): 38–42.
———. *L'affaire impôt sur la fortune.* Istanbul: Libra Kitap, 2010.
———. *Model Citizens of the State: The Jews of Turkey during the Multi-Party Period.* Translated by Paul Bessemer. Madison, NJ: Fairleigh Dickinson University Press, 2012.
———. "Perceptions of the Holocaust in Turkey." In *Perceptions of the Holocaust in Europe and Muslim Communities: Sources, Comparison, and Educational Challenge,* edited by Günther Jikeli and Joëlle Allouche-Benayoun, 61–70. London: Springer Science, 2012.
———. "Sachsenhausen temerküz kampı'nın Türk ziyaretçileri." *Toplumsal Tarih* 151 (July 2006): 38–43.
———. *A Scapegoat for All Seasons: The Dönmes or Crypto-Jews of Turkey.* Translated from Turkish by Paul Bessemer. Istanbul: Isis, 2008.
———. "Talat Paşa'nın kemiklerini mi? Nazi fırınları mı?" *Toplumsal Tarih* 150 (June 2006): 42–47.
———. *Türkiye'de Holokost tüketimi, 1989–2017.* Istanbul: Libra, 2017.
———. *The "Varlik Vergisi" Affair: A Study on its Legacy—Selected Documents.* Istanbul: Isis, 2005.
———, ed. *Varlık vergisi: Hatıralar—tanıklıklar.* Istanbul: Libra Kitap, 2012.
———, ed. *The Wealth Tax (Varlık Vergisi) Affair—Documents from the British National Archives.* Istanbul: Libra Kitap, 2012.
Barkey, Karen. *Empire of Difference: The Ottomans in Comparative Perspective.* Cambridge: Cambridge University Press, 2008.
Baron, Salo Wittmayer. *A Social and Religious History of the Jews,* 2nd revised ed. 18 vols. New York: Columbia University Press, 1952–1983.
Bashkin, Orit. *New Babylonians: A History of Jews in Modern Iraq.* Stanford, CA: Stanford University Press, 2012.
Bayraktar, Seyhan. "The Grammar of Denial: State, Society, and Turkish-Armenian Relations." Roundtable, One Hundred Years of Denial: The Armenian Genocide, *International Journal of Middle East Studies* 47, no. 4 (2015): 783–790.
Behmoaras, Lizi, ed. *Türkiye'de aydınların gözüyle Yahudiler.* Istanbul: Gözlem, 1993.
Beinin, Joel. *The Dispersion of Egyptian Jewry: Culture, Politics, and the Formation of the Modern Diaspora.* Berkeley: University of California Press, 1998.
Benayahu, Meir. *Rabi Eliyahu Kapsali, ish Kandiah: Rav manhig ve historyon.* Tel Aviv: Tel Aviv University Press, 1983.
Ben Aharon, Eldad. "A Unique Denial: Israel's Foreign Policy and the Armenian Genocide." *British Journal of Middle East Studies* 42, no. 4 (2015): 638–654.
Benbassa, Esther and Jean-Christophe Attias. *The Jew and the Other.* Translated by G. M. Goshgarian. Ithaca: Cornell University Press, 2004.
Benbassa, Esther and Aron Rodrigue. *The Jews of the Balkans: The Judeo-Spanish Community, 15th to 20th Centuries.* Oxford: Blackwell, 1995.
———. *Sephardi Jewry: A History of the Judeo-Spanish Community, 14th-20th Centuries.* Berkeley: University of California Press, 2000.
Bener, Yiğit, ed. *İçimizdeki Ermeni (1915-2015).* Istanbul: Can, 2015.
Ben-Naeh, Yaron. *Jews in the Realm of the Sultans: Ottoman Jewish Society in the Seventeenth Century.* Translated by Yohai Goell. Texts and Studies in Medieval and Early Modern Judaism 22. Tübingen: Mohr Siebeck, 2008.
Benveniste, Henriette-Rika. "The Idea of Exile: Jewish Accounts and the Historiography of Salonika Revisited." In *Jewish Communities Between the East and West, 15th-20th*

Centuries: Economy, Society, Politics, Culture, edited by L. Papastefanaki and A. Machaira, 31–53. Ioannina: Isnafi, 2016.

Berlin, Charles. "A Sixteenth-Century Hebrew Chronicle of the Ottoman Empire: The Seder Eliyahu Zuta of Elijah Capsali and its Message." In *Studies in Jewish Bibliography, History, and Literature in Honor of I. Edward Kiev*, edited by Charles Berlin, 21–44. New York: KTAV, 1971.

Besalel, Yusuf. *Osmanlı ve Türk Yahudileri*. Istanbul: Gözlem, 1999.

Bilu, Yoram and André Levy. "Nostalgia and Ambivalence: The Reconstruction of Jewish-Muslim Relations in Oulad Mansour." In *Sephardi and Middle Eastern Jewries: History & Culture in The Modern Era*, edited by Harvey E. Goldberg, 288–311. Bloomington: Indiana University Press, 1996.

Bleda, Mithat Şükrü. *İmparatorluğun çöküşü*. Istanbul: Remzi, 1979.

Bloxham, Donald. *The Great Game of Genocide: Imperialism, Nationalism, and the Destruction of the Ottoman Armenians*. Oxford: Oxford University Press, 2007.

Bornstein-Makovetsky, Leah. "Non-Urban Social Encounters between Jews and Muslims in the Ottoman Empire during the 16th through 18th Centuries." In *Jews and Muslims in the Islamic World*, edited by Zvi Zohar, 1–18. Bethesda: University of Maryland Press, 2012.

Boum, Aomar. *Memories of Absence: How Muslims Remember Jews in Morocco*. Stanford, CA: Stanford University Press, 2014.

Bowman, Steven. *The Jews of Byzantium, 1204–1453*. University: University of Alabama Press, 1985.

Boyarin, Jonathan. *The Unconverted Self: Jews, Indians, and The Identity of Christian Europe*. Chicago: University of Chicago Press, 2009.

Bozarslan, Hamit. "Kemalism, Westernization, and Anti-Liberalism." In *Turkey Beyond Nationalism: Towards Post-Nationalist Identities*, edited by Hans-Lukas Kieser, 28–36. London: I.B. Tauris, 2006.

Bozkurt, Gülnihal. "An Overview on the Ottoman Empire-Jewish Relations." *Der Islam* 71, no. 2 (1994): 255–279.

Brann, Ross. *Power in the Portrayal: Representations of Jews and Muslims in Eleventh- and Twelfth-Century Spain*. Princeton, NJ: Princeton University Press, 2009.

Braude, Benjamin. "Myths and Realities of Turkish-Jewish Contacts." In *Turkish-Jewish Encounters: Studies on Turkish-Jewish Relations through the Ages*, edited by Mehmet Tütüncü, 15–28. Haarlem, the Netherlands: SOTA Research Centre for Turkestan, Azerbaijan, Crimea, Caucasus and Siberia, 2001.

Brink-Danan, Marcy. *Jewish Life in 21st-Century Turkey: The Other Side of Tolerance*. Bloomington: Indiana University Press, 2012.

Brotton, Jerry. *This Orient Isle: Elizabethan England and the Early Modern World*. London: Allen Lane, 2016.

Çavuşoğlu, Mevlüt. "Message on International Holocaust Remembrance Day." Republic of Turkey Ministry for EU Affairs. January 27, 2015. https://www.ab.gov.tr/49393_en.html.

Çelik, Adnan and Namık Kemal Dinç. *Yüzyıllık ah! Toplumsal hafızanın izinde 1915 Diyarbekir*. Istanbul: İsmail Beşikci Vakfı, 2015.

Çelik, Adnan and Ergin Öpengin. "The Armenian Genocide in the Kurdish Novel: Restructuring Identity through Collective Memory." *European Journal of Turkish Studies* (Online), Complete List, 2016, 2–17.

Cemal, Hasan. *1915: The Armenian Genocide*. London: Gomidas Institute, 2015.

———. *1915: Ermeni soykırımı*. Istanbul: Everest, 2012.

Chazan, Robert. *Medieval Stereotypes and Modern Antisemitism.* Berkeley: University of California Press, 1997.

Cohen, Jeremy. *The Evolution of Medieval Anti-Judaism.* Ithaca, NY: Cornell University Press, 1982.

——. "The Muslim Connection or On the Changing Role of the Jew in High Medieval Theology." In *From Witness to Witchcraft: Jews and Judaism in Medieval Christian Thought*, edited by Jeremy Cohen, Wolfenbütteler Mittelalter-Studien Band 11, 141–162. Wiesbaden: Harrassowitz Verlag, 1996.

Cohen, Julia Phillips. *Becoming Ottomans: Sephardi Jews and Imperial Citizenship in the Modern Era.* Oxford: Oxford University Press, 2014.

——. "Halal and Kosher: Jews and Muslims as Political and Economic Allies." *AJS Perspectives*, The Muslim Issue (Spring 2012): 40–41.

Cohen, Julia Phillips and Sarah Abrevaya Stein. "Sephardic Scholarly Worlds: Toward a Novel Geography of Modern Jewish History." *Jewish Quarterly Review* 100, no. 3 (2010): 349–384.

Cohen, Mark R. "Foreword." In Bernard Lewis, *The Jews of Islam*, xiii–xxiii. Princeton, NJ: Princeton University Press, 2014.

——. "The 'Golden Age' of Jewish-Muslim Relations: Myth and Reality." In *A History of Jewish-Muslim Relations: From the Origins to the Present Day*, edited by Abdelwahab Meddeb and Benjamin Stora, translated by Jane Marie Todd and Michael B. Smith, 28–38. Princeton, NJ: Princeton University Press, 2013.

——. "Historical Memory and History in the Memoirs of Iraqi Jews." In Eli Yassif, et al., eds., *Ot LeTova: Essays in Honor of Professor Tova Rosen* (Beer Sheva: Dvir, 2012), 110–137.

——. "Islam and the Jews: Myth, Counter-Myth, History." *Jerusalem Quarterly* 38 (1986): 125–137.

——. "The Jews under Islam: From the Rise of Islam to Sabbatai Zevi." In *Bibliographical Essays in Medieval Jewish Studies* (New York, 1976), 169–229, reprinted with a supplement as Princeton Near East Paper Number 32 (Princeton, 1981).

——. "The Neo-Lachrymose Conception of Jewish-Arab History." *Tikkun* 6, no. 3 (May/June 1991): 55–60.

——. *Under Crescent & Cross: The Jew in the Middle Ages.* Princeton, NJ: Princeton University Press 1994, revised edition 2008.

Cutler, Allan Harris and Helen Elmquist Cutler. *The Jew as Ally of the Muslim: Medieval Roots of Anti-Semitism.* Notre Dame, IN: University of Notre Dame Press, 1986.

Dadrian, Vahakn N. *Key Elements in the Turkish Denial of the Armenian Genocide.* Cambridge, MA: Zoryan Institute, 1999.

Dadrian, Vahakn and Taner Akçam. *Judgement at Istanbul: The Armenian Genocide Trials.* New York: Berghahn Books, 2011.

Daniel, Norman. *Islam and the West: The Making of an Image.* Edinburgh: University Press, 1960.

Dankoff, Robert. *An Ottoman Mentality: The World of Evliya Çelebi.* Leiden: Brill, 2006.

Danon, Abraham. "Sur Sabbatai Cevi et sa secte." *Revue des études Juives* 37 (1898): 103–110.

Daskalakis-Giontis, Mihalis. "Defining Neighbours: Greeks and Dönme in Joseph Nehama's *History of the Israelites of Salonica*." MA thesis in Hebrew and Jewish Studies, University College London, 2015.

Demir, Hülya and Rıdvan Akar. *İstanbul'un son sürgünleri.* Istanbul: İletişim, 1994.

Dubnow, Simon. *History of the Jews.* Translated by Moshe Spiegel. 5 vols. South Brunswick, N.J.: Thomas Yoseloff, 1967–1973.

Dumont, Paul. "Jewish Communities in Turkey during the Last Decades of the Nineteenth Century in the Light of the Archives of the Alliance Israélite Universelle." In vol. 1 of *Christians and Jews in the Ottoman Empire: The Functioning of a Plural Society*, edited by Benjamin Braude and Bernard Lewis, 209–242. New York: Holmes & Meier, 1982.

Efron, John. *German Jewry and the Allure of the Sephardic*. Princeton, NJ: Princeton University Press, 2015.

Eissenstat, Howard. "Children of Özal: The New Face of Turkish Studies." *Journal of the Ottoman and Turkish Studies Association* 1, no. 1–2 (2014): 23–35.

Erkin, Behiç. *Hâtırat 1876–1958*. Ankara: Türk Tarih Kurumu, 2011.

"Eyewitness to Massacres of Armenians in Istanbul (1896)." In *Sephardi Lives: A Documentary History, 1700–1950*, edited by Sarah Stein and Julia Cohen, 134–139. Stanford, CA: Stanford University Press, 2014.

Ford, Henry. *The International Jew: The World's Foremost Problem*. Vol. 1. Dearborn, MI: Dearborn Publishing Company, 1920.

Franco, Moïse. *Essai sur l'histoire des Israélites de l'Empire ottoman depuis les origenes jusqu'à nos jours*. Paris: A. Durlacher, 1897.

Friedman, Isaiah. *Germany, Turkey, and Zionism, 1897–1918*. Oxford: Oxford University Press, 1977.

Galanté, Abraham. *Appendice à l'Histoire des Juifs de Rhodes, Chio, Cos etc., fin tragique des communautés Juives de Rhodes et de Cos oeuvre du brigandage Hitlerien*. Istanbul: Kağıt ve Basım İşleri, 1948.

———. *Documents officiels Turcs concernant les Juifs de Turquie*. Istanbul: Haim Rozio, 1931.

———. *Don Joseph Nassi, Duc de Naxos, d'après de nouveaux documents*. Conférence faite à la Société Bene B'rith le Samedi 15 Fevrier 1913, Constantinople: Fratelli Haim.

———. *Esther Kyra d'après de nouveaux documents: Contribution a l'Histoire des Juifs de Turquie*. Istanbul: Fratelli Haim, 1926.

———. *Histoire des Juifs d'Istanbul: Depuis la prise de cette ville, en 1453, par Fatih Mehmed II, jusqu'à nos jours*. Vol. 1. Istanbul: Imprimerie Hüsnütabiat, 1941.

———. *Medicins Juifs au service de la Turquie*. Istanbul: M. Babok, 1938.

———. *Nouveaux documents sur Sabbetaï Sevi: Organisation et us et coutumes de ses adeptes*. Istanbul: Fratelli Haim, 1935.

———. *Rôle économique des Juifs d'Istanbul*. Istanbul, Impr. Hüsnütabiat, 1942.

Galanti, Avram. *Iki uydurma eser: I. Siyon önderlerinin protokoları, II. Beynelmilel Yahudi: Tarihi, siyasi, tenkidi tetkik*. Istanbul: Kağıt ve Basım İşleri, 1948.

———. *Türkler ve Yahudiler: Tarihî, siyasî tetkik*. Rev. 2nd ed. Istanbul: Tan Matbaası, 1947.

Galip, Özlem. *Imagining Kurdistan: Identity, Culture and Society*. London: I.B. Tauris, 2015.

García-Arenal, Mercedes. "The Jews of Al-Andalus." In *A History of Jewish-Muslim Relations: From the Origins to the Present Day*, edited by Abdelwahab Meddeb and Benjamin Stora, translated by Jane Marie Todd and Michael B. Smith, 111–129. Princeton, NJ: Princeton University Press, 2013.

Gazi Mustafa Kemal (Atatürk). *Atatürk'ün söylev ve demçeleri I–III*. Ankara: Atatürk Kültür Dil ve Tarih Yüksek Kurumu, 1997.

Gerber, Haim. Introduction to *Crossing Borders: Jews and Muslims in Ottoman Law, Economy and Society*, 7–34. Istanbul: Isis, 2008.

Gerber, Jane. *The Jews of Spain: A History of the Sephardic Experience*. New York: New York University Press, 1992.

Göçek, Fatma Müge. "Defining the Parameters of a Post-Nationalist Turkish Historiography Through the Case of the Anatolian Armenians." In *Turkey Beyond Nationalism:*

Towards Post-Nationalist Identities, edited by Hans-Lukas Kieser, 85–103. London: I.B. Tauris, 2006.

———. *Denial of Violence: Ottoman Past, Turkish Present, and Collective Violence against the Armenians, 1789–2009*. Oxford: Oxford University Press, 2014.

———. "Reading Genocide: Turkish Historiography on 1915." In *A Question of Genocide: Armenian and Turks at the End of the Ottoman Empire*, edited by Ronald Grigor Suny, Fatma Müge Göçek, and Norman M. Naimark, 42–52. Oxford: Oxford University Press, 2011.

———. *The Transformation of Turkey: Redefining State and Society from the Ottoman Empire to the Modern Era*. London: I.B. Tauris, 2011.

Goitein, Shlomo Dov. *Jews and Arabs: Their Contacts through the Ages*. New York: Schocken, (1955) 1973.

———. *A Mediterranean Society: The Jewish Communities of the Arab World as Portrayed in the Documents of the Cairo Geniza*. 6 vols. Berkeley: University of California Press, 1967–1993.

Gökbilgin, M. Tayyib. *XV-XVI asırlarda Edirne ve Paşa livası*. Istanbul, 1952.

Goldish, Matt. *Sabbatean Prophets*. Cambridge, MA: Harvard University Press, 2004.

Goodblatt, Morris. *Jewish Life in Turkey in the XVIth Century as Reflected in the Legal Writings of Samuel De Medina*. New York: Jewish Theological Seminary of America, 1952.

Graetz, Heinrich. *History of the Jews*. Translated by B. Löwy. 11 volumes. Philadelphia: Jewish Publication Society of America, 1891–1898.

Güleryüz, Naim. *The History of the Turkish Jews*. Condensed from a lecture by the author. Revised 2nd ed. Istanbul: Rekor, 1992.

———. *The Turkish Jews: 700 Years of Togetherness*. Istanbul: Gözlem, 2009.

———. "Turkish Jews: Turkish-Jewish Friendship over 500 Years." http://www.turkyahudileri.com/index.php/en/12-turkish-jewish-community

———. *Türk Yahudileri tarihi I: 20. yüzyılın başına kadar*. Istanbul: Gözlem, 1993.

Gürel, Ziya. "Kurtuluş savaşında demiryolculuk." *Belleten* 44, no. 175 (July 1980): 539–573.

Gürün, Kâmuran. *Ermeni dosyası*. Ankara: Türk Tarih Kurumu, 1983.

———. *Fırtınalı yıllar dışişleri müsteşarlığı anıları*. Istanbul: Milliyet, 1995.

Gutman, David. "Review: Ottoman Historiography and the End of the Genocide Taboo: Writing the Armenian Genocide into Late Ottoman History." *Journal of the Ottoman and Turkish Studies Association* 2, no. 1 (2015): 167–183.

Guttstadt, Corry. *Die Türkei, die Juden und der Holocaust*. Hamburg: Assoziation A, 2009.

———. *Turkey, the Jews, and the Holocaust*. Translated from German by Kathleen M. Dell'Orto, Sabine Bartel, and Michelle Miles. Cambridge: Cambridge University Press, 2013.

———. *Türkiye, Yahudiler ve Holokost*. Istanbul: İletişim, 2012.

Guttstadt, Corry, Thomas Lutz, Bernd Rother, and Yessica San Román, eds. *Bystanders, Rescuers or Perpetrators? The Neutral Countries and the Shoah*. International Holocaust Remembrance Alliance series, vol. 2. Berlin: Metropol, 2016.

Hacker, Joseph. "Ottoman Policy toward the Jews and Jewish Attitudes towards the Ottomans during the Fifteenth Century." In vol. 1 of *Christians and Jews in the Ottoman Empire: The Functioning of a Plural Society*, edited by Benjamin Braude and Bernard Lewis, 117–126. New York: Holmes & Meier, 1982.

———. "The *Sürgün* System and Jewish Society in the Ottoman Empire during the Fifteenth to Seventeenth Centuries." In *Ottoman and Turkish Jewry: Community and Leadership*, edited by Aron Rodrigue, 1–65. Bloomington: Indiana University Press, 1992.

Haim Nahum: A Sephardic Chief Rabbi in Politics, 1892–1923. Edited with an introduction by Esther Benbassa. Translated from the French by Miriam Kochan. Tuscaloosa: University of Alabama Press, 1995.

Haker, Erol. *Bir zamanlar Kırklareli'de Yahudiler yaşardı . . . Kırklarelili Adato ailesin'in öyküsü*. Translated by Natali Medina. Istanbul: İletişim, 2002.

——. *From Istanbul to Jerusalem: The Itinerary of a Young Turkish Jew*. Istanbul: Isis, 2003.

——. *Once Upon a Time Jews Lived in Kırklareli: The Story of the Adato Family*. Istanbul: Isis, 2003.

Hakko, Vitali. *Hayatım. Vakko*. Istanbul: Şedele, 1997.

——. *My Life: Vakko*. Istanbul: Libra, 2011.

Halevi-Wise, Yael, ed. *Sephardism: Spanish Jewish History and the Modern Literary Imagination*. Stanford, CA: Stanford University Press, 2012.

Henry Morgenthau Papers, Box 14–15, Reel 13–14, Correspondence with Wise, Stephen S. (Stephen Samuel), 1874–1949, Special Correspondence, Manuscript Division, Library of Congress, Washington, DC.

Hovannisian, Richard. "The Critic's View: Beyond Revisionism." *International Journal of Middle East Studies* 9, no. 3 (1978): 379–388.

——. *Denial of the Armenian Genocide in Comparison with Holocaust Denial*. Yerevan: National Academy of Sciences, 2004.

İhsanoğlu, Ekmelleddin. *A Culture of Peaceful Coexistence: Early Islamic and Ottoman Turkish Examples*. Istanbul: Research Centre for Islamic History, Art, and Culture, 2004.

Inalcik, Halil. "Foundations of Ottoman Jewish Cooperation." In *Jews, Turks, Ottomans: A Shared History, Fifteenth Through the Twentieth Century*, edited by Avigdor Levy, 3–14. Syracuse, NY: Syracuse University Press, 2002.

——. "How to Read 'Ashık Pasha-zade's History." In *Studies in Ottoman History in Honour of Professor V.L. Ménage*, edited by C. Heywood and C. Imber , 139–156. Istanbul: Isis, 1994.

İpşirli, Mehmed. "Mustafa Selânikî and His History." *Tarih Enstitüsü Dergisi* 9 (January 1978): 417–472.

Itzkowitz, Norman. Review of *Germany and the Ottoman Empire 1914–1918* by Ulrich Trumpener. *Middle East Journal* 22, no. 4 (1968): 515–517.

Jacobs, Martin. "Exposed to All the Currents of the Mediterranean: A Sixteenth-Century Venetian Rabbi on Muslim History." *AJS Review* 29, no. 1 (April 2005): 33–60.

——. "An Ex-Sabbatean's Remorse? Sambari's Polemics against Islam." *Jewish Quarterly Review* 97, no. 3 (2007): 347–378.

——. *Islamische Geschichte in jüdischen Chroniken: Hebräische Historiographie des 16. und 17. Jahrhunderts*. Texts and Studies in Medieval and Early Modern Judaism 18. Tübingen: Mohr Siebeck, 2004.

——. "Joseph ha-Kohen, Paolo Giovio, and Sixteenth-Century Historiography." In *Cultural Intermediaries: Jewish Intellectuals in Early-Modern Italy*, edited by David B. Ruderman and Giuseppe Veltri, 67–85. Philadelphia: University of Pennsylvania Press, 2004.

Kalderon, Albert. *Abraham Galante: A Biography*. New York: Sepher-Hermon, 1983.

Kaligian, Dikran. "Anatomy of Denial: Manipulating Sources and Manufacturing a Rebellion." *Genocide Studies International* 8, no. 2 (2014): 208–223.

Kalmar, Ivan. "Benjamin Disraeli: Romantic Orientalist." *Comparative Studies in Society & History* 47, no. 2 (April 2005): 348–371.

Kalmar, Ivan Davidson and Derek Penslar. "Orientalism and the Jews: An Introduction." In *Orientalism and the Jews*, edited by Ivan Davidson Kalmar and Derek Penslar, xiv–xl. Lebanon, NH: University Press of New England, 2004.

Kamhi, Jak. *Gördüklerim yaşadıklarım*. Istanbul: Remzi, 2013.

———. "Letter to Abraham H. Foxman." August 22, 2007. Available on the website of the Turkish Coalition of America, http://www.tc-america.org/issues-information /armenian-issue/letter-to-abraham-386.htm.

———. *What I've Seen What I've Experienced*. Edited by Heath Lowry. Istanbul: Bahçeşehir University Press, 2013.

Karpat, Kemal H. *The Ottoman Mosaic: Exploring Models for Peace by Re-Exploring the Past*. Seattle: Cune, 2010.

Kieser, Hans-Lukas. "Dr. Mehmed Reshid (1873–1919): A Political Doctor." In *Der Völkermord an den Armeniern und die Shoah/The Armenian Genocide and the Shoah*, edited by Hans-Lukas Kieser and Dominik Schaller, 245–280. Zurich: Chronos Verlag, 2002.

Kıvırcık, Emir. *Büyükelçi: Yirmi bin insanı Nazi soykırımından kurtaran, Kurtuluş Savaşı kahramanı bir Türk'ün ve şerefli ulusunun tarihi değiştiren öyküsü!* Istanbul: GOA, 2007.

———. *The Turkish Ambassador*. CreateSpace Independent Publishing Platform, 2011.

Konuk, Kader. *East West Mimesis: Auerbach in Turkey*. Stanford, CA: Stanford University Press, 2010.

Kulin, Ayşe. *Kanadı kırık kuşlar*. Istanbul: Everest, 2016.

———. *The Last Train to Istanbul*. Translated by John Baker. Istanbul: Everest, 2006.

———. *Nefes nefese*. Istanbul: Remzi, 2002.

Landau, Jacob. "Hebrew Sources for the Socio-Economic History of the Ottoman Empire." *Der Islam* 54, no. 2 (1977): 205–212.

———. "Relations between Jews and Non-Jews in the Late Ottoman Empire: Some Characteristics." In *The Jews of the Ottoman Empire*, edited with an introduction by Avigdor Levy, 539–546. Princeton, NJ: Darwin Press, 1994.

———. *Tekinalp: Turkish Patriot, 1883–1961*. Istanbul: Nederlands Historisch-Archaeologisch Instituut, 1984.

Langmuir, Gavin. *History, Religion, and Antisemitism*. Berkeley: University of California Press, 1990.

Lassner, Jacob. *Jews, Christians, and the Abode of Islam: Modern Scholarship, Medieval Realities*. Chicago: University of Chicago Press, 2012.

———. "Joseph Sambari on Muhammad and the Origins of Islam: A Learned Rabbi Confronts Muslim Apologetics and a Christian Polemical Tradition." In Jacob Lassner, *The Middle East Remembered: Forged Identities, Competing Narratives, Contested Spaces*. Ann Arbor: University of Michigan Press, 2000, 341–385.

Lehmann, Matthias. *Emissaries from the Holy Land: The Sephardic Diaspora and the Practice of Pan-Judaism in the Eighteenth Century*. Stanford, CA: Stanford University Press, 2014.

Lellouch, Benjamin. "Eliyahu Capsali, Jewish Cantor of the Ottomans." In *A History of Jewish-Muslim Relations: From the Origins to the Present Day*, edited by Abdelwahab Meddeb and Benjamin Stora, translated by Jane Marie Todd and Michael B. Smith, 200–202. Princeton: Princeton University Press, 2013.

Letter from Léon Sémach, Bursa, to the central office of the Alliance Israélite Universelle, Paris, October 11, 1915. Translated from French into English as "A Report on the

Deportation of Armenians from Bursa (1915)." In *Sephardi Lives: A Documentary History, 1700–1950*, edited by Sarah Stein and Julia Cohen, 158–160. Stanford, CA: Stanford University Press, 2014.

Letters of Salo Baron in New York to Abraham Galanté in Istanbul, February 13 and April 24, 1936. The Central Archives for the History of the Jewish People (Jerusalem), Galanté Papers, P-112/45. Reproduced in *Sephardi Lives: A Documentary History, 1700–1950*, edited by Sarah Stein and Julia Cohen, 411–413. Stanford, CA: Stanford University Press, 2014.

Levi, Avner. *Türkiye Cumhuriyetinde Yahudiler: Hukukî ve siyasi durumları*. Edited by Rıfat N. Bali. Istanbul: İletişim, 1996.

Levi, Mario. *İstanbul bir masaldı*. Istanbul: Remzi, 1999.

———. *Istanbul Was a Fairy Tale*. Translated by Ender Gürol. Champaign, IL: Dalkey Archive, 2014.

Levy, Avigdor. Introduction to *The Jews of the Ottoman Empire*, edited by Avigdor Levy, 1–150. Princeton, NJ: Darwin Press, 1994.

———, ed. *Jews, Turks, Ottomans: A Shared History, Fifteenth Through the Twentieth Century*. Syracuse, NY: Syracuse University Press, 2002.

———, ed. *The Jews of the Ottoman Empire*. Princeton, NJ: Darwin Press, 1994.

———. *The Sephardim in the Ottoman Empire*. Princeton, NJ: Darwin Press, 1992.

Levy, Lital. "A Republic of Letters without a Republic?" *AJS Perspectives* (Fall 2010): 24–26.

———. "Self and the City: Literary Representations of Jewish Baghdad." *Prooftexts* 26 (2006): 163–211.

Lewis, Bernard. *The Crisis of Islam: Holy War and Unholy Terror*. New York: Random House, 2003.

———. *The Emergence of Modern Turkey*. 1st ed. Oxford: Oxford University Press, 1961.

———. *The Emergence of Modern Turkey*. 2nd ed. Oxford: Oxford University Press, 1968.

———. *The Emergence of Modern Turkey*, 3rd ed. Oxford: Oxford University Press, 2002.

———. *The Jews of Islam*. Princeton, NJ: Princeton University Press, 1984.

———. *Notes and documents from the Turkish Archives: A Contribution to the History of the Jews in the Ottoman Empire*. Oriental Notes and Studies. Jerusalem 1952.

———. "The Privilege Granted by Mehmed II to His Physician." *Bulletin of the School of Oriental and African Studies* 14, no. 3 (1952): 550–563.

———. "The Pro-Islamic Jews." *Judaism* 17, no. 4 (Fall 1968): 391–404.

———. "The Revolt of Islam." *New Yorker*. November 19, 2001.

———. "The Roots of Muslim Rage." *Atlantic Monthly*. September 1990.

———. *What Went Wrong? Western Impact and Middle Eastern Response*. New York: Oxford University Press, 2002.

Lewis, Bernard with Buntzie Ellis Churchill. *Notes on a Century: Reflections of a Middle East Historian*. New York: Viking, 2012.

Lewy, Guenter. *The Armenian Massacres in Ottoman Turkey: A Disputed Genocide*. Salt Lake City: University of Utah Press, 2005.

Lichtheim, Richard. *Rückkehr: Lebenserinnerungen aus der Frühzeit des deutschen Zionismus*. Stuttgart: Deutsche Verlags-Anstalt, 1970.

Lipstadt, Deborah. *Denying the Holocaust: The Growing Assault on Truth and Memory*. New York: Free Press, 1993.

Lowry, Heath. *The Story Behind Henry Morgenthau's Story*. Istanbul: Isis, 1990.

Mallet, Laurent-Olivier. *La Turquie, les Turcs et les Juifs: Histoire, représentations, discours et stratégies*. Istanbul: Les Éditions Isis, 2008.

Mamigonian, Marc A. "Academic Denial of the Armenian Genocide in American Scholarship: Denialism as Manufactured Controversy." *Genocide Studies International* 9, no. 1 (2015): 61–82.

Ma'oz, Moshe. "Communal Conflicts in Ottoman Syria during the Reform Era: The Role of Political and Economic Factors." In vol. 2 of *Christians and Jews in the Ottoman Empire: The Functioning of a Plural Society,* edited by Benjamin Braude and Bernard Lewis, 91–105. New York: Holmes & Meier, 1982.

Masters, Bruce. *Christians and Jews in the Ottoman Arab World: The Roots of Sectarianism.* Cambridge: Cambridge University Press, 2001.

Mastnak, Tomaž. *Crusading Peace: Christendom, the Muslim World, and Western Political Order.* Berkeley: University of California Press, 2002.

———. "Western Hostility toward Muslims: A History of the Present." In *Islamophobia/ Islamophilia: Beyond the Politics of Enemy and Friend,* edited by Andrew Shryock, 29–52. Bloomington: Indiana University Press, 2010.

Matar, Nabil. *Turks, Moors and Englishmen in the Age of Discovery.* New York: Columbia University Press, 2000.

Mazower, Mark. *Salonica: City of Ghosts: Christians, Muslims, and Jews, 1430–1950.* New York: Vintage, 2006.

McCarthy, Justin, Esat Arslan, Ömer Turan, and Cemalettin Taşkıran. *The Armenian Rebellion at Van.* Salt Lake City: University of Utah Press, 2006.

McCarthy, Justin, Bilâl Şimşir, Heath Lowry, and Mim Kemal Öke. *Armenians in the Ottoman Empire and Modern Turkey, 1912–1926.* Istanbul: Boğaziçi University Press, 1984.

McCarthy, Justin, Ömer Turan, and Cemalettin Taşkıran. *Sasun: The History of an 1890s Armenian Revolt.* Salt Lake City: University of Utah Press, 2014.

Melson, Robert. *Revolution and Genocide: On the Origins of the Armenian Genocide and Holocaust.* Chicago: University of Chicago Press, 1996.

Menocal, Maria. *The Ornament of the World: How Muslims, Christians, and Jews Created a Culture of Tolerance in Medieval Spain.* New York: Back Bay Books, 2003.

Miller, Judith. *One by One, by One: Facing the Holocaust.* New York: Simon and Schuster, 1990.

Moiz Kohen/Munis Tekinalp. "Die Juden in den Balkanländern." *Monatsschrift der österreichisch-israelitischen Union,* 25, no. 9–10 (September–October 1913): 16–24.

Moore, R. I. *The First European Revolution, c. 970–1215.* Oxford: Blackwell, 2000.

———. *The Formation of a Persecuting Society: Authority and Deviance in Western Europe, 950–1250,* 3rd ed. London: Wiley-Blackwell, 2007.

Mordtmann, Johannes H. "Die jüdischen Kira im Serai der Sultane." *Mitteilungen des Seminars für orientalische Sprachen: Westasiatische Studien* 32, no. 2 (1929): 1–38.

Morgenthau, Henry. *Ambassador Morgenthau's Story.* New York: Doubleday, 1918.

Naar, Devin. "Fashioning the "Mother of Israel": The Ottoman Jewish Historical Narrative and the Image of Jewish Salonica." *Jewish History* 28, no. 3 (2014): 337–372.

———. *Jewish Salonica: Between the Ottoman Empire and Modern Greece.* Stanford Studies in Jewish History and Culture. Edited by David Biale and Sara Abrevaya Stein. Stanford, CA: Stanford University Press, 2016.

Néhama, Joseph, ed. *In Memoriam: Hommage aux victimes Juives des Nazis en Grèce,* Tome II. Salonique: Communauté Israélite de Thessalonique, 1949.

———. *Dictionnaire du judéo-espagnol.* Madrid: Consejo Superior de Investigaciones Científicas, 1977.

———. *Histoire des Israélites de Salonique*. Tome I. *La communauté Romaniote, Les Sefardis et leur dispersion*. Paris: Librairie Durlacher/Salonique: Librairie Molho, 1935.

———. *Histoire des Israélites de Salonique*. Tome II, *La communauté Sefaradite, période d'installation (1492–1536)* Paris: Librairie Durlacher/Salonique: Librairie Molho, 1935.

———. *Histoire des Israélites de Salonique*. Tome III. *L'age d'or du Sefaradisme Salonicien (1536–1593)* (first volume) Paris: Librairie Durlacher/Salonique: Librairie Molho, 1936.

———. *Histoire des Israélites de Salonique*. Tome IV, *L'age d'or du Sefaradisme Salonicien (1536–1593)* (second volume) Paris: Librairie Durlacher/Salonique: Librairie Molho, 1936.

———. "Sabbataï Sevi et les Sabbatéens de Salonique." *Revue des Écoles de l'Alliance Israélite* 3 (1902): 289–323.

Neyzi, Leyla. *İstanbul'da hatırlamak ve unutmak: Birey, bellek ve aidiyet*. Istanbul: Tarih Vakfı, 1999.

Nirenberg, David. *Anti-Judaism: The Western Tradition*. New York: Norton, 2013.

———. *Communities of Violence: Persecution of Minorities in the Middle Age*. Princeton, NJ: Princeton University Press, 1996.

———. "Love Between Muslims and Jews in Medieval Spain: A Triangular Affair." In *Jews, Muslims, and Christians in and around the Crown of Aragon: Essays in Honor of Professor Elena Lourie*, edited by Harvey Hames, 127–155. Leiden: Brill, 2004.

———. "What Can Medieval Spain Teach Us About Muslim-Jewish Relations?" *CCAR Journal/A Reform Jewish Quarterly* (Spring/Summer 2002): 17–36.

Novikoff, Alex. "Between Tolerance and Intolerance in Medieval Spain: The Historiographic Enigma." *Medieval Encounters* 11, nos. 1–2 (2005): 7–36.

Ojalvo, Denis. "Le Lobbysme juif en Turquie." MA thesis, Galatasaray University, 2005.

———. "Türk Yahudileri lobiciliği." http://www.turkyahudileri.com/index.php/tr/makale-ve -tezler/114-turk-yahudi-lobiciligi-1.

"Ottoman Empire." In vol. 16 of *Encyclopaedia Judaica Jerusalem*, 1530–1554. Keter: Jerusalem, 1971.

Özyürek, Esra. Introduction to *The Politics of Public Memory in Turkey*, edited by Esra Özyürek, 1–15. Syracuse, NY: Syracuse University Press, 2007.

———. *Nostalgia for the Modern: State Secularism and Everyday Politics in Turkey*. Durham, NC: Duke University Press, 2006.

———, ed. *Politics of Public Memory in Turkey*. Syracuse, NY: Syracuse University Press, 2007.

———, ed. *Unuttukları ve hatırladıklarıyla Turkiye'nin toplumsal hafızası*. Istanbul: İletişim, 2002.

Parla, Taha. *Türkiye'de siyasal kültürün resmi kaynakları, Cilt I: Atatürk'ün nutuk'u*. Istanbul: İletişim, 1994.

Pasto, James. "Islam's 'Strange Secret Sharer': Orientalism, Judaism, and the Jewish Question." *Comparative Studies in Society & History* 40, no. 3 (July 1998): 437–474.

Paudice, Aleida. *Between Several Worlds: The Life and Writings of Elia Capsali: The Historical Works of a 16th-Century Cretan Rabbi*. Forum Europäische Geschichte 7. Munich: Martin Meidenbauer, 2010.

Peirce, Leslie. *The Imperial Harem: Women and Sovereignty in the Ottoman Empire*. Oxford: Oxford University Press, 1993.

Pinto, Bensiyon. *Anlatmasam olmazdı: Geniş toplumda Yahudi olmak* (I had to tell it: To be Jewish in Turkish society). Istanbul: Doğan, 2008.

———. *Jude sein in der Türkei: Erinnerungen des Ehrenvorsitzenden der jüdischen Gemeinde der Türkei Bensiyon Pinto*. Translated by Richard Wittman. Würzburg: Ergon, 2010.

———. *My Life as a Turkish Jew: Memoirs of the President of the Turkish-Jewish Community, 1989–2004.* Interviewed by Tülay Güler. Edited by Leyla Engin Arık. Translated by Nicole Pope. Kindle edition, 2011.

Quataert, Donald. "The Massacres of Ottoman Armenians and the Writing of Ottoman History." *Journal of Interdisciplinary History* 37, no. 2 (2006): 249–259.

———. *The Ottoman Empire, 1700–1922.* Cambridge: Cambridge University Press, 2000.

Ray, Jonathan. "Beyond Tolerance and Persecution: Reassessing Our Approach to Medieval Convivencia." *Jewish Social Studies* 11, no. 2 (Winter 2005): 1–18.

Reisman, Arnold. *An Ambassador and a Mensch: The Story of a Turkish Diplomat in Vichy France.* CreateSpace Independent Publishing Platform, 2010.

Rodinson, Maxime. *Europe and the Mystique of Islam.* Translated by Roger Veinus (1980). London: I.B. Tauris, 1988.

Rodrigue, Aron. "Difference and Tolerance in the Ottoman Empire." *Stanford Humanities Review* 5, no. 1 (1995): 81–90.

———. *French Jews, Turkish Jews: The Alliance Israélite Universelle and the Politics of Jewish Schooling, 1860–1925.* Bloomington: Indiana University Press, 1990.

———. *Jews and Muslims: Images of Sephardi and Eastern Jewries in Modern Times.* Seattle: University of Washington Press, 2003.

———. "The Mass Destruction of Armenians and Jews in the 20th Century in Historical Perspective." In *Der Völkermord an den Armeniern und die Shoah/The Armenian Genocide and the Shoah*, edited by Hans-Lukas Kieser and Dominik Schaller, 303–316. Zurich: Chronos Verlag, 2002.

Rosanes, Salamon Abraham. *Korot ha-Yehudim be-Turkiyah ve-artsot ha-kedem.* Vol. 1–3. Husitin, 1907, 1910–1911, 1913–1914.

———. *Korot ha-Yehudim be-Turkiyah ve-artsot ha-kedem.* Vol. 4–5. Sofia, 1933–1934, 1936–1937.

———. *Korot ha-Yehudim be-Turkiyah ve-artsot ha-kedem.* Vol. 6. Jerusalem, 1945.

Rosanes, Shlomo (Salamon). *Divrei yamei Israel be-Togarma ('al-pi mekorot rishonim), Helek rishon: Yamei ha-gerushim ve ha-nedurim ve hityashvut ha-plitim be-Togarma (1300–1520)* (History of the Jews of Turkey according to the earliest sources, Part I: The period of the [Spanish & other] expulsions, migrations and settlement of the refugees in Turkey, 1300–1520). 2nd revised ed. Tel Aviv: Dvir, 1930.

Roth, Cecil. *Dona Gracia of the House of Nasi: A Jewish Renaissance Woman.* Philadelphia: Jewish Publication Society of America, 1948.

———. *A Short History of the Jewish People.* Illustrated edition, revised and enlarged. London: East and West Library, 1948.

Rothberg, Michael. *Multidirectional Memory: Remembering the Holocaust in the Age of Decolonization.* Stanford, CA: Stanford University Press, 2009.

Rozen, Minna. *A History of the Jewish Community in the Istanbul: The Formative Years, 1453–1566.* Brill: Leiden, 2002.

Sachar, Howard. *Farewell España: The World of the Sephardim Remembered.* New York: Vintage, 1995.

Sachsenhausen Concentration Camp, 1936–1945: Events and Developments. Edited by Günter Morsch and Astrid Ley. Schriftenreihe der Stiftung Brandenburgische Gedenkstätten Band 24. Berlin: Metropol, 2011.

Said, Edward W. *Orientalism.* New York: Vintage, 1978.

Şaul, Eli. *From Balat to Bat Yam: Memoirs of a Turkish Jew.* Istanbul: Libra, 2012.

———. *Balat'tan Bat-Yam'a.* Edited by Rıfat N. Bali and Birsen Talay. Istanbul: İletişim, 1999.

Schapkow, Carsten. *Role Model and Countermodel: The Golden Age of Iberian Jewry and German Jewish Culture During the Era of Emancipation.* Translated by Corey Twitchell. London: Lexington Books, 2016.

Scheindlin, Raymond. "Hasdai ibn Shaprut." In *A History of Jewish-Muslim Relations: From the Origins to the Present Day,* edited by Abdelwahab Meddeb and Benjamin Stora, translated by Jane Marie Todd and Michael B. Smith, 134–135. Princeton, NJ: Princeton University Press, 2013.

———. "Samuel ibn Naghrela." In *A History of Jewish-Muslim Relations: From the Origins to the Present Day,* edited by Abdelwahab Meddeb and Benjamin Stora, translated by Jane Marie Todd and Michael B. Smith, 132–133. Princeton, NJ: Princeton University Press, 2013.

Schmidt, Jan. Review of Martin Jacobs, *Islamische Geschichte in jüdischen Chroniken. Journal of Early Modern History* 8, no. 3–4 (2004): 443–447.

Schmitt, Carl. *The Concept of the Political.* Chicago: The University of Chicago Press, 1996.

Scholem, Gershom. *Sabbatai Sevi: The Mystical Messiah.* Translated by R. J. Zwi Werblowsky. Princeton, NJ: Princeton University Press, 1973.

Seltzer, Robert M. "Dubnow, Simon." *The YIVO Encyclopaedia of Jews in Eastern Europe.* http://www.yivoencyclopedia.org/article.aspx/Dubnow_Simon.

Şeni, Nora. "Survival of the Jewish Community in Turkey." In *A History of Jewish-Muslim Relations: From the Origins to the Present Day,* edited by Abdelwahab Meddeb and Benjamin Stora, translated by Jane Marie Todd and Michael B. Smith, 490–494. Princeton, NJ: Princeton University Press, 2013.

Sewell, William H. Jr. *Logics of History: Social Theory and Social Transformation.* Chicago: University of Chicago Press, 2005.

Shafak, Elif. *The Bastard of Istanbul.* New York: Viking, 2006.

Shannon, Jonathan. "Performing al-Andalus, Remembering al-Andalus: Mediterranean Soundings from Mashriq and Maghrib." *Journal of American Folklore* 120 (2007): 308–334.

Shapiro, Henry. "Legitimizing the Ottoman Sultanate in Early Modern Greek." *Journal of Turkish Studies* 40 (2013): 327–351.

Shapiro, James. *Shakespeare and the Jews.* New York: Columbia University Press, 1997.

Shaw, Stanford J. "Christian Anti-Semitism in the Ottoman Empire." *Belleten* 54 (1990): 1073–1149.

———. *The Jews of the Ottoman Empire and the Turkish Republic.* New York: New York University Press, 1991.

———. *Turkey and the Holocaust: Turkey's Role in Rescuing Turkish and European Jewry from Nazi Persecution, 1933–1945.* New York: New York University Press, 1993.

———. "Turkey and the Jews of Europe during World War II." In *Turkish-Jewish Encounters: Studies on Turkish-Jewish Relations through the Ages,* edited by Mehmet Tütüncü, 309–325. Haarlem, the Netherlands: SOTA Research Centre for Turkestan, Azerbaijan, Crimea, Caucasus and Siberia, 2001.

Shaw, Stanford J. and Ezel Kural Shaw. *History of the Ottoman Empire and Modern Turkey.* Vol. 2, *Reform, Revolution, and Republic: The Rise of Modern Turkey, 1808–1975.* Cambridge: Cambridge University Press, 1977.

Shmuelevitz, Aryeh. "Capsali as a Source for Ottoman History 1450-1523." *International Journal of Middle East Studies* 9 (1978): 339–344.

———. "Jewish-Muslim Relations in the Writings of Rabbi Eliyahu Capsali." In Hebrew. *Pe'amim* 61 (1994), 75–82.

Shohat, Ella. "Rethinking Jews and Muslims: Quincentennial Reflections." *Middle East Report* 178 (1992): 25–29.

———. "Taboo Memories, Diasporic Visions: Columbus, Palestine, and Arab-Jews." In Ella Shohat, *Taboo Memories, Diasporic Voices*, 201–232. Durham, NC: Duke University Press, 2006.

Shryock, Andrew. "Introduction: Islam as an Object of Fear and Affection." In *Islamophobia/ Islamophilia: Beyond the Politics of Friend and Enemy*, edited by Andrew Shryock, 1–25. Bloomington: Indiana University Press, 2010.

Shtober, Shimon. Introduction to *Sefer divre Yosef le-Rabbi Yosef Sambari*, 13–55. In Hebrew, English abstract, ii–ix. Jerusalem: Ben-Tzvi Institute, 1994.

———. "Islam and Sabbateanism in the Chronicle Sefer Divrei Yosef." In *Jews and Muslims in the Islamic World*, edited by Bernard Dov Cooperman and Zvi Zohar, 321–334. Bethesda: University Press of Maryland, 2013.

Şimşir, Bilâl, ed. *British Documents on Ottoman Armenians*. Ankara: Türk Tarih Kurumu Basımevi, 1989.

———. *Ermeni meselesi 1774–2005*. Ankara: Bilgi, 2005.

———. *Şehit diplomatlarımız*. Ankara: Bilgi, 2001.

———. *Türk Yahudiler: Avrupa ırkçılarına karşı Türkiye'nin mücadelesi*. 2 vols. Ankara: Bilgi, 2010.

Skolnik, Jonathan. *Jewish Pasts, German Fictions: History, Memory, and Minority Culture in Germany, 1824–1955*. Stanford, CA: Stanford University Press, 2014.

Smith, Roger, Eric Markusen, and Robert Jay Lifton, "Professional Ethics and the Denial of Armenian Genocide." *Holocaust and Genocide Studies* 9, no. 1 (Spring 1995): 1–22.

Soifer, Maya. "Beyond Convivencia: Critical Reflections on the Historiography of Interfaith Relations in Christian Spain," *Journal of Medieval Iberian Studies* 1, no. 1 (2009): 19–35.

Somekh, Sasson. *Baghdad, Yesterday: The Making of an Arab Jew*. New York: Ibis, 2007.

Sonyel, Salahi. *The Assyrians of Turkey: Victims of Major Power Policy*. Ankara: Türk Tarihi Kurumu, 2001.

———. "The Fifth Centenary of the First Jewish Migrations to the Ottoman Empire." *Belleten* 56, no. 215 (April 1992): 207–212.

———. *The Great War and the Tragedy of Anatolia*. Ankara: Türk Tarihi Kurumu, 2001.

———. *İngiliz gizli belgelerine göre Adana'da vuku bulan Türk-Ermeni olayları* (Temmuz 1908-Aralık 1909). Ankara: Türk Tarihi Kurumu, 2014.

———. *Minorities and the Destruction of the Ottoman Empire*. Ankara: Türk Tarihi Kurumu, 1993.

———. *Osmanlı Ermenileri büyük güçler diplomasisinin kurbanları*. Istanbul: Remzi, 2009.

———. "Turco-Armenian Relations in the Context of the Jewish Holocaust." *Belleten* 54, no. 210 (August 1990): 757–772.

———. "Turco-Jewish Relations during the First World War and Turkey's War of Liberation." In *Turkish-Jewish Encounters: Studies on Turkish-Jewish Relations Through the Ages*, edited by Mehmet Tütüncü, 225–238. Haarlem, the Netherlands: SOTA, Research Centre for Turkestan, Azerbaijan, Crimea, Caucasus and Siberia, 2001.

Southern, Richard W. *Western Views of Islam in the Middle Ages*. Cambridge, MA: Harvard University Press, 1962.

Stanislawski, Michael. "Salo Wittmayer Baron: Demystifying Jewish History." *Columbia University Alumi Magazine* (Winter 2005), http://www.columbia.edu/cu/alumni /Magazine/Winter2005/llbaron.html.

Starr, Deborah. "Sensing the City: Representations of Cairo's *Harat al-Yahud*." *Prooftexts* 26 (2006): 138–162.

Stillman, Norman. "History." In *The Jews of Arab Lands: A History and Source Book*, edited by Norman Stillman, 3–110. Philadelphia: The Jewish Publication Society of America, 1979.

———. *The Jews of Arab Lands in Modern Times: A History and Source Book*. Philadelphia: Jewish Publication Society of America, 1991.

———. "Myth, Counter-Myth, and Distortion." *Tikkun* 6, no. 3 (May-June 1991): 60–64.

Stora, Benjamin. "The Crémieux Decree." In *A History of Jewish-Muslim Relations: From the Origins to the Present Day*, edited by Abdelwahab Meddeb and Benjamin Stora, translated by Jane Marie Todd and Michael B. Smith, 286–291. Princeton, NJ: Princeton University Press, 2013.

Suny, Ronald Grigor. *"They Can Live in the Desert but Nowhere Else": A History of the Armenian Genocide*. Princeton, NJ: Princeton University Press, 2015.

———. "Truth in Telling: Reconciling Realities in the Genocide of the Ottoman Armenians." *American Historical Review* 114, no. 4 (October 2009): 930–946.

———. "Writing Genocide: The Fate of the Ottoman Armenians." In *A Question of Genocide: Armenians and Turks at the End of the Ottoman Empire*, edited by Ronald Grigor Suny, Fatma Müge Göçek, and Norman M. Naimark, 15–41. Oxford: Oxford University Press, 2011.

Suny, Ronald and Fatma Müge Göçek. "Introduction: Leaving it to the Historians." In *A Question of Genocide: Armenian and Turks at the End of the Ottoman Empire*, edited by Ronald Grigor Suny, Fatma Müge Göçek, and Norman M. Naimark, 3–14. Oxford: Oxford University Press, 2011.

Tezcan, Baki. *The Second Ottoman Empire: Political and Social Transformation in the Early Modern World*. Cambridge: Cambridge University Press, 2010.

Thomas, Lewis V. and Richard N. Frye. *The United States and Turkey and Iran*. Cambridge, MA: Harvard University Press, 1951.

Toktaş, Şule. "Perceptions of Anti-Semitism among Turkish Jews." *Turkish Studies* 7, no. 2 (2006): 203–223.

Tolan, John. *Saracens: Islam in the Medieval European Imagination*. New York: Columbia University Press, 2002.

———. *Sons of Ishmael: Muslims through European Eyes in the Middle Ages*. Gainesville: University Press of Florida, 2008.

Tütüncü, Mehmet. Introduction to *Turkish-Jewish Encounters: Studies on Turkish-Jewish Relations through the Ages*, edited by Mehmet Tütüncü, 9–12. Haarlem, the Netherlands: SOTA Research Centre for Turkestan, Azerbaijan, Crimea, Caucasus and Siberia, 2001.

Udovitch, Abraham and Lucette Valensi, *The Last Arab Jews: The Communities of Jerba Tunisia*. New York: Harwood, 1984.

Ulgen, Fatma. "Reading Mustafa Kemal Ataturk on the Armenian Genocide of 1915." *Patterns of Prejudice* 44, no. 4 (2010): 369–391.

Üngür, Uğur Ümit, ed. *Genocide: New Perspectives on its Causes, Courses, and Consequences*. Amsterdam: Amsterdam University Press, 2016.

———. *The Making of Modern Turkey: Nation and State in Eastern Anatolia, 1913–1950.* Oxford: Oxford University Press, 2012.

———. Review of Burak Arlıel, *The Turkish Passport.* H-Genocide, H-Net Reviews. March 2012. URL: http://www.h-net.org/reviews/showrev.php?id=35380.

Üngür, Uğur Ümit and Mehmet Polatel, eds. *Confiscation and Destruction: The Young Turk Seizure of Armenian Property.* London: Bloomsbury Academic, 2013.

Veinstein, Gilles. "Jews and Muslims in Ottoman Territory before the Expulsion from Spain." In *A History of Jewish-Muslim Relations: From the Origins to the Present Day,* edited by Abdelwahab Meddeb and Benjamin Stora, translated by Jane Marie Todd and Michael B. Smith, 164–169. Princeton, NJ: Princeton University Press, 2013.

———. "Jews and Muslims in the Ottoman Empire." In *A History of Jewish-Muslim Relations: From the Origins to the Present Day,* edited by Abdelwahab Meddeb and Benjamin Stora, translated by Jane Marie Todd and Michael B. Smith, 171–195. Princeton, NJ: Princeton University Press, 2013.

———. "Trois questions sur un massacre." *L'Histoire,* no.187 (April 1995): 40–41.

Wien, Peter. "Coming to Terms with the Past: German Academia and Historical Relations between the Arab Lands and Nazi Germany." *International Journal of Middle East Studies* 42, no. 2 (May 2010): 311–321.

Winter, Michael. "The Relations of Egyptian Jews with the Authorities and with the Non-Jewish Society." In *The Jews of Ottoman Egypt (1517–1914),* edited by Jacob Landau, in Hebrew, 371–420. Jerusalem: Misgav Yerushalayim, 1988.

Wolf, Kenneth. "*Convivencia* in Medieval Spain: A Brief History of an Idea." *Religion Compass* 3, no. 1 (2009): 72–85.

Yelda. *Çoğunluk aydınların'da ırkçılık.* Istanbul: Belge, 1998.

———. *İstanbul'da, Diyarbakır'da azalırken.* Istanbul: Belge, 1996.

Yerushalmi, Yosef Haim. *Zakhor: Jewish History & Jewish Memory.* Seattle: University of Washington Press, 1982.

Zürcher, Erik. "Renewal and Silence: Postwar Unionist and Kemalist Rhetoric on the Armenian Genocide." In *A Question of Genocide: Armenian and Turks at the End of the Ottoman Empire,* edited by Ronald Grigor Suny, Fatma Müge Göçek, and Norman M. Naimark, 306–316. Oxford: Oxford University Press, 2011.

———. "The Role of Historians of Turkey in the Study of the Armenian Genocide." *Centre for Policy and Research on Turkey (ResearchTurkey)* 4 (2015): 12–17.

Films, Journals, Media, Newspapers, and Television

Ağaoğlu, Adalet, Ahmet Altan, Oya Baydar, Murat Belge, Hasan Cemal, Cengiz Çandar, Perihan Mağden, and Bejan Matur. "A Letter to the Armenians." P24: Platform for Independent Journalism (website). http://platform24.org/en/articles/270/a-letter-to-the -armenians.

Akgüneş, Gürkan. "Diş hekimine infaz." *Milliyet,* August 22, 2003, 5.

"AK Partili vekil açıkladı: Gülen'in babası Ermeni." Haber7.com, November 2, 2016. http:// www.haber7.com/guncel/haber/2201612-ak-partili-vekil-acikladi-gulenin-babasi -ermeni.

Akyol, Mustafa. "Unraveling the AKP's 'Mastermind' Conspiracy Theory." *Al-Monitor,* March 19, 2015. http://www.al-monitor.com/pulse/originals/2015/03/turkey-zion -protocols-akp-version.html.

"Armenian Allegations: Myth and Reality." Testimony delivered by Professor Justin McCarthy before the House Committee on International Relations, May 15, 1996.

"Armenian Genocide PBS debate." YouTube video, 26:27. From a debate panel televised by PBS on April 17, 2006. Posted by "Ellen Salmonson." February 11, 2017. https://www.youtube.com/watch?v=dO03QlxWZ5Q.

Arsu, Sebnem. "Seminar on 1915 Massacre of Armenians to Go Ahead." *New York Times*, September 24, 2005.

Arsu, Sebnem and Dexter Filkins. "20 in Istanbul Die in Bombings at Synagogues." *New York Times*, November 16, 2003.

"Bakan Eroğlu: Gülen, Yahudi mezarlığına gömülecek." Siyasihaber3.org, December 9, 2016. http://siyasihaber4.org/bakan-eroglu-gulen-yahudi-mezarligina-gomulecek.

Benhabib, Seyla. "In Turkey, A History Lesson in Peace." Opinion. *The New York Times*, November 18, 2003.

"Biz, Ermenileri Yahudiler gibi durup dururken kesmeye başlamadık." CNNTürk. "Aykırı Sorular," February 3, 2014.

Burak Arlıel, dir. *The Turkish Passport*. Imaj, Interfilm Istanbul, Turkey, 2011. https://web.archive.org/web/20120425034845/http://www.theturkishpassport.com/holocaust_story.asp.

Catinchi, Phillipe-Jean. "Gilles Veinstein, historien, spécialiste de l'Empire ottoman." *Le Monde*, February 12, 2013.

"Cecil Roth 1899–1970." Oxford Jewish Heritage Committee (website). http://www.oxfordjewishheritage.co.uk/resources/further-reading/170-cecil-roth-1899-1970.

"Crude Bomb Explodes at UCLA Professor's Home." *Los Angeles Times*, October 4, 1977, page D1.

"Cumhurbaşkanı Erdoğan: FETÖ tam bir maşa, onun üstünde üst akıl var." *Haber 10*, July 31, 2016.

"Cumhurbaşkanı Erdoğan: Milli seferberlik ilan ediyorum." CNNTurk, December 14, 2016.

Demir, Gül and Niki Gamm. "Jak Kamhi: A Man of Exemplary Character and Determination." *Hürriyet Daily News*, August 18, 2007.

Dink, Hrant. "Gerçek maskaralık." *Agos*, October 20, 2000.

Durmuş, Yusuf Ziya. "Edirne Synagogue Reopens Its Doors After Restoration." *Daily Sabah*, March 27, 2015.

Erdoğan, Eyüp. "Turks Saved Jews from Nazi Holocaust." *Turkish Daily News*, October 25, 2008.

"Erdoğan Lashes Out at Foreign Media Ahead of Turkey Polls." AFP (Agence France-Presse), June 6, 2015.

Erdoğan, Recep Tayyip. Address to the Council of Foreign Relations, New York, September 23, 2014. Presidency of the Republic of Turkey (website). https://tccb.gov.tr/en/news/542/3249/president-erdogan-addresses-cfr.html.

"Erdoğan'dan Yahudi açılımı." *Hürriyet*, October 7, 2009.

"Erdoğan's Campaign of Hate Speech: Case of Targeting the Gülen Movement, 2013–2017." Stockholm Center for Freedom, 2017. https://stockholmcf.org/wp-content/uploads/2017/06/Erdogans-Vile-Campaign-Of-Hate-Speech-Case-Study-Targeting-Of-The-Gulen-Movement_2017.pdf.

"Erdoğan: Üst akıl Fethullah Gülen değil." *Timeturk*, July 31, 2016.

"'Fethullahçı Terör Örgütü' suçlaması." *Milliyet*, April 4, 2015.

"Fethullah Gülen'le ilgili şok bir belge daha." *A Haber*, April 8, 2015.

"Fethullah Gülen Sabetayist mi?" *Odatv*, August 23, 2016.

Fisk, Robert. "Turkish Money Fails to Blot Out the Stain of Genocide." *The Independent*, January 17, 1998.

Gravé-Lazi, Lidar and Herb Keinon. "Knesset Committee Recognizes Armenian Genocide." *Jerusalem Post*, August 3, 2016.

Greenblatt, Jonathan. "ADL on the Armenian Genocide." ADL Blog. Anti-Defamation League, May 13, 2016. https://www.adl.org/blog/adl-on-the-armenian-genocide.

Greenhouse, Emily. "The Armenian Past of Taksim Square." *New Yorker*, June 28, 2013.

"Gülen babadan Ermeni anadan Yahudi'dir!" *Yeni Akit*, August 16, 2016.

"Heureux comme un juif en Turquie." *Le nouvel observateur* 2092, December 9, 2004.

Honon, William. "Princeton Is Accused of Fronting for the Turkish Government." *New York Times*, May 22, 1996.

Khatchadourian, Raffi. "A Century of Silence: A Family Survives the Armenian Genocide and its Long Aftermath." *New Yorker*, January 5, 2015.

Koptaş, Rober. "Cinayetin değil, inkârın özrünü savunuyorum." *Agos*, February 2, 2012.

Korkmaz, Tamer. "Rabin'in oğlu Fetullah bunalımda!" *Yeni Şafak*, August 12, 2016.

———. "Sakladım, gizli tuttum, söylemedim, uyuttum!" *Yeni Şafak*, August 23, 2016.

Lewis, Bernard. Speech at the National Press Club, Washington, DC. Broadcast on C-Span, March 25, 2002.

Manşetüstü, *Yeni Akit*, October 28, 2015; November 11 and 12, 2015; July 17, 2016; February 11, 2017.

Molinas, İvo. "Hangi 'soykırım'?" *Şalom*, June 10, 1998.

———. "Holokost ve soykırım." *Şalom*, June 8, 2016.

———. "Soykırım endüstrisi." *Şalom*, January 9, 2008.

"Neve Şalom'a hain terör saldırısı!" *Cumhuriyet*, September 6, 1986.

"Neve Şalom'a ilk saldırı değil." *Hürriyet*, November 11, 2013.

"Osmanlı torunuyuz mazlum yanındayız." *Hürriyet*, January 7, 2009.

"Öcalan'dan Ermenilere mektup: Bize yardımcı olun." *Radikal*, January 30, 2014.

Parkinson, Joe. "Dismay Over Turkish Rates." *Wall Street Journal*, January 12, 2012.

"Pis bir Yahudi mahallesi idi." *Şalom*, December 9, 2016.

"Prime Minister Erdoğan Reiterates 'No Genocide' in Darfur." *Today's Zaman*, November 9, 2009.

"Prime Minister Erdogan Tells ADL That 'Anti-Semitism Has No Place in Turkey.'" ADL Press Release, June 10, 2005.

"Prof. Dr. Stanford J. Shaw vefat etti." *Şalom*, December 20, 2006, http://arsiv.salom.com.tr /news/detail/4397-Prof-Dr-Stanford-J-Shaw-vefat-etti.aspx.

Ramoğlu (Güney), Ersin. "Karay Yahudisi Fethullah Gülen." *Sabah*, December 28, 2016.

"Second Arrest Warrant Issued for Gülen." *Hürriyet Daily News*, February 24, 2015.

"Seven Jailed for Turkey Bombings." *BBC News*, February 17, 2007.

Shaheen, Kareem. "Revealed: The Terror and Torment of Turkey's Jailed Journalists." *Guardian*, March 23, 2017.

———. "Turkey Sentences Journalists to Life in Jail Over Coup Attempt." *Guardian*, February 16, 2018.

Tanış, Tolga. "US Jewish Group Demands PM Erdoğan Return Award." *Hürriyet Daily News*, July 24, 2014.

Tarih Vakfı, 100. yılda 1915'e ve bugüne bakışlar: "Tehcir-taktil-soykırım: 1915–2015," Karin Karakaşlı, Rober Koptaş, Zakarya Mildanoğlu. http://tarihvakfi.org.tr/Etkinlik /persembekonusmalari/1.

Tremblay, Pinar. "Is Gulen an Armenian?" *Al-Monitor*, August 12, 2016.

"Turkey Issues Arrest Warrant for Erdogan Rival Fethullah Gülen." *Guardian*, December 19, 2014.

"Turkish-Armenian Writer Shot Dead." *BBC News*, January 19, 2007.

"Turkish Jews Disavow 'Genocide' Move." *Today's Zaman*, August 23, 2007.

"Turkish Jewish Museum Reopens after Update." *Hürriyet Daily News*, February 27, 2016.

"Türkiye'nin tutumu örnek gösterildi." *Şalom*, March 6, 1985.

"Türkiye'yi dunyaya tanıttılar." *Hürriyet*, November 29, 1988;

"TüTAV ödülleri sahiplerini buldu." *Güneş*, November 29, 1988.

Ünlü, Ferhat. "Çağımızın Sabetay Sevi'si: Fethullah Gülen." *Sabah*, October 4, 2015.

Uzer, Umut. "Ermeni meselesine farklı bir bakış." *Şalom*, May 27, 2015.

———. "The Fallacies of the Armenian Nationalist Narrative." *Jerusalem Post*, April 27, 2015.

———. "Hayal ve gerçek arasında Balakian'ın kara köpeği." *Şalom*, April 27, 2016.

"Üzeyir Garih öldürüldü." *Hürriyet*, August 25, 2001.

Vick, Karl. "Al Qaeda's Hand in Istanbul Plot: Turks Met with Bin Laden." *Washington Post*, February 13, 2007.

———. "Turkey Charges Acclaimed Author." *Washington Post*, September 1, 2005.

Yavuz, M. Hakan ve Umut Uzer. "Ermeni meselesi, devlet ve aydınlar." *Zaman*, Yorum, February 23, 2013.

Internet Sources

Avlaremoz: www.avlaremoz.com.

International Holocaust Remembrance Alliance: https://www.holocaustremembrance.com/international-holocaust-remembrance-alliance.

Üst akıl belgeseli/"Mastermind" anti-Semitic conspiracy theory documentary: https://www.youtube.com/watch?v=Zqw2eZ1K6Uw.

Raoul Wallenberg Center: http://www.raoulwallenberg.net.

Sachsenhausen Concentration Camp: https://www.sachsenhausen-sbg.de/en/.

Sephardic house: https://web.archive.org/web/20140307003335/http://www.turkyahudileri.com/content/view/2883/287/.

Sephardic House: Institute for Researching and Promoting Sephardic History and Culture at the Center for Jewish History in New York: https://web.archive.org/web/20010220164801/http:/www.sephardichouse.org:80/quincentennial-foundation.html.

Turkish census: http://www.worldjewishcongress.org/en/about/communities/TR.

Turkish Jewish Community: http://www.turkyahudileri.com/index.php/en/12-turkish-jewish-community.

Wannsee Conference: https://www.ghwk.de/en/.

INDEX

and antisemitic stereotypes, 176; and
downplaying of anti-Jewish violence, 105;
and emergence of critical Turkish Jewish
voices, 217–23, 224; and framework of
study, 20, 22; and "Holocaust heroism"
tales, 192, 198–99; and idealized accounts
of Muslim-Jewish harmony, 278; influence
of writings, 89–103; and Jewish messianism, 57; and life stories of Turkish Jews,
254; and Ottoman myths in Turkish
Republic, 81–82; and Ottoman tolerance
narrative, 186n40; and Quincentennial
Foundation's influence on historiography,
161–63, 164; on Sabbatian movement,
109n49; and utopian accounts of Ottoman
rule, 106
Gallipoli, 75
Garih, Üzeyir, 157–58
General History of the Jews, A (Dubnow),
90–91
"genocide" term, viii. *See also* Armenian
genocide; Holocaust
Gerber, Haim, 104
German Jews: and author's background and
research, vii–viii; and early Ottoman Jewish historians, 57; and efforts to recognize
Armenian genocide, 289; and emergence
of critical Turkish Jewish voices, 225, 282;
and Graetz's idealization of Ottoman
rulers, 67; and "Holocaust heroism" tales,
191–92, 210n38; and influence of Galanté's
writings, 88; and life stories of Turkish
Jews, 264; and lobbying against the Armenian genocide, 129, 133; and Sephardic
model of acculturation, 53–54; and Turk-
ish lobbying efforts, 141
German-Turkish Friendship Treaty, 256
Gerson, V., 61
Geschichte der Juden, 54
Gestapo, 193–94, 202, 222, 230
Gezi protests, 294
Giacomo of Gaeta, 99, 103–4
Gladstone, William, 29n77
global warming denialism, 208
Göçek, Fatma Müge, ix–x, 3, 283–84
Gog and Magog, 39
Goodblatt, Morris, 50n64
"good Muslims/bad Muslims" trope, 6

Graetz, Heinrich: and agenda of Quincentennial Foundation, 167–68; and Covo's
writings, 58; and Franco's history of Ottoman Jewry, 63; on the French Revolution,
69n9; and idealized accounts of Ottoman
rule, 67; and influence of Galanté's writings, 84, 90–91, 93; influence on Jewish
historians outside Turkey, 97–102; and
medieval model of Islamic tolerance,
69n1; and Quincentennial Foundation's
influence on historiography, 162–63; and
Sephardic model of acculturation, 53–56
Granada, Spain, 6, 30, 31
Grand National Assembly, 83, 88
"gratitude" narrative: and agenda of
Quincentennial Foundation, 156, 158,
168, 183; and Armenian uprisings, 71n58;
and author's background and research,
xiii; and Baron's writings, 99; and early
Jewish accounts of sultanic saviors, 39, 41;
and emergence of critical Turkish Jewish
voices, 216, 228, 235, 240n60, 280; and
Erdoğan's rhetoric, 296; and framework
of study, 20, 22–23; and Franco's history
of Ottoman Jewry, 64; and Galanté's
writings, 86; and genocide denialism,
2; and "Holocaust heroism" tales, 195,
198, 199–201; and idealized accounts of
Muslim-Jewish harmony, 277; and "Jew
as the friend" discourse, 181; and Jewish
messianism, 45; and Jewish-Muslim
alliance in Ottoman Empire, 60; and
Jewish/Ottoman relations, 77; and Jewish patriotism, 58–59; and life stories of
Turkish Jews, 254, 267–68, 291n31; and
lobbying against the Armenian genocide,
127, 131, 133; and Nahum's leadership, 66;
and Néhama's writings, 95; and Ottoman
myths in Turkish Republic, 81–82; and
Quincentennial Foundation agenda, 214;
and Roth's writings, 97–98; and Turkish
lobbying efforts, 145; and utopian accounts of Ottoman rule, 106
Great Britain, 192
Great Eastern Islamic Raiders' Front,
272n102
Great Synagogue, Edirne, Turkey, 293
Greco-Ottoman war of 1897, 60, 62, 121

MARC DAVID BAER is Professor of international history at the London School of Economics and Political Science. He earned his doctorate from the University of Chicago. Dr. Baer is the author of *Honored by the Glory of Islam: Conversion and Conquest in Ottoman Europe*, which won the Albert Hourani Prize from the Middle East Studies Association of North America, and *The Dönme: Jewish Converts, Muslim Revolutionaries, and Secular Turks*.

9 780253 045416